Genealogical Abstracts from
The Telephone

1889-1896
Loudoun County
Virginia

Patricia B. Duncan

Heritage Books
2008

HERITAGE BOOKS
AN IMPRINT OF HERITAGE BOOKS, INC.

Books, CDs, and more—Worldwide

For our listing of thousands of titles see our website
at
www.HeritageBooks.com

Published 2008 by
HERITAGE BOOKS, INC.
Publishing Division
100 Railroad Ave. #104
Westminster, Maryland 21157

Copyright © 2008 Patricia B. Duncan

All rights reserved. No part of this book may be reproduced or transmitted in any form or by any means, electronic or mechanical, including photocopying, recording or by any information storage and retrieval system without written permission from the author, except for the inclusion of brief quotations in a review.

International Standard Book Numbers
Paperbound: 978-0-7884-4587-3
Clothbound: 978-0-7884-7701-0

INTRODUCTION

This book provides abstracts of articles containing genealogical or other historical information from *The Telephone* newspapers of Loudoun County, Virginia.

Microfilms of the following Loudoun County newspapers are available through the Interlibrary Loan service of the Library of Virginia.

The Democratic Mirror and *The Mirror* newspapers:
(Library of Virginia Reel Series 284)

17 Jun 1857 - 4 Dec 1861
14 Jun 1865 - 31 Dec 1874
12 Jul 1865 – 31 Oct 1878
7 Jan 1875 - 25 Feb 1879
6 Feb 1879 - 15 Nov 1883
1 Jan 1880 - 27 Dec 1883
24 Jan 1884 - 27 Dec 1888
3 Jan 1889 - 31 Dec 1891
7 Jan 1892 - 20 Dec 1894
3 Jan 1895 - 16 Dec 1897
6 Jan 1898 - 27 Dec 1900
3 Jan 1884 - 31 Oct 1901
1 Jan 1901 - 7 Aug 1902
4 Jun 1908 - 24 Dec 1919
4 Jul 1913 - 22 Dec 1916

The Loudoun Telephone newspapers:
(Library of Virginia Reel Series 363)

7 Jan 1881 - 26 Dec 1884
2 Jan 1885 - 21 Dec 1888
4 Jan 1889 - 25 Dec 1891
1 Jan 1892 - 28 Apr 1893
4 May 1894 - 11 Sep 1896

Some of the above reels show overlapping dates. Although some issues appeared on both reels, most reels contain mainly issues that do not appear in the other reels. There are also a number of missing issues in each series.

The front page of each issue usually consisted of business cards and general entertainment articles. Subsequent pages contained advertisements and legal notices, local general and personal news, obituaries, marriage announcements, and some national and international news.

Although some entries in this book are the complete article, many are shortened abstracts. Marriage announcements and obituaries were sometimes long and flowery, and parts have been omitted here.

Abbreviations may have been used in these abstracts. Administrator/Administratrix may be abbreviated as Admr. and Executor/Executrix as Exor. Ages are often shortened to year month day (y m d.) Months are sometimes abbreviated and dau. might be used as an abbreviation for daughter.

As with any transcription of records, it is advisable to obtain a copy of the original document to verify the accuracy. Although every effort is made to transcribe accurately, mistakes are inevitable.

Special thanks to the Library of Virginia and the Special Collections Library of Albuquerque, New Mexico.

THE TELEPHONE
Published at Hamilton, Loudoun Co, Va
by Yardley T. Brown

Friday, 4 January 1889   Vol. XI, No. 36

Wm. RUNER, a colored man, was killed one day last week by being thrown against the saw in Col. R. H. DULANY's saw mill, in the southern part of the County.

Herndon: The death of Mabel, daughter of Wm. M. and Sadie GARRETT.

Bushrod PIGGOTT of Silcott Springs died at his home last Tuesday night. For several months he has been in poor health. His remains were interred at Lincoln, yesterday. He leaves a wife and little one. He was about 43 years of age.

Married: At the residence of the bride's parents, Fairfax C. H., Va., on Monday, Dec. 24, 1888, by Rev. O. C. BEALL, Mr. George R. WOODARD, of Fairfax C. H. (formerly of Leesburg) to Miss Alice GAINES, dau. of George W. GAINES, Esq.

Died: Joshua RUSSELL, at his home in Frederick Co Md, on the 31st of 12th month 1888, in the 95th year of his age.

Friday, 11 January 1889   Vol. XI, No. 37

Aldie: A. L. B. ZEREGA is in New York for the funeral of his father.

Aldie: Mrs. Wm. B. CARTER died at her home on Dec. 31st.

Mr. Joshua P. BROWN, son of Wm. H. BROWN, and Miss Nellie DUVAL, of Martinsburg, were married in the M. E. Church South, at that place on Wednesday evening, Jan. 2d.

Herndon: The body of Mrs. DeREAMER, was carried to Washington for interment. She died at the residence of her son-in-law Mr. Carl ROESER, near this place.

Lovettsville: Cards are out for the marriage of Mr. Newton STONE and Miss Ada RODEFFER. The ceremony will be performed at the Lutheran church, on Thursday next, Rev. P. H. MILLER officiating, assisted by Rev. S. J. RINKER and Dr. SCHINDLER.

Jos. H. SHERRARD, of Winchester, died in that city last Sunday in the 89th year of his age.

Married: At the residence of the bride's father, Mr. T. O. WYNDHAM, on the 18th of Dec 1888, by Rev. J. H. MOORE, Mr. Chas. A. WILLIAMS, of Loudoun, and Miss Annie C. WYNDHAM, of Clarke Co.

Married: Jan. 5th 1889, at the residence of the bride's parents, In Fairfax Co. by Rev. S. A. BALL, Samuel M. JENKINS to Maggie V. DAILY.

Married: Dec. 19th '88, by Rev. Dr. SCHINDLER, at the home of the bride, Mr. George W. MYERS, to Miss Mary V. SPRING, both of Loudoun.

Married: Dec. 20th '88, by the same at the home of the bride, Mr. W.
G. BISER, to Miss Lydia C. COOPER, both of Loudoun.
Married: Dec. 27th 1888, by the same, at New Jerusalem Church,
Mr. Luther B. BOGER, to Miss Lulu B. BEATY, both of Loudoun.
Died: At "Sunny Side," the residence of her daughter, in Loudoun
Co, Dec. 28, 1888, Mrs. Catharine COOKSEY, aged 70 years.
Died: Mrs. Lucy SKINNER, wife of the late James SKINNER, died at
her home near Middleburg, Nov. 11th 1888, in the 68th year of
age. For about 44 years she has identified with the Methodist
Church.
Died: At his residence, near Silcott's Springs, Jan. 1st, 1889,
Bushrod PIGGOTT, aged 43 years. Member of The Society of
Friends. Interred in their burial grounds at Lincoln.

Friday, 18 January 1889   Vol. XI, No. 38

On the 10th inst., Mr. Ivan C. BRADFIELD and Miss Carrie
MORELAND, of Loudoun, were married in Washington.
Miss Imogene JAMES, dau. of William JAMES, of Washington, but
formerly of Waterford, died at the latter place last Sunday
morning, and her remains were interred Monday afternoon.
Mr. Levi NIXON died at his home two miles east of Hamilton, last
Tuesday evening, the result of a stroke of paralysis, on Friday.
This was the third attack, the first about two years ago. The
same disease had caused the death of three brothers. Interred at
Leesburg yesterday. He was 65 years of age.
Herndon: Mr. Harry THOMAS, formerly from Loudoun, who has
made his home during the past year or two with Mr. Daniel
BORDEN, of Spring Vale, was taken to a hospital in Washington
on Thursday of last week where he died during the night.
Jan. Ct.: C. J. C. MAFFETT qualified as guardian of Lillie B.
CRAVEN. Wills of Wm. T. HUNT dec'd, Smith REED dec'd,
Jacob BODMER dec'd and ___ CLAGETT dec'd were admitted
to probate. Wm. B. POTTS qualified as Admr. of Jane E. POTTS
dec'd. A. G. CHAMBLIN qualified as guardian of Clara
CHAMBLIN. Application of Joshua G. MORAN for pension
allowed. Wm. PIGGOTT qualified as Admr. of Bushrod
PIGGOTT dec'd. A. B. CHAMBLIN qualified as Admr. of Eveline
B. CHAMBLIN dec'd. Jas. B. SCHOOLEY and A. J. BRADFIELD
as notaries public. Estate of Mrs. Louisa F. MINOR committed to
Sheriff. Estate of Townsend J. McVEIGH committed to Sheriff.
The wedding of Miss Ada RODEFFER and Mr. Newton M. STONE
was celebrated in St. Johns Lutheran Church, Lovettsville, on
Thursday the 10th inst. at 1 p.m. ... Ushers: Messrs Ray
SCHAFF, W. G. BISER, Hugh RODEFFER and Bush STONE,
the latter the brother of the groom. Bridesmaids and groomsmen:
Miss Lucy COMPHER and Mr. Kirke JOHNSON; Miss Lulu

COMPHER and Mr. Elmer DOTY; Miss Anna RODEFFER and Mr. John CHAMBLIN; Miss Effie LINDSAY and Mr. George HAYNE. The bride's dress was a most elaborate production of the dressmaker's skill, made of brown silk and plush, with hat to match. The bridesmaids wore dresses of cream albatross cloth, and the groomsmen black cut-a-way coats and black trowsers with satin neckties and kid gloves to match the dresses. The marriage was performed by Rev. P. H. MILLER.

Married: At. St. John's Lutheran Church, Lovettsville, Jan. 10, 1889, Mr. Newton M. STONE and Miss Ada V. RODEFFER, Rev. P. H. MILLER, of Westminster, Md, officiating.

Married: Jan. 7th, at the M. E. Parsonage, Leesburg, by Rev. D. C. HEDRICK, Mr. Charles HIGDON and Miss Sallie COOKSEY, all of Loudoun.

Died: Of typhoid pneumonia, Dec. 22nd, Clinton Clyde BALLENGER, son of Edgar and Dorcas O. BALLENGER, aged 13y 3m.

Friday, 25 January 1889   Vol. XI, No. 39

The remains of the late F. M. HENDERSON, who died at Staunton a year or two ago, were brought to this town last Thursday, and laid at final rest in the family lot in Union Cemetery.

Miss Hallie O. WOODWARD, of Charlottsville, who teaches school in Loudoun, and who is a first cousin to President-elect HARRISON and Colonel MOSBY, was married in Washington city last week to Mr. S. D. HICKS Jr. of Richmond.

James J. WEST, a well known temperance speaker, formerly of Jefferson Co, but recently a citizen of Illinois, fell from the third story window of a hotel at Harper's Ferry and died.

At 4 o'clock Thursday evening, Dec. 13th 1888, the marriage of Miss Sommerville A., dau. of the late Morgan ROWZEE, of this Co., and Mr. Milton SCHOOLEY, of Waterford. The bride wore a green henrietta cloth dress trimmed in plush and in her hair she wore a wreath of orange blossoms. The groom on the sunny side of forty. The ceremony performed by Rev. J. E. ARMSTRONG.

Married: By Rev. J. R. BRIDGES, on Jan. 17th 1889, David BLAIR, of Clay Co., Kentucky, to Miss Nancy COCKRILLE, of Loudoun.

Friday, 1 February 1889   Vol. XI, No. 40

Married: Jan. 24th at the house of Mr. Ed SPRING, near Taylortown, by Rev. D. SCHINDLER, Mr. John HUNTER and Miss Jannie E. A. POTTERFIELD, both of Loudoun.

Married: At the Parsonage of the M. E. Church, South, Middleburg, Jan. 9th, by Rev. C. M. BROWN, Chas. H. SMITH and Rosa J. SELBAUGH, both of Loudoun.

Died: Miss Nannie POTTS, at the home of her brother, J. O. POTTS, in Hillsboro, Jan. 24th after a lingering illness, aged about 40 years.
Died: At his home in Hughesville, on the evening of the 18th of Jan. after prolonged suffering, Wm. T. HUNT in the 39 year of his age.
Died: Jan. 22nd, at her residence near Mountain Gap, Mrs. Elizabeth J. DANIEL, in the 54th year of her age.
Mr. Saml. H. LOVE sold his farm, located 2 miles SE of Hillsboro, to Jack BAKER, a worthy colored man. BAKER was formerly a slave of the late Jonah HATCHER, and after being liberated he remained in that gentleman's employ and foreman of the farm, while his wife was doing domestic duty in the HATCHER home.
Mrs. Linsay COPELAND died at her home, near Silcott Springs, last Wednesday, of cancer of the stomach.

Friday, 8 February 1889   Vol. XI, No. 41

Died: Mary Randolph, only child of Randolph and Nannie RHODES, near Leesburg, Feb. 2nd, aged nearly 6 years.
J. Fenton JACKSON died at his home in Frederick Co. at 4 a.m. on Wednesday and will be buried today. The deceased was 70y 5m 9d old.
Charles Rupert PAXTON died at his home "Carlheim," near Leesburg, last Friday about 1 p.m., from angina pectoris. The funeral took place from the home of the deceased at 11:30 Monday morning, conducted by Rev. R. T. DAVIS, of the Episcopal Church, of which he was a member, assisted by Rev. Mr. TUSTIN, of Bloomesburg, Pa. Remains were borne to Union Cemetery. Mr. P. lacked one month of being 73 years of age.
Waterford: Mr. Saml. WRIGHT and Miss ___ PAXSON were married at the Presbyterian Parsonage, by Rev. L. B. TURNBULL, Wednesday afternoon, Feb. 6.
Died, Feb 2d, 1889, near Covington, Newton Co, Georgia, at the home of her husband, E. F. POTTS, late of Hillsboro, this county, Mrs. Gennie D. POTTS, after a long and painful illness. The deceased was a sister of Mrs. T. F. GAVER and dau. of Prof. J. H. DANIEL, of Washington, DC, where his remains were brought and interred in the father's family lot, in Glenwood Cemetery.

Friday, 15 February 1889   Vol. XI, No. 42

Eli STOCKS, an old resident of the Neersville neighborhood, died on the 11th inst.
Dr. H. W. GREGG, formerly of Loudoun, died at his home in Hamilton, Texas, on Jan. 1st.
Miss Mary JOHNS, from near Pittsburg, Pa, is visiting at the home of her uncle, Jos. H. JEWETT, at Lincoln.

The divorce suit of THROCKMORTON vs THROCKMORTON was decided a few days ago by the Judge KEITH in favor of the defendant.

Feb. Ct.: Wills of Chas. R. PAXTON, Saml. ANKERS and H. Clay COOPER admitted to probate. Emly A. MOXLEY qualified as Ex. of Benj. F. MOXLEY dec'd.

Charles Rupert PAXTON was born on 2 Mar 1816 in Cattawissa, Columbia Co, Pa. As a young man he was a civil engineer on the Erie RR. He later purchased lands in Alleghany Co, NY ... About 1870 he came to Loudoun and purchased 1,200 of the old "Exeter" estate near Leesburg.

Died: Near Mt. Gilead, Jan. 21st, M. Katie, dau. of Wm. H. and F. C. D. JOHNSON aged 17y 10m 28d.

Died: George JORDAN, at his home in Philomont, Feb. 7th, of consumption and Bright's disease, in the 46th year of his age.

Died: Matilda STOCKS, wife of Mahlon STOCKS, near Hillsboro, of pneumonia, Feb. 8.

Friday, 22 February 1889   Vol. XI, No. 43

Mr. L. M. McGAVACK recently visited Mr. and Mrs. Millard JANNEY, the latter his sister, in Roanoke.

Herndon: Mrs. Wm. AYRE, who had a knitting needle penetrate her ear, several years since, died on Monday the 11th inst.

Waterford: Daniel BOYD, our old colored citizens died in Washington on the 16th. His remains were brought back and interred in Friends burying ground.

Died: At the home of her husband, about 3 miles S of Leesburg, on Friday, Feb. 15th 1889, Mrs. Jane Francis HOGELAND, wife of Mr. John J. HOGELAND, in the 71st year of her age. Her remains were interred in Union Cemetery, Leesburg, on Sunday.

Died: At the residence of her daughter, Mrs. M. E. JOHNSTON, at Sterling, on Sunday, Feb 17th at 3 p.m., Mrs. Mary CAMP, after an illness of two weeks, in the 69th year of her age.

Died: At the residence of her aunt, in Frederick Co Md, on the 9th of February, Mary R., second daughter of F. M. and Maggie L. MYERS (and grand daughter of Spencer MINOR dec'd of Loudoun) in the 18th year of her age.

Friday, 1 March 1889   Vol. XI, No. 44

Mr. and Mrs. John STRASBERGER (latter formerly Miss Freddie HOGE, of this vicinity) will removed from Chicago to Nebraska on account of Mr. S's health.

Woodburn, Feb 21: Marriage of Miss Lou. WHITE, daughter of Levi WHITE, to Mr. Edward ROE, of Zanesville, Ohio, which took place today, at the residence of the bride's parents. The bride wore a neat fitting costume of dark green cloth, and in her hand carried a beautiful bouquet of choice flowers. The ceremony was performed by Elder E. V. WHITE. They will make their home in Zanesville, Ohio.

Bolington: Samuel WRIGHT Sr. died at the residence of his son-in-law, Tilghman COOPER, near Lovettsville, last week. His remains were interred in the cemetery at Waterford.

Lost Corner: Margaret FULTON, "Aunt Peggy," of this county, died near here last Sunday morning. She was 95 years of age and had been vigorous until a few months ago.

Friday, 8 March 1889   Vol. XI, No. 45

Died: Mr. Clarence HEAD, at his home in Leesburg, March 2d, of typhoid pneumonia, aged 33 years.

Died: Jas. GRUBB, at his home near Hillsboro, March 1st at an advanced age.

Died: Mrs. Mary L. BROWN, wife of Chas. L. BROWN, at her home near Lovettsville, Feb. 22d in the 59th year of her age.

Friday, 15 March 1889   Vol. XI, No. 46

We understand that Mr. Wm. STEVENSON living near Aldie, committed suicide last Monday evening, March 11, by hanging himself in his own barn. He was some 70 years old and had been in bad health for a good many years.

Miss Alice MEANS died at 5 a.m. last Saturday morning at the home of her mother, near Washington and her remains were interred by the side of her father, in Georgetown Cemetery, on Sunday afternoon.

Mr. Joseph HOWELL, living at Mt. Gilead, died suddenly on Saturday, March 2nd about 3 p.m. He leaves a wife and seven children.

Capt. W. P. SMITH of Leesburg died suddenly of heart disease on the 7th inst., aged 69 years. He was walking on the street when he suddenly fell and died. His remains were interred in Union Cemetery on Sunday.

Louis H. POWELL, a member of the Leesburg bar, died last Friday morning after a lingering illness, in the 41st year of his age. His funeral took place Sunday afternoon, Rev. Dr. DAVIS officiating.

Mrs. Carita SWAN died last Monday at the untimely age of 22 years, leaving an infant son. The deceased was a daughter of Dr. J. F. MASON, of this county.

March Ct.: Wills of James GRUBB, Elizabeth H. THRASHER, Augustus ZEREGA and Antoni WILSON admitted to probate. Letters of administration on the estate of S. M. GIBSON, R. Emma GIBSON Admx.

Wm. P. TAVENNER died at his home near Philomont, on the 8th inst., having been sick only a few days, with pneumonia. He leaves a wife and children.

Died: Mrs. M. COS, at St. Paris, Ohio, Feb. 5th aged 84 years. Some years ago she was the second wife of Joseph STEPHENS of Va. and step mother of J. J. STEPHENS, of this county, who traveled through that country in 1860 and found a noble mother.

Died: Mrs. Maria MOBERLY at the residence of her son-in-law, Geo. W. WATERS, in Loudoun Valley, aged 80y 9m.

Friday, 22 March 1889   Vol. XI, No. 47

On Monday last Mr. John H. DAVIS who lived about 3 miles from this place, near the Centerville pike, went into the woods to select timber for railroad ties, fell and died. He was subject to epileptic fits, and was about 65 years old. *Fairfax Herald*.

J. W. JOHNSON, formerly of Leesburg but now residing in Washington was married to Miss Mamie E. EASTWOOD of that city on the 14th inst.

On the afternoon of the 14th at Hedgewood, the home of Thomas R. and Elen H. SMITH, the marriage of their eldest daughter, Anna T., to Eli ELLIOTT, of West Liberty town. At five o'clock the bridal party, consisting of J. RUSSELL, brother of the bride, in the roll of "best man," and Miss Sarah L. HAINES, of Maryland, followed by the contracting couple, entered the parlor. The reading of the certificate by Laura SMITH in the manner of the Society of Friends. The bride, in white adored with Brussell's lace, smylax and rose buds, against a background of blooming plants. They will live in West Liberty.

Jay WINSTON, 16 years old, died at the home of his mother at Carlin's mill, Fairfax Co yesterday evening of a spinal trouble. He had been blind for a number of years and was taken sick at the D. D. and B. Institute in Staunton. His body will be sent to Middleburg and will be buried beside his father in the cemetery there.

Bolington: George BAKER of Morrisonville, buried his youngest child last week, aged 1 year.

Waterford: Tuesday evening the wedding of Mrs. L. Kate RICKARD to Mr. John PAXSON.

A telegram was received on the 20th from Springfield, Mo. announcing the sudden death of Harriet HAINES, wife of Abraham HAINES, and daughter of the late Ann M. RADCLIFFE of this place.

Death of Mrs. M. A. STANSBURY at her home in Leesburg on Thursday night last. She was the widow of the late J. J. STANSBURY, who died a short time ago. She was a member of the M. E. Church South.

Married: At the residence of the bride's uncle, Mr. N. H. BARTLETT, near Lovettsville, Mar. 14th '89 by Rev. P. N. MILLER, of Westminster, Md, Mr. Elmer E. ARNOLD, of Washington Co, Md, and Miss Rebecca H. V. BARTLETT of Loudoun Co.

Married: On Tuesday, March 5th at the home of the bride's mother in Baltimore, Md, by the Rev. W. T. EVANS, Miss Olivia KERN and Emory V. CHINN, junior partner of the mercantile firm of CHINN Bros., Lovettsville.

Married: At the residence of the bride's parents, on the 18th, by the Rev. G. W. POPKINS, Mr. A. M. HAYNES to Miss Annie M. THRIFT, all of Loudoun.

Friday, 29 March 1889   Vol. XI, No. 48

Mr. John W. ESKRIDGE, of Fauquier Co, died suddenly at his home near Bristersburg on Saturday morning last. He was a member of the Ninth Va Cavalry and served throughout the entire war. He was a brother of Mrs. W. H. CARLIN, of this city.

Mrs. Louis D. WINE died at her home in Hyattsville, Md, last Monday morning. She was a dau. of the late Robert McCREARY, of Gettysburg Pa.

Married: At the home of the bride, in Waterford, by Rev. SCHINDLER, Mr. John PAXSON and Mrs. L. Kate RICKARD, both of Loudoun.

Died: George REDMAN, near Hillsboro, Mar. 22, 1889, of pneumonia aged 80 years.

Friday, 5 April 1889   Vol. XI, No. 49

Married: At Tankerfield, Mar. 27th, by Rev. D. SCHINDLER, Mr. Richard T. NEWTON and Miss Mary F. KIDWELL, both of Loudoun.

Died: In Miami, Mo., March 19th, Albert HARDING, aged 71 years, formerly of Loudoun.

Died: Mrs. Olivia MYERS, wife of Thos. J. MYERS, and daughter of David and Elizabeth STEADMAN, born in Leesburg, Feb. 9th 1842, died at the residence of her husband, near Taylortown, Va, April 1st 1889 in the 48th year of age.

Died: At his home in Lincoln, March 29th '89 of consumption, Peter COSBERRY, aged 28 years. He leaves a young wife. His funeral was preached by Rev. W. H. GAINS, of Middleburg.

Mr. Henry MAFFETT died at his residence near Ball's Mill, on Thursday morning last, in the 84th year of his age. He was a successful farmer, and leaves a comfortable estate.

On Saturday morning last, the wife of Thomas F. CORNWELL, a young farmer residing a couple of miles west of Hillsboro, passed away. She leaves 4 small children the youngest but three weeks old. She was formerly from Rappahannock Co. to which place the body was taken for burial. About 3 o'clock on the morning of the same day, their neighbor of the adjoining farm died before a doctor could be gotten. It is believed that rheumatism went to his heart. He was in the 62 year of his age. His remains were interred at Salem church, on Sunday afternoon. Among those in attendance at the funeral was William, 20 year old son of John P. DERRY, who upon his return home was kicked by his horse and the following evening died.

Neersville: On Sunday evening, March 31st, Willie A., son of John P. DERRY, was kicked in the left side by a young horse and lingered until Monday evening when he died. He was born April 1st, 1869 and died April 1st 1889, being just 20 years of age.

Friday, 12 April 1889   Vol. XI, No. 50

Gov. LEE has removed the political disabilities of Chas. A. NEWLON, who was convicted of felony in Loudoun Co and was pardoned on the 15th of February.

Mr. Robert KILGOUR has, after a visit to his father's James M. KILGOUR, started to Italy and other foreign counties in the interest of the same firm for which he has been traveling for several years.

Married: At the residence of the bride's parents, Loudoun, Mar. 31st 1889, Mr. Lewis J. VIRTS to Miss Minnie B. RILEY, daughter of Mr. Jas. W. RILEY.

Co. Ct.: Wills of Henry MAFFETT, Elizabeth J. DANIEL and Louis H. POWELL admitted to probate. Administrations of estates of Emma TAVENNER and Ebenezer J. CONARD granted. Estates of Thos. APPLE and Isaac D. BUDD committed to Sheriff.

Friday, 19 April 1889   Vol. XI, No. 51

Mr. James KINCHELO, of Fauquier and Miss Annie GIBSON, dau. of Mr. John GIBSON, of Loudoun, were married in Middleburg on Tuesday, of last week.

Cards are out for the marriage of Rev. Carter PAGE, rector of Christ Church, Goresville, to Miss Nannie Banbury, dau. of Col. Wm. GIDDINGS, of this county, on April 25th 1889, at Christ Church.

Lincoln: Last Saturday morning, Aquila JANNEY, an aged man of this neighborhood was found dead in his room, at the residence of his son, Dr. Edgar JANNEY, of Washington. Interred here by the side of his wife, in Friends burying ground Sunday afternoon. He was an Elder of Goose Creek Meeting. His death was supposed to have been caused by apoplexy.

Death of Aquila JANNEY occurred at the home of his son, Dr. Edgar JANNEY, in Washington last Friday evening. Death declared caused by embolism, an effection of the heart similar to apoplexy. His body was brought to Lincoln on Saturday and on

Sunday afternoon his funeral took place from Friends Meeting House. He was nearly 84 years old. He was the last of a family of brothers, including the late John JANNEY.

Died: Mrs. Elizabeth FAWLEY, wife of Jeremiah FAWLEY, died at her home, near Goresville, April the 11th 1889, of pneumonia, aged 43 years.

Miss Ellen D. ARCHER, late of our vicinity, was married to Mr. Jas. H. DORRITEE, in Washington on the 18th inst. They will locate in Baltimore where Mr. D. is engaged in business.

Father of Mrs. Edgar H. PAXSON in this vicinity from a Baltimore paper: The funeral of Stephen D. COULBOURN, who died on Tuesday, in the 80th year of his age took place yesterday. Interment was at Greenmount Cemetery. He was an old merchant of this city, having come here from Somerset Co. in 1844, and engaged in grocery and commission business.

Friday, 26 April 1889   Vol. XI, No. 52

Miss Annie L. GARRETT died Tuesday evening at her home near Silcott Springs where her funeral will take place this morning. Interment at Forth [North] Fork.

Bolington: Rinard JACOBS of this vicinity died on Friday of last week. His remains were interred in the St. Paul burying ground on Sunday.

Lenah: On Monday last, the decayed remains of Mrs. Mary HIBBS, wife of Maj. Wm. HIBBS, was removed from their resting place at Gum Spring, and buried at Mt. Zion.

It is announced that Mr. Dennie HIGGINS, of Farmwell and Miss Katie PALMER, of Gum Spring, will be married at the latter named place tomorrow.

Lenah, Apr 23: The marriage of Mr. Wilmer HUTCHISON, of Pleasant Valley to Miss Clara KARNER, of Gum Spring, this morning at 10 o'clock, performed by Rev. Mr. COE of Farmwell. the bride was attired in a peacock blue surah silk. ...

Married: At the Parsonage, April 24th, by Rev. W. G. EGGLESTON, Mr. Joseph HIBBS, of Prince William Co., to Miss Hattie BEACH of Loudoun Co.

Married: At the residence of John H. ALEXANDER, Esq., Leesburg, on Tuesday, April 23d 1889, by Rev. C. T. HERNDON, Dr. Edward A. DUNCAN, of Washington DC, and Miss Alice W. BOND, daughter of the late Asa M. BOND, of Waterford.

Married: At the residence of Jno. H. ALEXANDER, Esq., in Leesburg, on Tuesday, April 23d, 1889, by Rev. C. T. HERNDON, Mr. A. T. SHAWEN and Miss Amanda C. BERRY, all of Loudoun.

Died: Daniel MORIARTY, of Loudoun, in Washington City, of consumption, in the 27th year of his age.

Friday, 3 May 1889   Vol. XII, No. 1

Mr. Richard WHITE who has been ill for more than a year, died at his mother's residence near Clarks Gap, on last Friday evening, April 26th, in the 40th year of age.

The wife of Josiah WOOD died last Tuesday evening. Interred in the Methodist burying ground in Hamilton, on Thursday May 2d. She leaves a husband and several children.

Lenah, April 30th: The marriage of Mr. Dennie HIGGINS to Miss Katie PALMER, took place as announced at the bride's parent's on Wednesday morning last, at 11:30 o'clock. The bridesmaids were Misses Fannie PALMER, Fannie WILLIAMS, Mary MEYERS and Mollie MAFFETT. They were united by Col. E. V. WHITE of Leesburg. Miss PALMER is of Gum Spring. ...

Friday, 10 May 1889   Vol. XII, No. 2

Married: May 2d 1880, at Lutheran Parsonage, Lovettsville by Dr. D. SCHINDLER, Mr. William H. FILLER and Miss Jennie HUNTER, both of Loudoun.

Col. Geo. W. CARTER returned to the ministry. He is a native of Loudoun and a brother of Armstead CARTER Esq.

Died: Near Centreville, Fairfax Co, April 28th, Elizabeth T., wife of Henry SWART, in the 68th year of her age.

Died: At his home near Leesburg, Richard T. WHITE, on April 27th 1889. He was a member of the M. E. Church, South.

Friday, 17 May 1889   Vol. XII, No. 3

May Ct.: Will of John McCABE admitted to probate. N. H. KENT qualified as Admr. wwa of Margarat A. STANSBURY dec'd. Estate of R. Y. MORAN, John KEEN and J. W. KEEN committed to Sheriff. John H. HUGHES and W. R. CHINN qualified as Notary Public.

Godfrey SHELLHORNE of Loudoun died near Farmwell on Tuesday. He came to Leesburg from Germany many years ago.

Elizabeth Mathews RUSSELL, widow of Caleb RUSSELL, formerly a resident of Loudoun, died at the home of her son, Theodore RUSSELL, in Henry County, Iowa, on the 5th inst. She was a sister of Rebecca BIRDSALL, who lives near Lincoln. She was probably 80 years old and a long suffer of asthma. Life long member of the Society of Friends. Since above writing received letter - Born May 17th 1805 (84 years ago today) and married June 8th 1843. She with her husband moved to Iowa in 1854.

Mr. John McCABE, the father of Charles P. McCABE and grandfather of Judge J. B. McCABE, of Leesburg, died at the residence of his son, in this town, on Thursday last, in the 92 year of his age. He was one of the soldiers of the war of 1812 leaving but one, Dr. DRAKE, of Leesburg, living in this section who went through the trying scenes of that period.

Friday, 24 May 1889 Vol. XII, No. 4

A married license was issued in Washington, on Wednesday, to Francis T. LOWE and Maggie E. THOMPSON, both of Dover, Loudoun Co.

Albert CHANDLEE died at his home near Sandy Spring, Md, last Monday morning. For 2 or 3 years he had been in ill health. He was a member of the Society of Friends. His father, who survives him, is in the 99th year of his age.

Mr. R. H. KITIS and Miss Ida PORTER were married last night in the M. E. Church. She is the daughter of Rev. A. J. PORTER, Presiding elder. The groom is from Old Point. Both are member of the Good Templars. The ceremony was performed by Rev. J. S. WICKLINE, assisted by Rev. S. A. BALL, both Good Templars. They will locate in Philadelphia. *Alexandria Gazette*

George GRIFFIN, colored, was run over by a train on the W. & O. road just north of this city early yesterday morning and died a few hours afterwards. GRIFFIN and a colored girl named Francis BRISCO had been to a dance where they indulged too freely in liquor.

Married: At the M. E. Parsonage, Herndon, by Rev. S. A. BALL, May 16th, Mr. Mark COCKRILL and Miss Maude C. P. MOXLEY, both of Fairfax Co.

Married: At the Episcopal Rectory in Baltimore, on Thursday, May 16th 1889, by Rev. George A. LEAKIN, Mr. Edgar W. BIRKBY, of Leesburg, and Miss Mamie BAILEY, of Baltimore.

Married: May 2nd 1889, at Lutheran parsonage, Lovettsville, by Dr. D. SCHINDLER, Mr. William B. FILLER and Miss Jennie HUNTER, both of Loudoun Co.

Married: In Salem, May 8, 1889, by the Rev. J. R. BRIDGES, J. E. BLAIR, of Richmond, to Mrs. A. P. VENABLE, sister of officiating minister.

Died: In Richmond, Saturday, May 18th at 1:35 p.m., Mary Amanda Bentley, wife of Dr. Richard Heath DABNEY, of the University of Indiana, and the youngest child of E. B. BENTLEY, of that city.

Died: At the home of her son, John F. KIDWELL, near Herndon station, Fairfax Co, on the morning of April 20th 1889, Mrs. Ann KIDWELL in the 66th year of age.

Friday, 31 May 1889 Vol. XII, No. 5

The little child of Mr. Henry FURR died about a week ago of diphtheria. Another child has since been afflicted.

Friday, 7 June 1889   Vol. XII, No. 6

Sketch: Mr. Louis D. WINE, prominent in business in Washington. He is a native of Loudoun Co Va and began life as a school teacher. ... He has a fine country residence at Hyattsville, Md, known as Ravenswood.

Sketch: Wm. H. SAUNDERS, son of Mr. Henry SAUNDERS, near Leesburg, and now Junior member of the real estate firm of John SHERMAN & Co. He came to Washington in August 1887. ...

A daughter of Mr. Sidnor BENNETT, who died at Clarksburg, Md, was buried at Catoctin Free Church yesterday.

Mr. Lucien POWELL returned to his old home on Wednesday. He is employed in New York by speculators in works of art.

The two remaining children of Mr. Henry FURR died from diphtheria, were buried yesterday at Leesburg Cemetery. They both died on Wednesday morning at about 4 and 9 o'clock.

Mr. Wm. KENT, at Short Hill, fell dead near his home last Tuesday morning, of heart disease.

Philomont: Mr. B. F. BROWN who has been in declining health for several years, died at his brother-in-law BUTTER's Monday evening about 7 o'clock. His remains were interred in the Friends burying ground at Lincoln Wednesday.

Married: At the bride's mother's near Morrisonville, by Rev. C. F. BEALES, May 21st '89, Mr. David E. JACOBS and Miss R. J. HUNTER, both of Loudoun Co.

Friday, 14 June 1889   Vol. XII, No. 7

Died: William CLENDENNING, at his home near Hillsboro, June 10th, with pneumonia, in the 46th year of his age.

Died: At Daysville, Loudoun Co, May 2d, 1889, Mrs. R. Virginia HAVENNER, wife of B. T. HAVENER, in the 41st year of her age.

Col. John M. RICHARDSON, formerly of Loudoun Co, died at Tucson, Arizona, May 1st, and was buried near his home, at Carthage, Mo., on May 5th. He left Loudoun for Missouri, and subsequently served in the Union army where he gained the position of Colonel. A few months since he went to Arizona in hopes of improving his health. His wife also died only a few months ago. He was 68 year of age.

Waterford: Mrs. Anna McKINNEY, wife of Mr. J. W. McKINNEY, who has been in ill health for several months, died at her home early yesterday morning.

Waterford: Miss Virginia BENNETT, daughter of Sydnor BENNETT, died very suddenly at Rockville, Md, on the 4th inst.

Mrs. Margaret DULIN, widow of the late Alfred DULIN, of this county, and mother of Mr. George C. DULIN, died at Cool Springs, Md, on Monday last, in the 77th year of her age. Her remains were interred in Union Cemetery, Leesburg.

June Ct.: Xlberta [Alberta] J. PIGGOTT qualified as guardian of Mary E. PIGGOTT. Estates of Julius MASON and Maria MASON committed to sheriff. Will of Wm. H. STEPHENSON admitted to probate. G. B. GIBSON and Jos. A. GIBSON qualified Admr. of John N. GIBSON. Albert MILHOLIN qualified as Admr. of B. F. BROWN dec'd.

Friday, 21 June 1889   Vol. XII, No. 8

Died: At Sterling, June 14th, 1889, Goldie Rozella, daughter of W. S. and Mattie R. WILEY, aged 13 months.

Died: Mrs. Hattie B. GLASCOCK, of Washington, widow of the late Capt. Alfred GLASCOCK, died at the home of her mother, Mrs. Orra M. FADELY, in Leesburg, on Monday evening last, in about the 44th year of her age.

Died: Mrs. Margaret DULIN, relict of the late Albred [Alfred] DULIN at Silver Springs, Montgomery Co Md, June 9th '89, in the 78th year of her age. For most of her life a resident of Loudoun and for many years a member of M. E. Church, South, of Leesburg.

Lenah: Death of Mr. John CHINN, who died after retiring Friday evening. Heart disease is supposed to have been the cause of his death. His remains were interred in the family burying ground, Sunday morning at 10 o'clock.

Friday, 28 June 1889   Vol. XII, No. 9

Last two pages missing, no marriages or deaths.

Friday, 5 July 1889   Vol. XII, No. 10

Announcement Wednesday morning, July 3d, of the death of Mr. William CLINE during the night before (daughter-in-law and granddaughter in home with him.) He was the senior member of the Hardware firm of Cline & Sons of Leesburg and a member of the M. E. Church, South. He died in the 72d year of his age. Interment in Union Cemetery Friday afternoon.

On the farm of Col. J. R. BRINTON, about one mile S of Leesburg, last Tuesday morning, Mr. S. A. CAMPBELL and Mr. S. E. HORSEMAN who were employed on the farm were driving a flock of sheep in pen. A prop that supported the roof was knocked out of position and stuck Mr. HORSEMAN on the head and causing almost instant death. He was 33 years old and leaves a wife and one child.

Died at the home of her father in Waterford, June 12, 1889, Mrs. Annie B. McKINNEY, aged 32y 10m 20d. She leaves a husband and three small children.

Died: Nellie JAMES, June 29th 1889, infant daughter of John E. and Alberta JAMES aged 10m 23d.

Died: On Saturday, June 22nd, 1889, at Whitehall, the residence of her uncle, T. S. TITUS, of cholera infantum, Virginia, daughter of Clinton and Lennie E. HOSKINSON, aged 8m 9d.

Died: In Washington city, on Friday June 18th 1889, at 12 o'clock, after a long and painful illness, Samuel TITUS, husband of Martha A. TITUS, in the 75th year of his age.

Died: At the residence of his brother, Edwin DAVIS, near Farmwell, June 19th 1889, Mr. Robert L. DAVIS.

Friday, 12 July 1889   Vol. XII, No. 11

Kersey HOLMES (son of the late Dr. Jesse HOLMES) and wife are visiting, they reside at Kearney, Neb.

Charley WILLIAMS, of Lovettsville, buried his oldest child on Wednesday, the 10th inst., aged 12 years.

Married: On the Harper's Ferry bridge, June 25th 1889, by Rev. Jas M. STEVENSON, Mr. Jas. D. COPELAND of Loudoun to Miss Lizzie WALDRON, of Connecticut.

Died: Morris Lee BROWN, infant son of Dr. and Mrs. L. A. BROWN, of Leesburg, July 4th 1889, aged 3m 6d.

Friday, 19 July 1889   Vol. XII, No. 12

No marriages or deaths.

Friday, 26 July 1889   Vol. XII, No. 13

Mr. H. E. ALTMAN, of Loudoun, and Miss Hattie MARTIN of Fauquier co were married in Baltimore on Sunday last.

Mrs. Mary E. LOTT, relict of the late Parkenson L. LOTT, died in Leesburg, Thursday night of last week.

Lenah: Mr. L. E. HUTCHISON, a formerly resident of this county, lost one of his children last week.

Lenah: We record the death of Mrs. Jno. WILSON on 17th inst. She has been a sufferer for about 14 years. Her remains were interred in the family burying ground, near Middleburg, on Friday.

Married: Married at the residence of the bride's father, near Oatland, July 17th, 1889, by Rev. C. T. HERNDON, Miss Lillie DODD and Mr. W. G. GIBSON, all of Loudoun.

Died: Near Snickersville, Thursday, July 11th 1889, Mary Eleen [Ellen?], infant dau. of John B. and Bettie SANTENYERS, aged 11d.

Died: Near Leesburg, on July 17th '89, after a lingering illness for several months, Mrs. Lucy L., beloved wife of David GAINS, and daughter of the late Thomas A. and Precilla C. GAINS, near Middleburg, in the 44th year of her age.

Died: At "Newstard" near Bloomfield, July 19th 1889, of cholera infantum, Richard Chamblin, son of Henry and Lizzie FRASIER, aged 7m 2d.

Died: On the morning of July 19th '89, Ella, baby of Henry and Cossie JANNEY, a few months old.

Friday, 2 August 1889   Vol. XII, No. 14

Mrs. Mary B. BALL, wife of G. W. BALL, formerly of Loudoun, died at her home in Alexandria, last week.

Rebecca M. THOMAS, of Sandy Md, died at Mountain Lake Park on the morning of the 24th inst., after an illness of only two days. Her son, Dr. Frank THOMAS, and family, had just sailed for Europe.

Philomont: Miss Mary TATE, an elderly lady who for many years has been afflicted with paralysis, died at W. H. TAYLOR's Monday evening and was interred in the Friends burying ground at Lincoln, Wednesday.

Mrs. Mary HUTCHISON, consort of the late Beverly HUTCHISON Esq., departed this life at the residence of her son, Ludwell HUTCHISON, near Little River, on the 26th inst., after a long and painful illness. she was in her 79th year. Interred in family burying ground Sunday morning.

Mary TATE, who lived near Philomont, died on Monday about 12 m. Member of the Society of Friends, and was buried in their burying ground on Wednesday.

Birth: A son, to M. E. CHURCH and wife, of Falls Church, July 26th.

Friday, 9 August 1889   Vol. XII, No. 15

Mr. Wm. N. McVEIGH, uncle of Mrs. D. KEEN, died in Alexandria recently, aged 80 years. Born in Loudoun, but moved to Alexandria when 8 years of age, and spent his long life almost entirely there.

Mr. Samuel H. MULLEN, of this town, and for several years past a member of the police force, died Sunday morning in the 64th year of his age.

Mr. D. H. VANDEVANTER and Miss Carrie HOUGH, of Waterford, drove to Hamilton and proceeded to the Parsonage and inquired for Rev. EGGLESTON. He being absent, Rev Henry BRANCH united them in marriage. [two days earlier]

Married: At the residence of Mr. W. E. GARRETT, in Leesburg, on Monday morning, Aug 5th 1889, by Rev. G. W. POPKINS, Mr. W. R. SHARPE, of Toledo, Ohio, and Miss Ollie WEILER, of Washington DC.

Died: At "Clover Hill," Fairfax Co, on Monday, July 29th 1889, of dysentery, Orion, son of L. E. and Bettie HUTCHISON, in the 5th year of his age.

Died: Near Hillsboro, Thursday, July 18, 1889, Gracie Lee, infant dau. of Luther J. and Emma HOLTSCLAW, aged 5 months.

Died: At his residence near Mt. Gilead, on the 29th inst., in the 51st year of his age, Charles E. TAYLOR, after a short illness.

Died: Nancy WEADON, near Lincoln, July 29th after a lingering
illness of several months, aged 76 years.

Friday, 16 August 1889   Vol. XII, No. 16

John WILDMAN and wife, of Bucks Co. Pa are visiting at the
childhood home of the latter, the residence of her brother-in-law,
Thos. BROWN, near Lincoln, accompanied by a granddaughter,
Miss Sallie TWINING.

Bolington: John STEWART died at his home, last Sunday, after a
lingering illness. His remains were laid to rest in the Rehoboth
burying ground on Monday.

George COOPER, a brother of John COOPER, near Morrisonville,
died on Tuesday 20th inst.

Died: Near Mt. Hope Church, July 31st 1889, Mary Margaret, infant
dau. of Burr T. and Malvina G. ALEXANDER, aged six months.

Died: Clara Blanch GRUBB, infant daughter of L. M. and Maggie V.
GRUBB, died at the residence of Benj. GRUBB, near
Taylortown, July 13th, 1888, aged 10m 21d.

Died: Mr. F. M. COLE, near Middleburg, Aug. 11th '89, aged 65
years.

Died: Mrs. Jane JONES, wife of Mr. Burr JONES, at Mt. Gilead, Aug.
10th '89, of chronic diarrhea, in the 56th year of her age.

Married: On Aug. 9th '89, in Frederick city, by Rev. Mr. DEIHL, John
C. MOORE to Miss Katie MYERS, both of Loudoun.

Friday, 30 August 1889   Vol. XII, No. 18

Died: Thomas KIDWELL, at his home, 3 miles NW of Lovettsville, on
Tuesday night, Aug. 12th in the 65th year of his age. He was
taken suddenly ill about 7 p.m. with piercing pains in his breast,
and passed away at 11 o'clock.

A marriage license was issued in Washington a few days ago to Mr.
Geo. W. DARR, of Loudoun, and Miss Lorinda SPINDLE, of
Fairfax.

A serious accident last Saturday, in which a child of Isaac
JACKSON was killed. The horse attached to the car in which
JACKSON's wife and child and sister-in-law were riding was
frightened and upset the car, killing the child instantly.

Friday, 6 September 1889   Vol. XII, No. 19

Miss Gertie GRIFFITH of Round Hill died last Thursday, aged about
22 years. Her remains were sent to Washington for interment.

Mrs. Dr. WELTY and family left on Tuesday enroute to join her
husband and oldest son at their new home, on the Shoshonee
Indian Agency, in Wyoming.

Friday, 13 September 1889   Vol. XII, No. 20

Announced Sunday morning that Thomas H. GORE died, at his home in Washington, after a short illness of about a week. He was born in Hughesville, 51 years ago. During the past 6 or 7 years he has, with his brother-in-law, Rodney JANNEY, been successfully conducting a business in Washington. The remains were brought back to his native soil on Monday and the funeral conducted at Friends meeting house, in Lincoln, at 4 o'clock on that day.

Lenah: We report that death of Mr. Jno. H. FERGUSON, formerly of this county, who died at his residence in Washington on the 3rd inst. His remains were brought to Loudoun and interred in Mt. Zion Cemetery.

Sept. Ct.: Will of Samuel W. GEORGE Sr. admitted to probate. Estate of John W. STEWART dec'd committed to sheriff. V. V. PURSELL appointed committee of Robt. OSBURN. Estate of Mary BROWN committed to sheriff and powers of Chas. J. BROWN Exor. revoked. Will of Achsah W. SMITH admitted to probate and estate committed to sheriff. Geo. W. TITUS qualified as Admr. of Geo. COOPER. Tom HAMILTON (colored) found guilty of intent to kill another colored man and given 5 years.

Died: James T. SCHOOLEY, at the residence of his parents, in Waterford, 8th month 25th 1889, in the 11th year of his age.

Friday, 20 September 1889   Vol. XII, No. 21

Mr. William CRAVEN died at the residence of his nephew, E. J. C. MOFFETT, near Arcola, on the 11th inst., at an advanced age.

Sept. Ct.: Estates of John JANNEY and John L. JORDAN committed to sheriff.

Catastrophe occurred near Union last Tuesday causing the death, by drowning, of Misses ATWELL and KATOR, from Alexandria and Georgetown, who were visiting at Union, when crossing Moore's ford.

Died: At the husband's residence near Mountsville, Mrs. Sallie M. GOUCHNAUER, wife of W. L. GOCHNAUR, departed this life Sunday, Sept. 1st 1889, aged 50 years.

Friday, 27 September 1889   Vol. XII, No. 22

The Alexandria *Gazette* of last Thursday announced the death on that day of Mr. G. Frank KELLY, of which Loudoun Co was his native soil. He had been sick for some time at the Alexandria House where he made his home. For many years he was a senior member of the well known firm Kelly & Carr, which was dissolved only a few months ago.

Mr. Milton PANGLE departed this life, at his residence about 3 miles SE of Arcola, on Monday morning last, in the 65th year of his

age. He moved from upper Loudoun into this section some 5 or 6
years ago. His daughters are accomplished women.
Last Tuesday morning, about 9 a.m., Mr. James M. WALLACE died
very suddenly at his home in Hamilton. He had only been home
a few days from a visit to some of his children in Massachusetts.
On Thursday the remains were taken to Leesburg and buried in
Union Cemetery, nearly 80 years fro the time of his birth. About
three years ago Mr. WALLACE married Mrs. Mary WHITE, of
this vicinity, and settled in Hamilton. He was for a time a Justice
of the Peace in this district and later a Director in the Loudoun
National Bank. He was a first cousin of Gen. Lew. WALLACE.
On Tuesday morning Mrs. Sarah BOND, relict of the late Edward
BOND, died at the home of her daughter, Mrs. Laura SHUEY, in
the town of Waterford. She had reached the ripe age of 80 odd
years. On Wednesday the body was laid to rest in the Friends
burying ground.
Died: Winona Somers, son of Joseph T. & Sarah DIVINE, at their
home in Waterford, Sept. 17th, aged 6y 3m 25d.
Died: Near Gum Spring, Va, Sept. 11th 1889, after a short illness,
William Holmes CRAVEN, in the 68th year of his age.
Died: Cleveland TINSMAN, near Upperville, Sept. 19th 1889, of brain
affection, youngest son of J. M. and S. J. TINSMAN.

Friday, 4 October 1889   Vol. XII, No. 23

The funeral of Mrs. Mary BURCH, wife of Edgar F. BURCH, of this
county, who died last Saturday, took place from St. James
Episcopal church Tuesday morning, Rev. Dr. DAVIS officiating.
The remains were interred in Union Cemetery.
Died: At his home near Hillsboro July 29th, Samuel, second son of
Ann and the late Thomas McARTER, in the 32nd year of his age.
Died: In Leesburg, on Friday night, Sept. 20th, after a short illness of
dysentery, at the residence of her grandmother Mrs. Catharine
RYAN, Katie Celestine CROSS, oldest child of William and
Annie V. CROSS, aged 9y 6m 18d.
Married: Mr. Klein WRIGHT and Miss Virginia Lee HOUGH were
married at the Episcopal parsonage in Anacostia by the Rev. W.
G. DAVENPORT at 3 o'clock Tuesday afternoon, Sept. 17th. The
bride wore a dress of gray Henrietta cloth and was attended by
Miss Mamie QUIGLEY.
Married: Sept. 26 '89, by Rev. Dr. SCHINDLER, at the hand of Mr.
Charles BROWN, near Lovettsville, Mr. Luther McKINNEY to
Miss C. Virginia CRUMBAKER both of Loudoun Co.

Friday, 11 October 1889   Vol. XII, No. 24

Married: On the 1st of October, at the St. James Hotel, Washington DC, Mr. G. H. HORSEMAN to Miss Eva V. MUNDAY, by the Rev. G. W. POPKINS.

Mrs. Annie ELLIOTT returned to the home of her father, Thomas R. SMITH, from her new home in West Liberty, Iowa.

Miss Frances FAUNTLEROY, dau. of the late Capt. Charles M. FAUNTLEROY, of Leesburg, was married at Oakland Plantation, Rapides parish, La, Wednesday last to Mr. Charles CHAFFE Jr.

Sterling: Marriages yesterday by Rev. W. C. P. COLE: Wm. MORGAN and Miss Sallie WALKER, Chas. H. ADAMS and Miss Blanche WOODS, and Mary PHILLIPS [?? – female name] and Miss Rose BROWN.

Sterling: rumor also say John BLINCOE and Miss B. THAYER were married also.

Sterling: We also had a death here yesterday, a 3 year old daughter of E. M. ALEXANDER.

Neersville: On Sunday evening the 6th, Jessie, the 5 year old dau. of Mr. N. J. CULLEN, was literally roasted alive. Mrs. CULLEN went to the barn to milk, leaving Jessie and her two small brothers in the house. She returned to find the child in the doorway completely enveloped in flames. She died about 11 o'clock Sunday. It is supposed the children had taken an oil can from a shelf and were pouring oil into the stove and it exploded.

Mrs. Baily COCKERILL, an aged widow, who lived about 4 miles S of Leesburg, was frightened to death last Saturday night. Her son-in-law, David BLAIR, went home drunk and assaulted his wife. The old lady interfered when BLAIR threatened to kill her, and went to get his pistol. She rushed from the house and an unmarried daughter ran after her. She died a short time later.

Jacob SCOTT, of Waterford, died last Saturday morning at the home of Mr. Geo. SCHOOLEY, where he had been living for some time. For years he was subject to epileptic fits. He was 85 years of age. The funeral took place on the Sabbath at Friends Meeting House. ...

Mr. Geo. LAYCOCK, of the firm of Tavenner & Laycock, and Miss Ella G. JOHNSON were united in marriage at the home of the latter, in Washington, at 3:30 p.m. yesterday, by the Rev. Mr. GREEN, of that city.

Friday, 18 October 1889   Vol. XII, No. 25

Emma DUTTON, wife of John B. DUTTON, of Waterford, sick for many months, died at 3 o'clock this morning. Funeral Sunday 10 a.m.

Mr. C. B. HESS died suddenly at his home, in Leesburg, last Monday night. He leaves a wife and child.

Oct. Ct.: Wills of Jas. M. WALLACE dec'd, Jacob SCOTT dec'd, M. M. ROGERS dec'd, Wm. KOLB and Susan Ann VIRTS dec'd admitted to probate. Estate of Abel WARFORD dec'd committed to Sheriff.

Married: On the 3d inst., at the residence of the officiating clergyman, by the Rev. Dr. Nelson HEAD, Mr. C. F. HAWLING to Miss Mollie M. BROWN, all of Loudoun.

Died: Sept. 30th 1889, Mrs. Fannie THOMPSON, wife of Eli THOMPSON, in the 26th year of her age. She leaves 4 stepdaughters and a babe two weeks old.

Died: William H. ADAMS, on Sunday morning, Oct. 6th, at his residence, near Morrisonville, after a short and painful illness, in the 74th year of his age.

Friday, 25 October 1889   Vol. XII, No. 26

The wife of Ham. WOOD, a well known colored man, was buried yesterday.

Dr. Albert GRAY, uncle of Jno. GRAY, of Leesburg, died in Baltimore on the 21st inst.

Emma S. DUTTON, wife of John B. DUTTON, died at her home in Waterford, on the morning of the 18th inst. after 18 months of acute physical suffering which robbed her of her sight. About 3 weeks before her death she was attacked by consumption of the bowels. She was in the 83 year of her age. On the Sabbath her remains were taken to the Friends Meeting House and laid to rest in the grave yard nearby.

Friday, 1 November 1889   Vol. XII, No. 27

Cards are out for the marriage of Mr. E. H. HIRST, of Purcellville, to Miss Annie Almira CASE, of Washington, at Trinity Church, in that city, on Thursday, Nov. 14th.

Mrs. Mary CLARKE died suddenly one day last week, of heart trouble. Interred at Short Hill.

Mr. Richard T. BENTLEY died yesterday at Bloomfield, near Sandy Springs, Md., in the 71st year of his age. At the time of his death he was president of the Sandy Springs Savings Bank and Montgomery Co. mutual fire insurance com. Member of the Society of Friends.

Died: At "Grafton," Clarke Co., the residence of her husband, on Saturday night, Oct. 26th 1889, of pneumonia, Evelyn Byrd LEE, and dau. of the late Wm. Byrd PAGE, of "Pagebrook" Clarke Co and Eliza Mayo Atkinson, his wife. Her remains were followed to the cemetery at the "Old Chapel," on Tuesday, the 29th inst.

Died: Aug. 2d 1889, Roy Raxford, third child of Laura R. and D. S. GREGG, aged 8m 20d.

Last Wednesday evening, as May LEITH, a niece of Mrs. Thos. ROGERS was returning from school to the home of her aunt, she was met in the woods about ½ a mile S of town by Orion ANDERSON, a colored boy in the employ of Mr. Samuel ROGERS, who attacked her with a bag over his head. ... When he was arrested she could not identify him and was released. She is probably 14 years of age and ANDERSON is about 17.

Friday, 8 November 1889   Vol. XII, No. 28

Cards are out for the marriage of Mr. Arthur HOEBER and Miss Mary G. WILDMAN dau. of Mr. J. W. WILDMAN, of Leesburg, at St. James Episcopal church in that town on the 20th inst.

Dr. R. W. JANNEY, son of the late Geo. JANNEY of Hamilton, died at his home in Waterford last Monday night, after a protracted illness of consumption. He was probably 35 years of age, a physician of good repute. He left a wife and child.

We receive a report that ANDERSON, the colored boy who attempted an assault upon May LEITH, near Hamilton, one week ago, was taken from the Leesburg jail, last night and lynched. [see article last issue]

Married: Oct. 24th 1889, at the M. E. Church, South, Berryville, by the Rev. Wm. E. WOOLF, Jos. A. BALDWIN, of Loudoun and Ella J. HARDESTY, of Clarke County.

Married: In Lexington, Dawson Co, Nebraska, at the residence and by Rev. F. R. WOTRING, on Wednesday, Oct. 9th 1889, Mr. Nimrod E. SLACK to Miss Jennie F. MOORE, of Nebraska. Mr. SLACK is a native of Loudoun and successful farmer.

Died: Mrs. Mary WOOD, wife of Hamilton WOOD, died at her home, near Hamilton, Oct. 22d in the 46th year of her age.

Friday, 5 November 1889   Vol. XII, No. 29

Death of Mr. Lewin T. JONES occurred on Thursday of last week, at his home near Waterford, of apoplexy. He was a valued member of the Waterford Farmers Club. He was about 65 years of age. His remains were interred in Union Cemetery, at Leesburg on Saturday, Rev. H. BRANCH officiating.

The marriage of Mr. E. H. HIRST of Purcellville and Miss Anna Almira CASE, of Washington, took place on Wednesday.

Mr. Balie TAYLOR and Miss Clara OSBURN were married at the home of the bride's father, Mr. Jos. OSBORN, near Purcellville, on Tuesday.

Mr. J. A. M. MILLER of Hamilton and Miss Bettie BRAMHALL, near Morrisonville, were married on the 4th inst.

Mr. Levi CUMMINS and Miss Sallie WIGHTMAN were united about three weeks since.

Cards are out for the marriage of Mr. Albert SCANLAND, of Fairfax, and Miss Rosa CHAMBLIN, of Hamilton.
Nov. Ct.: Edgar McCRAY qualified as Admr. of Dr. R. W. JANNEY dec'd. C. Powell NOLAND qualified as Admr. of Susan C. NOLAND dec'd. Wills of Elizabeth SHUMAKER, Mary E. CLARK and Burr P. NOLAND admitted to probate.
Married: On Wednesday morning, Nov. 13th 1889, at the residence of Mrs. Orra M. FADELY, grandmother of the bride, by Rev. B. W. BOND, Mr. David L. GRAYSON, of Chatanooga, Tenn, and Miss May, dau. of the late Capt. Alfred GLASCOCK, of this county.
Married: On Wednesday, Nov. 6, by the Rev. J. P. CAMPBELL, of Faith Presbyterian Church, David A. BRECKENRIDGE, of Leesburg, to Miss Estelle E. SIMS, of Washington DC.
Married: Oct. 9th '89, at the parsonage of the M. E. Church, South, by Rev. B. W. BOND, James SKILLMAN and Annie POLLARD.
Married: At the parsonage of the M. E. Church, South, Leesburg, on Tuesday, Nov. 5th, by Rev. B. W. BOND, Chas. T. MORIARTY and Kate CLARK, all of Loudoun.

Friday, 22 November 1889   Vol. XII, No. 30

At the new Baptist church yesterday, marriage of Mr. Albert T. SCANDLAN, of Dunn Loring, Fairfax Co, and Miss Rosa CHAMBLIN, of Hamilton. ... Little maids of honor, Hazel KEEN and Marbel WILMARTH, in white, with dresses en train. Bridesmaids, Misses Laura CHAMBLIN, Phila CRAIG and Lulu WHARTON accompanied by groomsmen Messrs. Wilmer HAMPTON, Walter CHAMBLIN and Arthur NICHOLS. Rev. C. T. HERNDON performed the marriage rites of the Baptist Church.
On the morning of Nov. 12th, at the home of Mr. and Mrs. J. C. OSBURN, the marriage of their oldest dau., Clara, to Mr. Bailey TAYLOR. Wedding party: Mr. Joe LODGE and Miss Ella WEBSTER; Mr. Joe L. LODGE and Miss Beau WALKER; Mr. Will WILSON and Miss Florence WELSH; Mr. Howard WELSH and Miss Blanch TAYLOR; Mr. Harry TAYLOR and Miss Jessie OSBURN. Rev. I. B. LAKE performed the ceremony. ...
Married: Nov 5th by Rev. I. B. LAKE, Miss Alice OSBURN, at the home of her brother, Mr. Volney OSBURN, near Snickersville, to Mr. Edward SINGLETON, of Georgia.
Died: Mrs. Annie JACOBS, wife of L. T. JACOBS, at her home in Philomont, Nov. 9th in the 38th year of her age. She leaves a little babe and other children.
Died: At the residence of Mrs. Mary WHITE, at Hillsboro, in this county, on Nov. 7th 1889, Miss Cornelia WHITE, in the 82nd year of her age.

Died: Walter Gerome WILEY, at his home in Sterling, Oct. 31st 1889, aged 30y 10m.

Died: On Nov. 5th 1889, from an attack of diphtheria, Mary Elma COLE, little daughter of Kendric B. and Jennie COLE, of North Fork, at the age of 10y 7m.

Friday, 29 November 1889   Vol. XII, No. 31

John F. SMITH of Lovettsville, has moved his family to Hyattsville, near Washington DC where he has engaged for three years in carpentering.

Married: In Leesburg, on Tuesday, Nov. 26th 1889, by Rev. N. HEAD, D.D., Mr. Arthur MULLEN and Miss Ada BROOKS, daughter of the late Philip W. BROOKS, all of this place.

Died: At her home, at Luckett's Cross Roads, on the 10th of Oct '89, Mary LUCKETT, widow of the late Wm. C. LUCKETT in the 77th year of her age.

Friday, 6 December 1889   Vol. XII, No. 32

Last Saturday night 11:30, Solomon RUSE passed away. He passed his 91st birthday in last Sept. Three daughters resided with him. The funeral took place at noon on Tuesday at the Hamilton M. E. Church, South where he was a member for 50 years. He was born on a farm near where Hamilton's X roads is now located, in the vicinity of Morrisonville. His parents, Michael and Elizabeth RUSE, were both raised in that neighborhood. He had ten children, all of whom lived to be very old people, except 1 daughter who died when 15 years old. All the remaining nine are married, none more than once except one sister, who was married three times and she was the only one of the family with no children. Mrs. Katie HIXON, a sister living in Ohio, died a few years ago at the age of 102, and another in the same state, lived to be 91 or more. Many years ago he removed to the neighborhood of Hamilton and located on the farm now owned by Mr. HELM, where he worked at his trade, that of blacksmithing. He afterward moved to Wm. TAVENNER place and worked in the old stone shop, which was torn down only a few years ago. He then moved his shop to the place now occupied by Mr. Thos. SCHOOLEY, in Hamilton, and purchased the farm just north of town, now owned by Hiram TAVENNER. In 1841 he sold all of this farm except a few acres which surrounded his home near the Depot. Twenty years ago next Feb his wife passed over to join two of her children gone before; but 7 children are still living.

Married: At the residence of ??? ??xander [John H. ALEXANDER in Mirror], in Leesburg on Nov. 27th 1889 by the Rev. ?? [C. T.

HERNDON on marriage register], Mr. D. H. TITUS and Miss Hattie V. WHITE, all of Loudoun. [part covered and unreadable]
Married: On the 27th inst., near Lovettsville, by the Rev. St. J. RINKER, Mr. Kenny C. CHINN and Miss Emma V. SOUDER, dau: of Mr. Geo. P. SOUDER, all of Loudoun.
Married: On Monday, Nov. 18, 1889, by Rev. A. R. REILEY, Fenelon D. HAY, of Washington DC, to Bessie E. SURVICK, of Leesburg.
Married: At the residence of the bride's father, J. T. SKINNER, Octavia, Neb., Nov. 23, 1889, Rev. BENTLEY officiating, Prof. M. M. SMITH, formerly of Highland Co, O., to Miss Alice SKINNER, formerly of Loudoun. Both are leading educators of Nebraska.
Died: In Washington, on Sunday, Dec. 1, 1889, at 7:39 p.m., Margaret A. POLAND, widow of the late Alexander POLAND. Interment at Leesburg, on Thursday 5th instant.
Died: On Sunday, Dec. 1, 1889, Edgar COOPER, son of John W. and Sarah A. COOPER, aged 13y 5m 6d.

Friday, 13 December 1889   Vol. XII, No. 33

It is rumored that Dr. Harry WILSON and his sister, Emily, formerly of Lincoln, but now living in Tenn., will both be married soon.
Arthur W. PHILLIPS, of Waterford, married Miss Letitia Annie GOSSLING, of Frankfort, Pa, at the home of the bride's parents in that town on Thanksgiving day. They will reside on his farm near Waterford.
Henry D. HOLLINGSWORTH, son of C. L. HOLLINGSWORTH, of Waterford, who has resided in California for several years married Miss Carrie BOND, who recently left Waterford, at the home of the bride's brother, T. H. BOND, in Stockton, Cal, on the 10th ult. They will reside at Jolon, Monterrey Co., in the southern part of the state where Henry is engaged in farming, or ranching as they call it there.
Miss Ellen MEANS, youngest daughter of the late Capt. Samuel MEANS, of Waterford, was married to Wm. T. HACKETT, of Baltimore, in that city, on the 28th ult. They returned to the home of the bride's mother, at Brooks Sta., DC, near which the groom has been employed for some time.
Dec. Ct: Annie S. FRY qualified as guardian of John T. FRY, Malinda E. FRY, and Wm. B. FRY. R. W. GRUBB qualified as Admr. of Eliza JANNEY dec'd. W. R. JONES qualified as Admr. of Lewen T. JONES dec'd. Estate of Wm. H. STEPHENSON dec'd committed to Sheriff. Wills of Elizabeth and Mary TATE admitted to probate.
Bolington: Mr. Josephus FRY and Miss Jennie WENNER was consummated last week, Rev. SCHINDLER officiating.

Daniel ADAMS, of the vicinity of Wheatland, died on Thursday of last week, aged 79 years. His remains were interred in the Rehoboth burying ground on Saturday.

Married: At New Jerusalem church, Dec. 4th, by Rev. Daniel SCHINDLER, Mr. Josephus M. FRY to Miss Mary V. WENNER, both of Loudoun.

Married: Nov. 28th in Trinity Methodist church, Paris, Va, by Rev. J. C. DICE, Rev. J. C. JONES, paster of Grace M. C. Church, South, Washington DC, and Miss Ada Warren, daughter of Douglas GIBSON, Esq.

Died: Mrs. Julia A., wife of Samuel SLATER, and only sister of Peter A. FRY, died at the residence of her husband, 3 miles E of Lovettsville, on Monday morning Dec. 2d, 1889. Aged 65 years.

Died: At the residence of her son, Mr. Thos. G. ELGIN, near Leesburg, on Thursday night, Dec. 10th 1889, Mrs. Mary J. ELGIN, widow of the late Francis ELGIN, in the 85th year of her age.

Friday, 20 December 1889   Vol. XII, No. 34

License was issued in Washington, yesterday, for the marriage of Henry E. JENIFER of Md. and Carrie A. ROLLINS, of Leesburg.

Mr. R. J. C. THOMPSON of Leesburg died at his home in this town, about midnight Tuesday, in the 79th year of his age. He had been a resident of Leesburg for nearly 60 years, having settled here in 1831. He leaves an aged widow.

Maj. Jas. F. DIVINE, the "Old War Horse" of the temperance cause, died at the home of his daughter, in Washington, on Thursday of last week, in the 73d year of age, and was buried on Saturday, at Leesburg, where he had resided during most of his life. He was one of the pioneer temperance reformers of this section, his principal work was done in the order of Good Templars.

Friday, 27 December 1889   Vol. XII, No. 35

Married: Dec. 19th 1889, at Mr. I. ELGIN's by Rev. J. C. DINWIDDIE, Robert L. DONOHOE to Miss Florence ELGIN.

Married: On the 18th inst., at the Methodist parsonage, Leesburg, by the Rev. Dr. HEAD, Mr. Wm. A. BEANS, and Miss Martha J. WYNKOOP, all of Loudoun.

Married: On the 18th inst., in the Baptist Church, North Fork, by the Rev. C. T. HERNDON, Mr. Thomas MORIARITY and Miss Roberta B. BELL, all of Loudoun.

Married: At the residence of Mr. James H. LAYCOCK, on the 19th inst., by the Rev. C. T. HERNDON, Mr. Oscar M. KEPHART and Miss Mattie E. LAYCOCK, all of Loudoun.

Married: At the residence of the bride's parents, Mr. Charles
JENKINS, his oldest daughter, Miss Ella A. JENKINS, to Mr.
Harry C. FILLER, by the Rev. G. W. POPKINS on the 18th.
Died: Rachel GYDER, at her residence near the Marble Quarry,
Loudoun Co, Dec. 20th 1889, in the 97th year of age. Interred at
North Fork, Dec. 27th.
Mountain Gap: The marriage of Mr. Oscar M. KEPHART and Miss
Mattie E. LAYCOCK took place at the house of the bride.
Neersville: Last Sunday evening, Mr. W. H. SAGLE, drove to the
residence of W. B. RILEY, Esq. to take Miss Lottie EDWARDS
out for a drive, and went to Hillsboro to the residence of Rev.
DULANEY who married them.

Friday, 3 January 1890   Vol. XII, No. 36

A marriage license was issued last Monday in Washington, to
Thomas P. MARKS, of Loudoun, and Kate L. SMITH, of
Alexandria.
Married: At the residence of Wm. E. GARRETT, in Leesburg, on
Dec. 24, 1889, by Rev. Dr. HEAD, Mr. A. P. HUMMER and Miss
C. C. BURDETTE, all of Loudoun.
Married: In Charlestown, Dec. 9th, 1889, by Rev. Dr. A. C.
HOPKINS, Joseph A. CARLISLE, of Loudoun, to Miss Florence
E. BROWNE.
Married: At the Reformed Church, Lovettsville, Dec. 23rd by the Rev.
M. [H.] St. G. [J.] RINKER, Mr. Wallace G. EVERHART to Miss
Eppie EVERHART, all of Loudoun Co.
Married: In the M. E. Church at Lovettsville, Dec. 24th, by Rev. D. C.
HEDRICK, A. Eugene HOUSEHOLDER and Miss M. Ella
COOPER, all of Loudoun Co.
Married: Dec. 24th '89, by Rev. D. C. HEDRICK, Samuel HAWS and
Miss Mollie BAKER.
Died: At the residence of her brother, near Farmwell, on Thursday,
Dec. 19, '89, Miss Hannah Virginia CLOWE, in the 69th year of
age. Interred in Union Cemetery, Leesburg.

Friday, 10 January 1890   Vol. XII, No. 37

A marriage license was recently issued in Washington to Richard R.
HARRIS and Ella J. NEAL of Leesburg.
Rumors in Round Hill to the effect that Miss Jennie LUNSFORD of
that place and George W. GULICK of Kansas will be married in
the near future.
Mrs. Louisa, relict of the Rev. Travis HERNDON, passed away at
the residence of her niece at Round Hill, on last Sunday, at the
advanced age of 87 years. Interred at Middleburg.
On Monday of last week, while two sons of Chas. BAKER near
Taylortown, were out hunting, one of them slipped and

discharged the gun and the load took effect in the head and neck of his brother, who died in a few minutes.

Death: Near Lovettsville, on the 23rd of Dec 1889, Michael WIARD, aged 93 years.

Death: At Morrisonville, Dec. 23, 1889, Mr. Jno. PRICE, in 76th year of his age. He was one of Harper's Ferry's merchants until the beginning of the war.

Married: In Washington DC, Jan. 2, 1890, by Rev. S. W. HADDAWAY, Willie L. ELGIN and Mollie T. RODGERS.

Married: On the 2d inst., at the residence of Capt. Wm. E. GARRETT, Leesburg, by the Rev. Dr. Nelson HEAD, Mr. J. W. BROWN to Mrs. Frances O. BROWN, all of Loudoun.

Married: By the Rev. John WOOLF, at his residence on the 31st of Dec 1889, Mr. Chas. E. LONGERBEAM to Miss Sarah C. REED.

Died: At the residence of her brother, near Farmwell, on Thursday, Dec. 19, '89, Miss Hannah Virginia CLOWE, in the 69th year of age. Interred in Union Cemetery, Leesburg.

Mr. Chas. GARDNER departed this life the 31st of Dec. in the 87th year of his age. The funeral was conducted by the Rev. G. W. POPKINS.

Friday, 17 January 1890   Vol. XII, No. 38

Samuel C. HOLMES, who death is announced in this paper, was a son of the late William HOLMES.

The death Monday last, of E. H. CHAMBERS, of Harpers Ferry. He was father of Mrs. C. W. LITTLEJOHN, of Leesburg. We do not know his age, but he was well up in the eighties.

Co. Ct.: Wills of Louisa H. L. HERNDON, Solomon RUSE and Elizabeth COMPHER were admitted to probate. Estate of R. L. DAVIS and Wm. T. CLENDENNING were committed to the Sheriff.

Ruth Hannah SMITH, widow of the late John SMITH, died suddenly about 10 o'clock last night, at the home of her son-in-law, David BIRDSALL, at an advance age. Funeral tomorrow (Sat.) at Lincoln, 2:30 p.m.

Mrs. Ann CRUZEN, widow of the late Wm. CRUZEN, of the Harper's Ferry U. S. Arsenal, died last Monday in her 95th year. She leaves nine children, 31 grandchildren, 43 great grandchildren and one great-great grandchild. She was born in Harper's Ferry on July 26, 1786. Two of her brothers fought in the Revolutionary War. She was among the earliest settlers of Harper's Ferry. Her youngest child, John R. CRUSEN, is now sheriff of Cumberland. The first grave that existed in Harper's Ferry was dug by a brother of hers.

Died: Samuel C. HOLMES, on the 11th inst., at his residence in Dover, Deleware, of pneumonia, formerly of Loudoun.

Died: On Jan. 8, '90, in Washington, Marvin Paul, son of Wm. D. and Mary E. EASTERDAY, aged ten years.
Died: At Sterling, Jan. 1, '90, Eugenia, only daughter of B. A. and Sallie N. SHREVE, aged 3y 1m.
Died: At the residence of her husband, Oscar TAYLOR, at Fall River, Kansas, Jan. 3, 1890, Mrs. Ella F. TAYLOR, daughter of the late Luther A. TRASHER [THRASHER], of Loudoun.

Friday, 24 January 1890   Vol. XII, No. 39

C. E. LUNSFORD, formerly of Round Hill, lost a little child in Alexandria on the 21st, of pneumonia. She was buried at Catoctin, Wednesday.
Last Wednesday, at the home of Mr. J. H. ORRISON, the marriage of his sister Miss Loretta ORRISON to Mr. John WRIGHT of Fauquier Co. At 1 p.m. Rev. W. G. EGGLESTON performed the ceremony. Mr. Will MYERS and Miss Nora THOMAS acted as attendants. They will reside near Orlean, Fauquier Co.
On Sunday evening, January 19th, Mr. Thos. AYERS, died at his home near "Oak Hill." His remains were interred in the Union Cemetery, Leesburg, Tuesday evening.

Friday, 31 January 1890   Vol. XII, No. 40

Old Kitty CHAMP, relict of the late Joseph CHAMP, aged colored woman, died at Swamp Poodle, last Monday night.
Cards are out for the marriage at St. James Episcopal Church, Leesburg, at 7 p.m. Tuesday, Feb. 18th 1890, of Miss Annie, dau. of the late R. M. BENTLY, and Mr. Howard SCRIBNER, of Philadelphia.
Mrs. Delia DONOHOE, wife of Mr. John C. DONOHOE, died at her home in this town, on Saturday evening last, after one week's illness, of catarrhal pneumonia, in the 48th year of her age. She was a member of the M. E. Church, South. Her funeral took place on Monday, Rev. B. W. BOND, Dr. N. HEAD and D. C. HEDRICK officiating. Interred in Union Cemetery.
Neersville: John G. EDWARDS was married to Miss Virginia MILLS, of Brownsville, Md, last Thursday.
Death of Mrs. Edgar HIRST occurred Wednesday afternoon at the home of her parents, in Washington, from which only a few weeks since she went forth a bride. She went to Washington last Sunday morning, death cause by neuralgia of the stomach. The body will be brought up this (Friday) morning and the funeral will take place at Friends Meeting House, at Lincoln, at 12 o'clock.
Married: On the 22d inst, at Short Hill Baptist Church, by A. A. P. NEEL, J. Hoover ADAMS and Mary E. JENKINS, both of this county.

Died: In Washington DC, Jan. 23, 1890, Samuel MORRISON, aged 65 years.

Died: At Mt. Gilead, Jan. 16th 1890, John W. DENNIS, aged 53y 3m.

Died: Wm. Summers OSBURN, son of Mary and the late Mortimer OSBURN, at his home in Baltimore, on the morning of the 21st, in the 42d year of his age.

Died: At her par[en]ts home near Union, Jan. 23d, 1890, Rosa Myrtle, infant daughter of J. Clay and Emma JENKINS, aged 4m.

Died: On Wednesday, Jan. 29, 1890, at 9:45 a.m., Annie Almira, wife of Edgar Heston HIRST and dau. of W. W. and Mary F. CASE, at the home of the latter in Washington DC.

Died: Flavius C., only son of Jno. J. OTLEY, at his home near Silcott Springs in the 16th year of his age.

Mrs. Annie SMALLWOOD, wife of F. M. SMALLWOOD and dau. of Wm. C. and Amelia MORGAN, of Clark Co, departed this life of typhoid pneumonia, at the residence of Thos. L. HUMPHREY, Loudoun Co, Jan. 14th, 1880 [1890]. Her funeral was preached by Rev. J. C. DICE, of Loudoun circuit, buried in the Ebenezer cemetery. Leaves a husband and three small children.

Friday, 7 February 1890   Vol. XII, No. 41

[*Baltimore Sun* of Wednesday] Anna M. HYNSON, widow of Benjamin T. HYNSON and daughter of Edward and Maria KENLY, at her home in Baltimore, on Monday.

[*Baltimore Sun* of Wednesday] On the same day, in New York city, Anna S., wife of Ezra LIPPINCOTT, and daughter of the late Jas. SUTTON.

Farmwell: Frank N. FURR died after a long struggle with typhoid pneumonia. He was the owner of the celebrated "Flash".

Herbert OSBORN, treasurer of Loudoun Co, died at his home in Leesburg, last Tuesday, in his 47th year, of pneumonia. Leaves a wife and three children. Member of the Knights of Pythias and Masonic fraternities, and an official of the M. E. Church, South. Funeral took place yesterday (Thursday) at Union Cemetery, Leesburg.

[*Baltimore American*] Death of Mahlon CHANDLEE took place at his home near Sandy Spring, Md, on Wednesday. He passed his 99th birthday on the 23d of last December.

The wedding of Mr. J. E. WILLIAMS and Miss Libbie J. WELLS occurred here [Denver Col.] Jan. 28. Both were formerly residents of Sterling, Va.

Died: At the residence of her husband, near Snickersville, Jan. 28th, 1890, Marietta, wife of James ALDER, aged 46 years.

Died: In Atlanta, Ga., Jan. 27th '90, at the residence of her son, Thos. H. HOGE, Mrs. Mary A. HOGE, relict of the late Thos. HOGE, of Loudoun.

Died: Mary J. BUTTS, wife of Oliver G. BUTTS, near Harpers Ferry, Feb. 2d, 1890, in the 65th year of her age. She leaves several children.

Friday, 14 February 1890   Vol. XII, No. 42

Mr. John B. MORRIS, formerly of Rose Mount, Clarke Co, died in Richmond Thursday the 6th. He was totally blind.

Chas. L. HOLLINGSWORTH sold his farm at Waterford to Will JAMES, and with wife and daughter expect to take a trip to California where two of his sons reside.

Wm. H. GRAY died at the home of his son, Rev. Arthur P. GRAY, at Amherst C. H., Va, on the 8th inst., in the 85th year of his age. Native of Loudoun. Brought to Leesburg for interment.

Wm. DODD and his wife, residing near Mountsville – Mrs. DODD died on Monday the 19th inst, and her husband died the next day, Tuesday, the 11th. Both had passed their three score and ten.

Mrs. Elizabeth McCRAY, wife of Wm. McCRAY, died at her home, near Hamilton, last Sunday about 11 o'clock. On Tuesday her remains were interred at the Friends burying ground, at Lincoln. She would have been 76 years of age in April next.

Feb. Ct.: Administrations granted on the estates of Frank N. FURR dec'd, Amos HUGHES dec'd, Geo. W. FLING dec'd, Catherine CHAMP dec'd and Wm. SMITH dec'd. Will of Herbert OSBURN dec'd admitted to probate. C. C. GAVER qualified as Notary Public. Estate of Wm. E. LUCKETT committed to sheriff.

Married: At the residence of Ish MYERS, Feb. 6, 1890, by Rev. D. C. HEDRICK, Mr. Jos. W. CORDELL to Miss Amanda E. STOUT, all of Loudoun.

Married: On the 5th inst., near North Fork, by Rev. C. T. HERNDON, Robt. WILLIAMS to Maud SPALDING, all of Loudoun.

Died: At her home, near Philomont, Feb. 5th 1890, Mrs. Delilah BEAVERS, widow of the late Thos. BEAVERS, in the 84th year of her age.

Died: Mrs. Catharine CHAMP, widow of the late Joseph L. CHAMP, at her home near Hamilton, Jan. 27th in the 73d year of her age.

Friday, 21 February 1890   Vol. XII, No. 43

Just as the meeting at that place was dismissed, last Sabbath, a funeral cortege arrived with the body of Mary WALTERS, whose death occurred on Friday, at the residence of her sister, near Philomont.

Tolliver BOLYN also received the final summons on Friday. He was attacked by the grippe about two weeks before and went to the home of his brother, Somerfield BOLYN, near Lincoln, where he died on Friday. He had been continuously employed in Purcell's store in Purcellville for probably half of his about sixty years.

Eli J. HOGE of Hughesville and member of Society of Friends, died at 6 p.m. on Tuesday. On Thursday at 3 p.m. he was borne to Friends Meeting house at Lincoln and laid in the graveyard.

At "Oakland Green" the residence of William H. and Martha J. BROWN, on the morning of the 18th inst., the marriage of their dau. Susan P., to Fayette WELSH. Bridal party: Will H. WILSON and Lizzie B. SMITH; Thomas J. BROWN and Thamsin NICHOLS; Will WELSH and Mary E. HOGE; Ross CRAVEN and Florence WELSH; followed by the bride and groom. She was attired in dark green silk, carrying a bouquet of flowers. The ceremony of the Society of Friends was recited.

Bolington: Mr. John WRIGHT, who has been an invalid for the last year, died on Wednesday of last week. Interred in the burying ground at Mt Olivet on Friday.

Bolington: Miss Mary LEWIS, of our village, died after a lingering illness, last Saturday night. Interred in the Rehoboth Cemetery on Monday.

Lenah: Thos. MANLEY, an aged and honorable colored citizen, died on the 12th inst.

Lenah: Henry B. HUTCHISON Esq. died at his residence 2 miles SW of Lenah, on the 3rd inst., of pneumonia.

Married: On the 12th inst., at the residence of the bride's father, by Rev. C. T. HERNDON, Howard THOMPSON to Mary E. TRUSSELL, all of Loudoun.

Married: On Jan. 15th '90 at the home of the bride, by Rev. J. E. ZERGER, Flavius J. HOWELL, of Round Hill, to Miss Florence J. MICHAEL, of near Mountain Dale, Frederick Co, Md.

Died: On Feb. 11th 1890, Charlotte E. DENHAM, daughter of L. H. DENHAM and the late Caroline DENHAM, at her late residence, 463 G. St, NW, Washington DC.

Died: At the home of her sister, Elizabeth GREBB, near Philomont on the 14th of second month, Mary N. WALTERS, in the 58th year of age.

Friday, 28 February 1890 Vol. XII, No. 44

Mrs. Jane ORRISON died near Sterling last Saturday.

Mr. S. R. TILLETT and Miss Mollie THOMAS were married in Baltimore on Tuesday.

Death of Honora M., wife of Chas. E. SCHOOLEY, at Wichita, Kan., on the 10th inst. She was a granddaughter of Dr. MARLOW, who formerly resided at Lovettsville.

Fairfax: Mr. Frank REID died at Langly on Friday morning of last week.

Fairfax: Mr. KIDWELL died on Saturday morning near Spring Vale, from three tumors in his stomach.

Fairfax: Mrs. Jane SWEENEY, relict of the late John H. SWEENEY, died at Annandale, on Thursday, the 13th, aged 84 years.
Fairfax: A little dau. of Mr. MILLARD, near Calvin Run, was burned to death last week by her dress catching fire from a stove.
Fairfax: The infant child of Mr. and Mrs. Wm. M. GARRETT was buried on Wednesday, the 19th inst.

Friday, 7 March 1890   Vol. XII, No. 45

Mr. Charles E. MOUNT died at his home near Mountsville last Saturday morning, of pneumonia, which resulted from an attack of the prevailing epidemic. Although an officer in the confederate army, he has been identified with the Republican party. He was probably 60 odd years of age.
Last Tuesday the lifeless body of Mrs. Charles LEMON (nee Maggie TALLEY) arrived from her late home in Mecklenburg Co. and was laid to rest in the Friends burying ground at Lincoln. About 3 or 4 years ago she and her husband removed from Loudoun to Mecklenburg.
Died: At her parents' home, near Goresville, Feb. 18th '90, Una Moran, infant dau. of John H. and Lillie M. MISKELL, of convulsion, aged 2m 11d.

Friday, 14 March 1890   Vol. XII, No. 46

Mr. David EATON and Miss Mary C. RITICOR were united in marriage at Mt. Zion, on Feb 25th by Elder BADGER.
Mrs. I. P. WARNER went to Montgomery Co. Md, last Saturday to attend the funeral of her mother, Mrs. Elizabeth PUMPHREY, who died at her home in that county on Friday. She was 70 odd years of age.
Hiram N. TAVENNER died at his home in Hamilton yesterday morning, at about ten o'clock after a brief illness. He was a native of Loudoun and during the past half century he has resided in Hamilton and had he lived until the coming May he would have been 83 years of age. His wife, who was a native of New England, preceded him to the grave about a score of years ago. The funeral will take place tomorrow (Sat.) at 10:00 a.m.
Calvin COATS, living near Waterford, died last Monday from the effects of cancer of month, aged 78 years. His wife was lying very ill and death is likely.
[part missing] Farmwell, last Friday, little boy Jessie ELLIOT ... his brother accidentally discharged ??? and the ball passed through his head killing him almost instantly.
March Ct.: Wills of Reuben JENKINS, Mary J. ELGIN, Ruth H. SMITH, Thos. W. AYRES and William DOOD [DODD] dec'd admitted to probate. Isaac FLETCHER qualified as Admr. of Mary E. FLETCHER dec'd. Estates of Wm. GODFREY, John

CRIDLER, Peter SKINNER and James HARRIS committed to Sheriff. Geo. D. HOGE qualified as Admr. of Delilah H. BEAVERS dec'd.

Friday, 21 March 1890   Vol. XII, No. 47

Mrs. Sarah A. BENEDUM died at her home in Hamilton, of pneumonia about 10 o'clock yesterday morning, after an illness of about ten days, aged 69 years. Funeral services will take place tomorrow at 1 p.m. and interment at Leesburg cemetery.

Miss Mollie LUCKETT died at the home of her father, Samuel C. LUCKETT, in Waterford, last Sabbath, after a protracted illness of several months.

Llewelyn RUSSELL, eldest son of the late Caleb RUSSELL, formerly of Loudoun, died at his home in New Albany, Indiana of tumor of the stomach, on the 5th inst.

Mr. Jonathan KEEN, living near Bloomfield, met his death last Friday. He was riding on horseback, a few miles from his home, on Thursday and while passing a team he fell fro the horse his head striking the ground and his lower limbs falling in front of the wagon wheels. On Sunday his body was taken to Berryville for interment. He was a man of scholarly attainments and although a farmer, he lived among his books. He leaves a wife and one son, several other children having preceded him to the grave. He was about 63 or 64 years of age.

Married: At the Reformed Church, Lovettsville, on the 6th inst., by the Rev. H. St. J. RINKER, Mr. Charles BOOTH to Miss Fannie B. GREEN, all of Loudoun.

Died: On Feb. 15th 1890, Mrs. Jane E. ORRISON, at the residence of her son-in-law, J. W. WHALEY, Sterling.

Died: At her residence near Lovettsville, the 9th inst. Mrs. Isaac FRY, in the 78th year of her age.

Friday, 28 March 1890   Vol. XII, No. 48

James MITCHELL, worthy colored man died near Clarkes Gap, on Wednesday. He was taken suddenly ill just a week before.

On Wednesday evening, the death of Mr. William CLOWE, formerly of upper Loudoun. He fell from a wagon and expired immediately, due to heart trouble.

Mrs. Dolly SNOOTS of Morrisonville died last week, after a lingering illness, aged 90 years. She had been an invalid for several years. Leaves six children, several grandchildren and great grandchildren. Mother of ten children, four of whom, with her husband, preceded her to the tomb. Member of the Lutheran church for 56 years. Interred in the Lutheran burying ground near Lovettsville; services by Dr. SCHINDLER.

Isaac FRY has broken up housekeeping since the death of his wife. He will make his home with his son, Samuel H. FRY, and his daughter Rebecca has gone to her sister, Mrs. Jennie SMITH, of Hyattsville, Md.

Mr. W. H. HUNTER, teacher of Water's School, on Thursday evening persuaded Miss Clara FREY to accompany him to the residence of Rev. Dr. SCHINDLER and they were married.

Died at her home near Little River, of pneumonia, on the 22d inst., Mrs. Chloe CHINN, consort of the late John L. CHINN. Mrs. CHINN's illness was painful but brief. She was seized with La Grippe, then relapsed into pneumonia. Her remains were interred in the family burying ground Monday evening.

Mrs. Sarah A. E. PRESGRAVE, wife of J. T. PRESGRAVE, died at the residence of her husband, near Pleasant Valley, Mar. 21st, 1890, of bilious fever and extreme torpidity of the liver, in the 56th year of her age. She had eight children. Her funeral was preached by Rev. MEADE and she was laid away near Arcola.

Married: On the 20th inst., at the residence of Mr. Wm. SEATON, near Purcellville, by Rev. J. S. WICKLINE, Mr. Samuel J. SMITH and Miss Ella SEATON.

Married: On Tuesday, Mar. 25th at the home of the bride, Mr. Luckett COMPHER to Miss Lutie BEANS, all of Loudoun.

Married: At New Jerusalem church, Mar. 20th by Rev. Dr. SCHINDLER, Mr. William A. HUNTER to Miss Claretta M. FRY, both of Loudoun Co.

Friday, 4 April 1890   Vol. XII, No. 49

Mrs. Annie LACY, wife of B. F. LACY, residing near Clark's Gap, died in Leesburg last Monday morning. She was paralyzed some time ago. On Tuesday her remains were taken to Waterford and funeral services were conducted in the Baptist Church, by Rev. Chas. HERNDON. She was a daughter of Mr. Silas CORBIN, of Waterford.

Dr. CHANCELLOR on Wednesday morning informed us that he was just returning from the funeral of his brother-in-law, William ELLZEY, who died at his home, Mount Middleton, in lower Loudoun, last Sunday morning, and was buried in the family burying ground, on Wednesday. Death was caused by diseased lungs, resulting from an attack of the grippe, about two months ago. He was 52 years of age.

Last Wednesday evening it was reported that Nimrod TAVENNER had dropped dead at his home about half a mile north of the Depot. About 5 o'clock he went out to the wood pile and was found lying on the ground. In the 78th year of his age. Funeral will take place today (Friday) meeting at the house at 2 p.m.

Herndon: Mr. L. D. BALLOU, who was stricken with paralysis while at the breakfast table, on Sunday morning last, died at 12:30 p.m. on Wednesday. He leaves a wife and a son about 18 years old.

Died: Martha HACKLEY, wife of Wm. H. HACKLEY at her home near Harpers Ferry, in Loudoun, March 25th, aged 63 years. Member of the M. E. Church for 40 years.

Friday, 11 April 1890   Vol. XII, No. 50

The death of Mr. Armstead SILCOTT, sick for a short time. He was in his 68th year.

Mr. C. Matt BALL, formerly of this county, but for a number of years a resident of Alamosa, Colorado, married Miss Bertha M. GAINES, at that place on Wednesday, April 2, 1890.

Died: At his home, in Memphis, Tenn., on the 20th of March last, John C. MILLS, in the 65th year of his age. Born and raised in Leesburg and moved to Memphis about 35 years ago.

Died: At the home of his son-in-law, Mr. Chas. W. HEFFNER, in Frederick Co, Md, on March 28, 1890, of paralysis of the throat, John McKIMMEY, aged 75y 24d. He leaves six children and many grandchildren.

Died: At her home, near Farmwell, on Sunday, April 6, 1890, Mrs. Annie E. DOWNS, wife of Mr. Stephen DOWNS, aged 32y 1m 2d.

Friday, 18 April 1890   Vol. XII, No. 51

John W. WILDMAN, merchant of Leesburg, departed this life last Monday evening at 5 o'clock, in his 70th year. When the public school system was established in Va he was appointed superintendent of schools of Loudoun Co. He was afflicted with pulmonary trouble. Funeral was conducted at his late residence on Wednesday evening by Rev. Dr. DAVIS, of the Episcopal Church, of which he was an officer. Interred in Union Cemetery.

Co. Ct.: Wills of Jno. PRICE, Colvin COATS, Thos. SETTLE, Eli J. HOGE, Hiram N. TAVENNER, Mary M. KERN, Rachel HAVENNER, Mary S. DANA, Henry B. HUTCHISON and Michael WIARD admitted to probate. F. W. CHINN qualified as Admr. of Jno. L. CHINN dec'd. G. Ludwell SEATON appointed committee of Jos. G. EACHES. Powers of V. V. PURSELL committee of Robt. OSBURN revoked.

Herndon: Mr. Allison THOMPSON, father of William THOMPSON, late Mayor of Hamilton, walked from his home to this village on Tuesday last, a distance of 6 miles. He is about 84 years old. His wife died on the 30th of March last, at the age of 77. They had been married and lived together 59y 6m. They having living at this time 82 grandchildren and 58 great grandchildren.

Married: In Washington DC, March 6th 1890, in the M. E. Church, South, by Rev. S. W. HADDAWAY, Mr. Charles J. GATES, of Washington, and Miss Ada CURRY, formerly of Leesburg.

Married: On the 8th inst., at the residence of Mr. Geo. W. SCHOOLEY, in Waterford, by Rev. J. S. WICKLINE, Mr. Elliot S. DONALDSON and Miss Emma S. SPURGEON, both of Loudoun.

Friday, 25 April 1890   Vol. XII, No. 52

John SHRIOCK died at his home, near Farmwell last Tuesday morning.

Last Monday Mr. Joseph HOLT, who formerly lived in Hamilton, arrived here and removed from the Methodist grave yard the remains of Mrs. Manly HAINES, which were buried there about 10 years ago and on Tuesday proceeded with them to Baltimore Co, Md and reinterred by the side of Mr. HAINES, who died and was buried there about 2 years after the death of his wife. They were the parents of Mrs. HOLT. Messrs. Holt & Haines conducted a store here for several years.

Last Saturday a hearse bearing the remains of Joab OSBURN passed through our town enroute to Leesburg where they were interred in Union Cemetery. He died near Snickersville on Thursday. He was the father of late Herbert OSBURN, Treasurer of our county, who died only a few weeks ago. He was 84 years of age.

D. H. VANDEVANTER married Miss Carrie HOUGH, daughter of L. E. HOUGH, of Waterford on Wednesday morning, in Leesburg, by Rev. J. C. DINWIDDIE.

Miss Leslie WOOD, dau. of the late Thomas WOOD, of Frederick co., and Mr. E. Clarance JORDAN, son of the late E. C. JORDAN, proprietor of JORDAN's White Sulphur Springs, were married here yesterday morning. The ceremony took place in Christ Episcopal Church, performed by Rev. Nelson P. DAME. ...

Bloomfield: the death of little Wade HAMPTON, son of John HAMPTON Esq., caused by some splinters of a broken slate piercing one of his limbs.

Warrenton: Judge Thomas B. RICE, born in 1806 and who lived at one time in Upperville, died at his adopted home, Carlenville, Ill. where he had resided over 50 years. He has a number of nephews and nieces in the neighborhood of Orlean.

Fauquier Co: Mr. John SQUIRES who lives near The Plaines was thrown from his horse near Halfway on Sunday last and killed. He was about 70 years of age. Buried yesterday in Middleburg.

Married: At the residence of the bride, near Poolsville, Md, on Tuesday, April 15th 1890, by Rev. B. W. BOND, of Leesburg, Mr.

John C. CARR, of Loudoun, and Miss Nora J. GOTT, of the former place.

Married: April 13th 1890, by Rev. John WOOLF, at the residence of Mr. Landon REED, Mr. Thomas REED to Miss Rebecca REED, all of Loudoun.

Married: April 16th '90, by Rev. John WOOLF, at his residence, Mr. Jas. UTTERBACK to Miss Florence G. BROWN, all of Loudoun.

Died: At the residence of his son-in-law in Leesburg on Tuesday morning, April 22d 1890, Mr. Geo. F. WOODWARD in the 78th year of his age.

Died: Friday night, April 18th, 1890, at Farmwell, Mrs. Harriet E. HIGGINS, in the 60th year of her age. Her funeral was preached on the following Sabbath in the Presbyterian church at Farmwell, Burial was at Belmont Church.

Died: April 1st, 1890, Mrs. Sallie SNOOTS aged 69 years, wife of Presley SNOOTS.

Died: Alice Louisa SPRING, wife of David W. SPRING, was born Feb. 2d, 1864, died April 17th 1890. She was a member of the M. E. Church. She leaves one son and a devoted husband.

Friday, 2 May 1890 Vol. XIII, No. 1

Maj. Henry J. ROGERS, brother of the late Milton ROGERS (who lived near Aldie) died in New York last Wednesday.

Mrs. Ann DIVINE, wife of C. F. DIVINE, died suddenly at her home in Waterford, one day last week.

Samuel LOVE, a son of Eli LOVE, living near Hillsboro, met a tragic death last Saturday evening by falling from his horse and breaking his neck. ... In his pocket were two bottles of "Schnapps".

George MURREY (colored), son of Samuel MURRAY, of Lincoln, removed to St. Clare, N. J., in September '87 with his family. In October last he returned on a visit to his parents. He returned to St. Clare to find his wife had started for New York in the company with Lacy ???x, formerly of Snickersville, George's nephew who was boarding with him at the time, taking all his money. He was so upset he was placed in an asylumn. His mother brought him home in February but he was again put in an asylum. [paper creased]

Waterford: Henry ALLEN, middle aged colored man a member of the Odd Fellows Lodge of this place died suddenly at the house of ??nson [Henson?] YOUNG near here. The funeral took place at 2 p.m. on Monday preached by Rev. J. T. OWINGS. [paper creased]

Thornton WHITACRE died at his home, near Lincoln, at 11 o'clock in the evening of the 24th inst. thus rounding up a life of about ¾ of

a century, of diabetes. On Saturday afternoon his funeral took place at Lincoln. He had no family.
Lenah: Nelson SUTTLE, only brother of the late Thos. SUTTLE expired during Friday night, very suddenly. He was about 70 years of age. He leaves considerable property which will probably descend to his servants as he was without relatives. His remains were interred in the burying ground near his residence on Sunday.
Died: On Thursday morning, April 10, 1890, at the home of Mrs. Mattie WILEY, her only child, little Walter Ray aged 6m 15.

Friday, 9 May 1890   Vol. XIII, No. 2

Died: Miss Katie MANN, daughter of Samuel and Mary MANN, at their residence near Lovettsville, on April 29th, in the 15th year of her age. The corps was conveyed to Mt. Olivet, where Rev. J. S. WICKLINE conducted funeral services.
Warrenton, May 4: Rev. A. D. POLLOCK, D.D., died here yesterday afternoon, age 81. He was a prominent Presbyterian clergyman, a native of Pa and first cousin to Gov. POLLOCK of that State. He came to Va 60 years ago and married a daughter of Charles LEE. His eldest son, Major Thomas POLLOCK, was killed at Gettysburg and his body never recovered.

Friday, 16 May 1890   Vol. XIII, No. 3

Co. Ct.: Wills of Newton SETTLE dec'd and Thornton WHITACRE dec'd admitted to probate. Jno. W. FURR qualified as Notary Public. Estate of Daniel PAYNE (col.) committed to sheriff. Geo. C LYON qualified as Admr. of Mary E. LYON dec'd. W. S. SUMMERS qualified as Admr. of Sanford COCKERILLE dec'd Summerfield BOLYN qualified as Admr. of T. M. BOLYN dec'd. Wm. J. STONE qualified as Admr. of Michael WIARD dec'd. Eva R. SWANK qualified as Guardian of Sarah E. and Jno. W. SWANK. A. H. DAVIS, col'd., licensed to celebrate the rite of matrimony.
Harpers Ferry: An increase of pension has been granted James BLINCO of this place.
Philomont: Mrs. Ruth BALDWIN, mother of the late Dr. M. K. BALDWIN, is visiting her grandson, Dr. L. L. CHAMBLIN. She is in her 97th year.

Friday, 23 May 1890   Vol. XIII, No. 4

John WELSH, son of Seldon WELSH (formerly of Hamilton) died at the home of his father, in Middleburg, on Wednesday of last week. He was studying for the ministry, at Randolph Macon College.

Col. Robert J. T. WHITE died at the home of his sister Mrs. MILTON, in Hamilton, last Sunday morning, after a lingering illness, in the 69th year of his age, doubtless the result of an accident which befell him about 4 years ago when he was thrown violently from his horse and a slight attack of paralysis followed. He was a native of Loudoun. ... At one time he removed to Little Rock, Ark. where he held the office of Secretary of State under two gubernatorial regimes of MURPHY and CLAYTON. Where there his wife (a sister of Dr. TAYLOR, of Hillsboro) died and he returned with his family to Loudoun and located on a farm near Hillsboro. During the war he was a Union man and subsequently identified with the Republican party.

State Senator HEATON died at his home in Leesburg last Saturday night of appolexy. Born in Loudoun. In 1881 he was elected to represent the district in the State Senate and re-elected in 1885 and 89. On Tuesday his remains were interred at Short Hill.

Mrs. Mary MYERS, wife of Wm. MYERS, died at her home, near Hughesville, last Sunday evening, in the 69th year of her age of cholera morbus. Interred at Lincoln on Tuesday.

Friday, 30 May 1890   Vol. XIII, No. 5

Farmwell, May 27: Rev. Saml. BROWN died at this place at about 10 a.m. today in the 75th year of his age, having been born Feb. 11th 1816 in that part of the county known as "Between the Hills." For 58 years a member of the Methodist Episcopal Church.

Cards are out for the marriage of Mr. Henry GORDON to Miss HADDAY.

Mrs. Albert BEST died at her home, near Hillsboro, one day last week.

Mr. H. G. DULANEY, the millionaire of Welbourne, is reported critically ill in Marsailles France. His sister, Mrs. NEVILLE and Miss Lean WHITING (his cousin) are on their way.

Mrs. Jane CORBIN died at Willisville on the 9th inst. having reached her three score years and ten. Some years ago she had a paralytic stroke. Member of the M. E. Church for 40 years.

Married: May 15, 1890, by Rev. John WOOLF, at his residence, Mr. Jerome B. GRAY and Miss Julia GOUGH, all of Loudoun.

Married: In Leesburg, on Saturday, May 24th 1890, by Rev. B. W. BOND, Jno. RICE and Alice C. RECTOR, all of Loudoun.

Died: At the residence of her son-in-law, Mr. Phillip HOWSER, at Farmwell, Apr. 16, 1890, Mrs. Harriet HIGGINS, in the 61st year of her age.

Friday, 6 June 1890   Vol. XIII, No. 6

Edgar LICKEY died last Saturday evening, in about the 28th year of his age. Interred at Short Hill burying ground on Monday.

Round Hill: Jos. A. LODGE of this place was married on Tuesday to Miss Lucy COMPHER at the home of her father, Mr. John COMPHER, near Waterford.

Round Hill, June 5: Yesterday, A. L. MOORE, of Round Hill and Miss Laura NICHOLS, dau. of Mr. Jas. NICHOLS, were united in the holy bonds at Ebenezer Church, Rev. I. B. LAKE officiating.

Friday, 13 June 1890   Vol. XIII, No. 7

Bolington: On Monday morning, the 9th inst., Mrs. James PONTON, while suffering from temporary derangement of mind, came near being burned to death. She arose early in the morning, procured some corn husks and saturated them with coal oil and set fire to them and then leaped into the flames. We learn that Mrs. P. died on Tuesday at 11 a.m. and was interred at Mt Olivet yesterday. She leaves 4 children, one a babe only 4m old.

T. C. BAKER of Purcellville married Miss Lizzie T. BROWN, performed last Tuesday at the residence of the bride's mother, in Washington City, by the Rev. S. H. GREEN, Pastor of Calvary Baptist Church.

Friday, 20 June 1890   Vol. XIII, No. 8

Mary, youngest daughter of C. G. and Ella DAVIS, died at the home of her parents in Lincoln last Monday evening. she had not fully recovered from the effect of measles when she fell to disentery. She was about 12 years of age.

Mary B., wife of F. H. FRITTS, died at her home in Purcellville, last Friday, aged 34y 10m, of the effects of the Grippe.

Two prominent business men were married to Baltimore ladies last week: Mr. Jos. D. BAKER (Pres. of the People National Bank of Leesburg) on Thursday married to Miss Virginia H. MERKELL. They will reside in Frederick. On Friday Stilson HUTCHINS, the leading newspaper man of Washington, married to Miss Rosa B. KEELING.

Co. Ct.: N. R. HEATON qualified as Admr. dbn wwa on the estates of Louisa M. HEATON, Eliza R. BEARD and Jas. HEATON dec'd. Will of Henry HEATON dec'd admitted to probate, N. R. HEATON Exor. Will of Amanda T. BEST dec'd admitted to probate, E Clinton POTTS Exor. Nimrod S. ALLEN qualified as Admr. of Mary SMITH dec'd. Estate of Wm. BUTTS, and Saml. MORRISON committed to Sheriff. Henry T. JANNEY qualified as Exor. of Thornton WHITACRE dec'd.

John MOFFET, of Fauquier Co, died on Tuesday, of last week, aged 96 years.

Thos. WILLIAMSON of Fauquier was found dead in his yard last Thursday morning. He was formerly a merchant in Warrenton.

Friday, 27 June 1890   Vol. XIII, No. 9

Judge Henry W. THOMAS died at his home at Fairfax C. H., last Sunday and his remains were interred on Monday. He was in the 78th year of his age. He was a whig and then a democrat. ...

Jerre HAVENNER of Hamilton was stricken with paralysis last Tuesday and died on the following day. He had almost reached his 90th milestone. Interred at Harmony churchyard yesterday afternoon.

Fairfax: Mr. Allison THOMPSON, father of the late W. W. THOMPSON, of Hamilton, died on Wednesday morning. He was about 85 years of age.

Fairfax: Miss Fannie LEE, dau. of Cassius F. LEE, died quite suddenly, on Wednesday morning, at the residence of Mrs. CASTLEMAN, with whom she was boarding.

John McGUIRE, eldest son of Dr. J. M. G. McGUIRE, of Clarke Co, was drowned at Hawk's Nest, W. Va, Monday while bathing.

Married: At the residence of the bride's father, near Mountsville, on Wednesday, June 25th 1890, by Rev. R. T. DAVIS, D.D., Mr. Chas. W. S. TURNER, of Rockingham Co, and Miss M. Elizabeth, dau. of Francis M. CARTER Esq. of Loudoun.

Married: At the residence of the bride's father, in Leesburg, on Wednesday, June 25th 1890, by Rev. B. W. BOND, Mr. Nixon SAMPSELL to Miss Maiza PERRY, both of Leesburg.

Married: At the rectory in Leesburg on July 16th 1890, by Rev. Dr. R. T. DAVIS, Mr. Herbert CURRY to Miss Ida GATES, both of Loudoun.

Friday, 4 July 1890   Vol. XIII, No. 10

Mrs. J. W. HARPER, sister of the late Dr. A. P. BROWN, of Upperville, died at Front Royal, on the 21st ult.

Mrs. Ruth E. ODELL, with son and daughter, accompanied by Dr. S. T. NOLAND's widow and her two daughters, arrived from Delphi, Indiana last Friday to spend the summer with her father, Maj. Geo. W. NOLAND, near Round Hill.

Married: At 914 New York Ave., Washington City, on Thursday, June 26th 1890, Rev. J. T. WIGHTMAN, pastor of Mt. Vernon Place, M. E. Church, South, Mr. Wm. HEAD, and Miss Florence M. ATTWELL, dau. of Mr. Ewell ATTWELL, both of Leesburg.

Married: At Christ Church, Goresville, on Wednesday morning, July 2d 1890, Rev. W. G. HAMMOND, pastor of Middleburg circuit, M. E. Church, South, and Miss Ellen R. GIDDINGS, daughter of Col. Wm. GIDDINGS, Rev. Nelson HEAD, D.D., and Rev. Carter PAGE officiating, all of Loudoun.

Friday, 11 July 1890   Vol. XIII, No. 11

Mr. Selden PEACH died suddenly in Upperville last Saturday, heart disease was probably the cause. He was one of the board of directors of the M. F. Ins. Co. of Loudoun.

A son of Rodney MITCHELL, colored, aged about 10 years, was struck by a locomotive on the W. & O. near Paeonian Springs last Saturday and may be fatally injured.

Mrs. Nannie T. ELGIN, wife of Benj. ELGIN and daughter of the late Judge Henry W. THOMAS died in Alexandria on the 3d inst., from nervous prostration brought on by the death of her father one week before.

Died: At her home in Bloomfield, on Sunday, June 8th 1890, at the residence of her uncle, H. H. TAYLOR, little Louise, infant child of Leven T. JACOBS, aged 7m 15d.

Died: Mrs. Mary J. WALDREN, wife of Mr. Hiram C. WALDRON, died at her home near Harpers Ferry, June 26th, after an illness of 4 months from tumor and dropsy, aged 48y 7m. At age 14 she joined the Methodist Episcopal Church. The remains were taken to Mt. Olivet, services by pastor Rev. J. S. WICKLINE.

Friday, 18 July 1890   Vol. XIII, No. 12

Lot TAVENNER, an old citizen, died at his home near Lincoln, Wednesday evening, and his body will be interred today, meeting at the house at 10 a.m.

Mrs. Mary Ann NIXON, widow of the late George NIXON, committed suicide by hanging on Thursday last, at the residence of Mr. Ed. HAWLEY, about 2 miles S of Leesburg. She was about 75 years of age and had been twice in her lifetime an inmate of the asylum. Interred in the Presbyterian church yard, Leesburg, on Friday evening, the Rev. B. W. BOND officiating.

July Ct.: Will of Adam COOPER dec'd admitted to probate. Wm. H. LUCKETT qualified as Admr. of Mary B. LUCKETT dec'd. H. N. RECTOR and W. J. LUCK qualified as Admrs. of Samuel RECTOR dec'd. Estate of William CLOWE committed to Sheriff.

Miss Mary E. FOSTER, aunt of Capt. J. W. FOSTER, died at The Plains, Fauquier Co, last Friday, when one of the shafts came loose from the axle of the carriage and upset the vehicle. She was thrown out and sustained injuries from which death ensured. She leaves a valuable estate.

Mr. Chas. RICHARDSON, of Pittsfield, Mass, and Miss Clara, dau. of Rev. Dr. MASON, pastor of the Congregational church, were married by him, in the church at 11 o'clock Wednesday morning the 16th inst.

Friday, 25 July 1890   Vol. XIII, No. 13

Died: Near Morrisonville, July 4th, 1890, after a brief illness, Mabel, infant daughter of Geo. W. and Rosa B. CASE, aged 11m 5d.

Departed this life, July 4th, 1890, Mrs. Christian SHRY, aged 70y 3m 24d.

Died: On Tuesday, July 7th, 1890, of cholera infantum, Randolph F. MYERS, infant son of E. F. MYERS, aged 8m 28d.

Mrs. S. Ella BEALES, wife of J. E. BEALES and dau. of Mortimer BEALES, died at her home, in town, about 9 o'clock Monday evening, after an illness of about three weeks, in the 29th year of her age. About 2 years ago she joined the M. E. Church South. She leaves a husband and little child. The funeral took place on Wednesday, at Harmony church.

Friday, 1 August 1890   Vol. XIII, No. 14

Mrs. John W. MORAN, mother of W. H. W. MORAN, of Hamilton, died at her home near Farmwell, last Saturday evening, of typhoid fever, aged 45.

Last Friday afternoon, Rev. Joseph HELM died at the home of his son-in-law, Mr. Lewis SHUMATE, near Leesburg. He had been ailing for about two weeks with bowel trouble and a hemorrhage. He was born in vicinity of Hagerstown, MD, but in early life lived in Georgetown. He found a wife in this vicinity, Miss Mary E. CARR, sister of the late David CARR. He was a member of the M. E. Church, South, and a founder of the first church of that denomination in The Grove. He was 84 years of age. The funeral took place at the home of Mr. SHUMATE, on Saturday afternoon, conducted by Rev. Dr. HEAD, assisted by Rev. W. G. EGGLESTON, interment in Union Cemetery, Leesburg.

J. R. BAKER, proprietor of the Hamilton drug store, died at 4 o'clock this morning of congestion of the brain. He was reported sick with typhoid fever. Interment will probably be made at Laurel Md. He was nearly 45 years of age.

Mrs. Noble B. PEACOCK died at her home near Wheatland, Tuesday morning, and her remains were interred at Catoctin Church, Wednesday afternoon.

L. N. HOUGH, of Waterford, on Tuesday drove to vicinity of Hamilton, took Miss Lucy PRESTON into his carriage and proceeded to Leesburg, where they were married at the Presbyterian manse, by the Rev. J. C. DINWIDDIE. Mr. H. was paralyzed in one side a few months since and has not yet recovered.

Griffith PAXSON died at his home near Waterford, on the 21st inst. in the 81st year of his age. Interred in the burying ground at Waterford n Wednesday of last week.

Friday, 8 August 1890   Vol. XIII, No. 15

Oliver R. DAVIS died at the residence of his parents at Lincoln, on the 5th inst., in the 49th year of his age, after an illness of over two months.

Died: Eli A. LOVE, of Hillsboro neighborhood. He was about 85 years, about 2 years ago a stroke of paralysis robbed him of much of his vitality, until death occurred last Friday at about 11 a.m. Burial at the Friends burying ground at Waterford last Sabbath.

James M. WALKER died at his home in Waterford, on the night of the 24th ult. Born about 72 years ago and spent all his life at Waterford. Treasurer of the Mutual Fire Insurance Company. Burial at the Friends buying ground at Waterford last Sabbath.

Friday, 15 August 1890   Vol. XIII, No. 16

Co. Ct.: Wills of Jos. HELM, Ann E. GAYNOR, Henrietta BENEDICT, Mahlon JAMES, and Jas. M. WALKER were admitted to probate. H. H. RUSSELL appointed curator of estate of J. R. BAKER dec'd. Wm. PIGGOTT qualified as Admr. of Lott TAVENNER dec'd. E. V. WHITE qualified as Admr. of Wm. H. CLOWE dec'd. John H. SHRY qualified as Admr. of Christina SHRY dec'd.

Hillsboro: Dr. John LOVE, of Ohio, brother of the late Eli A. LOVE, died last week.

Rev. D. W. HILL, of the Va. Conference M. E. Church, died at the parsonage at Annex, Augusta Co., Va on July 23d. He was 32 years old. His remains were taken to Monroe Co. W Va for interment. His widow is a sister of Rev. J. S. WICKLINE, of Hillsboro.

Friday, 22 August 1890   Vol. XIII, No. 17

L. W. S. HOUGH, a leading merchant of Leesburg, died at his home in that town last Saturday night in the 71st year of his age. Funeral Monday afternoon.

Jesse H. BROWN (son of David BROWN) who was raised on the farm now tenanted by J. W. ORRISON, just N of town, is stopping off from an excursion to Boston (from his home in Indianapolis). He left here about 30 years ago and located in Richmond Ind.

Mrs. Susan MYERS, wife of Fenton MYERS, died at her home in Hamilton at 1:40 o'clock this morning. She had a fall last Winter, which injured her hips and she never fully recovered. Death by disease of liver and stomach. She was 59 years of age. Interment tomorrow (Sat) in Hamilton.

Friday, 29 August 1890   Vol. XIII, No. 18

Last Tuesday evening a shadow fell across the threshold of Mr. and Mrs. Rodney ARNETT, in Hamilton. A life which only a few days before brought a new ray of light into their home went out again and left it darker than before.
On Thursday of last week, Miss Fanuyl, the 16 year old dau. of Mr. C. A. NEWTON, proprietor of the Hotel Catoctin, at Leesburg, died at that house.

Friday, 5 September 1890   Vol. XIII, No. 19

Mamie, youngest daughter of the late Smith HIRST, died at her home in Lincoln, Wednesday morning. She was about 17 years of age. Death was probably cause by internal hemorrhage.

Friday, 12 September 1890   Vol. XIII, No. 20

Rev. Elias WELTY, father of Dr. WELTY, late of our town, died at his home in Baltimore on the 4th inst., aged about 70 years. He was, many years ago, stationed at Leesburg.
Sept. Ct.: Wills of Emily DIVINE, Jos. GOCHNAUER and Amy A. BEANS admitted to probate. Wm. F. COOPER qualified as committee of W. GARRET. Robt. R. and Samuel H. LOVE qualified as Admr. of Eli A. LOVE dec'd. Estate of John MITCHELL committed to Sheriff.
Last Tuesday at 11:30 at Lincoln a funeral of Elias HUGHES, who departed this life at his home near Hughesville, last Saturday, aged about 65 years. The casket was taken into the Friends Meeting house.
Last Tuesday at 2:00 at the Friends Meeting house in Lincoln, the funeral of Olivia Bradfie[l]d NICHOLS, wife of Isaac NICHOLS, who departed this life at 8 o'clock Sabbath evening, after a protracted illness. Disease of kidneys and bladder was the immediate cause of death. She was in her 82d year.
Died, after a lingering illness of several months, Job SMITH, aged 73 years. He departed this life last Tuesday, the 2d inst. His remains were laid to rest on Thursday in the Union Cemetery, Lovettsville, services by Rev. St. John RINKER.

Friday, 19 September 1890   Vol. XIII, No. 21

Benton NICHOLS arrived at Lincoln on Thursday of last week, direct from California, summoned by the illness of his mother, Olivia NICHOLS, but did not arrive in time for the funeral.
Miss Fannie POWELL, second daughter of Mr. G. POWELL, died at her home, near the depot about 4 o'clock this morning, of typhoid fever. She was about 18 years of age.

Died, suddenly at her home in Lincoln, Sept. 3rd 1890, of disease of the heart, Mamie L., daughter of Smith and Mary Frances HIRST, aged 18 years. Member of the M. E. Church.

Friday, 26 September 1890   Vol. XIII, No. 22

Sarah McCLELLAND, wife of William McCLELLAND, died at her home, in Lincoln, last Friday night, 10 o'clock. She was stricken down with paralysis of the brain and death quickly ensued. Funeral was held at the house on Sabbath afternoon, and her body laid to rest in Friends burying ground.

Friday, 3 October 1890   Vol. XIII, No. 23

Miss Susan TAVENNER, sister of the late Mahlon TAVENNER, died at the home of her niece, Mrs. Jas. B. PEUGH yesterday, at 10 a.m., aged 82 years. Her death resulted from a stroke of paralysis which afflicted her about two weeks since. Funeral takes place today, meeting at the house at 2 p.m.

Miss Ann SHUMAKER died last Sunday, at the residence of Thomas BALL, near Morrisonville. Interred in the Arnold Grove burying ground, on Tuesday.

Hillsboro: three funerals in this neighborhood on Tuesday the 23d: Mr. John CHAMBLIN, Mrs. FRITTS and Miss Ann SHUMAKER.

Mrs. Shep. HARRISON's of Fairfax, was the scene of a wedding Tuesday evening. Her daughter, Miss Carrie, and Mr. Charles CHAPEN, of Washington were united in marriage at 8 o'clock, by the Rev. Mr. SAUNDERS, cousin of the bride. the bride was attired in white and carried a lovely cluster of pink roses. Miss Minnie CHAPIN, Mr. Geo. TOWNSEND, Miss Carrie TOWNSEND and Dr. Edw. DETEWILER officiated as bridesmaids and groomsmen. They will reside in Washington.

Married: At the residence of the bride's father in Leesburg, on the 19th of Sept. 1890, by Rev. B. W. BOND, D.D., Miss Bertha L., dau. of Mr. Chas. A. CLINE, and Mr. Francis H. S. MORRISON, son of Col. J. H. MORRISON, of Lexington, Va and grandson of the late Gen. F. H. SMITH, of the Va. Military Institute.

Died: At the residence of his father, Ellzey CHAMBLIN, near Mechanicsville, John CHAMBLIN on Sept. 26th, 1890, aged 44y 11m 26d, of cancer.

Died: Sept. 11th, at her home near Lincoln, Fannie, daughter of Wm. H. and Martha FLETCHER, in the 17th year of her age.

Died: Harvey ELLMORE died at his home near Old Farmwell, Sept. 11th, 1890, aged 15y 3m 11d.

Died: At his home near Centreville, Fairfax Co., Sept. 22nd 1890, Henry S. SWART, in the 70th year of his age. He leaves one daughter and four sons to mourn.

Friday, 10 October 1890   Vol. XIII, No. 24

Cards are out for the marriage of Dr. Chas. G. GIDDINGS, formerly of Goresville, in this county, and Miss Maud D. CRICKTON, of Atlanta, Ga, which is to take place on Wednesday Oct 15th 1890, at St. Luke's Cathedral in that city.

A pretty wedding took place at Harmony Church on Wednesday, Mr. Will MYERS, formerly of Hughesville (but lately more inclined to be a resident of Hamilton) and Miss Nora THOMAS, daughter of Mr. and Mrs. R. W. THOMAS. ... Ushers Messrs Will THOMAS and Edgar WILEY, followed by Mr. Frank MYERS (brother and best man) and Miss Mary HATCHER, bridesmaid. Performed by Rev. W. G. EGGLESTON.

Friday, 17 October 1890   Vol. XIII, No. 25

Mrs. Susan RINKER, widow of the late John L. RINKER, died at her home in Leesburg, Tuesday night Oct. 14th in the 75th year of her age.

Mrs. G. W. LAYCOCK went to Washington yesterday, to be present at the marriage of her brother, Mr. Frank JOHNSON, to Mrs. May EWER, which was to take place at 7:30 last evening.

Oct. Ct.: Mary E. CONARD Admx. of Jno. W. CONARD dec'd executed new bond. R. R. WALKER qualified as Admr. dbn wwa of Jacob SCOTT dec'd. Wills of Leven BICHARDS [RICHARDS] and Elias HUGHES admitted to probate. Geo. W. SMITH qualified as Admr. of Job SMITH dec'd. Estates of Portia R. DORSEY and Oswell CARTER committed to Sheriff.

Bolington: Miss Margaret FRY died quite suddenly at Frederick EAMICH's last Saturday. Interred in the Union Cemetery near Lovettsville, on Sunday, services by Rev. St. J. RINKER.

Friday, 24 October 1890   Vol. XIII, No. 26

Larry T. CULAN, who had carved his own tombstone, died at Harpers Ferry on Saturday aged 77 years.

Miss Lizzie MOSBY died at the residence of her sister, Mrs. RUSSELL, near Bedford City, Tuesday, after a short illness. She was a sister of Col. John S. MOSBY.

Married: At the Methodist Parsonage, in Hamilton, by the Rev. W. G. EGGLESTON, Pastor, Mr. Robert E. TRENARY, to Miss Julia CARLISLE, both of Loudoun.

Friday, 31 October 1890   Vol. XIII, No. 27

Miss Flora, dau. of Mr. Aaron BEANS (formerly of Waterford) married in their Ohio home to Mr. S. GOULDING, an engineer on the Hocking Valley and Toledo RR.

A few days ago, Almeta (age 5 years) the only daughter of E. Sheldon and Bettie A. ARNOLD, died of scarlet fever.
Mrs. Emma GWATHMEY, of New London Ct. who was visiting her sister, Mrs. J. T. TRIBBY, of this place, last summer, started Sept 1st for Ala. to visit her parents, Mr. S. HINDMAN, Tuscumbia, Ala. and to meet her husband Mr. R. GWARTHMEY a commercial traveller in La, but two weeks ago while out driving she was thrown from the carriage and died. She leaves three little daughters and her husband.
Died: Near Neersville, Oct. 9th, 1890, after a brief illness, Almeta M., only daughter of E. Sheldon and Bettie M. ARNOLD, aged 5y 8m 17d. Funeral services conducted by W. S. WICKLINE in place of Rev. W. D. NICOLL the Lutheran minister.

Friday, 7 November 1890   Vol. XIII, No. 28

The death of T. Walker FRED, son of Frank L. FRED, at his home in Indian Territory, on Wednesday of last week.
A little child of W. H. W. MORAN died last Sunday, of spinal meningitis, at the home of its parents, in Hamilton and its body was interred at Leesburg on Monday.
Mrs. Susan SHAFER, who had passed 4 score, died at her home in Hamilton, on Wednesday, and her body will be interred at Arnold Grove today. Services at the house at 10 a.m.
Round Hill: A pretty wedding at the residence of Mr. Amos BEANS, the home of the bride, the parties being Mr. Charles SPRING, of Leesburg, and Miss Alice BEANS, Rev. DINWIDDIE, of the Presbyterian Church officiating. The attendants were Mr. Adin WHITE and Miss Martha BEANS, sister of the bride; Mr. Joseph A. BEANS, brother of the groom; Mr. Armstead THOMAS and Miss Florrie LAYCOCK, cousin of the bride. The bride wore a suit of fawn colored Faille Francaise and plush, with hat to match and carrying a bouquet of roses.
Thomas SANBOWER, an aged citizen living near the Berlin ferry, died quite suddenly one day last week.

Friday, 14 November 1890   Vol. XIII, No. 29

Mr. Hal G. DULANY died at his home at Welbourne last Saturday, at 8 a.m. in the 37th year of his age. He had returned only about two weeks before from Europe where he had been about two years. It is reported that the original cause of his illness was an operation performed to remove from his throat an orange seed. The funeral took place Sunday evening at 3 p.m., interment in a private burying ground on his estate. He was wealthy, having interested the estates of Lady HUNTON, of England, besides valuable property of his immediate family.

Friday, 21 November 1890   Vol. XIII, No. 30

Nov. Ct.: L. H. POTTERFIELD qualified as Admr. of Thos. SANBOWER dec'd. Estates of J. D. GIBSON dec'd and Nancy T. BENTON dec'd committed to Sheriff. A. J. BRADFIELD qualified as guardian of Maria H. and W. A. METZGER.

Neersville: Miss Virginia POTTS, daughter of Jonathan POTTS, was buried at Salem Cemetery two weeks ago, of typhoid fever. She was 17 years old.

Neersville: One week ago the same burial ground received the body of Joseph P. DERRY, aged 27, son of Mrs. Virginia DERRY, of typhoid fever.

Neersville: Arthur, a young son of Abner M. and Belle CONARD, was interred at St. Paul Cemetery, yesterday, death cause by diphtheria.

Friday, 21 November 1890   Vol. XIII, No. 30

H. Tudor TUCKER, brother of Hon. J. Randolph TUCKER, died suddenly at the Soldier's Home, Richmond, Va on Monday, aged 65 years. He resided several years in Middleburg. He was a bachelor.

The death of Mrs. Chas. SILCOTT, after a lingering illness, last evening at 7:10 o'clock. She leaves a husband and two children. Meeting at the house tomorrow at 10 o'clock a.m., funeral services at Harmony Church at 11 o'clock.

Dr. L. F. HOUGH and Miss Nannie GORE were married at the home of the bride's parents (Mr. and Mrs. Albert GORE) on Wednesday at 3 p.m., by Rev. C. T. HERNDON.

Friday, 28 November 1890   Vol. XIII, No. 31

Marriage of Mr. Joseph CRIM and Miss Annie E. CARIE, dau. of James CARIE, a former resident of this vicinity (Bolington) but now of the vicinity of Daubs Station, Frederick Co Md, took place at the residence of the bride's parents, on the evening of the 20th inst., Rev. J. L. WICKLINE officiating.

Friday, 5 December 1890   Vol. XIII, No. 32

Mr. Daniel SHAFFER died at his home in Hamilton yesterday morning at 5 o'clock, aged about 40 years. He was a sufferer of rheumatism. His remains will be interred today at Arnold Grove, meeting at the house at 10 a.m.

Friday, 12 December 1890   Vol. XIII, No. 33

Rebecca MILLER, daughter of Wm. MILLER of Alexandria, died at her home in that city last Saturday night after a long illness.

Harriet STEER, widow of the late Samuel L. STEER, died at her home in Waterford, on the 7th of the 12th month [last Sabbath] in the 84th year of her age. She was the last member of one of Waterford's most prominent families. She leaves several children. Her body was laid to rest on Tuesday in the burying ground of the Friends, of which she was a devoted member.

Mr. John HERNE died at Round Hill last Saturday morning about 8 o'clock. He was thrown from a horse while racing on the turnpike on the 27th of last month and remained unconscious until last Saturday when he died. His remains were interred at Short Hill burying ground. He leaves a wife and 10 children.

Co. Ct.: Wills of H. Grafton DULANY dec'd, Basil SHOEMAKER dec'd and Susan TAVENNER dec'd admitted to probate. S. T. NICHOLS and H. M. DAVIS qualified as Admrs. of Isaac NICHOLS dec'd. The estate of J. R. BAKER committed to Sheriff. A. B. MOORE qualified as Admr. wwa of James H. ROGERS dec'd. Mr. E. McLIN minister of Lutheran Church, licensed to celebrate rites of matrimony.

Opinion of court in divorce case of Monena N. HAMPTON against J. N. HAMPTON. Wife admitted being unfaithful under threats of husband. Divorce granted.

Fairfax: Mr. Amos CROUNSE lost a 3w old child about 2 weeks ago.

Hillsboro: Mrs. Elizabeth VIRTS died at the residence of Mr. Samuel TRIBY, on the 3rd inst. Her remains were taken to Rehobeth and the funeral preached by the pastor and she was buried where she had been a member of the church for 50 years. Aged 76.

Mrs. Simon SANBOWER, living near Lovettsville, fell dead on Friday last, while out milking, She was 66 years old.

Bolington: Mrs. Betsy VIRTS, formerly of the vicinity of Waterford, died quite suddenly last week. She was taken sick on Sunday and died on Wednesday. Her remains were interred in the Rehoboth burying ground, services by Rev. J. S. WICKLINE.

Bolington: Mrs. Simon SANBOWER died very suddenly on Friday evening of last week. She died of heart disease. Her remains were interred in the Union Cemetery on Sunday, services by Rev. M. E. McLINN.

Married: On the 4th instant, in Washington, Rev. A. G. APPELL, united in marriage Miss Ida M. LESLIE, of Loudoun and Dr. George T. SHOWER, Baltimore.

Died: Died at his home at Silcotts Springs, Nov. 28, 1890, Basil W. SHOEMAKER in the 74th year of his age.

Died: At her home in Waterford, Nov. 29, 1890, of paralysis, Ida A. wife of Robt. W. HOUGH, after an illness of several weeks. She was a member of the M. E. Church. She leaves a husband and one little girl.

Friday, 19 December 1890   Vol. XIII, No. 34

Samuel O. BROWN, son of Isaac BROWN, took sick with catarrhal fever on the 3rd inst., which developed into typhoid, at his boarding place in Georgetown, where he was located in the employ of JOHNSON Bros. dealers in coal. He died last Saturday morning at 6 o'clock. He was nearly 27 years of age. Funeral at his boyhood home in Lincoln, buried in the burying ground of the Friends, of which he was a member.

Mrs. Catherine A. ENGLISH, wife of Mr. Charles A. ENGLISH, agent of the W. & O. RR at Leesburg, died at the residence of her husband in this town, about 9 o'clock last Monday night.

Cards are out for the marriage of Miss Rata, daughter of Mr. W. W. DIVINE Jr. and Mr. Chas. R. NORRIS, son of Jos. L. Lorris [NORRIS] which is to take place today (Thursday) afternoon, at the residence of the bride's parents in this town.

Ross CRAVEN and Grace HOGE were to have been married at the residence of the bride's father, Jesse HOGE, at Hughesville yesterday, and we presume that event took place.

Mr. Preston GOCHNAURER and Miss Annie GIBSON will be married in the church, at this place, next Wednesday evening, at 7 o'clock; the latter is the daughter of Owen GIBSON, who has rented the house of J. W. LONGCAR.

Philomont: Last week Mrs. Susan R. KERCHEVAL enlisted for life with Mr. Townsend SEATON, of Unison Va, Dr. I. B. LAKE officiated. At 10 p.m. the groom took his bride to his residence, some 4 miles distant.

Philomont: This week Mr. Orland CHAMBLIN will lead Miss Lula, daughter of our merchant, Mr. J. B. VANSICKLER to the alter and Rev. Mr. DICE will preside.

Friday, 26 December 1890   Vol. XIII, No. 35

Mary A., wife of David CARLISLE, died at the home of Morgan BEAVERS, near Paxons, last Sunday, in the 84th year of her age.

Jessie, the 2 year old daughter of Albert K. CHAMBLIN, died at the home of the latter's sister, Mrs. Mollie WALKER, near Round Hill, last week of pneumonia.

Died: Israel VIRTS, at his residence in Waterford, Dec. 13th, of consumption, in the 44th year of his age.

Friday, 2 January 1891   Vol. XIII, No. 36

Marriage license was issued in Washington, on Tuesday, to N. M. SOLOMON of Loudoun, and Martha WALKER, of Alexandria.

An infant daughter of Mr. and Mrs. W. A. McFARLAND died on Tuesday and laid to rest in Harmony graveyard yesterday.

Thamsin JANNEY sketch: Death mentioned in the last issue. Born 3d mo 16th 1840 in Richmond Va, her family afterward moving to "Forest Mills," near Lincoln, in this county. In 1869 she went with her family (her father having been appointed agent at the Pawnee Indian Agency in the West) to what was then the far West. Frail from infancy. After two years stay in the West the family returned to their Va home, where in 1875 she began the study of medicine. She died on the 17th of the 12th month.

Samuel THOMPSON was killed by the discharge of a gun in the hands of another colored man named Charles JOHNSON, on Christmas morning, near Silcott Springs.

Miss Owen EVERHART, daughter of Jno. B. EVERHART, near Harpers Ferry, died on the 21st inst., of typhoid fever. She was a member of the M. E. Church at Ebenezer.

Bolington: Manerva SCOTT died last Tuesday. Interred in the Rehobeth burying ground, on Wednesday, services by Rev. J. H. WILSON.

Mrs. Sallie SHUMAKER, an aged lady of the vicinity of Lovettsville, passed away on Tuesday morning the 23d inst.

Married: In Charlestown, Dec. 22 1890, by Rev. Miles S. READ, Mr. Harry G. DOOLEY, of Charlestown, and Miss Ida E. FRANKLIN, of Leesburg.

Married: Dec 23d 1890, of Parsonage M. E. Church, South, Leesburg, by Rev. B. W. BOND, John PUMPHREY and Orra J. WIGHTMAN, all of this county.

Died: Mr. Charles M. COFFMAN and Miss Sallie CONNER, at the Methodist Episcopal Parsonage, in Hillsboro, by Rev J. S. WICKLINE, both of Loudoun.

Died: Mr. Theodore M. FOLLIN and Miss Rosa B. RILEY, both of Hillsboro, at the residence of Mr. Craven LAY, by Rev. J. S. WICKLINE.

Died: On the 9th of Dec. 1890, Johnnie, son of Alonzo and Annie B. DINSMORE, aged 1y 8m.

Friday, 9 January 1891   Vol. XIII, No. 37

Married: Jan 6th 1891, at the residence of the bride, by Rev. B. W. BOND, Benjamin F. SPARROUGH, of Washington DC, to Miss Cella E. PHILLIPS, of Leesburg.

Married: On Wednesday, Dec 31st 1890, at the Presbyterian Manse in Leesburg, by Rev. J. C. DINWIDDIE, Mr. Chas. T. LAWSON to Miss Bertie L. COOKSEY, both of Loudoun.

Married: On the 31st inst., by the Rev. John WOOLF at his residence, at 6 o'clock, in the morning, Mr. Hunter W. LUCIUS to Miss Mattie F. DUNBAR, all of Loudoun.

The remains of Luther GOODHART, son of Mr. Chas. GOODHART, of this county, reached his parent's home on Monday, and were interred in the burying ground at Taylortown on Tuesday. He was an employe of the Norfolk & Western RR and in Oct last at Pearisburg was caught between the cars and mangled. He survived until a few days ago when death came to his relief. He was in the 20th year of his age.

Mrs. Thos. LATHAM died at her residence near Hickory Grove, on the 27th ult., at the advanced age of 70 years.

Robert Newton PANGLE, son of the late Milton PANGLE, died of consumption, at his residence near Arcola, on Dec. 15th. Mr. PANGLE was in his 32d year and leaves a wife and two children.

On Dec. 26, Miss Lucy ADAMS died of the same fatal disease, at the residence of her uncle J. H. ADAMS, near this village. She was a member of the Methodist Church. Interred in the Middleburg Cemetery.

Friday, 16 January 1891   Vol. XIII, No. 38

The little son of Mr. R. M. PRESTON, Teller of the Peoples National Bank, aged six years, died on the 2d inst. Their oldest son died on the 23d of December.

On the 5th inst., while Cloey PINKET, wife of Lewis PINKET, was passing along the road at North Fork, she dropped in the road and expired within five minutes. She was 66 years old and supposed died of heart trouble. Her funeral sermon was preached by Rev. Zack REED, in the old Church at North Fork, of which she was a member.

Jan. Ct.: Will of Annie E. STONE dec'd admitted to probate. G. P. HUNTER qualified as Admr. of Elizabeth VIRTS dec'd.

Friday, 23 January 1891   Vol. XIII, No. 39

Died: Mrs. Eleanor GULLATT, born Nov. 19, 1801, died Tuesday 13th at 6:30 o'clock a.m. at her home near Spink's Ferry, in the 90th year of her age.

Died: Mrs. Harriet A. VIRTS, wife of Mortimer M. VIRTS, in Hillsboro, Monday evening Jan. 19th, aged 48 years.

In Memoriam: Andrew Luther GOODHART aged 19y 6m 3d, son of Chas. W. GOODHART of Taylortown, died at Pearsburg, Va, on the 4th of Jan 1891 of injuries received by being thrown from a train on branch of N. & W. RR, near Pearisburg, Va, on the 6th of Oct. 1890.

[Winfield, Iowa Beacon, Jan. 9] Jonathan H. SCHOOLEY was born Aug. 2nd 1824, in Loudoun Co Va. His father was a farmer and also carried on a blacksmith shop. When the Mexican war broke out he enlisted 1 Jun 1846 in Co. F. First Reg. Mounted Rifles. Was in every battle from Vera Cruse to Mexico. ... Shortly after his return Oct. 22, 1849 at Baltimore Co Md, he married Emily Jane PRICE. Four children were born: Cornelius, Thomas,

The Telephone
Friday, 23 January 1891   Vol. XIII, No. 39

Susan and Laura, all of whom are living. He and family moved to Henry Co, Iowa, April 1855 and commenced farming. His wife died April 1860 and in May 1861 he enlisted in Co F, Seventh Reg. Missouri Vols. Made 1st Sgt. in March 1851. Promoted to 2nd Lt. of Co K, same Reg. Nov. 26th 1862 resigned on account of poor health. Jan. 1st 1863 was again married to an English lady, Hellen LENNOX, July 23, 1863, entered Co. E. Eighth Reg. Iowa Cav. as its 1st Sgt. and remained during the war. April 14, 1877 his wife died, leaving six children: Florence, Sherman, Emma, Alfred, Walter and Grace (one having died in infancy)... He died on the evening of 23rd of Dec. and on Christmas was laid to rest in the Friends' burial ground by the side of loved ones gone before.

Mrs. Wm. FERGUSON, dau. of the late John STROTHER, died suddenly in Snickersville, on Monday, of last week.

Mrs. Mary E. McVEIGH, mother of Mrs. Dr. KEEN, died at the home of the latter yesterday morning at 10 a.m. after a protracted illness. Funeral at the residence of Dr. KEEN, tomorrow (Sat.) at 10 o'clock.

Sidnor BENNETT, of Waterford neighborhood, died at his home in that place on the 14th inst. He had been failing for some time and about two weeks ago was attacked by pneumonia. He was probably nearly 80 years of age. His fourth wife and several children survive.

Rev. Chas. T. HERNDON, of the Hamilton Baptist church, and Miss Sallie J. ADAMS were united in marriage on Wednesday, at the home of the latter in Middleburg. They will make their home in Hamilton.

A marriage license was issued in Washington on Thursday to Calhoun ALLNUTT, of Loudoun, and Carrie O. COST.

Cards are out for the marriage of Miss Sally WOOD and Mr. Lewis NIXON, which will take place on Jan. 29th at 12 o'clock at the Church of the Covenant in Washington DC.

Mr. and Mrs. Thos. JANNEY have issued cards for the marriage of their daughter, Ethel Hyams, to Mr. Paul A. ANDREWS, which is to take place Tuesday evening, Feb. 3d '81 at the Arlington Hotel, Washington DC.

Herndon: Mrs. M. M. CASTLEMAN, who has been Principal of the Female Seminary here, died yesterday. She was a member of Episcopal Church.

Married: At the Parsonage of the M. E. Church, South, in Leesburg, on Wednesday, Jan. 21st 1891, by Rev. B. W. BOND, D.D., Mr. Chas. A. FRAME and Miss Susan C. DAVIS, all of Loudoun.

Friday, 30 January 1891   Vol. XIII, No. 40

Middleburg: Mrs. Lettie SHORTS died last Wednesday morning. She was about 29 years of age and a member of the Ashbury M. E. Church. Funeral sermon preached by her pastor, Rev. W. H. GAINES. She leaves a husband (Henry SHORTS also a member of that church), six little children, a mother and father, several sisters and brothers.

Friday, 6 February 1891   Vol. XIII, No. 41

Mrs. Maria POWELL, of this county, died at their residence of her daughter, Mrs. WYER, in Warrenton, on Tuesday of last week.
Mrs. Maria L. POWELL died suddenly, of apoplexy, at the home of her son-in-law, Rev. H. H. WYER, in Warrenton, on Tuesday, of last week, aged 81 years. When she was stricken down her children and others were arriving to attend the wedding of her daughter, who bears her mother's name, which was to take place on the following day. The wedding was solomonized in a room adjoining the one in which the mother's body was resting. The daughter was united in marriage to Rev. W. D. THOMAS, Professor of Phylosophy in Richmond College.
Mrs. Minor LANHAM, after a protracted illness, died at her home, near Woodgrove, last Saturday in about the 60th year of her age. Interred at Short Hill burying ground, on Sunday.
Fairfax: Capt. Ozias BLANCHARD died on Tuesday the 3d inst. at the age of 86y 8m. Born in Cumberland Co., Maine May 24th 1804. His wife, who is still living, is a sister of Mr. W. D. SWEETSER, the present Postmaster at Herndon. In 1837 they moved from Cumberland to Piscataquis Co. ...
Burial at Leesburg, on Friday last, of Mr. Eley HEAD, brother of B. F. HEAD and half brother of Rev. Nelson and Geo. R. HEAD, of that town. He was in the 50th year of his age, and many years ago removed to Baltimore and Philadelphia. He served as 1st Lt. in the 5th U.S. Cavalry.
In Memory: of Mrs. Mary E. McVEIGH – March 9th 1816 – Jan. 22d 1891.
Died: Howard B. EDWARDS, at the residence of Mr. S. R. EDWARDS, in the Loudoun Valley, on Tuesday Jan. 21st, in the 6th year of age.

Friday, 13 February 1891   Vol. XIII, No. 42

A marriage license was granted last Tuesday, in Washington to Thos. C. BRADY and Mattie GRIMES, of Loudoun.
Mrs. Fannie WYNKOOP died at the home of her son, James WYNKOOP, near Round Hill, last Monday, in about the 80th year of her age. She leaves many relatives.

Feb. Ct.: Estate of Wm. BUTLER dec'd committed to sheriff. Mary C. COPELAND qualified as guardian of Robt. B. and Margaret E. DONALDSON. Will of Sy[d]nor BENNETT dec'd admitted to probate.

Miss Ella PIERPOINT who for 2 or 3 years has resided with kinfolks at T. BROWN's near Lincoln, was married at the home of her father, in Fairfax Co last Wednesday evening of Mr. ___ SPRING, formerly of Loudoun, but now a resident of Montana. They were attended by the bride's sister Bertie and Warner M. BROWN. The ceremony was performed by Rev. Saml. BALL of Herndon. They will reside in Montana.

Mrs. Rebecca FOLLEN, of our town, was united in marriage last evening to Mr. Johnson WHEELER, of Missouri, but formerly of Fauquier Co. The bride is a daughter of the late John TAVENNER. Ceremony performed at the home of the bride, on Church St., by her pastor, Rev. W. G. EGGLESTON.

Mr. John FAIRFAX, son of Mr. F. W. FAIRFAX, of Fairfax Co. and Miss Alice, daughter of Mr. Marmaduke REID, of Prince William Co. were married on Wednesday of last week.

Friday, 20 February 1891   Vol. XIII, No. 43

Mr. Thos. W. EDWARDS died at his home "Fruitland," near Leesburg, Wednesday morning, in the 76th year of age.

Mrs. Helen BOTELER, wife of Hon. Alexander R. BOTELER, who represented this district in Congress, before the war, died at her home in Shepherdstown, W Va on the 15th inst.

Mrs. Julia STROTHER, aged 82, died at her residence, near Paris, on Friday last.

Three of our young men start to Ohio this week: Messrs. Chas. and Edgar VIRTS and Ashby ALLENDER.

Wife of Dr. R. F. PORTER died at their home in Denton Co., Texas, on Feb. 5th 1891.

Friday, 27 February 1891   Vol. XIII, No. 44

Mrs. J. W. LUPTON, wife of the Rev. J. W. LUPTON, formerly in charge of the Presbyterian church in this town, died recently at the residence of her husband in Clarksville, Tenn.

Round Hill: Wm. SEATON, after a brief illness, died at his home, near this place, last Friday, in about the 60th year of his age. His remains were interred at Short Hill burying ground, on Saturday.

Died: At her residence near Round Hill, Jan. 30th 1891, Mrs. Sarah C. LANHAM, wife of Minor LANHAM, in the 64th year of age. Member of the Baptist Church.

Friday, 6 March 1891   Vol. XIII, No. 45

Mrs. J. W. LUPTON, wife of Rev. J. W. LUPTON, formerly in charge of the Presbyterian church in Leesburg, died recently at the residence of her husband in Clarksville, Tenn.

Annie M. JANNEY, wife of Joseph JANNEY and daughter of the late Samuel TOWNSEND, died at her home in Baltimore, about a week ago. Her remains were interred on Saturday. She was a member of the Society of Friends.

Mr. Edward C. TURNER of Fauquier Co, died last Tuesday at his home near The Plains, after a short illness in the 75th year of age. He was the father of the late Robt. TURNER, whose tragic death is still fresh upon our minds.

Mrs. Virginia E. GORMAN, relict of the late Dr. Robert GORMAN, died at the residence of her son-in-law, Mr. Goodiet MORGAN, in Petersburg, Ind. on the 10th ult., aged 59 years. Also, Miss Virginia Eleanor GORMAN, dau. of the above, died at the same place on Oct. 29th last. Aged 17 years.

Aldie: Mr. J. T. SIMPSON, of this town, died on the 25th ult. in the 58th year of age.

Friday, 13 March 1891   Vol. XIII, No. 46

March Ct.: Wills of Jno. TAYLOR, Eleanor GUILLATT, Thos. W. EDWARDS and Ann Douglass ROSE admitted to probate. C. C. GAVER qualified as guardian of Fred S., Curtis C., Edgar C., Rufus T. and S. A. R. LOVE. Robt. R. LOVE qualified as committee of Thos. E. LOVE. Mary McLOUGHLIN as guardian of Patrick, Catherine, and Alice McLOUGHLIN. Mary McLOUGHLIN qualified as Admx. of Thos. McLOUGHLIN dec'd. Estate of Sallie REED dec'd committed to Sheriff. David T. THOMPSON qualified as guardian of Mary H., Samuel and Summerfield THOMPSON. E. A. MILHOLLEN qualified as guardian of Chas. A. P. LUCIUS.

Philomont: Miss Maggie RESSER and Mr. Jas. ALDER were united in marriage last week.

James N. CORBIN, of Jefferson Co W Va celebrated his 101 birthday a few days ago. He is in excellent health.

Married: At the residence of the bride's parents, near Leesburg, on Feb. 11th 1891, by Rev. J. C. DINWIDDIE, Mr. Florian COMPHER, of Montana, to Miss Annie SPRING, dau. of Mr. Jefferson SPRING, of this county.

Mr. and Mrs. DULANY, a bridal party from Fauquier Co, will in a few days be dismissed from the W. Pa Hospital, Pittsburg where they have passed a 16 weeks' honeymoon. On Nov 14 last, they were almost fatally injured in a collision on the Pa RR, near New Florence. They were married on 12 Nov. at the home of bride Anne CARTER's family.

Friday, 20 March 1891   Vol. XIII, No. 47

Mrs. Nancy M. UTTERBACK, widow of W. N. UTTERBACK, died at Marshall, Fauquier Co, on Monday.

Zachariah SMITH, colored citizen of lower Fauquier Co, died on Feb 27th, aged 112 years.

Wm. P. ORRISON died at his home, in the west end of town yesterday morning, from the effects of something like paralysis, aged 76 years. His funeral will take place tomorrow, at Catoctin Free Church meeting at the house at 10 a.m.

Died: Jas. W. JONES, father of J. A. JONES, one of the TELEPHONE employees. He was taken sick last Monday morning, pneumonia soon developed. He was 70 odd years old and it was his first illness. Interment Saturday 1 p.m. at Harmony Church.

Friday, 20 March 1891   Vol. XIII, No. 47

Mrs. Louisa A. PARIS, colored, at her home near Lovettsville, on the 1st inst.

Jacob H. MANNING, of lower Loudoun, died at his home near Sterling last Friday aged 62 years.

Henry GORE, son of Albert GORE, of our town, started for Chicago yesterday, where he will be in the employ of Robert GRUBB, formerly of this county.

Cards are out for the marriage of Miss Birtha WELTY (dau. of Dr. F. H. WELTY, lately of our town) to Lt. Frederick V. KRIIG, 8th U. S. Infantry, on Tuesday 31st inst., 9 p.m. at the home of the bride's parents, Shoshonee Indian Agency, Wyoming.

Mrs. Fanny PLASTER, living near Trappe in this county, mother of Dr. Geo. E. and D. H. PLASTER, lacks but 7 months of being 100 years old, and is still in excellent health.

Mrs. NORRIS, wife of Mr. H. DeButts NORRIS, of Fauquier, died suddenly Wednesday morning of appoplexy, at the residence of her son-in-law, Mr. Wm. H. SAUNDERS, in Washington. One of her sons is in Peru.

Last Friday Henry OWENS, a colored minister from below Ball's Mill, was adjudged insane and sent to Central Asylum.

Friday, 27 March 1891   Vol. XIII, No. 48

No marriages or deaths.

Friday, 3 April 1891   Vol. XIII, No. 49

Marriage licenses were issued in Washington last Friday to Andrew W. CLEVELAND of Fairfax Co and Phebe C. HENSON, of Alexandria Co; John W. HALL of Loudoun and Annie E. HOLLADAY of Fauquier; Ernest L. THOMPSON and Blanche May THOMPSON, both of Fairfax Co, and to Adolphus WHITLAY and Sarah HARRISON of Fairfax.

Marriage license was issued in Washington Tuesday to G. F. PRESTON, of Loudoun Co and Georgie EGGLESTON of Boston.

A little son of Thos. WILEY, near Purcellville, died of pneumonia, yesterday. He was about 6 years old. All of Mr. WILEY's family have been ill.

Mr. Charles TRUSSELL, who has tenanted Mason JAMES' farm near Round Hill the past year, died at that place on Wednesday or Thursday, of consumption.

Mr. John MANN died Thursday at his home near Lovettsville in the 91st year of his age. He was among the pioneers of Loudoun Co. He leaves some five or six children among them being Rev. L. A. MANN, former pastor of Burkittsville charge, Middleton Lutheran church, and now located at Mercersburg, Pa; Mrs. Wm. Z. MAIN and Mrs. J. M. MILLER, of Knoxville, and Mrs. KALB, of Loudoun co.

Friday, 10 April 1891   Vol. XIII, No. 50

Mrs. Mahala VANSICKLER died at her home, near North Fork, Thursday of last week, in the 90th year of her age. She had been an invalid for 11 years, and a member of the Baptist Church.

John STOCKS, a weak-minded brother of Mrs. Gabrael WARNER, with whom he has made his home for many years, died last Monday morning. His remains were interred at Waterford.

Mr. Steven CONARD, of Illinois, and Miss Alice SHOEMAKER, daughter of Geo. SHOEMAKER, of Purcellville, left on the morning train Wednesday, for Washington, where they were married, thence went to Ill, their future home.

Mr. James COSTELLO died at the home of his son, near Upperville, in the 104th year of age. He was of Italian descent. He leaves several children, some of which are said to be over 70 years old.

T. W. FRANKLIN died at his home in our town about noon on Tuesday of cancer of the face. He was a member of Harmony church, in whose burying ground his remains were laid on Wednesday. Member of the Loudoun Rangers, a home guard in command of Capt. Saml. MEANS, during the late war. He was taken prisoner and incarcerated for some time in Libby Prison, where he contracted rheumatism which so disabled him that he was granted a pension.

Thursday evening of last week Round Hill was startled by the sudden death of Mr. A. M. TAYLOR, who while walking along the streets suddenly fell to the ground and expired in a few minutes. Mr. TAYLOR was over 73 years old, and had served as J. P. for some years, which office he held at the time of his death. He leaves an aged wife and several children.

Bolington: Archibald MORRISON, formerly of Morrisonville, but late of Nebraska writes to the Lutheran congregation here for aid due to two years of failed crops. He went from Loudoun some 12 or 15 years ago, to Illinois, and from there he went to Nebraska where he purchased a farm.

Mrs. Lawrence LEITH died at the residence of her brother-in-law, Mr. B. F. LEITH, near this place, on Sunday night, of dropsy. Interred in the Middleburg cemetery, Tuesday afternoon.

Died: Clarence, the oldest son of Thomas H. and Mary V. WILEY, died at his home, near Purcellville, on April 1st 1801 [1891], aged 6y 4m.

Friday, 17 April 1891   Vol. XIII, No. 51

Mr. Joseph W. HOWELL, near Round Hill, died at his home yesterday at noon, aged about 66 years. Funeral at the house tomorrow (Saturday) at 10 a.m.

Mr. Logan OSBORN, a wealthy stock raiser of Charlestown, W. Va, died last Monday night, at the National Hotel, Washington DC, where he spent winters. His wife, son, and 2 daughters and a number of grandchildren were with him when he died. He was attended by his son, Dr. OSBORN, of Charlestown, and Dr. CHAMBERLIN, of Washington. Native of this county, Mr. Wm. OSBORN, his brother, and Mrs. J. H. PURCELL, his sister, both living near Woodgrove. The remains were sent to Round Hill Wednesday, on 11:30 train and interred at the OSBORN burying ground at Short Hill.

Last Saturday morning, a little daughter of Mr. George HAMPTON (who lives at the "Dry Mill" about a mile east of Clarks Gap) aged about 8 years, went to the spring after a bucket of water and to do so had to cross the creek on a long. She fell in and her body was found washed ashore about a mile down stream and on the following day was interred in Harmony Churchyard.

April Ct.: Will of Chas. TRUSSELL dec'd admitted to probate. Wm. A. WOOLF qualified as Admr. of Jno. WOOLF dec'd. Jas. C. VANSICKLER qualified as Admr. of Mehala VANSICKLER dec'd. Virginia JACKSON qualified as Committee of Susan MANLY, a person of unsound mind. Nathan T. BROWN qualified as Notary Public.

Mrs. A. M. WHALEY, formerly of this county, died at the residence of her son-in-law, G. W. F. HUMMER, in Washington, on Monday last, aged 86 years.

The remains of Harry ACHER, who died at Norton, Kansas, reached Leesburg Monday morning and were conveyed to the residence of his grandfather, Capt. B. R. ATTWELL, and then to Union Cemetery to be laid beside those of his father, the late David ACHER, Rev. Dr. HEAD officiating.

Married: In Leesburg, on Wednesday, April 8th, by Rev. Nelson
HEAD, M. D. TAVENNER and Sarah A. POLLEN, all of
Loudoun.
Died: Lelia Bess, youngest child of Sandy and Venna SMITH, at
their home, near Philomont, April 9th, of consumption, in the 15th
year of her age. Interment in the Baptist burying ground, at
Lincoln. Her funeral sermon was preached by Rev. Armstead
FURR.
Died: On Saturday, April 4th, Jas. Edward, only child of James A.,,
and Ella ROLLINS, aged 10 days.
Died: At his home, at North Fork, April 9th, Cornelius C. SEATON, of
typhoid fever, aged 29y 3m.

Friday, 24 April 1891   Vol. XIII, No. 52

Mr. N. B. PEACOCK, returned yesterday with his second bride, Miss
Lola SHUEY, she having lived in Waterford many years, but for
some time has resided in Baltimore, where they were married on
Wednesday.
Lenah: Mrs. Martha MAFFETT, consort of the late Wm. MAFFETT,
died at the residence of her son, C. J. C. MAFFETT, near Gum
Spring, on Saturday night last, after a lingering illness of some
weeks. Funeral conducted by Rev. G. W. POPKINS, after which
her remains were placed to rest in the family burying ground.
Jefferson H. PANGLE died between 8 and 9 Monday morning in the
27th year of his age, of consumption. He leaves a mother and
several sisters and brothers. His remains were interred in the
family cemetery, Tuesday evening.
Ella, eldest daughter of Dr. Jas. WILLARD, of Lovettsville, after a
lingering illness, died on Friday of last week. Her remains were
laid to rest last Sunday morning, in the Union Cemetery, services
by Rev. M. E. McLINN.
Married: At the Methodist Parsonage in this place on Wednesday
morning, Apr 22d, by Rev. W. G. EGGLESTON, Mr. Jos. W.
BELL, of Clarke Co., and Miss Alice I. POSTON, of Loudoun.
Mrs. Julia JACKSON, an estimable colored lady, has recently
received a pension. Her son served in the Federal army during
the late war.

Friday, 1 May 1891   Vol. XIV, No. 1

Mrs. Eleanor Hill LEE, mother of Mrs. Henry HARRISON, of
Leesburg, died at her home in Washington last Monday, aged 72
years.
Marriage license for J. Benjamin HURST and L. Francis THRIFT, of
Loudoun, was issued in Washington on Tuesday.

Friday, 8 May 1891   Vol. XIV, No. 2

Mrs. JENKINS, wife of Wm. G. JENKINS, of Mt. Gilead, died at her home on Tuesday.

Wm. ARNETT, brother of Samuel ARNETT of our neighborhood, died at his home, near Snickersville last Monday. He was afflicted with paralysis on Saturday. Interment at Ebenezer on Wednesday. The deceased was in his 85th year.

Friday, 15 May 1891   Vol. XIV, No. 3

Mr. Geo. LEE, formerly of Loudoun, died at Waterfall, Prince William Co., on the 4th.

Wm. SCHOOLEY, of Waterford, died at the home of his son, near Downey's Mill last Saturday night, aged 69 years. He died about an hour after being attacked with apoplexy.

Falls Church: while involved in a quarrel about politics at Halls Hill, about 3 miles from this place, Charles CHINN was shot and instantly killed by Charles MURRAY, last Sunday. Both colored.

Robert R. WALKER, of Waterford, and Miss Lida NEEDLES were married in Philadelphia, the home of the bride, on the 6th inst. They will live in Waterford, on the C. L. HOLLINGSWORTH farm.

Little Belle, 3 year old dau. of Mr. J. R. BEUCHLER, of this town, died last Friday night after a brief illness of membranous croup.

Miss Zilpha RITICOR, died at the old family homestead, near Aldie, on Sunday, May 10th in the 85th year of her age. Member of the Old School Baptist Church. Interred in Mt. Zion burying ground on Monday, Elder BADGER officiating.

Friday, 22 May 1891   Vol. XIV, No. 4

Mr. Addison SHUGARS, of Washington, a former residence of this town, died at Freedman's Hospital in that city on Sunday last of pneumonia brought about by an attack of la gripe. His remains were taken to his father's home near Clark's Gap on Monday evening and were interred Tuesday.

Herndon: Mr. Geo. W. WILLIAMS, one of our oldest citizens, died at about 10 p.m. last night, after a sickness of about five weeks.

Aldie: Miss Zilpha RITICOR died at her home near this place, on the 10th inst., in the 85th year of her age. Her remains were interred in the burying ground at Mt. Zion, on the 12th, Elder J. N. BADGER conducting the funeral services.

Aldie: Mr. Francis CHINN, living near this place, is in his 98th year and remarkably healthy.

Friday, 29 May 1891   Vol. XIV, No. 5

Correct an error: late Wm. SCHOOLEY, he died at the home of his son near Bennett's X Roads and was aged 73y 3m 18d.

Married: At the Methodist Parsonage in Hamilton, May 24th, by Rev. W. G. EGGLESTON, Mr. Thomas I. KITCHEN to Miss Rosa P. BALLENGER, both of this county.
Died: Mrs. Christian EVERHART, at her home in the northern part of Loudoun, on Monday, May 18th, nearly 71 years of age. A week before her death she was attacked by apoplexy, while in her garden. Interment on Wednesday, services at the house and Lutheran church, conducted by Rev. M. E. McLINN.
Sunday last, at the Methodist church, the marriage of Mr. MAYPOLE and Miss CARLISLE, after the services.
Bolington: Mrs. Burr SIMPSON died at her home, near here, this Wednesday morning.
Prof. EISENBURG of Staunton, Va and Miss Mary RODEFFER will be married at the Lutheran Church, on Thursday of next week, at 8 a.m.

Friday, 5 June 1891   Vol. XIV, No. 6

Dr. John T. MASON, surgeon in the Confederate service, died in Baltimore yesterday. He was a son of the late Temple MASON, of Loudoun. Interred at Leesburg tomorrow, Wednesday.
Cards are out for the marriage of Miss Bessie JANNEY, to Mr. Wilmer KOZER, of Pa, at the home of her father, P. JANNEY, in Lincoln tomorrow.
A funeral cortege bearing Mrs. Nancy ORRISON, relict of the late Jonah ORRISON, passed through town yesterday enroute from the home of her son-in-law, Mr. Joseph JANNEY, at Purcellville, to Catoctin Free Church, where interment took place. She was in her 84th years. She was raised in the vicinity of Waterford.
Miss Margaret A. HAINES, sister of Mr. George W. HAINES, editor of the Charlestown (W. Va.) *Spirit of Jefferson*, died in that town Sunday last.

Friday, 12 June 1891   Vol. XIV, No. 7

Mr. Levi TAVENNER, of McLean, Ills, who emigrated from Loudoun back in the 30's, arrived in Loudoun to visit relatives around Hamilton, having been raised on the farm now owned by S. R. TILLETT, adjoining our town on the south.
"Tom" LUCAS, a colored mute, died at his home in Hamilton last Sunday, of some lung affection.
In the Bellafontaine, Ohio *Republican*, of April 23d, notice of the death of Mrs. Mary GREEN, of that place, who was the last surviving member of the family of John H. HOGE, a former resident of Loudoun County, death by paralysis.
Lincoln: At the home of Phineas JANNEY on Sunday the 6th inst., marriage of his daughter Bessie, to Mr. Wilmer KOZER, of Pa.

Mrs. Mary Jane NIXON, wife of Col. Joel L. NIXON, and mother of
the proprietors of the Linden Hotel, died at her home in this town
last Sunday morning, in the 70th year of her age.

Mr. Patrick HOGAN, farmer residing near Aldie, died last Friday
night at an advanced aged, after several months of suffering.

Along the west side of Short Hill, Mr. Armstead BUFFINGTON,
about 65 years of age, who lived along in a small house, was
found dead. His son, living in Harpers Ferry had asked someone
to check on him. It is supposed he had been dead ten days or
more. He was interred at Ebenezer Church. A few years ago he
had his right arm cut off by a train on the B. & O. RR and ever
since had lived the life of a hermit.

A quiet wedding took place at Salem church last Thursday, Mr.
Frank SHUMAKER and Miss Ella FILLER, Rev. DULANY
officiating.

Annie and Mollie VIRTS, dau. of W. H. VIRTS, a former citizen of
this county, but late of Tiffin Ohio, are visiting their uncle G. W.
VIRTS.

Co. Ct.: Wills of Maria L. POWELL dec'd and Rhoda SLOPER dec'd
admitted to probate. J. F. CRAIG guardian of J. Asa CRAIG
executed a new bond.

Wm. H. SMITH in Delaware Co., Ohio, formerly of Loudoun, having
removed there at the close of the war has a fine farm.

Friday, 19 June 1891   Vol. XIV, No. 8

Mr. George WHITE died at his home in our town last Tuesday
morning of cancer of the stomach. Funeral services were
conducted at the Methodist Church, by Rev. W. G.
EGGLESTON. He was just 54 years old on the day before he
died. His father died of cancer of the stomach, a brother now
living in the West has a cancer of his face, another brother has
serious hemorrhages and three sisters died of consumption. One
brother suffered a violent death at the hands of a confederate
soldier, who shot and killed him, at his home, near Leesburg.

People of Lincoln were shocked yesterday morning to hear that
Rodney DAVIS had been found dead in his bed. He was in his
84th years. His wife found him dead in bed, it is thought he died
between 12 and 4 o'clock. His funeral will take place this (Friday)
afternoon, with interment in the burying ground of the Friends of
which Society he was a member. He removed to Lincoln from
Alexandria when a comparatively young man. He was
postmaster of the post office at Lincoln until it was removed by
President CLEVELAND.

Golden wedding anniversary celebrated for Mr. and Mrs. C. Means
VANDEVA[N]TER on June 3rd at their home in Washington DC.

Co. Ct.: Will of Ziphe RITICOR dec'd admitted to probate and Robt. A. RITICOR qualified as her Admr.

Harpers Ferry: J. B. BECKWITH, who was born in Loudoun Co, died in Wood Co, this state, last week, aged 91 years.

The marriage of Miss Mary RODEFFER and Prof. EISENBURG, of Staunton, Va was accomplished at the Lutheran Church on Thursday, the 4th inst., Rev. M. E. McLINN officiating. ...

Bolington: Mrs. Edna AFFETT buried her youngest child on Sunday the 14th inst.

Bolington: Miss Lena RICE, after a short illness, died at the home of her father, at Brunswick, Md, on Sunday, 14th. Her remains were interred in the Union Cemetery at Lovettsville, on Monday.

Middleburg: Mr. and Mrs. Robert ROSS, colored, of Marshall, Va, on Sunday the 14th celebrated their silver wedding, at their residence. They were formerly of Lynchburg, Va.

Aldie June 17th: On Wednesday last, Mr. Thomas B. TYLER, of Chicago, wed Miss Martha, daughter of the late John F. SIMPSON, of this town. Rev. R. T. DAVIS, of Leesburg, performed the ceremony in the new Episcopal Church. They will reside in Chicago.

Friday, 26 June 1891   Vol. XIV, No. 9

The *Gazette* announces the death in Alexandria, on Tuesday evening, of Mr. James H. McVEIGH, who, when a young man, with his brother, the late Wm. N. McVEIGH, went to that city from Loudoun and engaged in business there. Mr. McV. was in the 85th year of his age.

Mrs. Eliza THOMPSON, widow of the late R. J. C. THOMPSON, of this place, died at her home on Loudoun St on Wednesday. About ten days ago she was stricken with paralysis. She was 83 years of age.

Friday, 3 July 1891   Vol. XIV, No. 10

Chas. W. WILLIAMS died at his home in Alexandria on Wednesday morning, June 24th 1891, in the 44th year of his age. He was a painter by trade and a few years ago resided awhile in Leesburg.

Harpers Ferry: The family of John McKERNAN, a conductor on the Valley branch of the B. & O., living near Brunswick, Md, was poisoned last week by eating cakes made of flour which was found in the road and given to Mrs. McKERNAN by a farmer named Daniel SHIFFER. One child has died. Mr. McKERNAN was a widower and married the widow of the late Scott REED, or REEDER.

Lydia JANNEY, widow of the late Asa M. JANNEY, died at her home in Lincoln, last Friday afternoon, in the 91st year of her age. On

Sabbath afternoon her funeral took place at Goose Creek meeting house, of Friends, of which she was a member.

Aldie: Mr. C. W. PALMER, of this town, died on Tuesday last, in about the 35th year of age, of consumption. Leaves a wife and three little children.

Died: At Falls Church, July 1st Methel, only daughter of Chas. D. and Julia CHURCH, aged 9y 1m 9d.

Milton B. DAVIS, aged 87 years, of Rappahannock Co, died in Fauquier Co. last week.

Friday, 10 July 1891   Vol. XIV, No. 11

Married: At the residence of the officiating minister in Leesburg, on July 7th 1891, by Rev. Dr. Nelson HEAD, Mr. Nelson W. BARNHOUSE to Miss Christina STOCKS, both of Loudoun.

Died: Mrs. Fanny FUR wife of Mr. Elzy FUR, at her home near Hillsboro, July 4th, in the 62d year of her age. For 20 years she was a member of the M. E. Church. She leaves a husband, six daughters and three sons.

Harpers Ferry: Arthur NASH, a son of the late Philip NASH, of this place, brakeman on the B. & O. was killed at Mt. Airy last week, having fallen under the moving train.

Friday, 17 July 1891   Vol. XIV, No. 12

N. D. OFFUTT, Esq. died at his residence at Rockville, Montgomery Co., on Tuesday, after a protracted illness, aged 68 years. During his early life he was engaged in railroad building in this state, Tenn and W. Va. ... He married a sister-in-law of Dr. R. H. EDWARDS of Leesburg.

Co. Ct.: Wills of Patrick HOGAN and Nancy ORRISON dec'd admitted to probate. Samuel S. SIMPSON qualified as guardian of J. FRENCH, T. B. and Augustus SIMPSON. J. C. COLEMAN appointed committed of Mary C. ROLES.

John W. ORRISON died last Thursday night at his home in Frederick Co Md, in the 63 year of his age. His remains were interred in the Rehoboth Cemetery on Saturday, services conducted by Rev. SLATER of the Lutheran Church.

Miss Fannie HILLEARY, of Lovettsville, after a lingering illness, died at the residence of her parents last Friday night. Interment at Union Cemetery.

Herndon: Mr. Charles KITCHEN, a former resident of this place but for the past few years residing in Washington, died on Saturday last and was brought to this place and buried on Monday.

Friday, 24 July 1891   Vol. XIV, No. 13

Narcissa L. SCHOOLEY, an invalid for many years, was found dead in her bed yesterday morning at the home of her brother,

Reuben SCHOOLEY, in Waterford. She was 67 years of age. Funeral will take place from the house tomorrow (Sat.) at 10 a.m.

Friday, 31 July 1891   Vol. XIV, No. 14

Miss Betsy BRANDON, an old lady, died in Philomont last Tuesday night.

Died: Mrs. Louisa A. NELSON, at her home at Lenah, aged 80 years. Member of the M. E. Church.

Friday, 7 August 1891   Vol. XIV, No. 15

Died: At her late residence near Mt. Gilead, on the 22nd day of July 1891, Mrs. Miranda JOHNSON, in the 73rd year of her age.

Fauquier: On Saturday last a little son of Mr. Wm. REED near Delaplane fell out of a persimmon tree and shortly afterwards died.

Herndon: Mr. and Mrs. Wm. GARRETT lost a child nearly one year old, on Saturday last, and Mr. and Mrs. T. E. REED lost a 14 month old on Sunday, both of Cholora Infantum.

Harpers Ferry: Miss Rebecca PETERKIN, daughter of Rev. Dr. PETERKIN and sister of Bishop PETERKIN, of W. Va, died at Cumberland, Md, last Sunday night. Miss PETERKIN founded the Hospital of Sheltering Arms in Richmond Va.

Friday, 14 August 1891   Vol. XIV, No. 16

Marriage license was issued to George W. TARLTON and Halie M. JACOBS, of this county, in Washington, last Friday.

Aug. Ct.: Wills of John W. DAVIS dec'd, Sallie MITCHELL dec'd and Geo. W. WHITE dec'd admitted to probate. Jas. W. ELGIN qualified as Admr. of Mary J. ELGIN dec'd. Estates of Thos. MANLY and Fannie OVERHALL dec'd committed to sheriff. Jas. W. HOGAN qualified as Admr. of Nicholas HOGAN dec'd. Estate of E. B. FADELEY dec'd committed to Sheriff. Rev John J. BAILLIE licensed to celebrate the rite of matrimony.

Philomont: Miss Mary SAFFEL who was injured by a fall, has died. Interred at Rossels Chapel, Rev. Mr. BUSH officiating.

Friday, 21 August 1891   Vol. XIV, No. 17

Miss Hattie LEWIS, daughter of Mrs. Ann S. LEWIS, died at her mother's residence in Leesburg last Sunday, after a protracted illness. Her funeral took place Monday afternoon, Rev. J. C. DINWIDDIE officiating. Interment in Union Cemetery.

Mr. Wm. H. FORSYTH, of Leesburg, died at his home in this town last night, August 18th, in about the 78th year of age.

Marriage license was issued on Wednesday to B. F. STOUFFER of Pt. of Rocks and Sarah J. MITZLER, of Allentown, Pa. Also to John Wm. RICE and Clara V. REYNOLDS, of Fairfax.

We regret to learn that Mr. and Mrs. Richard BROWN, who are now visiting the home of the latter's father Samuel P. BROWN, have recently lost a little child, less than 1 year old, to death.

Friday, 28 August 1891   Vol. XIV, No. 18

Mr. Joseph LAYCOCK died at his home, near Woodburn, last Sunday night, in the 90th year of age. Funeral at the Grove, conducted by Rev. W. G. EGGLESTON on Tuesday.

In the Lincoln neighborhood, the marriage of Edward B. RAWSON and Miss Marianna SMITH, took place at the residence of the bride's father, Edward J. SMITH, yesterday at 1 p.m.

Friday, 4 September 1891   Vol. XIV, No. 19

Death of Miss Laura WOOD, daughter of Daniel T. WOOD, of Frederick Co., in Washington, where she had been for medical treatment. Funeral at the home of her parents today.

On Thursday of last week, Meadow Brook, the home of Edward J. SMITH, near Lincoln, was the scene of the marriage of his daughter Marianna SMITH to Edward B. RAWSON. The marriage certificate, as read by her uncle Wm. BROWN, had 65 names afterward signed. They will reside in New York city, where Mr. RAWSON is Vice Principal in the Friend's Academy.

Friday, 11 September 1891   Vol. XIV, No. 20

Wm. N. HOUGH died at his residence near Hillsboro on the 7th inst. at the ripe old age of 79 years. Interment on Wednesday at Arnold Grove.

Married: In Middleburg, on Thursday, Sept. 3rd 1891, Rev. Robt. S. CARTER, of Big Stone Gap, Va, to Bessie Lloyd, daughter of the late Burr P. NOLAND, of this county, Rt. Rev. Thos. U. DUDLEY, officiating.

In Washington DC, Sept. 5th 1891, by Rev. Dr. MOFFETT, Ella ASHLEY, daughter of Wm. ASHLEY, Chicago, and W. B. CLINE, son of C. A. CLINE, of Leesburg.

Middleburg: Mr. Edward RUSSELL was buried here Saturday, Sept. 5th.

Friday, 18 September 1891   Vol. XIV, No. 21

Died: At her home near North Fork, Catherine, consort of Wm. DOUGLASS, aged 27 years. She leaves a husband and four children.

The Telephone
Friday, 25 September 1891   Vol. XIV, No. 22

Died: In Washington, DC, on Saturday, Aug. 29th, of paralysis, Mr. George W. FEASTER, in the 63rd year of his age.
Co. Ct.: Will of Jos. LAYCOCK dec'd admitted to probate. Thomas H. PIGGOTT qualified as guardian of T. W. NICHOLS and M. B. NICHOLS. Cassandra CARTER qualified as Admx. of Wm. M. CARTER dec'd. John H. NELSON qualified as guardian of Arthur Fairfax DIVINE and Jessie DIVINE. Estates of Robt. J. C. THOMPSON and Eliza THOMPSON dec'd committed to sheriff. John F. GULICK qualified as Admr. of Armida SWARTZ dec'd dbn wwa.
Dr. R. Tasker MITCHELL, Va physician, died suddenly from heart disease in the store of S. C. MILBURN, at Catlett's, Fauquier Co, on Friday. He was about 60 years of age.
Frank T. SMART, formerly of Leesburg, died in New Mexico on Aug 28, aged 34 years. He was a son of the late Fayette SMART, so widely known to the patrons of the Big Spring Mills before the war, and a grandson of the late Dr. F. T. DRAKE.

Friday, 25 September 1891   Vol. XIV, No. 22

Mrs. Hannah NIXON, relict of the late Asbury NIXON, died at her home about 2 miles E of Hamilton, Wednesday morning, aged 80 years. Funeral services at her home, yesterday, conducted by Rev. W. G. EGGLESTON, remains interred at Waterford.
The home of William H. and Martha Jane BROWN, near Lincoln was the scene Wednesday of their golden wedding anniversary. Nathan T., eldest son, read a short address.
Dr. Francis LAMBERT died at his residence in Gum Spring, this evening (Sept. 22).

Friday, 2 October 1891   Vol. XIV, No. 23

Mr. William BAER, of Bolivar, Frederick Co, Md, 77 years old, has a son 54 years old and a dau. but one week old. He has a second wife and is the father of 16 children, 11 of whom are living. He is a Republican and one of the children is named James Grant, another Rutherford B. Hayes and another Dolly Garfield. He expected to name the new comer Benjamin Harrison, but it will have to bear Mrs. HARRISON's name.

Friday, 9 October 1891   Vol. XIV, No. 24

Mr. W. H. DAVIS and Miss Lillian SIMPSON were married at the home of the bride's father, Henson SIMPSON Esq. on Wednesday.
Marriage licenses were issued from the Clerks Office of this county, for the marriage Oct. 7th of Mr. Jos. A. LODGE of Snickersville to Miss Lelia MILHOLLEN, of Philomont; and Mr. W. S. DAVIS, of Purcellville to Miss Lillian E. SIMPSON, North Fork.

Friday, 16 October 1891   Vol. XIV, No. 25

Co. Ct.: Wills of Herod Harvey DUNBAR dec'd and Emanuel RUSE dec'd admitted to probate. Brewis RUSSELL qualified as Admr. of Robt. E. RUSSELL dec'd. H. Kate WALTMAN qualified as Admx. of M. V. B. WALTMAN dec'd. Frank L. FUTZ of the M. E. Church, South, Thos. K. CROMER of the Reformed Church licensed to celebrate the rites of matrimony. Estate of Laura V. HILL committed to Sheriff.

Mr. L. Henry LUCKETT, eldest son of the late Ludwell LUCKETT, died suddenly at his home at Grange Camp, Fairfax Co, of heart disease, in about the 63rd year of his age.

Mrs. Emily S. KELLER died of paralysis, at her home in Palmyra, Mo, on Tuesday, the 5th of Oct., in the 70th year of her age. She was the eldest dau. of the late Col. John SIMPSON, of Loudoun.

Gen. W. H. F. LEE, died at his home, "Ravensworth," near Alexandria last evening.

Friday, 23 October 1891   Vol. XIV, No. 26

Mortimer BEALES died on Saturday last, at his home in our town. He was 72 years of age. Interred in the burying ground of Harmony Methodist Church, where he was a member.

Circuit Ct.: Will of Robt. OSBURN dec'd admitted probate. Some months after his death a will was found in a rail pile near Mr. JENKIN's house with whom Mr. O. lived and where he had probably lost it. The will was in the testator's hand writing, proved and admitted to probate. N. J. PURSELL qualified as Admr. wwa of Robert OSBURN dec'd. L. H. POTTERFIELD qualified as Admr. of Duana SANBOWER dec'd.

Mr. J. W. McKINNEY and Miss Jennie HOUGH were married at the residence of the bride's father John HOUGH Esq. on the 15th inst. Rev. SCOTT officiating.

Falls Church: Albert DIXON, a colored man living near here, died last Sunday, it is said he was 107 years old.

The death of Congressman William Henry Fitzhugh LEE occurred at 2:30 p.m. on Thursday 15th inst. at his home, 12 miles from Alexandria, due to valvular disease of the heart. The funeral took place at "Ravensworth" at 4 p.m. Saturday. He was the second son of Gen. Robert E. LEE, was born at Arlington, VA, the 31st of May 1838. ...

Mrs. Edmund BERKLEY, wife of Col. Edmund BERKLEY, of Haymarket, Prince William Co., died last Saturday. She was the mother of Capt. Edmund BERKLEY, superintendent of the Richmond and Danville division of the Richmond and Danville system.

Living near Fairfax Court House, Mrs. Jane JOHNSON, now in her 96th year. She is the grand-daughter of John SUMMERS, who died in 1796, aged 102 years, and is the widow of 3 husbands.

Friday, 30 October 1891   Vol. XIV, No. 27

Mrs. Thomas W. DICKY, an aged lady, died at her residence near Round Hill last Friday evening.

Mr. H. M. KINGSLEY of our town received a telegram from Waverly, Iowa, Monday evening, announcing the death of his mother, Mrs. S. H. KINGSLEY.

Mrs. Fannie PLASTER, residing near the Trapp, will celebrate her 100th birthday tomorrow.

Marriage of Mr. Ernest E. DAVIS, near Roanoke, Va, formerly of Lincoln, and Miss Jennie ADIE. The bride was attired in pale heliotrope silk exceedingly elegant, embellished with pearl passementeric around the neck, and down the front of bodice was worn a full ruffle of pink chiffon, with gloves same shade of her dress and carried a bunch of pink and white roses.

Died: Margaret J. MILLER as Aashton [Ashton?] Md, Oct. 22d 1891, in the 69th year of her age.

Died of consumption, in Purcellville, Oct. 12th, Mrs. Fannie A. WEADON, aged 47 years.

Mrs. ___ RADCLIFFE, who lived at Janney's Mill, was buried here on Thursday.

Died in Brooklyn Naval Hospital, Saturday, Oct. 17th 1891, Floyd Craven JAMES, son of Robt. M. JAMES, in the 20th year of his age. Floyd enlisted in U. S. Navy in July 1889, from an explosion of gas. ... He was buried with military honors in the Naval Cemetery in Brooklyn, Sunday Oct. 18th.

Friday, 6 November 1891   Vol. XIV, No. 28

Stephen S. HAIGHT, of this county, whose attempted marriage in Baltimore with Henrietta LUCAS, a colored woman, was granted a marriage license in Washington, on Monday last.

At the home of Chas. E. WARNER Esq, 2 miles N of town, the marriage of his daughter, Annie G. to Joshua P. HATCHER. Rev. W. G. EGGLESTON, of the M. E. Church South, performed the ceremony. Mr. Charles PAXSON was best man and Miss Mary HATCHER, sister of the groom, was bridesmaid. The bride was attired in a traveling suit of blue Bedford Cord with jewell trimmings and carried in her hand a beautiful bunch of white chrysanthemums.

Died in Pilot Point, Texas, Oct 27th '91, Dr. Robert F. PORTER, son of John F. PORTER, of Neersville, Va. In March '90 he married Miss W. ROSS, the only daughter of O. A. ROSS Esq., a merchant of Pilot Point, Texas. After 11 months his wife died after an illness of two weeks, on Feb. 5th. In Sept. he contracted typhoid fever. He was 27 years of age.

Friday, 13 November 1891   Vol. XIV, No. 29

Mr. Laban LODGE, formerly of this county, but now a resident of Bannock, Ohio is visiting relatives in Round Hill.

The marriage of Miss Martha LOVELESS, of this town, and Mr. Isaac B. WEBSTER, of Washington DC at the residence of Mr. T. W. WEADON, last Wednesday evening, at 6:30, Rev. W. G. EGGLESTON, officiating. Mr. C. W. WEADON, of Hyattsville, Md was best man with Miss Julia McFARLAND, the bride's maid of honor. The bride was attired in a golden brown suit and wore a lovely cluster of Marcheil Neil roses pinned at the waist. She carried a bunch of the same. Miss McFARLAND carried white chrysanthemums. They will reside in Washington DC.

Co. Ct.: Will of Washington DAY colored, admitted to probate. Estates of Jas. McDONOUGH, Marie S. TAVENNER and Emanuel RUSE committed to Sheriff. H. H. RUSSELL, Sheriff, appointed curator of estate of Thos. A. HAVENNER, dec'd. Robt. W. WASHINGTON qualified as Admr. of Geo. WASHINGTON dec'd.

Lenah: Elijah SINCLAIR, oldest son of James and Elizabeth SINCLAIR, died of consumption on the 5th inst. His remains were interred at Mt. Zion church Saturday.

Friday, 20 November 1891   Vol. XIV, No. 30

A marriage license was issued in Washington, Saturday to A. F. DUGGER, of Richmond, and F. Leola JAMES, of Round Hill.

A marriage license was issued in Washington Tuesday to Francis A. GAVER and Lydia V. JONES of Loudoun.

On Monday a marriage license was issued from the clerks office to Frank N. WELLS, of Washington, and Miss Jane H. GARRETT, of Sterling, in this county.

Mr. Wm. RUSSELL and Miss Mollie COMPHER, were to have been married at 10:30 yesterday at the home of the bride's father, John COMPHER Esq. near Waterford.

Mrs. Elizabeth SILCOTT, wife of Mortimer SILCOTT, died at her residence in this town on Saturday morning last, at the advanced age of 74 years. Funeral services at the house on Tuesday conducted by Rev. W. G. EGGLESTON, remains interred in Harmony burying ground. She had been an invalid for several years.

Miss Hattie E. RUSSELL and Mr. Thos. E. BLACKFORD was married at the Episcopal church, Sharpsburg, Md. on Wednesday, the 11th inst. The bride is a cousin of Mr. C. W. LITTLEJOHN, of this town and formerly lived at Hillsboro.

J. W. MARTIN died very suddenly while at breakfast, of heart disease, at his home near New Baltimore, on the 31st ult.
Died at her residence in Loudoun, Nov. 7th, Mrs. Joseph COMPHER, aged 73 years. She was a member of N. J. Evangelical Lutheran church for at least half a century.
We are informed that Mrs. J. W. KINES was a victim of a tragedy at Calverton, Fauquier Co., was formerly a Loudoun lady. Her maiden name was SMITH. Lee R. HEFLIN, a colored man, was arrested and charged with murder. The house was set on fire. Lizzie KINES, 8 years old, was pulled out of the building, dead, with a deep wound between her eyes, etc. Annie, age 10 years was burnt almost unrecognizable. Mrs. KINES skull had been crushed and her feet burned off. No traces of the youngest child, Gilbert, 4 years old, could be found.

Friday, 27 November 1891   Vol. XIV, No. 31

Mrs. Mary J. MOCK, formerly of Loudoun, and sister of the late James W. JONES, died at her home, in Charlestown, W Va, Tuesday evening in the 72d year of her age.
John GRAY died suddenly at the home of J. Y. BASSELL, in Leesburg on Thursday of last week.
In Fauquier, Mrs. J. W. KINES – her maiden name was Jennie SMITH, daughter of Jacob SMITH, who died some 40 years ago, leaving a wife and three daughter, within the vicinity of Neersville, this County. Eighteen years ago, the youngest daughter married J. W. KINES and settled near Calverton. KINES died very suddenly about 1 year ago, leaving his wife and three children.
A marriage took place yesterday at 5:30 p.m. at the residence of Wm. WEADON, this town. Miss Medora KUHLMAN was wedded to C. Wm. WARNER, Rev. W. G. EGGLESTON, of the M. E. Church, South, officiating. Miss Julia McFARLAND as maid of honor and Mr. A. C. WHITE was best man.
Roy W. VENNA is famous and possibly rich. He is a colored man living near Leesburg. Not long since he had a dream that there were valuable deposits of mineral paints on Dr. Shirley CARTER's fine farm "Morven" the home of the late ex-Gov. SWAN, about 3 miles N of Leesburg.
Mr. Eli THOMPSON's daughter, aged 12 years, died of diphtheria some days ago.
Bolington: John COATS (colored) was buried in the Rehoboth burying ground last Sunday. He served as a slave of Joshua WHITE, until the close of the war, since then he saved some of his earnings and left a little home for those he left behind. He died at age 75 years.

Martinsburg W Va, Nov. 21: At 4:30 p.m. today, Rev John LANDSTREET died, after an illness of three years, from an affection of the heart, aged 74 years. He was a member of the Baltimore Conference of the M. E. Church South since 1847. He was chaplain of the First Confederate Cavalry of Va. His native place was Baltimore, where his father, John LANDSTREET, for many years was engaged in merchandizing. The funeral will take place Monday from the M. E. Church. Interment will be in Greenhill Cemetery. He was married in Virginia, leaves a wife, four sons and three daughters.

Friday, 4 December 1891   Vol. XIV, No. 32

Mr. Frank WEADON brought home a bride last Wednesday evening, Miss Mollie PRESGRAVE, whom he was that day married in Washington City.

Hon. Wm. F. MERCIER died at his home near Hamilton, early Wednesday morning, the result of a paralytic stroke with which he was afflicted last Saturday morning, in the 78th year of his age. He was born in or near Baltimore, and came to Loudoun when a young man. He connected with the M. E. Church. Miss Hannah CARR, dau. of the late David CARR, who, with three sons, survived him. When California gold fever spread over the country, he joined, locating a ranch adjoining the village which is now San Francisco. Ill health of his wife prompted his return to Virginia. Funeral will take place this morning, at the residence of his son, C. C. MERCIER, at 10 o'clock, interment in Union Cemetery at Leesburg.

Josiah CARPENTER, oldest inhabitant of West Virginia, died at his residence in Preston County on Monday. Estimates of his age place him at 120 years or more. He claimed to have been born in Loudoun Co in 1032 [1732?] and was therefore, 159 years old. He claimed to remember Braddock's defeat and to have served as a teamster at that time. He has one daughter still living who is over 80.

Mr. William SMALLWOOD accidently shot himself yesterday causing almost instant death. He was at Eubank's Mill where he had been helping to make cider and while descending the steps with a gun in his hand, some way it discharged. He leaves a wife and five children, the youngest only one week old.

Herndon, Dec. 3: Death of Mrs. A. J. DOWNING, this morning about 5 o'clock.

Philomont: Miss "Dixie" MILHOLLEN unites today with Mr. J. D. LUNT, a prominent druggist of Alexandria Va.

Philomont: Jno. P. EVANS, an old soldier of the Mexican war, died a short time since.

Friday, 11 December 1891   Vol. XIV, No. 33

Marriage license issued in Washington on Tuesday, to Robert S. VANDEVANTER, of this county and Columbia B. FOSTER, of Norfolk.

Mrs. Ada PARKER, at her home near Philomont, Dec. 7th, in the 38th year of her age. Funeral preached by Rev Zack RIED. She leaves a husband.

Friday, 18 December 1891   Vol. XIV, No. 34

William H. WILSON and Elizabeth B. SMITH, both of Loudoun, were married in Washington DC on the 16th inst. He is a son of Isaac WILSON and she a daughter of Edward J. SMITH.

Dec. Ct.: Estates of S. L. and Carnelius [Cornelius] L. HODGSON dec'd committed to Sheriff. J. H. CLAPHAM appointed committee of Elizabeth CLAPHAM. E. A. MILHOLLEN appointed guardian of Kate LUCIUS. S. E. ROGERS resigned as guardian of Edward McV DUNBAR, L. M. McGAVACK appointed in his place. Will of John GRAY dec'd admitted to probate, Ed. NICHOLS qualified as Admr. wwa.

Cards are out for the marriage on Wednesday, Dec. 23, 1891, of Mr. R. Lee DENNISON and Miss Lizzie, daughter of Mr. Chas. E. POWELL, of this county.

Wedding celebrated yesterday at the residence of John G. HERNDON, Miss Maggie HERNDON to Mr. Fairfax MITCHEL, of Lancaster Co, Rev. Chas. HERNDON officiating.

[Alexandria Gazette] Death of Miss Ida T. SPRIGG at twilight hour on Sunday evening last of consumption and heart trouble, in the 24th year of her age. She had been a member of Little River Baptist Church. On Tuesday her remains were followed to the family burying ground.

Marriage on the 8th inst. of Henry S. SMITH, of Sterling, to Miss Louisa West SOMERVILL, of Washington DC. This is either the 4th or 5th trip to the altar for Mr. SMITH.

John MANLEY, colored, has been granted a pension of $8 per month for injuries received during the late war.

Friday, 25 December 1891   Vol. XIV, No. 35

Mrs. Addison HAINES and Anzie HUNT both died at Hughesville on Wednesday. The former was over 80 years of age. Her funeral will take place at 10 a.m. today. The latter was sorely afflicted with a cancer. Her remains will be interred on Saturday.

Mr. R. L. DENNISON of Washington and Miss Lizzie POWELL were married at the home of the bride's father, Mr. Chas. E. POWELL, at Leesburg, on Wednesday, Elder E. V. WHITE, officiating.

Mr. Edward NICHOLS qualified as Admr. of estate of the late John GRAY. He leaves his estate to his cousin Miss Etta BASSELL.

Mr. Beverley J. BOND, of Baltimore, brother of Rev. Dr. BOND, Leesburg, was buried in Lorraine cemetery on Thursday of last week. The Rev. Dr. Samuel ROGERS conducted the services.

Mr. Wm. W. DIVINE died at his home in Leesburg on Wednesday morning, aged 77. He was born and spent his life in this town. He was the brother of the late James. F. DIVINE.

Miss Lute, daughter of Nathan ALLDER, died at her home near Snickersville, last Saturday, after an illness of but two days. Her remains were buried at Short Hill burying ground.

Mrs. Sarah A. SANDERS, widow of the late Mayor Wilson C. SANDERS, died at her home near Goresville, on Monday last, in about the 82nd year of her age. Interment in Union Cemetery on Wednesday.

The remains of Mrs. STANTON, wife of Hon. Frederick P. STANTON, who died at her home, "Belmont," in this county, on Saturday were interred in Union Cemetery, Leesburg, on Monday, Rev. D. DAVIS officiating.

Friday, 1 January 1892   Vol. XIV, No. 36

William MYERS, one of our oldest citizens, died at the home of his brother Jacob, near Waterford, on the 5th ult. He was born on Dec. 20, 1806, hence if he had lived fifteen days longer he would have been 86 years old. He had been in frail health and quite helpless for two or three years. His remains were interred at Catoctin church.

Bolington, Va, Dec. 30 – On Wednesday of last week, Dr. Dan B. WILLARD and Miss Emma JOHNSON were united in the bonds of holy matrimony, at the home of the bride's father, C. W. JOHNSTON, Rev. M. E. McLINN officiating. After partaking of refreshments they were driven to Brunswick, where they took the train enroute to New York, where they will spend a few days. Upon returning they will make their abode at Goresville, where the Doctor is practicing his profession.

A double wedding took place at the Lutheran church on Tuesday, 29th inst. The contracting parties were Mr. John KALB and Miss Linnie FRY; Mr. John FRY and Miss Nettie FRY. At 10 o'clock, the appointed hour, the bridal parties arrived and were ushered up to the audience chamber. As they marched up the centre aisle, a wedding march was rendered by Mr. W. D. VINCEL. At the chancel rail they were met by Rev. M. E. McLINN who performed the ceremony which made two hearts beat as one. They immediately repaired to the basement of the church, where they received the congratulations of friends, after which Mr. KALB and his bride were driven to Brunswick, where they took the train enroute to Washington DC, where they will spend a few days with friends in the city. I did not learn whether Mr. FRY took the train or not.

There is also a double wedding to take place at the Lutheran Church today, with Ella VIRTS and Miss Ella BOGER; Mr. William WIARD and Miss ___ COOPER as the contracting parties.

Ely AXLINE's youngest child died yesterday, with diptheria.

The remains of Mr. Lewis HAWLING, son of the late Lewis HAWLING, of this county, and brother of Mr. Chas. T. and Wm. HAWLING, were brought to Leesburg on Sunday and interred beside those of his father in Union Cemetery, Dr. DAVIS officiating.

Mr. Hanson HARDY, residing a few miles east of Leesburg died very suddenly last Thursday afternoon, of congestion of the lungs. He was in town the early part of the day, somewhat complaining, but left for home, where he was taken suddenly ill after his arrival, and died in a few minutes. He leaves a wife and several children.

Mrs. Ann TURNER, wife of Mr. Richard TURNER, of this town, died rather suddenly last Sunday, in about the 63rd year of her age. For some time past Mrs. TURNER had not been in robust health but up to 2 o'clock on Sunday, she was moving about in her usual health. At that hour, she was taken suddenly ill with a fainting spell, and soon became unconscious, in which condition she remained until 8 o'clock.

Mrs. Harriet WYCKOFF, relict of the late Nicholas WYCKOFF, a highly esteemed lady and for many years a leading member of Mt. Zion Church, died at her residence, near Gum Spring, last Saturday morning, in the 87th year of her age.

Marriages: In the parlor of the Linden Hotel, Leesburg, on Wednesday morning, Dec 29, 1891, by Rev. B. W. BOND, Mr. John L. DAYMUDE and Miss Lizzie CROSEN, all of Loudoun. At Ketoctin church, Dec. 23d, by Rev. C. T. HERNDON, Mr. William McDANIEL and Miss Irene SEATON, all of Loudoun. At the residence of the bride's mother, at Mountain Gap, Dec 23d, by Rev. J. J. BAILLIE, W. J. GOUCH and Miss Julia BRADLEY, of Loudoun County.

At the residence of his parents near Union, Dec. 12th 1891, of congestion of the lungs, J. J. KEEN, beloved son of C. F. and Lizzie KEEN. On the morning of Dec. 12, 1891, "little Jesse" beloved son and only child of Charles and Lizzie KEEN, who for nearly six years was tenderly cared for and loved with a love that can only come from parental hearts.

A few days ago a young man named Homer SHAW, living near Nokesville, Prince William County, was preparing to go gunning and had placed his gun against a support, when a dog which was to accompany him knocked against it, causing it to fall and discharge, the lead lodging in the young man's foot and resulting in his death.

Mr. B. LANSFORD died at New Baltimore on the 17th aged 67 years.

Friday, 8 January 1892   Vol. XIV, No. 37

The Clarke *Courier* states that Mr. Robert MORRIS of Aldie was married to Miss Sallie C. MORRIS, near Berryville, on the 22nd ult.

Marriage licenses were issued in Washington on Monday to S. Elton VERTS and Ella V. BOGER, and Howard WILLIAMS and Leah CORNELL, all of Loudoun county. Also Sylvester FOX and Emma F. WHALLEY, both of Fairfax.

Mrs. Hannah WHITE, widow of the late George WHITE, died very suddenly at her home in Hamilton, about half past twelve o'clock on Monday. After eating her dinner she went to her room on the second floor. In a little while those below heard her call, and on going up to her room found her lying across a sofa unconscious and in a short time she breathed her last. Death was evidently caused by heart trouble. She had not been well for some time and realized that the end of her life was near, frequently speaking of it to her friends. Her funeral conducted by her pastor, Rev. W. G. EGGLESTON, at Harmony church, was numerously attended Wednesday afternoon, and her body was laid to rest in the burying ground near by where, only a few months ago, her husband preceded her. The deceased was, we believe, generally esteemed for her kind disposition and christian character. She was in the 50th year of her age.

Miss Mary CLINE a sister to the late Alfred and Wm. CLINE, died at her home in this town last Friday night in her 70th year.

Mr. Mortime MOORE, a worthy citizen of this country, died at his home near Philomont, last Friday, after a few days illness, in about the 60th year of his age.

Armistead Mason ELGIN, died at his home in Mobile, Ala., on Friday, Dec. 4th 1891, in the 75th year of his age. Mr. ELGIN was a native of this county, and a son of Chas. ELGIN, who many years ago was sheriff of Loudoun. He still has a number of relatives living here.

Mr. Wm. T. T. MASON, son of the late Wm. Temple MASON, of Temple Hall, near this place, died at Baltimore last week in the 72th year of his age. His remains were brought to Leesburg on Saturday, and laid at rest in Union Cemetery.

Miss Roberta CARSON, daughter of Mr. Jacob CARSON, residing near Goresville, in this county, was taken with the grippe last Thursday night. Pneumonia set in on Saturday, and about 8 o'clock Sunday night she was a corpse. Interment in Union Cemetery on Thursday. We understand that Mr. CARSON's entire family, consisting of himself, his wife, and four children, are all down with the same disease.

Deaths: Lee MACON, at Robert BRENT's near Lincoln, Dec. 19th in the 74th year of his age. Luke CHAMP, at his home in Mountsville, Dec. 21st in the 70th year of his age.

Marriages: At the Methodist Parsonage, in Hamilton, by Rev. W. G. EGGLESTON, Mr. Arthur SEATON and Miss Mary E. SEATON, both of Loudoun. At the city hall in Washington DC, on Tuesday, Dec. 29, 1891, at 11 o'clock a.m., Mr. John HAWS to Miss Jennie HAWS, both of Alexandria, Va.

Miss Celia PRESGRAVE was today united in marriage to Mr. Walter LOVELESS, of Washington DC, at the residence of the bride's father, J. T. PRESGRAVE, near Pleasant Valley, Rev. M. SUTTON officiating. The bride is a sister of Mr. E. W. PRESGRAVE, of our town.

News has just reached this place to the effect that Mr. Peter SMITH, the details of whose serious accident were given in the last issue of the TELEPHONE, died today at about 11 a.m. He regained consciousness on the day following his injury and remained so until within a few hours of his death. Mr. SMITH was just in the prime of life and was one of our most energetic and popular citizens. For many years he has been a member of the M. E. Church, South, and his honest, christian life had made him many friends. He leaves and aged father and mother, a wife and four children and several sisters and brothers to mourn his departure. His remains will be interest in the Union cemetery at Middleburg, Thursday evening.

Mr. Frank SIMPSON, near Paxsons, went to Alexandria Wednesday, at which place he was united in marriage with Miss Florence MILBURN, daughter of E. MILBURN, formerly of this place. On the night of the above named day the bridal couple arrived at this place and thence proceeded to the home of the groom's father, where they were given a reception.

Friday, 15 January 1892   Vol. XIV, No. 38

Mrs. LYNN, wife of Mr. Wm. LYNN, died Tuesday. She had been a member of the Catholic church for a number of years and the funeral rites will be performed by the Priest today.

Mr. Fenton HAMPTON passed away Tuesday night. His death was caused by the complication of diseases, superindiced by La Grippe. He was about 65 years old.

Yesterday, at 11:30, Mrs. Fannie Lloyd PLASTER departed this life at her home at Snickersville, surrounded by her numerous friends and relatives. Mrs. PLASTER was probably the oldest person then living in the State of Virginia. She was born at Rectortown Fauquier Co. on Monday, Oct. 31, 1791, consequently, at her death she was over 100 years old. She connected herself with the M. E. Church in 1703 [1803?] and has faithfully sustained her relations with the Church 88 years, and was thought to be the oldest Methodist in the U.S. – possibly in the world. She was married to Henry PLASTER, a farmer of this county, Nov. 15th 1816, with whom she lived 97 years on the same farm, near Unison, until his death, in 1883 at the age of 90.

M. T. MARCUS, of this place, and Mrs. DAFFER, widow of John DAFFER, will be married to day, at the bride's home, near Snickersville.

Mrs. Ida POTTS beloved wife of John T. POTTS, of Kellers W Va, was buried at St. Paul today, a victim of pneumonia; a sad death, as she had been married but a short time and had just moved into their new house, finished at Christmas.

The residence of Maj. and Mrs. J. F. LOVE, on Thirteenth Street, NW, Washington, DC, was the scene, Thursday evening, Jan. 7th of one of the prettiest weddings which have taken place at the National Capital this winter, when Miss Dora, eldest daughter of Major and Mrs. LOVE, was united in marriage with Mr. S. L. RICHARDS, a Washington newspaper correspondent, formerly a member of "*The Post*" editorial staff. ... The ceremony was performed by Rev. E. B. BAILY, a Presbyterian divine from the Capital and took place in the center of the parlors, where the wedding party was met by the bride's parents. The bride was attired in a beautiful fawn colored traveling dress, richly trimmed with brown fringe and disc and carried a bouquet of pure white bridal roses. she entered on the arm of the groom who were the conventional black and was attended by her sister and cousin, Misses Ada LOVE and Katie MANNING, each carrying bouquets of LaFrance roses. ... Many of the guests were from Loudoun County, where Major and Mrs. LOVE resided for years previous to their removal to Washington. The groom is also a native Virginia. On returning from their bridal tour, Mr. and Mrs. RICHARDS will reside at 505, 13th St. NW.

Mr. J. E. BEALES and Miss Fannie BENNETT, daughter of Wm. BENNETT, of Waterford, were married last evening, at the residence of Mrs. BEALES, Rev. W. G. EGGLESTON officiating.

The lifeless form of Mrs. A. T. SCANLAND (nee CHAMBLIN) who went away from our town, a happy bride, about two years ago, was brought back yesterday for interment. She died at her home near Falls Church on Wednesday.

At the Orthodox Friends meetings house, at Lincoln, Wednesday noon last, occurred the wedding of Mr. Walter H. HIRST and Miss M. Lacy BEANS, daughter of Mr. H. P. BEANS, near Wheatland. The church was tastefully decorated with potted plants. The bride was becoming attired in a blue Bedford cord dress; she carried in her hand a beautiful bouquet of LaFrance roses. After the beautiful and impressive ceremony of the Society of Friends, the happy couple left on the east bound train for Washington DC, and the South.

Wills of Wm. MYERS, dec'd, Jas. J. OTLEY, dec'd, Wm. G. JENKINS, dec'd, admitted to probate.

Estates of A. C. TRUNDLE and John M. MORAN committed to sheriff.

The case of Joseph DYE, charged with participation in the murder of the KINES family, was concluded in the court at Warrenton last Saturday, resulting in a verdict of guilty in the first degree. the exhibition before the jury on Friday of the head of one of the murdered KINES children had a marked effect. The evidence against DYE was strong. Various motives for the murder are assigned: HEFLIN's folks claim that DYE came after him at this home in Stafford, and hired him to do the murder. Judge LIPSCOMB sentences HEFLIN and DYE to be hanged on the 19th of March between the hours of 6 and 8 o'clock in the morning.

Friday, 22 January 1892   Vol. XIV, No. 39

Cards are out for the marriage of Mr. Edwin SHOEMAKER and Miss Permelia HIXON, at Mountain View, the residence of the bride's father, Mr. John H. HIXON.

Miss Rose HOUGH, near Waterford, was buried on Tuesday. She had gone to nurse a cousin, a Mrs. FURR, we believe, who was ill, and took sick and died there. Her mother went to the same place to care for her, and she too was taken sick and has been very ill. Mrs. FURR also continued very ill.

A very pretty wedding took place at Harmony M. E. Church, South, at noon Wednesday, the contracting parties being Mr. James WILLIS of Alexandria and Miss Mamie MYERS, the youngest daughter of C. F. MYERS, of our town. The church which was darkened and artificially illuminated and decorated with potted plants and flowers, was well filled at the appointed hour. A little later, about 12:30 the bridal party arrived and filed into the church to the sweet strains of a wedding march, by Miss Evolyn EGGLESTON. First the waiters: Mr. Samuel SIMPSON and Geneva HARDING, niece of the bride; Mr. R. WILLIS and Miss Annie WILEY; Mr. W. W. NIXON and Miss Lucy MYERS, sister of the bride. Then came the bride and groom, followed by their ushers, Messrs. Clarence TAVENNER and Edgar WILEY. The contracting couple were met at the chancel rail by the Pastor, Rev. W. G. EGGLESTON. Mr. and Mrs. WILLIS then proceeded to their carriages and were driven to the W & O railroad depot, where they boarded the 1:18 train enroute to Baltimore and elsewhere. They will locate in Alexandria, where the house for which Mr. WILLIS travels is located.

Mr. Joseph REED buried a little son on Saturday, the 16th.

Mr. Littleton TURNER and Miss Lucy ADAMS were united in marriage, in the presence of a few friends, at Little River church last Wednesday.

Mrs. Milton PANGLE, whose illness was recently mentioned in the TELEPHONE, died on the 10th inst. this is the fourth death which has occurred in that family within two years.

On Saturday last, at the residence of his father, near Arcola, Robt. H. LITTLE, of pneumonia, superinduced by an attack of La Grippe. Mr. LITTLE was about 35 years of age and was an exemplary and popular young man.

Yesterday, at the residence of her son, near Pleasant Valley, Mrs. Fannie HUTCHISON, consort of the late Sandford HUTCHISON. Mrs. HUTCHISON was among the oldest residence of this section being past four score years of age.

Following the announcement of Mrs. HUTCHISON's death, came tidings of the demise of Mr. David J. LEE, at his residence near Oatland. Mr. LEE was 48 years of age and the youngest son of Matthew P. LEE of this section.

Bolington, January 13 – Mrs. Adam COOPER died at her late residence, near Salem church, on the 11th inst. Her remains were interred at the Lutheran church yesterday.

The widow of the late John COATS (colored) was buried at the Rehoboth burying ground yesterday.

William WELCH died at his residence near here on last Thursday night. He had been quite feeble from old age for sometime and was taken with the grip a few days ago and soon yielded to the ravages of the disease. His remains were interred in the Catholic burying ground, at Petersville Md, on Sunday.

Mrs. Margaret A. GRUBB departed this life on Friday night of last week after a lingering illness she leaves a husband (Benjamin GRUBB) four daughters and three sons to mourn the loss of wife and mother. She had been a consistent member of the Lutheran church for a number of years. Her remains were interred in the Union cemetery, near Lovettsville, on Sunday afternoon.

Mrs. William SLATER died of that dread disease consumption, at the residence of her brother-in-law, Smith REED, aged about 35 years. Her remains were laid to rest in the Union cemetery, today.

Mr. Thomas B. BEALL, for many years a well-known and popular school teacher of Jefferson county, W Va, died Saturday last, in the eighty first year of his age.

Rev. Patterson FLETCHER, pastor of the Presbyterian church at Broadway, Rockingham county, died Sunday after a short illness of pneumonia. He was formerly pastor of the Presbyterian church at Duffields, W Va.

Friday, 29 January 1892   Vol. XIV, No. 30

Mr. Thomas M. WILSON, a prominent citizen of Norfolk, died in that city on the 20th inst. He formerly practiced law in Fauquier and Loudoun counties, as partner of Beverly DOUGLAS.

Dr. H. E. WALKER, who was a native of Loudoun and for several years a resident of Hamilton, died at his home in Washington, last Monday and his body was laid in its final resting place, in Washington yesterday.

J. L. McINTOSH, who is well known as an ex-Treasurer of Loudoun county, died at his home in Leesburg last Friday night, after a brief illness of erysipelas.

Mr. Bushrod OSBORNE, father of Mr. Jos. OSBORNE, near Purcellville, died last Tuesday. He was an aged man, but the exact number of his years we have not learned.

Lindsey COPELAND, another aged citizen, died at his home near Purcellville, on Wednesday.

It was Mr. Frank HIBBS whose rumored death on Thursday of last week was mentioned in the last issue. He had just returned from Chicago where he had been to purchased a lot of stock cattle. Pneumonia, superinduced by Grip was the cause of his death. We were informed yesterday that a sister of Mr. HIBBS died on Tuesday, and that his widow is very ill.

A colored man named John SMITH, living near Purcellville, went to Lincoln yesterday after a coffin for another of his children, this being the fifth one that has recently died.

We learn from the *Mirror* of the following deaths: Miss Mollie HOUGH, daughter of the late L. W. S. HOUGH, at her home in Leesburg, on Tuesday.

Mrs. Caroline TILLETT, at the residence of Mr. Rodney BEALES, in Leesburg, about 72 years of age.

Mr. John Wm. BEST, near Round Hill, [died] one day last week, at an advanced age.

John DUNN, near Coe's Mill [died] last week.

Hamilton had quite a surprise last Wednesday morning. Scarcely any one knew that W. C. WEADON was in town and no one was thinking of matrimony, until a number of carriages congregated at the residence of Mrs. B. A. McFARLAND. Parson EGGLESTON walked into the same place and "Clint" stepped across the street attired in attractive style. Mr. W. C. WEADON and Miss Julia McFARLAND were united in the bonds of wedlock, by the Rev. W. G. EGGLESTON, at the home of the bride's mother, in the presence of their immediate relatives. After the ceremony was performed and luncheon eaten they were driven to the depot, where they boarded the 1 o'clock train. They will locate near Mount Vernon, where Mr. WEADON is engaged on a large stock farm.

John HICKMAN, a former well-known resident of this vicinity, but late of Hagerstown Md, died at his residence there on Thursday of last week. His remains were laid to rest at Hagerstown, on Saturday.

Rev. M. E. McLINN's youngest child, aged about 3 years, died Saturday 23rd inst. Interment at the Lutheran Church, Tuesday, 26th inst.

Mrs. Benj. CROSS died Monday of LaGrippe, at an advanced age.

Willard FRANCIS, aged eight years, son of elder A. B. FRANCIS, died Sunday. Funeral today, at Mt. Zion church, conducted by Elder E. V. WHITE, of Leesburg.

Friday, 5 February 1892   Vol. XIV, No. 31

Marriages: At the residence of her parents, near Mt. Hope, on the 27th of January, 1892, Miss Mary E. GARDNER to Mr. Joseph R. BITZER, by the Rev. G. W. POPKINS.   At Mt. Hope church on Jan. 27th 1892, by the Rev. G. W. POPKINS, Miss Maud CROZEN to Mr. James POWER.

January 8th, 1892, at his residence in Hampshire county, West Va, Mr. Isaac G. NICHOLS, formerly of this county, aged 73y, 7m 10d. His remains were interred at Bethel Church, and his funeral sermon preached by Rev. Mr. HINGER, of the Evangelist church, of which he was a member.

Miss Polly FRITTS, died at the home of her nephew, Mr. Rodney MATTHEW, in Hillsboro, last Sunday, in the 77th year of her age. Interment on Monday.

A special to the TELEPHONE from Alexandria announced the sudden death of Mr. Allan C. HARMON of that City at 10 o'clock Tuesday night. Mr. HARMON was well known through the surrounding country as Secretary and Treasurer of the Independent Mutual Fire Ins. Co. of Fairfax County.

On the evening of Jan. 27th at the bride's residence, Dr. Eppa H. HEATON and Miss Mattie DADE were united in matrimony. Rev. KEEBLE carefully and securely tied the knot.

Mr. Mason DOWNS and Mrs. Rev. HOWELL, widow of the late Jos. HOWELL, were married in Leesburg Va a short time since.

The marriage of Miss Mabel VICKERS and Mr. Dan P. HOUSEHOLDER occurred Thursday afternoon (Jan. 7) at the residence of the bride's parents, Mr. and Mrs. J. M. VICKERS. The ceremony was performed by Rev. C. D. JACOBS, of the

Presbyterian church. The bride was attired in a dress of white silk with chiffon trimming; she wore a veil and carried roses. Miss Ida ADAMS, the made of honor, wore a dress of pale blue crepe de chine and carried pink roses. Dr. VANDEVANTER was the groom's best man. The bridal party, attended by the ushers, Will NORTHMORE, Frank NELSON, Fred VICKERS and Arthur WHITELEY, entered the room to the music of the wedding march, played by Mrs. BARNETT and stood within the bay window beneath an umbrella of ground pine and moss. The ceremony was performed by Rev. C. D. JACOBS. After ice cream and cake were served assistance being given by the bridesmaides, Misses Myrtle JOHNSTON, Fannie HAM, Emmie HASLAM, Rosa ROBINSON, Clara RAY and Bessie WADSWORTH.

Saco, Me., Jan. 27 – On of the most brilliant weddings ever celebrated in the society of this city was that this afternoon at the Saco Congregational church, when Miss Luella LEAVITT of Saco and Rev. T. Arthur FREY, pastor of the Pavillion church of Bidderford, were united in marriage. The groom was born in Lovettsville, Va, is a graduate of Yale, and is one of the brightest clergymen in Maine. The bride is the oldest daughter of Mr. and Mrs. Benjamin LEAVITT of this city. She is a graduate of Bradford Academy. ... [long article] The bridal party left on the evening train for Boston. On their return the newly-married couple will take up their residence at 25 Westworth St., in Beddeford.

Friday, 12 February 1892   Vol. XIV, No. 32

Mrs. __ RUSSELL, mother of Mr. Joseph RUSSELL, of Keep Tryst, Md, and Mr. George RUSSELL, of Loudoun county, Va, while on her way from the home of the former son to that of the latter, last Sunday afternoon, was stricken with apoplexy and fell in the street in Keep Tryst. The aged lady was dead. Mrs. RUSSELL was about seventy years of age.

Miss Gussie O. WHITE, who, with her mother, Mrs. Eliza J. WHITE, removed from Hillsboro, this county, to Baltimore City, less than three months since, was brought to her former home a corpse, on Wednesday last a victim to the prevailing epidemic. As the companion of her aged mother, the next of kin of her afflicted sister Mrs. J. O. POTTS, her sudden taking off was a great shock to the community. She was a most consistent member of the M. E. Church South. Interment in cemetery at Arnold Grove church. Services by her late Pastor, Rev. J. H. DULANEY.

Wills probated – that of Mollie S. HOUGH, Reuben DEAN, Lee SIMMS, Anzey HUNT, Alfred J. SPINKS, John DUNN, David J. LEE, Mary A. HAINES, Henry POLLARD, Jno. Wm. BEST, and C. E. DISHMAN.

T. E. LITTLE qualified as Admr. of R. H. LITTLE dec'd; Sarah Ellen SMITH and Jas. M. SMITH qualified as Admrs. of Peter SMITH dec'd; Robt. L. MYERS qualified as Admr. of Lindsay COPELAND dec'd; C. C. GAVER qualified as Admr. of Tobitha WATERS dec'd. Thos. H. PIGGOTT qualified as guardian of Martha B. PIGGOTT, Mary A. PIGGOTT, Sallie E. PIGGOTT and Thos. J. PIGGOTT. Estate of Mary E. FRY was committed to the Sheriff. On Wednesday Wallace GEORGE qualified as Executor of the late Jas. L. McINTOSH.

Mr. Francis CHINN died last night. He was the oldest citizen of this section and perhaps of the county, being in his 96th year.

Mr. Wm. SULLIVAN died at the residence of his son-in-law Dallas EURR [FURR], near Aldie last Friday. He was among the oldest citizens of that section.

Mrs. Rachel Ann JAMES departed this life, Feb. 3rd. She was 82y 2m 9d of age. Her funeral took place at the Methodist Church of this place Feb. 5th. She had been a member of the M. E. Church for 57 years. Rev. R. A. SCOTT conducted the services. His text was Matt. 27-52,53.

Mrs. Mary MOCK died Feb. 5th. Her age was 78y 26d. She has been afflicted with paralysis for some time. Rev. Mr. HERNDON conducted the service, which were held at the house.

The infant child of James PEACOCK died Monday night, ages about one week. The mother of the child is quite sick with a complication of diseases.

Mrs. Thomas J. COST, of Lovettsville, is lying critically ill with consumption. Her death is hourly expected.

Friday, 19 February 1892   Vol. XIV, No. 33

Mrs. James PEACOCK died at her home near Morrisonville, a few days ago. All of her children have been sick.

Harry M. CHEW, a brakeman on the B & O, fell from his train near Washington Junction a few days ago and received injuries from which he soon died.

The wife of Mr. Wm. HOFFMAN, near Bolivar, died of grippe on the 1st inst., leaving six small children, one an infant only a few months old. Her mother, Mrs. DIXON, of Halltown, is very ill.

Mr. John B. DUTTON breathed his last, in his home at Waterford surrounded by most of his children and other relatives. The result was a relapse, followed by pneumonia and heart trouble. John Biddison DUTTON was born in Baltimore county, Maryland and when quite a young man he came to Loudoun and located in Waterford., where he met and married Emma SCHOOLEY, who, after a long illness, through which he devotedly nursed her, passed on about three years ago. They had five children, one son and four daughters, all of whom were present at the father's funeral except one daughter who is residing in California. In his earlier business life he was engaged in merchandising. Subsequently he was one of the most active promoters of the Mutual Fire Insurance Company. On the Sabbath his remains were taken to the Friends Meeting House, where, through most of his life, he had been a devout worshipper. He was laid to rest in the graveyard nearby.

L. F. PALMER Sr., died at his residence, in Arcola, at 6 p.m., last Saturday. the direct cause of his death was pneumonia, and this fatal disease only confined him to his room one week. L. Frank PALMER was born Oct. 3d, 1829, near Gum Spring, this county, He was the fifth son of Philip and Prudence Virginia PALMER, to whom nine children were born. Early in life Mr. PALMER began the merchantile business at Gum Spring, which he successfully conducted until the war broke out. In 1861 his State called for his services and discontinuing business he gallantly shouldered his musket and enlisted with the Sixth Virginia Cavalry. He served his State faithfully, with bravery and distinction, until the end of the service. After the war he resumed his business at Gum Spring. He married Mary E. FERGUSON, Feb. 23rd, 1870, who with five children, now survives him. He conducted his business extensively until last October, when he retired, selling out his stock to his son-in-law, Dennis HIGGINS. His funeral took place from Mt. Zion Baptist Church at 2 p.m. Monday, Elder E. V. WHITE officiating.

The sad news has just been received of the death of Mrs. William RUSSELL. She has been sick for some time.

Friday, 26 February 1892   Vol. XIV, No. 34

A little child of Mr. Dan GREGG of Purcellville about three weeks ago died on Monday.

Wm. H. HOUGH died at his home near Waterford last Friday evening from the effects of an attack of the Grip. He was about 65 years of age. This is the third death in this family within a month, namely, two daughters and the Father. Mrs. James PEACOCK, whose death was mentioned last week was one of the daughters. The wife of the deceased, who was taken sick while absent from home attending her sick daughter, is still so ill that she has not, we understand, been informed of the death of her husband and other daughter.

The death of Mrs. Ann C. MILTON, mother of John and T. D. MILTON, which occurred at the home of her niece, in Alexandria, last Tuesday night, from the effect of a cancer. Her remains were brought up yesterday on the railroad to Purcellville, and from there to their last resting place in the burying ground at Arnold Grove. Only a few months ago the deceased left Hamilton to make her home in Alexandria. She was in the 73 year of her age.

The sad and rather sudden death of Mrs. James PEACOCK has cast a pall over this vicinity. On Friday she sat up for a couple of hours and also on Saturday morning for considerable time, and about 2 o'clock she passed peacefully away. She leaves a husband and three children to mourn the loss of an affectionate wife and a kind mother. The funeral was preached at the house by Rev. M. E. McLINN, on Monday, the 15th inst. Her remains were then born to their final resting place in the Catoctin burying ground.

The remains of George McHENRY, a former resident of this vicinity, but late of Baltimore, were brought from that city and interred at the Lutheran Church on the 15th last.

Friday, 4 March 1892   Vol. XIV, No. 35

The home and personal effects of Angie HUNT, at Hughesville, were sold at auction on Wednesday, A. C. VANDEVANTER auctioneer.

Mason THROCKMORTON, Esq., and Mrs. Martha C. OSBURN, both of this county, were married in Washington on Wednesday evening February 24th.

The Alexandria *Gazette* states that Miss Mary E. FOSTER, of Fauquier county, who died last week, possessed $80,00 [or $30,000] which, under the will of her aunt Mrs. James Edward FOSTER, will go to the eldest daughter of Capt. J. W. FOSTER, of Leesburg.

Died at her home in Leesburg, at 2 o'clock a.m., March 1st, 1892, after an illness of eight days duration. Mrs. Elizabeth G. GIST, widow of the late Henry C. GIST, in the 64th year of her age.

Mrs. Mary J. ADIE, after protracted suffering, died at her home at Sterling, in this county, on last Saturday, in the 53d year of her age. She was a widow of the late Jas. L. ADIE, of Missouri, and the mother of Mrs. Thos. HUTCHINSON, of this place.

Miss Norah MAFFETT and Mr. Jno. ANKERS were united in marriage in Mt. Hope church, yesterday, by Rev. Geo. W. POPKINS.

Mrs. Wm. B. AVERILLE died on Monday, at nearly 70 years of age, and Mrs. D. L. DETWILER, on Tuesday. Mrs. DETWILER was a year or two over 60. She was P.M. at Willard Post Office.

Friday, 11 March 1892   Vol. XIV, No. 36

The infant daughter of Edward and Anna H. BEST, died Wednesday afternoon, aged 5 months. Mr. BEST buried his father a few weeks ago.

Miss Mary LODGE died this (Thursday) morning at 5 o'clock. Funeral Saturday at 10 o'clock, from the residence of her brother, Mr. Nathan LODGE.

The funeral of Bula, the only child of Edgar and Anna H. BEST took place today.

Miss Gertie LOVE died at the home of her grandfather, Mr. Lewis TAYLOR, last Friday morning, and on Sunday her remains were laid to rest at Arnold Grove. She had been in broken health for several months, resulting in nervous prostration and death in convulsions.

Friday, 18 March 1892   Vol. XIV, No. 37

Mrs. Rosanna McDANIEL, wife of James McDANIEL, died Monday, Mar. 14th at Vernon Cottage, aged 98. Her funeral took place Wednesday morning. Several days before her death she made a request how she wished to be buried.

Wills of Sarah A. BARRETT, Ailsey E. SHRYOCK, Mary A. CLINE and Margaret A. JACKSON, dec'd admitted to probate. Will of Sarah A. DEAR dec'd admitted to probate. Jno. A. HAMPTON qualified as Admr. of Fenton HAMPTON dec'd. Be[n]j. F. HEAD qualified as Admr. of Wm. HEAD dec'd. Mary F. PALMER qualified as Admx. of Rachel A. JAMES. Estate of Amanda PAXTON committed to Sheriff.

Mrs. ___ LAWSON, wife of Mr. John LAWSON, died at her home about two miles east of Leesburg on Friday last. Interment in Union Cemetery on Saturday, Dr. Nelson HEAD officiating.

The eighteen month old child of Samuel RIDGEWAY died on Saturday of last week. Funeral services on Monday by Rev. McLINN, interment at Rehobeth burying ground.

Mrs. Martha S., widow of the late Capt. Ozias BLANCHARD died on Thursday, 10th instant, at the age of 83 years. She was the fourth of a family of eleven. Two only are left; one brother living in Maine, the other, W. D. SWEETSER, the present postmaster here. She, with several of her children, came her in 1869. Capt. B. followed, after remaining in Maine a while to close up his business. Of her family of ten children, but four are now living viz: Mrs. George L. HOWARD, of this vicinity, H. C. BLANCHARD, of South Dakota, Mrs. M. A. BARROWS, of Washington, DC, and H. W. BLANCHARD, of this town.

Friday, 25 March 1892   Vol. XIV, No. 38

Mr. John BOND, a young man yet in his teens, and Miss Ida MOBLEY, aged 15 years, both of this neighborhood, went to Hagerstown early last week, bent on getting married. Miss MOBLEY's mother telegraphed to prevent a marriage licence being issued and the chief of police was instructed to apprehend the youthful pair. He aneceeded but just arrived in time to witness the conclusion of the nuptial ceremony, for which the groom had secured license several days before.

R. B. ABEL and wife are in Martinsburg, W Va, attending the wedding of Miss Lillian E., accomplished daughter of John W. NEER, Esq., a prominent citizen of that place.

Mrs. Susan SHRIVER, popularly known as "Grandma" yielded to the insidious disease, La Grippe, on Sunday. She was born April 17th 1798, being almost 94 years of age. She resided with her son-in-law, John GRUBB, who married her only child, about half a century ago. She had nine grandchildren and forty-four great-grandchildren, all of whom are living in this state except four; Mrs. Wm. B.

GALLOWAY, living in Neb., being the most distant. Her remains were interred at Salem Church.

Mrs. Susan WATERS, beloved wife of Dr. J. F. WATERS, of Purcellville, was interred at St. Paul today.

Mrs. Hester COE, wife of Mr. Frank COE, died in Culpeper on Sunday. Mrs. COE, who with her husband resided for some time in Leesburg a year or two ago, is kindly remembered.

Friday, 1 April 1892   Vol. XIV, No. 39

Mr. Isaiah FISHER, who for many years was the efficient route agent on the W. O. & W., died at his home in Alexandria one day last week.

Mrs. Martha J. POTTS, formerly of this county, died at her residence in Washington DC, on Tuesday last, of heart disease.

Mrs. Emily J. HEAD, widow of the late Columbus HEAD, died at her home in this town last Thursday evening at an advanced age.

Mr. Garrett HULFISH, of Silcotts Springs, Va, buried his son today. This makes four boys that Mr. H. has followed to the grave. Edwin HULFISH, the young man buried today, was 19 years of age.

Miss Linnie BRUIN, aged 48 years, died at the residence of Henry WHITLOCK, in Aldie, last Sunday after an illness of nine weeks with pneumonia. A zealous member of the Episcopal church. Her remains were carried to Antioch church, Tuesday, for interment.

John Washington SAFFER, died at his residence near Centreville, Fairfax county, Tuesday night. The deceased was a brother of W. Thornton SAFFER, of this section.

Cards are out for the marriage on April 6th of Miss Lizzie SMITH, of Sterling and Mr. Nimrod ANDERSON, of this section.

We report the death of Mr. H. C. WALDRON, of this valley Saturday morning. He had been afflicted for some time with a cancer. In Nov. last, he went to Baltimore and had an operation performed by specialists in that city, but it did not good. Consistent member of Ebenezer M. E. Church. Interred on Sunday at Mt. Olivet M. E. Church.

Friday, 8 April 1892   Vol. XIV, No. 40

Marriage licensees were issued in Washington, Tuesday to Martin N. BUCHANAN, of Loudoun county, and Amelia MOSLEY.

Philomont, April 6 – Our community was shocked on Monday by an item in the papers announcing the sad death of Walter S. LAKE, at Bessemer, Alabama. Mr. LAKE was employed on the Sterling Dynamite works at that place and was suddenly killed by an explosion on the first day of April. The young man was a son of Thos. W. LAKE Esqr. He leaves a young widow to mourn his loss.

Mr. Harmon HAVENNER, of this county, died on Tuesday morning, after a few days illness, at his home in Broad Run District, in about the 36th year of his age.

Mrs. S. VANDEVANTER, widow of the late Cornelius VANDEVA[N]TER, formerly of this county, and daughter of the late Benjamine MORGAN of Clarke County, died of pneumonia at her home in Berryville, on the 26th of March. She was in her 56th year.

Miss Lizzie SMITH and Nimrod ANDERSON were united in marriage in Sterling yesterday. Only a few friends were present.

David AUSTIN, one of the oldest citizens of Martinsburg, died Thursday, aged 82 years.

Mrs. FOOTE, widow of the late Rev. Dr. FOOTE, of Romney, W. Va, died last week.

A marriage license was issued in Washington on Saturday to Lee BIRCH and Mittie E. LEE, both of Fairfax county.

Mrs. John SCOTT died at Warrenton last week. She was the wife of Major SCOTT, who was for nearly twenty years Commonwealth's attorney for Fauquier county.

Mr. Charles W. AISQUITH, druggist of Charlestown, W Va, died Saturday last. He served in the Second Virginia Infantry, Stonewall Brigade during the late war, and was badly wounded.

Rev. C. S. HEDGES, one of the oldest clergymen in the South, died Saturday in New Orleans of old age. He was 84 years old. He was born in Berkley county, Va and was a graduate of Virginia Theological Seminary.

Mrs. Philip HAXALL, formerly Miss TRIPLETT, died in Richmond recently, of a sudden attack of apoplexy. She was remotely the innocent cause of the famous MORDECAI-McCARTY duel which occurred in 1873.

Friday, 15 April 1892   Vol. XIV, No. 41

Richard, son of Thomas WARNER, of Morrisonville, was buried at the German Reform Church, near Lovettsville, one day last week. He was in Baltimore, where he was taken sick with measles, from which he seemed to be convalescent, when he ventured out and had a relapse, which proved fatal.

Round Hill, April 11, Mr. W. SCHOOLEY died suddenly last Saturday morning at 5 o'clock. He rested well during the night and was partly dressed when the summons came, like an electric shock, and he was no more. He was in his 70th year. He worked at his anvil all day Friday. Interred at Harmony church in Hamilton on Sunday.

Rev. J. C. DICE, familiarly known in our town as Father DICE, died at his home in Upperville, on the 5th inst., in the 72 year of his age. About fifteen years ago Mr. DICE was located in Hamilton. Remains were removed to Staunton and buried with Masonic ceremonies.

Loudoun Ct.: Wills of Sarah GEORGE, James W. HILL, Ann JONES, Louisa N. SIMPSON, and Wm. H. HOUGH dec'd admitted to probate. C. C. GAVER qualified as Guardian of Lucy R. TURNER. Nathan LODGE qualified at Admr. of L. Harmon HAVENNER dec'd.

Jno. F. SHRYOCK qualified as Guardian of Vera M., Bessie L. and Walter C. HAVENNER. Estates of Charles TRUSSELL and Alcinda RICHARDS committed to Sheriff. Ordinary licenses granted to Nixon Bros and John D. RYAN. Retail and bar-room licenses granted to C. R. LOWENBACH, Wm. H. BROOKS, Hickman & Bitzer, and Goodheart & Rollins.

Death: At Janesville, W Va, March 1, 1892 Mrs. Florence RATRIE, daughter of the late Dr. Francis LAMBERT of this county, in the 42 year of her age. In Leesburg, Friday, April 8, 1892 Samuel M. ROLLINS in the 47th year of his age. Carry J. POWER, oldest daughter of Charles and Sallie POWER, died at her home last Friday April 8, aged twenty years. She was taken with measles. She leaves her father, three sisters and four brothers to mourn her death, all of which are confined to their beds with the same disease. Today she was laid to rest beside her mother, who died about two years ago. Her funeral will take place at Mt. Hope church (where she will be buried) when her family is able to attend. She has been a member of the Baptist church for four years.

Miss Cora POWER, near Waxpool, died on Saturday last in about the eighteenth year of her age.

Mrs. Julia HUTCHISON, widow of the late Llewellyn HUTCHISON, died last Thursday, aged 83 years.

One day last week a colored girl, living at A. C. GEORGE's fell from an ox cart, on which she was riding, the wheel passing over her neck tearing the flesh in a horrible manner, exposing the arteries and jugular vein, from the effects of which she died in a few hours. She was about 12 years old.

Matthew SMITH, 78 years old, justice of the peace at Annandale, Fairfax county, died at the residence of his son, Mr. M. SMITH in Brooklyn, on the 6th inst. He was a native of England, but came to this country when a boy, and about 30 years ago bought a farm in Fairfax county, where he continued to reside.

Owen G. McDERMOTT, of Warren county, and Miss Annie SAFFELL of Fauquier, were engaged and the time for their marriage had been set, but owing to the illness of Mr. McDERMOTT the wedding had been postponed. A few days ago Miss SAFFELL learned that her lover was ill and she hastened to his bedside to find him dying. At once the necessary steps were taken for securing license, preacher &c, and inside of twelve hours Miss SAFFEL was maiden, wife and widow.

Friday, 22 April 1892   Vol. XIV, No. 42

County Ct: Rosa B. DISHMAN qualified as Guardian of Eddie E., Mary V. and Charles E. DISHMAN. Rosa B. DISHMAN, widow of Chas. E. DISHMAN, renounced the will of her late husband.

Died on April 14th at his residence in Brooklyn, NY, George LEE, eldest son of Dr. George LEE, dec'd, late of Leesburg, Va.

Mr. William FERGUSON died at his home in Washington on Sunday last, April 17th, of pneumonia, in the 59th year of his age. Mr. F. was a son-in-law of the late Maj. Jas. F. DIVINE, of this county. He was a gentleman of fine intelligence and for many years a valued employee in the U. S. Post office department. He leaves a widow and several children to mourn.

Philmont, Apr. 18 – Obadiah JACKSON, an old colored gentleman, received injuries on last Wednesday by being thrown from a cart, from which he died on Friday last. The deceased was buried at North Fork yesterday.

Bolington Apr. 20 – Mrs. Henry SNOOTS, after a short illness, departed this life on Friday the 15th inst. Her remains were laid to rest in the Rehobeth burying ground, on Sunday afternoon. The funeral sermon will be preached next Sunday 24th inst.

Friday, 29 April 1892   Vol. XV, No. 1

Mr. John R. McNEALEA, of Farmwell, died Wednesday morning of pneumonia.

A marriage licence was issued in Washington on Monday to Geo. A. FOWLE, of Alexandria, and Virginia TAYLOR, of Virginia.

Mr. Richard MARLOW, who resided between Leesburg and Pt. of Rocks, died suddenly at the latter named place on the 19th inst.

Another one of Mr. C. W. HARDING's children on Wednesday, at his home in Farmwell. One was buried about a week before. Measles was the cause of the double bereavement.

Information was received in this town on the 27th of the death of Mrs. Jennie LYNN, wife of Mr. H. Clay LYNN, formerly of this county, which occurred at her home in Richmond, on the 27th inst.

Lenah, April 27 – The youngest daughter of Mrs. Alice FLING, near Ryan, aged 14 years, died last Saturday after an illness of three days with pneumonia. Miss Susan HOLTZCLAW, who has been an invalid for several years, died at the residence of Mrs. Martha HOLTZCLAW, near Arcola, last Saturday. The funeral took place Monday afternoon.

Philomont, Apr 27 – Mrs. Margaret ORME, wife of Thomas ORME Sr., quietly breathed her last on the night of the 22d. She leaves her aged husband and the surviving son.

Friday, 6 May 1892   Vol. XV, No. 2

Mr. Charles POWER, well known in the vicinity of Farmwell, where he resided, died last Sunday. This is the third death which has occurred in that family quite recently. There are three other members of the household critically ill and their deaths daily expected. It is supposed that the trouble arises from the condition of the premises and the house wherein they reside. I was informed that the basement under the house contained several feet of water and that it was fast becoming stagnant.

John R. McNEALEA, whose death of pneumonia, at his home near Farmwell, was mentioned last week, was a citizen of distinction and an ex-Confederate veteran. He was born in this county in 1834. When quite young he enlisted in the U.S. Navy. After serving one year in the navy yard at Washington, he was shipped aboard a man-of-war to foreign countries. He had been upon this cruise about two years when the late war broke out and his vessel was ordered home. Arriving at New York, the crew were ordered to take the oath of allegiance. He refused, for which he was arrested and imprisoned. Making his escape he worked his way back to Virginia, where he joined the Eighth Va volunteers. Previous to 1863 he took part in five battles. In the winter of 1863 he was ordered with his division to North Carolina, where they beseiged General FOSTER. Returning to Va his division rejoined the Army of Northern Virginia, and marched with them to Gettysburg. He took part in that awful charge made by PICKETT's division on Gettysburg Heights. During that battle he was captured and sent to Johnson's Island. In January '65, he returned to the Confederacy a paroled prisoner, and followed LEE to Appomattox. He taught school for some years after the way, after which he went to work at his trade, which he continued until his death.

Circuit Ct.: Estate of Ann TURNER committed to Sheriff. Estate of Thomas EACHES committed to Sheriff.

Charles FOX, a native of Loudoun, uncle of Manly FOX, formerly of our town, died at his home in Iowa recently, at an advanced age. When a young man he was in the employ of "Aunt Sallie" BROWN, who then lived (we believed) on what is now known as the Mercier farm near Hamilton depot. He left Loudoun some thirty odd years ago and settled on the prairie, in Henry Co Iowa, where he remained until his death. He never married, and Mr. Manly FOX, now living at Vienna, Fairfax county, is his only living relative and heir.

Reverend Richard T. DAVIS, rector of St. James Episcopal Church, of Leesburg, passed from life last Tuesday morning in the 63rd year of his age. He had been unwell but a few days and not until the day before he died was his condition alarming. The funeral will take place today at the church where he has laborer for many years.

Jamestown, a proposed suburb of our village (Farmwell) has died in the midst of its days and the planner of the scheme has absconded.

Herndon, May 5 – Jerome, son of John F. OLIVER, died on Sunday evening. He had been sick all the past winter. He was about 17 years of age.

Marriages: On Monday, April 25, at Epiphany Church, Washington DC, by Rev. David BARR, George A. FOWLE, of Alexandria, and Virginia TAYLOR of Hillsboro, Loudoun County.

Deaths: Etta, the wife of Mr. Franklin A. THOMPSON, at Dranesville, Friday evening, April 22d 1892, ages 25y 2m 12d. She was converted a Christian the 16th of September 1879. Mrs. Rebecca FLING, at her home near Farmwell, on Monday, April 18th 1892, in the 45th year of her age. Nora FLING, April 23, 1892, at her home near Farmwell, in the 15th years of her age.

Friday, 13 May 1892 Vol. XV, No. 3

Mrs. Isabelle TAYLOR, wife of Mortimer TAYLOR, formerly of Loudoun, died in Baltimore last Sunday.

A special from Middleburg states that Stephen W. McCARTY, died at his home in Mountsville on the 3d inst., at the advanced age of 83 years.

Jesse PIGGOTT, an aged citizen, died on Monday at the Lot TAVENNER place, near Lincoln, where he had been boarding for some time. His remains were interred in Friends burying ground at Lincoln on Wednesday.

Ruthie, the youngest child of David H. and Rebecca BROWN, formerly of this vicinity, died at their home in Nebraska on the 1st last, aged about a year. Grip was the primary cause of her death.

Mrs. Lydia A. PRESTON, wife of Mr. Ed. PRESTON, and widow of the late ___ DILLON, died suddenly at her home in Purcellville, on Thursday of last week. It is reported that heart disease was the cause of her death. She was the mother of J. A. and J. W. DILLON of Purcellville.

New Straitsville, O., Apr. 29 – The home of Mr. A. BEANS was the center of attraction last eve, the occasion being the marriage of Miss Maggie, to Mr. E. P. ACHANER, a thriving young merchant of this city. The bride was beautifully attired in cream Bedford cord, trimmed and neatly draped with chiffon and ashes of rose velvet. Rev. SOUERS of the M. E. Church performed the ceremony.

County Ct.: Wills of Rev. R. T. DAVIS, dec'd and Mary TAVENNER, dec'd admitted to probate. Jos. A. DILLON qualified as Admr. of Lydia A. PRESTON. Estate of Emily J. HEAD committed to Sheriff. Corrie V. CLINE qualified as guardian of Gracie L., Alfred T., Mabel R. and Fannie B. CLINE. Ordinary licence granted to E. V. WHITE. Liquor licenses granted to Survick & Whitmore and Shryock and Presgraves.

Farmwell – Temple WORTMAN died suddenly at his home near this town last Saturday in the 42nd year of his age.

Friday, 20 May 1892 Vol. XV, No. 4

Mrs. J. S. STANLEY has issued cards for the marriage of her daughter Elsie Chichester HARRISON, to Mr. W. D. HEMPSTONE. The ceremony is to take place at 12 o'clock noon on Wednesday, June 1st, at St. James Episcopal church, Leesburg.

Death: Mr. Temple WORTMAN on the 28th of May 1892, in the 55th year of his age. He will be missed by his sister with whom he lived so long.

Miss Barbara BEACH, eldest daughter of Mr. Andrew BEACH, near Farmwell, departed this life on the 13th of May, 1892, aged 17y 4m 18d. She was a faithful member of the Mt. Hope Baptist Church. The funeral was preached in the Mt. Hope Baptist Church on Saturday the 14th by her pastor.

Prince William: Mr. Edward BRYANT and Miss Addie ESKRIDGE, both of this county, were married at Manassas on the 7th.

Friday, 27 May 1892   Vol. XV, No. 5

The *Mirror* announces the death of Mrs. Susan BIRKBY, widow of the late Thomas BIRKBY, at her home in Leesburg last Saturday, in the 66th year.

Farmwell: Mrs. Julia LOCK, who has been boarding in Sterling for several months, received word Wednesday morning of the death of her husband. He had started from his home in Colorado for Virginia, and died of heart failure, in Kansas City, Mo. His remains were brought to Charlestown W Va, and interred in the cemetery of that place. Mrs. LOCK has returned to Sterling where she will remain for the summer with her mother, Mrs. Julia TEBBS.

A very quiet but pretty wedding took place at the residence of Mr. Charles G. WALTER, Frederick, at 2 o'clock Thursday last (the 12th inst.) The parties to the contract were Mr. Cresford DIVINE and Miss Eugenia APPLE, both of Loudoun Co., Rev. Osbou[r]ne INGLE officiating according to the ritual of the Episcopal Church. The bride was tastefully dressed in steel Henrietta with hat and gloves to match and carried a bouquet of white carnations. The groom wore the usual black. After the ceremony they took the 2:55 train, B. & O. RR for their future home in Waterford.

Friday, 3 June 1892   Vol. XV, No. 6

Cards are out for the marriage of Miss Lula Estelle SCHOOLEY, daughter of Joseph E. SCHOOLEY, of Waterford, to Mr. William H. EVANS, of Norfolk. The ceremony will take place in Waterford Baptist church, Thursday, June 9th at 10 a.m. Reception from 8 to 11 p.m. Friday, June 10th Kemp Avenue, Atlantic City, Norfolk, VA.

From the Washington *Post* 1 June: The marriage of Miss Elsie Chichester HARRISON to Mr. W. Dade HEMPSTONE took place at noon today in St. James' Episcopal Church. The Rev. Walter P. GRIGGS, of Poolesville, Md Officiating. Mr. E. B. HARRISON was best man. The maid of honor was Miss Sadie HARRISON, sister of the bride. The bridesmaids were Misses Annie CROSS, Fanny

MARLOW, Bessie WATKINS, Ida SELLMAN, Jennie LYNCH, and Lalla HARRISON. The ushers were W. W. CHAMBLIN, Thomas SWANN, Frank CARTER, Thomas F. MASON, Arthur SHEETZ, and Otis WILLIAMS. The bride was given away by her uncle, Dr. R. H. EDWARDS.

E. Chas. ATWELL, a son of Ewell ATWELL, of Leesburg, was shot and almost instantly killed by an unknown negro, at Trinidad, D.C., about 12:30 last Saturday morning. The deceased was 21 years old and boarded at No. 219 second street, NE, Washington. He had lately been a brakeman on the Baltimore and Potomac railroad, but had recently taken a similar position on the Baltimore and Ohio road. ...

Deaths: Ann Amelia SHRIVER at the residence of her daughter, Hillsboro, on Saturday April 30th 1892, aged 80y 9m 3d; widow of David SHRIVER dec'd and mother of Mrs. C. C. GAVER.

The marriage of Miss Kathleen A. NOURSE to Dr. T. Melville TALBOTT was solemnized on Wednesday morning, at the Congressional church. The ushers, Dr. G. B. FADELEY and G. T. MANKIN preceding, then came the bride leaning on the arm of the groom. The bride's dress was tan colored cloth, trimmed with olive velvet and lace. Rev. Robert NOURSE (the bride's father) performed the ceremony. The bridal party left that evening for Atlantic city.

Mr. Edward EMBREY of Fauquier co, is 105 years old. At this age he is still very active and takes great interest in his farm work.

Friday, 10 June 1892   Vol. XV, No. 7

Deaths: Sue FRAME, wife of Charles FRAME near Purcellville, June 3rd 1892, in the 32nd year of her age.

Waterford Baptist church was crowded with visitors to witness the marriage of Miss Lula Estelle SCHOOLEY, the attractive daughter of Mr. J. E. SCHOOLEY of Waterford, to Mr. William H. EVANS, of Norfolk. The ushers Messrs. William E. PAXSON and Frank SILCOTT, followed by Miss Blanch BRABHAM with Mr. Robt. M. STEER, and Miss Emma STEER with Mr. Horace P. SCHOOLEY. Immediately after them came the bride and groom. The bride was attired in white India silk en train, trimmed in chiffon, and carried a lovely bouquet of Marcheil Neil roses. Miss STEER, the first made of honor, was dressed in white mulle and lace with empire sash, and carried bride roses. Miss BRABHAM wore a beautiful albatross, trimmed in lace and pearl, and carried a bouquet of roses. The groom, groomsmen and ushers were attired in black. The ceremony was rendered by Rev. C. T. HERNDON, of Herndon. They will reside in Norfolk.

Mr. T. A. VanDEUSON and Miss Maggie ROY, the latter residing in Alexandria, were united in the "happy bonds" last week. Dr. MASON of this place was called to Alexandria to tie the knot.

Friday, 17 June 1892   Vol. XV, No. 8

Jessie HOLMES, nephew of H. R. HOLMES, was to have been married last evening to Miss Rebecca WEBB, of Philadelphia.

Hester HOLMES, relict of the late Elisha HOLMES, died at the home of her son, Geo. W. HOLMES, near Woodburn, at eleven o'clock yesterday aged about 80 years. She had been in feeble health for some time.

Miss Julia SIMPSON, daughter of Capt. J. H. SIMPSON, was buried yesterday at North Fork. Funeral conducted by Rev. BITZER, of Leesburg, at the home of the deceased. She was a member of the Presbyterian church, and was probably 30 years of age.

Harlan BAKER died very suddenly last Friday, in Chester county Pa where he was visiting relatives. He was about 82 years of age. On Monday afternoon his remains were brought to Lincoln and interred in the Friends burying ground. Member of the Society of Friends.

Court: Wills of Ellzey CHAMBLIN dec'd and Wm. BALL dec'd admitted to probate. Estates of Mary E. COOPER and Geo. W. FLING committed to Sheriff. Jas. T. MORAN qualified as Admr. of John M. MORAN Jr. Rev. J. BARBER of the Baptist church licensed to celebrate the rites of matrimony.

Marriages: At the home of the bride, by W. G. EGGLESTON June 14th, Mr. W. R. NEWLON and Miss Florence R., daughter of J. Wm. LAYCOCK, all of Loudoun. On June 15th at the bride's home, by Rev. W. G. EGGLESTON, Mr. Oscar L. VAUGHN and Miss Rosa R. SANTMYER, all of Loudoun.

Friday, 24 June 1892   Vol. XV, No. 9

On Wednesday evening, at the residence of the bride's father, in Loudoun County, Mr. Norman REID, of Washington Grove, Montgomery County Md was married to Miss Lelia WALTMAN.

Sad intelligence of the death of Mrs. John M. DAVIS, nee WILMARTH, was announced by the Atlanta, Ga *Evening Herald*, of June 15th:

Last night at 12 o'clock Mrs. Bessie L. DAVIS, wife of Mr. J. M. DAVIS, died after a lingering illness. A native of Virginia and moved to Georgia only a short time ago. Member of the Episcopal church from childhood. She leaves a husband and one little girl.

Mr. Wm. SHUMAN, formerly of Middleburg died in Richmond on Wednesday, the 15th inst. in the 56th year of his age. His remains were taken to Loudoun county for interment.

Capt. Solomon HOGE, formerly of this county, died at his home near Morris, Ill., on May 30th in the 83d year of his age.

The wife of Mr. J. A. DEMONET, one of the proprietors of the new hotel which is being built on the Blue Ridge, died at her home in Washington last Friday night.

Esther Janney HOLMES, relict of the late Elisha HOLMES, departed this life at Green Hill, the old homestead, June 16th 1892, in her 76th year. Her remains were interred at Lincoln, in the Friends burying ground, of which Society she was a consistent member.

Friday, 1 July 1892   Vol. XV, No. 10

A marriage licence was issued in Washington Tuesday to Geo. C. HOUGH and Lillie C. HARPER, of this county.

The home of Mrs. Ella MATTHEW was the scene of a pretty home wedding Thursday morning 12 o'clock, June 23d, Miss Lula H. MATTHEW, daughter of the late Wm MATTHEW, of Loudoun, to Mr. Andrew WALL, vice president and manager of Fidelity Building, Loan and Investment Association, Washington DC by Rev. Geo. L. BITZER of the Presbyterian Church. The bride being in traveling costume attended by her sister, Miss Jessie MATTHEW, as maide of honor. After a beautiful ceremony lunch was served to relatives and a few most intimate friends. The party then left on the 1:35 train for New York, where they will take steamer Alaska for Liverpool, spending three months in England with parents of the groom.

On Monday evening last, Messrs. Leroy BLACKWELL, John SUDDITH, Howard YOUNG, A. P. BRADY and Geo. ALLISON went into the bar on the farm of Maj. T. Towson SMITH for protection from a storm. Lightning struck a post which extended to the roof and killed A. P. BRADY and George ALLISON instantly who were standing near or leaning against the post. Mr. BRADY is a young married man from Prince William county, near Gainesville, who leaves a wife and two children. Young ALLISON was unmarried and a son of Mr. Richard ALLISON. ALLISON was buried near his home.

Friday, 8 July 1892   Vol. XV, No. 11

On Wednesday morning our townsman, Burr P. FRED, departed this life at his home in this town. He had been afflicted with Bright's Disease for some time, and had been quite ill for several days, but it was thought that the immediate cause of his death was heart failure. Funeral services will be conducted at the house about 9 o'clock this morning, and interment later in the day at Middleburg.

Miss Sallie ROSS died of paralysis of the brain, at the home of her brother, Jno. T. ROSS, near the Trapp, on Wednesday of last week, aged 83 years.

Mr. James Henry HATHAWAY, one of the best known citizens of this and Fauquier counties, died at his home near Middleburg, last Saturday morning, aged 82 years.

Mr. Henry LEFEVRE, a citizen of Broad Run district, died at his home near Ryan, on Tuesday of last week. Mr. LEFEVRE was a member of the Loudoun Guards, Company C, during the war.

Mr. Chas. POWELL, residing about three miles south of Leesburg, on the L. & A. turnpike road, died at the residence of Joel CARRUTHERS, his partner in business, about three miles South-east of Aldie, Tuesday morning about 5 o'clock. Mr. POWELL was taken violently ill either Wednesday or Thursday morning of last week, while he was in that section on business, and never rallied from his first attack. His funeral took place from Mr. CARRUTHERS' residence at 10 o'clock Wednesday.

Rev. Dr. WILLIAMS, for several years Rector of St. James Episcopal Church, Leesburg, died Wednesday June 29th at Sudbrook Park, on the Western Md. Railroad, where he was spending the summer with his sister. The disease which caused his death was one which so baffled the physicians that a post-mortem was conducted by Prof. ATKINSON and Dr. BATCHELOR. It is indicated that he suffering from cancer of the stomach. He was buried in Georgetown DC, on Friday last.

The marriage of Miss Lillie HARPER, of this county, to Mr. George Clinton HOUGH, of Washington DC (formerly of Waterford) took place in Washington Ryland M. E. Church, Wednesday morning, June 29th, at half past ten o'clock. The bride wore a morning dress of soft white silk and chiffon and carried a large bouquet of white sweet peas, and clusters of the same were caught in her hair, while the groom, in a conventional morning costume, wore a boutoneire of the same sweet flowers. The ushers were Messrs. G. R. SEIFFERT, J. T. HOUGH and Frank HARPER, of Washington, and Mr. M. A. WATSON, of California. Mr. T. C. CALHOUN presided at the organ. They were met by Rev. J. A. PRICE who read the ceremony. At 12 o'clock Mr. and Mrs. HOUGH left Washington for an extended Northern town, after which they will reside at 1906 6th St. Le Droit Park, Washington DC.

Miss COURTNEY of Hume, and Mr. BLANKENBAKER, of Madison were married a few days ago. The bride was 82 years old and the groom 24. Miss COURTNEY gave Mr. BLANKENBAKER $7,500 to marry her, she had a horror of dying an old maid.

Friday, 15 July 1892   Vol. XV, No. 12

Mary Ann NICHOLS, wife of Joseph NICHOLS, died at 3 a.m. this morning at the residence of her son-in-law, Samuel N. BROWN, where her funeral will take place on Sunday, at 3 p.m. Death resulted from a brief illness of congestion of the lungs. She was in the 82nd year of her age.

County Ct: Wills of Esther J. HOLMES, L. F. SKILLMAN and John AULT admitted to probate. Wm. F. LYNN qualified as Admr. of Chas. E. POWELL dec'd. Lizzie CONNER qualified as Guardian of Sevella Lee, Wm. E. and Laura V. CONNOR, and Jesse Aberley. H. Kate WALTMAN qualified as Guardian of William G. WALTMAN. Estate of H. C. WALDRON committed to Sheriff.

Claton HOWARD, colored, who shot and killed C. E. ATWELL, of Leesburg, in Washington, May 28, has been captured and indicted for the crime.

Cards are out for the marriage of Miss Henrietta Benedict, daughter of John Y. BASSELL, of this town, to Mr. Henry Treat CRITTENDEN, of Columbus, Ohio. The ceremony is to take place on the 27th inst., at 8:30 p.m. in St. James Church, Leesburg.

Mr. L. F. SKILLMAN, a well known citizen of this county, died at his home near Aldie, on Saturday July 2d, in the 53d year of his age. Mr. S. had been in bad health for some time, but was well as usual up to within two days of his death. His remains were interred in the cemetery at Middleburg on Sunday, July 3d.

Mr. John Y. BASSELL, formerly of Leesburg, but at present engaged in business in St. Louis, arrived in Leesburg on Saturday last. He will remain until after the marriage of his daughter, which takes place on the 27th inst.

Friday, 22 July 1892   Vol. XV, No. 13

Deaths: Mrs. Catharine LIGGETT, in Waterford, July 9th 1892, at the residence of her son-in-law, Robert GRAHAM, aged 80y 5m.

Chilton SHUMATE died at his home in Fauquier county on the 11th of July, in the 96th year of his age.

Margaret Douglas, infant daughter of Wm. N. and Ella WISE, died at her parent's home in Leesburg last Sunday afternoon, aged 4m 25d.

Friday, 29 July 1892   Vol. XV, No. 14

Mrs. Ann HAY died last week, at the residence of her step-son, Geo. HAY, near Farmwell, at an advanced age.

Mrs. Lula FLETCHER, wife of Joshua FLETCHER and a sister of Capt. J. W. FOSTER, of this county, died at the residence of her father, Maj. T. R. FOSTER, at Marshall, Fauquier county, last Saturday.

Lincoln, July 28 – Little Harry, aged five years, son of Wm. MILLS, met with his death on Tuesday morning of this week. His father, who lives on Thomas R. SMITH's farm, was hauling with a large wagon and the little boy was riding on the off wheel horse, when he fell off, and before the wagon could be stopped the wheel ran over his head, killing him instantly. His remains were interred in Friends burying ground here, yesterday.

Cards are out for the marriage of James D. STEER, of Washington, to Mary, daughter of Jonah L. and Annie J. REES, of New York, on Aug. 11th. The ceremony will be performed in that city, at Friends Meeting House, after which the bride and groom will proceed to Washington DC, where in the evening of the same day they will have a reception at their future home.

Bolington, July 27 – After an illness of about three days, Mrs. Marietta ADAMS, a former resident of this vicinity, died at the home of her mother, in Washington DC, whither the family recently moved. She had been in delicate health for several years, and on Saturday night she passed peacefully away. Her remains were brought to Loudoun on Monday and laid to rest at Rehoboth, where she had been a consistent member for a number of years.

Friday, 5 August 1892   Vol. XV, No. 15

Brunswick – Engineer J. H. MILLER, of our town, met with a horrible death on Tuesday night July 14th. It seems that he had backed his train into a siding at the West End of Martinsburg yard to wait for express trains, Nos. 7 and 9. No. 7 passed, he then must have sat down on the track and going to sleep fell across the rail, for the next train within 20 minutes ran across his head killing him instantly.

Cards have been issued by Mrs. E. B. DuLANEY, formerly Miss Evelyn LEE, of Leesburg, announcing the marriage of her daughter, Miss Lee VILLARD, to Mr. B. Smith HILL, at Plainfield, New Hampshire.

Deaths: Of typhoid fever, of her home near Philomont, Daisy, beloved daughter of Sandy and Vines SMITH, July 21st in the eighteenth year of her age.

Friday, 12 August 1892   Vol. XV, No. 16

William E. SCHOOLEY, formerly of Waterford, this county, died at his home in Baltimore, last Friday, in the 82nd year of his age. His funeral took place on Monday.

Friday, 19 August 1892   Vol. XV, No. 17

Miss Mary UTTERBACK died at her home near Leesburg, last Friday, in about the 16th year of her age.

Friday, 26 August 1892   Vol. XV, No. 18

Mrs. Harriet N. PURCELL, wife of Rodney PURCELL, died at her home in Purcellville, Wednesday morning, resulting from a stroke of paralysis, last Saturday, which rendered her unconscious until she died. She was a sister of the late Senator HEATON. The funeral will take place today (Friday) at 11 a.m. Interment at Short Hill.

Howard WELSH, known in this vicinity, died at the home of his mother, Mrs. Albina WELSH, three miles south of Lincoln, last Thursday night, a victim of consumption. He was in the 40th year of his age. Interred in Friends burying ground, at Lincoln, on Sabbath morning.

Death: Miss Mary G. UTTERBACK, in the 10 year of her age. Mrs. Delila DONOHOE, a few miles south of Leesburg, on the 19th inst., about 84 years of age.

Death: Thomas BROOKS at the home of his mother, in Leesburg, on the 22nd inst., in the 19th year of his age. He was an employee in the *Washingtonian* office.

Death: Ruth F. ALLEN, daughter of Geo. W. and Albina P. ALLEN, near Harpers Ferry, July 29th aged 2y 9m.
Death: Mrs. Louisa RILEY, wife of Absolem RILEY, at her home near Harpers Ferry, August 5th, aged 72 years.
Col. Harrison M. SIMPSON died at his home in Fairfax County, Wednesday last, aged eighty years.

Friday, 2 September 1892   Vol. XV, No. 19

A marriage licence was issued in Washington last week to Mr. Frank G. GRAF, of Washington and Miss Ella CROSS, daughter of Jas. R. CROSS, of this county.
Mrs. Lavinia FAUNTLEROY, consort of the late Dr. J. T. FAUNTLEROY, of this county, died at her home in Leesburg last Tuesday evening, aged 79 years. Her remains were interred in Middleburg cemetery yesterday.
Mr. John H. SAUNDERS of this county died at his home in Leesburg, Tuesday evening, in about the 45th year of his age. His funeral took place yesterday afternoon, under the auspices of the Masonic fraternity, of which society he has long been a member.
A telegram was received here last Friday announcing the death of Ann BIRDSALL, at the home of her niece, Mrs. D. H. BROWN, near Genoa, Nebraska. She was probably over 80 years of age, and most of her long life was spent in Loudoun County.
Mr. James CARROLL, senior member of the Baltimore firm of Carroll, Adams & Co., dropped dead in his office last Friday. He was in his 74th year. The funeral took place at nine o'clock Monday morning from his residence, 615 Carrolton Ave., and a requiem mass was celebrated at St. Martin's Catholic Church, by Rev. T. J. BROYDRICK. The interment was in Bonnie Brae Cemetery. Mr. CARROLL, who was a native of Loudoun, spent much of the summer with his sister-in-law, Mrs. MENARD, near our town.
Mrs. Thomas J. WARNER, of Morrisonville, died very suddenly of heart disease one day last week. Her remains were interred in the Union Cemetery, near Lovettsville.
Philomont, Aug. 29 – Mr. Wm. TAVENNER, the oldest son of the widow of the late Wm. P. TAVENNER has died. He was laid to rest in the church yard at Lincoln today. He had been teaching for the past two years, and was expecting to attend college next season.

Friday, 9 September 1892   Vol. XV, No. 20

No death or marriage notices.

Friday, 16 September 1892   Vol. XV, No. 21

Last Tuesday night, as Mr. Geo. WIRE, of Lovettsville, was returning from Brunswick, after dark, he walked into an open draw of the canal bridge and was drowned.

Waterford: A little daughter of James WILLIAMS, aged fourteen months, which died of cholera infantum, was buried here on Monday.

Friday, 23 September 1892   Vol. XV, No. 22
No death or marriages notices.

Friday, 30 September 1892   Vol. XV, No. 23

A marriage licence was issued in Washington, this week, to Geo. MORAN, of Loudoun, and Margaret CROSEN, of Prince William.

Mrs. Hattie BROWN, daughter of the late John and Ruth Hannah SMITH, of this county, died at her home in Missouri, on the 18th inst. after an illness of several months.

Mr. and Mrs. Albert DAVIS left yesterday afternoon at attend the funeral of Mrs. DAVIS' father, Mr. Vincent AMBLER, who died at his home near Pleasant Valley, Fairfax county, on Wednesday, in the 82d year of his age.

Mr. Frank MYERS, of Hughesville, and Miss Cora WARNER, daughter of Isaac WARNER, Esq. will be joined in wedlock at the Methodist church on Wednesday, Oct. 5th at about twelve o'clock.

Col. J. M. McAFEE, of Falls Church, was thrown from a train on the W. & O. at the south end of Long Bridge, last Saturday morning and fatally injured. He was taken by a local train to Alexandria, where he died a few hours later.

The remains of Mrs. McVEIGH, wife of Mr. Frank McVEIGH of Falls Church, who died there Tuesday, were brought to Leesburg on Wednesday morning train, from whence they were conveyed to Middleburg for interment.

Mr. John W. HAMMERLY, an old citizen, died at his home in this town, about 9 o'clock last Saturday morning, in about his 74th year.

Friday, 7 October 1892   Vol. XV, No. 24

Edward L. RECTOR died at his home in this county one day last week, aged 55 years.

Robert COSTELLO, one of the oldest citizens of this county, died at his home, near Upperville, on the 22d ult. He leaves ten children, about sixty grand-children and four great-grandchildren.

Mr. Ashby HOLTZCLAW, of Arcola, and Miss Sallie L. COCKERILLE, of Fairfax County, were united in marriage by the Rev. Mr. SUTTON, in Dranesville church, Wednesday of last week.

The M. E. Church South, of this town, presented at high noon Wednesday with the beautiful decorations of rosemary, golden rod, ferns &c, the occasion being the marriage of Mr. Frank MYERS to Miss Cora WARNER, daughter of Mr. Isaac WARNER. The ceremony was performed by Rev. W. G. EGGLESTON, pastor of the church. Two ushers, Mr. Edgar MYERS, brother of the groom, and Mr. Theodore WARNER, brother of the bride; and Mr. George T.

SCHOOLEY, the best man, with Miss Frorence [Florence?] WARNER, sister of the bride, as maid of honor. The bride was attired in a handsome travelling dress of tan colored cloth, elegantly trimmed in velvet, with velvet hat to match, and carried a large bouquet of pure white cosmas. The maid of honor wore a becoming gown of the same handsome material as the bride's and carried a bouquet of pink cosmas. After the ceremony they left on the train for the Capitol City, and thence to Rockville Md. where they will spend about a week with the bride's relatives and friends.

Mr. Benjamin YOUNG, who for several years has been agent for White & Bro. at this place, died quite suddenly at the residence of Mr. Edgar TAVENNER, near town, last Monday night, in his 52d year. Shortly after 4:30 he was stricken with paralysis. Mr. Young was removed to Mr. TAVENNER's residence, where he was boarding, but death occurred about 12 o'clock. His remains were interred in the cemetery at Harmony church, in town, Wednesday afternoon.

Mr. John W. LICKEY, familiarly known as Capt. LICKEY, some 82 or 83 years old, died at the residence of his son-in-law, Mr. Alpheus JOHNSON, near Mt. Gilead, on Friday night, Sept. 30th. Funeral on October 2d. and "laid him away among the father's" in the old burial ground at North Fork.

Friday, 14 October 1892   Vol. XV, No. 25

County Ct.: Will of Samuel BANKS admitted to probate. W. F. BAST qualified as Admr. of Parmelia A. BEST. Walter L. COSTELLO qualified as Admr. of Robt. COSTELLO. A. C. WHITE qualified as Admr. of Hannah E. WHITE. James R. FOSTER appointed Guardian of Margaret FOSTER. S. L. PORTER qualified as Admr. of Henry S. WILLIAMS. John A. HAMPTON qualified as Admr. of James HAMPTON. Emily TAVENNER qualified as Admx. of Wm. L. TAVENNER. Ordinary license of John D. RYON transferred to Castle & Mullen. Jas. R. HOOE, attorney admitted to bar. Estate of Matilda FITZHUGH committed to Sheriff.

Friday, 21 October 1892   Vol. XV, No. 26

T. H. CARTER, a prominent citizen of Broad Run District, died at his home, near Lenah, on the 12th inst.

Mr. John A. ENGLISH, an uncle of Mr. Chas. A. ENGLISH, Station agent at Leesburg, was paralyzed last Thursday morning, at his home in Fredericksburg, and died that night. He was 73 years of age and unmarried.

In Hamilton was the marriage of Dr. Fenton M. NICHOLS, of Purcellville, and Mrs. Maria W. BENEDICT, who lives about two miles west of that place, which was solemnized at the Episcopal church, by Rev. J. W. KEEBLE, on Wednesday. The bride was attired in a very neat

travelling dress of dark blue cloth trimmed with velvet, and the groom wore a suit of black.
At the residence of the officiating clergyman, in Leesburg, on Tuesday Oct. 18, by Elder E. V. WHITE, marriage of Samuel E. COE and Gertrude SILMAN, all of Loudoun.
On the 12th inst. in the Methodist church in Snickersville, Mr. David BUTLER married Miss Annie KINES, both of this county.
Charles W. STULL and Etta Michael HUNTER, of Loudoun county, were married at the M. E. parsonage, Frederick Wednesday morning, by the Rev. A. J. GILL.
Miss Blanche FITZHUGH and Mr. H. F. HAINS, of Loudoun county, were married at the Presbyterian church on Monday last. The Rev. Mr. HOWISON, pastor of that church, performed the ceremony, assisted by the Rev. Mr. BOSMAN, of the Methodist church.
Mr. Frederick JAMES and Miss Rose HILL were quietly married, by the Rev. J. H. DULANY, at the residence of the bride's father, Joseph HILL, near Snickersville, Wednesday of last week.
On the afternoon of the same day, at Ebenezer church, Mr. Frank MOORE and Miss Lillie JAMES, daughter of T. Benton JAMES, were married by Rev. I. B. LAKE, D.D.
Circuit Ct.: Elwood SHOEMAKER qualified as Admr. of Sarah SHOEMAKER dec'd. Ed. E. GARRETT admitted to practice in Circuit Ct. Henry G. SCHULKE, a native of Germany, filed declaration of citizenship.
The home of the late Samuel M. JANNEY at Lincoln, was the scene of a very interesting occasion last Monday, the ninetieth birthday of Elizabeth JANNEY, relict of the distinguished historian of the Society of Friends. Grandson Samuel M. JANNEY Jr. presented her of a cane made of wood taken from the original Pennsylvania dwelling of William PENN.
Herndon, Oct 20th – The funeral of Edward TAYLOR, son of J. W. TAYLOR of this town, who was killed in the W. & O. yard in Alexandria on Saturday night last, while in discharge of his duties as conductor, was attended in the Congregational church here on Tuesday at eleven o'clock. Interment at Chestnut Grove Cemetery.
Alexandria Oct 18 – the body of Benjamin THOMPSON who lived near Langley, was found in the woods near Langley on last Monday. He had been shot through the body, and as his gun was lying beside him it is supposed he accidently shot himself. He was about seventeen years of age.

Friday, 28 October 1892　Vol. XV, No. 27

Mrs. L. A. DeLANEY, died at the residence of her son-in-law, T. L. WORSLEY, in Leesburg, Thursday evening of last week, in the 71st year of her age.

Mr. Edward A. JOHNSON, of Washington, formerly of Leesburg, brother of Mr. S. J. JOHNSON, of the latter named place, was married to Miss Rosa PRINCE, of Baltimore, on the 20th inst.

Bolington: Jacob STOUT, an aged citizen of this vicinity, who has been suffering for some time from a derangement of his mind, is now a raving maniac. Rumor says he will be taken to Leesburg and treated there.

Falls Church: Mr. W. H. LARNER, of New York, died at the residence of his other, Mrs. C. LARNER, Tuesday, Oct. 25th at 4:45 p.m.

Marriage licenses were issued from the county clerks office on Monday as follows: Robert W. OFFUTT, of W. Va, and Effie E. LINDSEY of Loudoun; W. C. GALLEHER and Maria L. ELGIN, both of this county, and on Tuesday W. R. KEELER and Laura L. COLE, both of Loudoun.

Wm. P. RATHIE, son of John B. and Sallie RATHIE, of Leesburg, died last Saturday morning, in the 28th year of his age.

The *Washingtonian* announces the death of Mrs. H. O. CLAGETT, wife of Capt. H. O. CLAGETT, mayor of Leesburg, which occurred at the residence of her mother, in Leesburg, Thursday morning of last week. About three weeks ago a tumor was taken from her right breast – the wound had healed over, but she was taken with remittent fever and died from heart failure. Her funeral took place from St. James Episcopal church, Saturday at 3 p.m., Rev. Carter PAGE officiating.

Friday, 4 November 1892   Vol. XV, No. 28

A marriage license was issued in Washington this week to Frank T. McPHERSON and Nora E. ELGIN, both of this county.

The *Star* reports that S. Virginia, wife of J. W. THOMPSON, formerly of Loudoun, died quite suddenly at her home in Washington on Wednesday.

The marriage of Miss Mary E. TAVENNER, daughter of Mr. Edgar TAVENNER, of this place, to Mr. A. H. CALLOW, a well known Baltimorean, is announced to take place in St. Pauls church in town at high noon the 16th inst.

In Mt. Olive (colored) Baptist church, at Lincoln, Wednesday at high noon J. Wm. BOYD, of Paeonian Springs, was married to Miss Jennie BROWN, in the presence of their relatives and a few intimate friends.

Bolington: Mrs. Eliza YAKEY of Tankerville died on last Saturday. Her remains were interred at the Reform burying ground on Monday. The sensation of the day is the marriage of Mr. Frank BAKER and Miss Minnie VIRTS which was consummated at the residence of the bride's parents, Isaac VIRTS, on Tuesday the 1st inst.

At high noon on Wednesday, October 26th at the residence of the bride's father, in Loudoun county, Miss Maud L. ELGIN and Mr. W. C.

GALLEHER were united in marriage by the Rev. Chas. T. HERNDON. The bride wore a becoming suit of tan color. The bridal party proceeded to Leesburg where they took passion on the 1:35 for Washington and South.

Deaths: Martha E. SWART, wife of A. L. SWART, at her home near Lenah, Sept. 30th in the 70th year of her age.

Friday, 11 November 1892   Vol. XV, No. 29

We learn that Mr. Chas. ETCHER, a citizen of Leesburg, died quite suddenly one day this week.

The late T. H. CARTER, of Broad Run district, who died intestate, left considerable property to which there are no known legal heirs.

It is reported that Mr. Furr WHITE, of Hughesville, and Miss Annie SIMPSON of North Fork will be married in the North Fork church on the 16th inst., at 11 a.m.

Wm. MARSHALL, citizen of this county, died at his home near Hughesville last Monday night.

On Tuesday evening last, at about 3 o'clock, at the residence of the bride's parents, near Lovettsville, Mr. Geo. S. BAKER was quietly married to Miss Minnie L. VIRTS, in the presence of their immediate friends, by Rev. M. E. McLINN, of the Lutheran church. They will go to housekeeping at once in Loudoun.

Friday, 18 November 1892   Vol. XV, No. 30

Marriage licence was issued in Washington on Tuesday to Chas. W. DEAN and Helen ALLEN, both of Loudoun county.

Dr. R. W. TAVENNER died at his home in Hillsboro on the 2nd inst.

A marriage licence was issued from the Clerk's office, in Leesburg to Mr. J. E. THOMPSON and Miss Lizzie SMITH, both of Loudoun.

Mr. Frank SMITH and sister, Miss Inez, left yesterday for Alexandria, to attend the marriage of their brother, Mr. Ed. SMITH, to Miss Sophia MARTIN of Alexandria, Va.

Nellie, the little nine year old daughter of Herbert L. JENKINS and a little son of J. P. FURR's both of Mt. Gilead, died a few days ago of diphtheria.

We presume that we were in error, last week, in announcing the death of Mr. Chas. ETCHER, of Leesburg since we find the following in the *Washingtonian*: Mr. James ETCHER, a brother of Mr. Chas. E. ETCHER, of Leesburg, died at his home near Sycolyn, on Monday last.

Archibald N. DOUGLASS, a citizen of Charlottesville, died last Saturday, aged 81 years. Mr. D. was a brother of the late Col. Chas. DOUGLASS, of Loudoun. Mr. D. was the owner of a fine estate in this county.

Mrs. Mary A. SCOTT, mother of Rev. R. A. SCOTT, died at her home in Lovettsville, on Monday night, of pneumonia. Her remains will be interred in the Rehobeth burying ground today.
County Ct: C. C. GAVER qualified as Admr. of R. W. TAVENNER dec'd. H. O. CLAGGETT qualified as Admr. of Jennie CLAGETT dec'd. H. H. RUSSELL Sheriff appointed curator of the estate of T. H. CARTER. H. H. RUSSELL sheriff appointed committee of B. G. CARTER. Robt. L. DONOHOE qualified Admr. of James ETCHER dec'd. L. M. McGAVACK as Guardian of Edward McV. DUNBAR gave additional bond. B. L. FOX qualified as committee of W. E. STEER. Owen L. THOMAS qualified at Notary Public. Estates of David BROWN and Chas. W. BLINCOE committed to Sheriff.
One of the most brilliant and pretty weddings of the year was celebrated in St. Paul's church in town, Wednesday at high noon. The bride was Miss Mary E. TAVENNER, daughter of Mr. Edgar TAVENNER, and Mr. Albert H. CALLOW, of Baltimore, was the happy groom. The bride entered on the arm of her father, and was accompanied by her sister, Miss Rose TAVENNER as maid of honor. She was met at the chancel by the groom and his best man, Mr. Al PRICHETT, of Baltimore. The bride wore a becoming travelling costume of brown broad cloth, neatly trimmed, and carried a pretty bouquet of La France roses. Her bridesmaid looked pretty in a tan colored dress of the same material. The ushers were Mr. Chas. TAVENNER, brother of the bride, and George MORRISON of Laurel Md. Rev. J. W. KEEBLE was the officiating clergyman. Immediately after the ceremony they boarded a train for an extended Southern tour. They will be at home at 2434 Madison Avenue Baltimore. where they will permanently reside.
A nuptual mass was celebrated at the residence of the bride's father, Joseph LACY, near Bloomfield, yesterday about 3 o'clock, when Miss Mary LACY and Mr. Turner J. ROSS were united in marriage. The ceremony was performed by Rev. Chas. SHIPLEY. The bride was dressed in white and carried roses. The bridesmaids were Misses Antonia FORD, Hattie LACY, Kate WALTMAN and Mildred LACY, all of whom were attired in becoming white costumes. The groomsmen were Messrs. J. H. ROSS, H. CHAMBLIN, P. LACY and Wade E. THOMAS. At the conclusion of the ceremony there were driven to the groom's home, near The Trapp, for a reception.
Mr. Furr WHITE and Miss Annis [Annie?] SIMPSON, daughter of Mr. Henson SIMPSON, of North Fork, were married on Wednesday, in North Fork Baptist church. After the ceremony they were driven to Leesburg, where they boarded the train for an extended bridal tour.
Mr. John L. LAKE, formerly of this county, and Miss Margaret E. FORREST were married in St. Patricks church, Washington, at 8 a.m. yesterday. They will be at home at "The Whitley," 941 H. Street, after December 5th.

The Telephone 111
Friday, 25 November 1892   Vol. XV, No. 31

On the 10th inst., in Washington city, Mrs. Sallie A. MUSE, formerly of Loudoun, was married to Mr. Jno. T. NICHOLS, of Massachusetts, Rev. George W. POPKINS, of this county, officiating.

Friday, 25 November 1892   Vol. XV, No. 31

Mr. Lee CHAMBLIN died at his home in or near Philomont last Tuesday. He was advanced in years, but his exact age we have not learned.

Marriage licenses were issued in Washington this week to John T. McNEALLEY of Brunswick Md and Delia P. JAMES of Waterford; Albert T. PRESTON and Minnie V. McMAHON, of Loudoun.

Cards are out for the marriage of Mr. B. Viers WHITE, of this town, and Miss Lillian CARTER, daughter of Mr. and Mrs. Samuel H. BROSIUS, of Baltimore. The ceremony is to take place Wednesday evening Nov. 30, 1892 at seven o'clock in the church of the Ascention, in that city.

Mr. R. J. CARTER of Maroa, Ills, is a brother of the late T. H. CARTER, of Broad Run district, and the only living legal heir to his estate. Mr. CARTER is a born Loudouner, but moved to the West when a boy and is now the efficient secretary of The Leavitt & Oglevee Co.

In the death of William WILLIAMS, which occurred at his home in Waterford on Wednesday morning this community has lost one of the most valued citizens. Born in the village where he died. One of the organizers of the Mutual Fire Insurance Company of Loudoun, from the time of its organization to his death, 37 years, was its president. The later years of his life were given in the ministry of the Society of Friends. The funeral will take place at 12:30 today at Friends Meeting House in Waterford. Interment in the burying ground nearby.

Mrs. Fannie MYERS, nee SHAWEN, wife of Capt. Frank MYERS, died quite suddenly at her home in Lincoln last Tuesday morning in the 48th year of her age. She had been in bad health for several months, but her death was very unexpected. She leaves a husband and several children. Her funeral took place yesterday from her late residence at 10 o'clock. Interment in the family burying ground at Ketoctin church, about two miles north of Hamilton.

Mr. Thos. B. COCKEY of Leesburg died at his residence in that place last Monday. He was 55 years of age. The *Mirror* says Mr. COCKEY was a native of Maryland, and on Wednesday morning his remains were taken to Baltimore, for interment and laid to rest beside others members of his family.

Mr. Arthur NICHOLS (son of S. T. NICHOLS) and Miss Florence M. WELSH, were united in marriage at the Methodist Parsonage, in Hamilton, by Rev. W. G. EGGLESTON, last Tuesday morning, after which they boarded the mid-day train on the W. O. & W. enroute to Washington, where Arthur has been employed for several years and where he has provided a new home for his bride.

Miss Emma McD. ROLPH, says the Baltimore *Sun*, was married to Dr. Joseph B. RATHIE, formerly of Leesburg, at 9 p.m. last Thursday, at the residence of the bride's mother, 743 West Fayette Street. The ceremony was performed by the Rev. C. C. GRIFFITH, rector of Ascension Protestant Episcopal church. Shortly after the ceremony they took the train for Cockeysville Md., their future home, where the groom is practicing medicine.

Mr. Jas. E. THOMPSON and Miss Lizzie SMITH were united in marriage at the residence of the bride's father, Wm. H. SMITH, near Mt. Hope, on the 16th inst., Rev. Geo. W. POPKINS officiating.

Mr. S. T. MATTHEW and Miss Margaret Gibson GOLDEN, both of lower Loudoun, were united in marriage at the residence of Millard T. BROAD near Leesburg, on the 16th inst., Rev. B. F. BALL officiating.

Married at the home of the bride's mother, Mrs. Sophia MARTIN, No. 115 south Alfred street, Thursday evening, November 17th, Edward SMITH, of Loudoun county, and Miss Sophia MARTIN, of this city. *Alex. Gazette.*

Deaths: William WILLIAMS, at his home in Waterford Va, at 8:45 a.m., 11 mo. 23 1892, aged 76y 5m 29d.

Friday, 2 December 1892   Vol. XV, No. 32

Mary, the ten year old daughter of Dr. BALDWIN, of North Fork, died Tuesday night of diphtheria.

Mr. John MORAN, formerly of this county, died at his home in Washington last Friday night of pneumonia, in the 24th year of his age. He was a brother of W. H. W. MORAN, of our town. His former home was in lower Loudoun, near Waxpool.

The *Washingtonian* says "on Sunday morning last, Miss Sallie BRANDON, living along in Philomont, since the death of her twin sister, was found dead lying in the middle of the floor. Died of old age or heart failure as supposed."

Rev. W. T. SCHOOLEY, formerly of this county, pastor of the Lee Street Methodist Church, Roanoke, has resigned to engage in business pursuits in Colorado.

Married Nov. 30th 1892 at "Sunny Side," the residence of the bride's mother near Hillsboro, Miss Mary H. HOUSE, daughter of Mary J. and E. C. H. HOUSE, deceased, to J. W. LOVE, of the same vicinity. The bride was attired in a dress of gray bedford cord, with trimmings of silver gray, and carried a bouquet of pink geraniums and white chrysanthemums. The ceremony was performed by Rev. J. H. DULANEY. After refreshments they were driven to the station at Purcellville where they took the 2:30 train for Washington.

In Lovettsville on Thanksgiving morning, the parties to the contract were Mr. Harry POTTERFIELD, son of Thos. L. POTTERFIELD, of Lovettsville and Miss Bertie J. FRY, eldest daughter of Mr. Charles FRY of S., near Lovettsville. The ceremony was performed by Rev.

T. K. CROMER, pastor of the Lovettsville Reformed church, the ceremony being commenced just as the ferry boat left the Virginia short and out there on the flowing waters of the Potomac, but in "Maryland, my Maryland" they were pronounced man and wife. The bride was attired in ta neat fitting "go away" suit of blue cloth, and hat and trimmings to match. They took the train for Washington on a bridal tour, returned Saturday morning and a wedding dinner will be given them at the residence of the groom's father in Lovettsville. They will reside in Lovettsville.

Miss Lillie Carter BROSIUS and Mr. B. V. WHITE were married at night in Ascension Protestant Episcopal Church, the Rev. Chas. G. GRIFFITH officiating. The bride' parents live at 1012 Lafayette avenue. The groom is a son of Col. E. V. WHITE, of the Confederate calvary service. The bride wore white cotele and carried lilies of the valley. The maid of honor, Miss Flossie GIDDINGS, of Loudoun county, Va, wore blue china silk and carried la France roses. The ushers were E. H. BROSIUS, James WEEDEN, of Washington; E. B. HARRISON and W. W. CHAMBLIN of Leesburg.

Mrs. C. M. GRIGSBY, widow of the late Col. A. S. GRIGSBY, of Fairfax county, died Tuesday in Pulaski county.

Friday, 9 December 1892   Vol. XV, No. 33

Col. and Mrs. E. V. WHITE have issued cards for the marriage of their daughter, Ada, to Mr. I. T. LONG, of Washington DC. The ceremony takes place at their residence in this town, Thursday afternoon, December 15th at 1 o'clock.

Charles STAUBS, son of Aaron STAUBS, was drowned in crossing the river at Harpers Ferry on Wednesday the 30th of November. He and three other young men got into a skiff, on the Ferry side, to cross over to the Loudoun side, and when about half way across the boat capsized. STAUBS could not swim. His body was found the same evening, and buried on Friday, December 2nd. He was about 20 years old and a brother of Mrs. James W. POTTS, near Mechanicsville.

On Wednesday afternoon, November 23, at 3 o'clock, in the private parlor of the Metropolitan Hotel, Washington DC, Mr. John T. McNEALLEY was married to Miss Delia P. JAMES, oldest daughter of Mr. Charles JAMES, of Waterford, Va, by Dr. J. G. BUTLER, pastor of St. Paul's Lutheran church. The bridal party was attended by Miss Jeanette JAMES, a sister of the bride, and Mr. E. C. SHAFER, a friend of the groom. Mr. Harry L. HILLEARY, of Manassas Va and Mr. E. M. GOVER and wife were also present. The happy couple returned to Brunswick Thanksgiving day and a dinner was partaken of at the groom's home at 3 o'clock.

Philomont: Mr. J. Lee CHAMBLIN, whose death was announced in the TELEPHONE, is still living, though critically ill. He is at the residence

of his son, R. C. L. CHAMBLIN. Mrs. Julia CHAMBLIN also
continues quite ill. Henry THURSTON, a worthy colored citizen,
died yesterday.
As we go to press, Mr. J. L. CHAMBLIN died at noon on Wednesday.
He was 81 years of age.
Lovettsville: Recently Mr. Harry POTTERFIELD and Miss Bertie FRY
were united in marriage; and on December 1st Mr. Samuel STREAM
and Miss Katie RICHIE were bound by the matrimonial tie, and on
the same day Mr. Edward FULENGANE [FILLENGANE] led to the
altar Miss Medora SWOPE.

Friday, 16 December 1892 Vol. XV, No. 34

Mrs. Samuel HOUGH died at her residence, near Purcellville last
Sunday night.
Mr. James McDANIEL of Purcellville neighborhood died last Friday
morning, in about the 63d year of his age. His funeral took place
from his late residence at 10 a.m. Saturday. Interment in Ketoctin
cemetery at 2 p.m. the same day.
Mrs. John H. WHITMORE died at her residence near Goresville last
Saturday evening, of heart trouble, in about the 67th year of her age.
She leaves a husband and several grown children, among them
Mrs. Herbert OSBOURN and Mrs. Albert VANDEVANTER, of this
section. Interred in the Union Cemetery, Leesburg, Monday.
Mr. Logan PURCELL, of Purcellville, who while coon hunting a few
weeks ago fell from a tree and sustained serious injuries was
removed to Garfield Hospital in Washington, last Friday for
treatment, where he died last Tuesday night. His remains were
brought home on the evening train Wednesday and interment took
place yesterday. He was about 28 years of age.
December Ct: Wills of Wm. WILLIAMS, Ellen J. McELROY, Wm.
McELROY and Edward W. RECTOR admitted to probate. Robt. R.
WALKER qualified as Admr. dbn wwa of Joshua PUSEY. Estate of
T. H. CARTER committed to the Sheriff. Jos. L. NORRIS qualified as
Admr. of Thos. B. COCKEY. Estate of Mort. J. BEALES committed
to Sheriff.
Herndon: Mrs. Mary D., wife of Mr. John F. OLIVER, died yesterday.
She has been sick several months and has seemed near her end for
some weeks.
R. Neville SAUNDERS, brother of Mr. Henry SAUNDERS, of this
county, died at his home in Washington city, at 4 o'clock last
Tuesday morning. Born and raised in Loudoun, but had been a
resident of Washington for nearly thirty years, most of which time
was spent as a clerk in the Auditor's Office of the P. O. Department.
He was partially paralyzed in his left side some years ago.
Mr. M. M. McCARTY, son of W. M. McCARTY, residing near "Oak Hill,"
about two miles northeast of Aldie, in this county, was found in a

dying condition on the Ball's Mill road, about 2½ miles north of Mt. Zion church, last Sunday afternoon. The cause of death has not been learned. The deceased was about 27 years of age.

A marriage license was granted in Washington last Monday to James H. WILKINS and Apple F. WALTON, both of Loudoun county.

Ada, youngest daughter of Col. E. V. WHITE, and Mr. I. T. LONG, of Charlottsville, were united in marriage at the residence of the bride's parents, in Leesburg, last Thursday afternoon, Elder A. B. FRANCIS officiating. After the ceremony the young people boarded the train for a trip through the Southern states.

Miss Annie L. BEALL died suddenly at the residence of Mr. H. P. BEANS, near Purcellville, where she was boarding last Wednesday morning about 11 o'clock. It was found that the passage from the stomach to the bowels had closed and was beyond the reach of medicine. A surgical operation was performed, removing from the neck of her stomach a huge tumor. About two years ago she taught in the Hamilton School. For several years she has been a member of the Society of Friends (Orthodox). She leaves a mother and two brothers, she was 23 years of age. Her funeral took place yesterday at 1 p.m. from Mr. BEANS' residence, interment in Friends burying ground, at Lincoln.

Mrs. Chas. MERCIER will be lay away today in Leesburg cemetery. Her death occurred in Washington at Columbia hospital at which place she had been under treatment for some weeks.

Bolington: George COOPER who was paralyzed about one year ago, had another stroke last week, from which he died. Cards are out for the marriage of Miss Lilly C. MOORE, of Georgetown, to Mr. Frank P. STONE, on Wednesday (today) 21st inst., at twelve o'clock at Herman Presbyterian church.

Lovettsville: Mr. George COOPER, an aged citizen near this place who received a severe stroke of paralysis about two years ago, died last Friday. Interred in the cemetery near this place on Saturday.

A dreadful tragedy occurred at Martinsburg, a small village near the Potomac, in Montgomery Co. Md last Sunday, resulting probably in the death of James WATERS, a young man, who was shot by his father, Dan'l. WATERS. The two had a dispute and the son knocked the father down.

Daniel H. SOWERS, well-known farmer of Clarke county, died last week.

Elijah CARTER, citizen of lower Fairfax, died at his home near Newington Thursday.

Friday, 30 December 1892   Vol. XV, No. 36

Philomont: Mr. Thos. JACKSON has buried another and the last one of his children. Diphtheria has robbed him of his two motherless children and left a lonesomeness in his heart.

The Fairfax county grant jury last week indicted Benj. D. UTTERBACK, Jr. for an assault on L. E. HUTCHISON, formerly of Unison, this county.

Mrs. Maria E. CARTER, wife of Capt. Jno. CARTER died on the 15th of Dec. at the residence of her son-in-law, Mr. C. F. RITICOR, at Oatlands, in the 63rd year of her age.

Mrs. Mary TAVENNER, wife of Mr. Benjamin TAVENNER, died at her home near Mountain Gap last Tuesday morning, in about the 45th year of her age.

Friday, 6 January 1893   Vol. XV, No. 37

Falls Church: Married at the Baptist church, Tuesday evening at 8 o'clock, by Rev. J. T. BARBER, father of the bride, Miss Emma Marie BARBER to Mr. Andrew C. SILL of Tennessee.

The Bethel M. E. church near Luckets Va was the scene of a ceremony at 6 p.m. on Thursday, Dec 22, when Mr. E. Frank FRY led Miss H. A. HOUGH to the altar. The ceremony was performed by Rev. R. N. SCOTT. The bride's maids, Misses Nannie D. FRY and Ella E. FRY preceded the bridal to the altar, attended by the groomsmen Messrs. George HOUGH and J. W. COOPER.

A marriage license was issued in Washington on Saturday to Jas. E. BROWN, of Loudoun, and Annie D. STROTHER.

Mr. Chas. E. ARNETT and Miss Mollie SHUGERS were quietly married by Rev. W. G. EGGLESTON, at the Methodist parsonage in Town, Wednesday evening.

During 1892 the clerk's office of this county issued 140 marriage licenses, 87 were to white, and 53 to colored persons.

Bolington Jan 4: A double wedding was consummated at the residence of John W. EAMICH in Morrisonville last Thursday the 29th inst. The contracting parties were Mr. P. CRIM, of Purcellville and Miss Ada EAMICH, and Mr. John SLENTZ and Miss Lou CRIM. Rev. J. HALPENNY officiated. The bridal parties went on a short tour to Frederick county Md. They returned home on Saturday.

Friday, 13 January 1893   Vol. XV, No. 38

Departed this life Tuesday, Dec 29th 1892, Mrs. Kate MERCIER, wife of C. C. MERCIER Esqr. and second daughter of the late Henry A. and Elizabeth BALL, of "Temple Hall," this county. In early womanhood she united with the Episcopal Church.

Annie Elizabeth GREEN, daughter of Fielding C. and Sophia GREEN, was born Jan. 1st 1872 and died Jan 2d 1893. She leaves a father, mother, four sisters and one brother.

Married: At Morrisonville, on Dec 28, by Rev. __ HALPENNY, Peter CRIM of Purcellville and Miss Ada B. EAMICH.

Married: At the same time and place by the same, Mr. John SLENTZ and Miss Lula CRIM.

Married: At the Baptist Parsonage in Hamilton, Jan. 5th 1893 by Rev. C. T. HERNDON, Miss Ollie A. McDANIEL and Chas. A. FRAME, both of Loudoun co.

Mrs. Rebecca VEALE, consort of the late Albert VEALE, died very suddenly of apoplexy, at the residence of her son-in-law, Chas. A. ARUNDELL, at Farmwell, last week.

Miss Phoebe A. HAWKINS, formerly of Hamilton, and Mr. G. W. BROWN, of Bergen county, New Jersey, were married in Washington on the 3d inst. by Rev. G. C. SMITH.

The matrimonial fever is still prevalent in Lovettsville. Mr. Amos HARRISON and Miss Minnie FRY were made one, in the Lutheran church by Rev. M. E. McLINN on the 28th of December; and on Jan. 4th at the home of the bride's parents, Mr. and Mrs. John W. COMPHER, Miss Millie COMPHER and Mr. Grant REED were united in marriage, by Rev. M. E. McLINN.

Annie SCHROGGINS, for several years past a teacher in the pubic colored school of this town, died at her home in Leesburg last Thursday after an illness of several weeks.

Marriage licenses were issued from the clerks office of this county this week to Robert C. HALL and Rebecca DeBUTTS, both of Loudoun; and to Wm. C. HEFLIN of Fauquier and Mary E. DODD of Loudoun.

Mrs. CHAMBERLAIN, wife of Dr. CHAMBERLAIN, of Middleburg, and sister of Mr. John H. ALEXANDER, of Leesburg, died at her home in Middleburg on Tuesday.

Thomas E. TAYLOR died 6th inst., was born in 1831 at the home where nearly his entire life was passed. He was educated in the neighborhood schools and with Benjamin HALLOWELL, at Alexandria. He came to the front of our county affairs about 1855. After the war he was a deputy sheriff under Samuel C. LUCKETT. He united in marriage with Mary J. PIGGOTT in 1867. There was born a daughter and a son, who did not survive childhood and a second son, Henry who was called home from Abington, Penn., too late to see his father alive. His remains were laid away beside his father's at Lincoln, from the old Friends Meeting House.

County Ct: Will of Elizabeth O. CARTER dec'd committed to probate. Estates of Edward MORRISON, Bernard HOUGH, Geo. MARLOW, Joshua REID, Robt. COE and Sarah CRAVEN committed to sheriff. Jackson M. MINOR qualified as Admr. of estate of Mary A. MINOR. Wm. S. SUMMERS qualified as Admr. dbn of Francis E. SHREVE. H. H. RUSSELL Sheriff appointed committee of Nelson BEAMER. R. M. PRESTON qualified as Notary Public. John M. CHAMBLIN qualified as Admr. of J. Lee CHAMBLIN dec'd. Ordinary license of Castle & Mullen, transferred to Chas. E. PERRY.

This community was shocked last Saturday morning at the death of Mr. Thos. A. SCHOOLEY about 4 o'clock this morning. The funeral took place from his late residence at 1 p.m. Monday, conducted by Rev. W. G. EGGLESTON, in the M. E. church, after which his remains were interred in the cemetery adjoining. Thomas A. SCHOOLEY was born near Waterford, November 25, 1824. He was the youngest child of Aaron and Betsey SCHOOLEY, to whom six children were born. Nov 18th 1846 he married Miss Hannah HOUGH. In 1848 he moved to Hamilton and occupied the house now owned by W. A. McFARLAND. Hamilton was then a village of five houses. In 1855 he formed a partnership with his brother, William, and opened a blacksmith shop. In 1860 he bought the property which he owned at the time of this death and moved thereon. He continued the blacksmith trade until 1880 when he turned the business over to his son, George. He was the father of eight children, seven of whom survive him. His wife died some eight years ago. Many years ago he united with the M. E. Church North. Within the past twenty months two of his brothers have died, both on Saturday morning and very suddenly.

Friday, 20 January 1893   Vol. XV, No. 39

Mr. R. C. HALL and Miss Bessie DeBUTTS were married at Welbourn, this county, on the 10th inst.

Mr. William BLONHAM and Miss Lena POLEN, both of eastern Loudoun, were united in marriage by Rev. B. F. BALL, in the Methodist parsonage, in Leesburg, on the 12th inst.

Mrs. Betsey GRUBB died at her home, near Hillsboro, on Wednesday evening at the remarkable age of 84 years. Her funeral will take place from her late residence at 10 a.m. to day. Interment at Salem.

Mrs. Martha J. BROWN, wife of William H. BROWN, died at her residence, near Janney's Mill, last Sunday morning in the 70th year of her age.

We learn that Mrs. Nancy HARPER, of Luckets, this county, died on Thursday last at the wonderful age of ninety-three.

Mr. William BEANS, partner in the livery business of Mr. J. T. HUNT, died Sunday. His remains were taken to Loudoun county on Monday for burial. *Charles Town Free Press.* Mr. BEANS was formerly a resident of this county and resided near Purcellville.

Mr. Isaac VANDEVANTER of this county died at his residence in the suburbs of Leesburg at about 2 p.m. Wednesday in the 86th year of his age. He leaves a wife and two children.

From the Richmond *Times* of last Saturday, Colonel James Monroe TALIAFERRO died in Leesburg on Sunday, in the 84th year of his age. Colonel TALIAFERRO was one of the old Virginia family, and was born in Oakland, King George county, Va August 1809. He was educated at West Point, and was a classmate of Generals Robert E.

LEE and Joseph E. JOHNSTON. He was the youngest son of a brilliant family, his brothers having figured in the war history of the country prominently. His oldest brother, John Wishart TALIAFERRO, was with Paul JONES on the Bon Homme Richard. Colonel TALIAFERRO formerly represented Suffolk and Prince William counties in the Virginia Senate.

In memory of Martha Jane BROWN. Born on the 13th of September 1822, daughter of Joshua and Sarah (WILSON) PANCOAST. She was married on 23 Sept 1841 to William Holmes BROWN, in Goose Creek Meeting House, where on the 17th of the present month family and friends met to pay last tribute.

Mrs. Jane SOUDER, wife of A. J. SOUDER, near this place, died last Sunday morning, after several weeks of suffering with pneumonia. Her remains were interred at the Reformed Church, Tuesday. She leaves a husband, three daughters and two sons.

A letter from Rochester, Illinois, informs us of the death of Mr. Jno. DAVIS, who died at that place on Jan. 2, '93. Mr. DAVIS was born in Loudoun County, near Mt. Gilead, in 1848. He leaves a wife and three children. His brothers and sisters in Loudoun are Mr. Benj. DAVIS, George W. DAVIS, Mrs. James M. HALL and Mrs. James TAVENNER.

Friday, 27 January 1893   Vol. XV, No. 40

Mr. Wm. PAYNE, of Washington and Miss Ella LYNCH, of Falls Church, were married Wednesday evening, at the residence of Mrs. LYNCH.

Mr. Theodore PAYNE, of Fairfax and Miss Monia NEWLON, of Falls Church, were married at the residence of Mr. A. C. NEWLON.

Esther WATERS, wife of Joseph WATERS (colored) of this town died last Sunday. Her funeral on Tuesday was largely attended by her colored friends.

Mr. Chas. A. ENGLISH, station agent at Leesburg, and Mrs. Nannie Claibourne LIGHTFOOT, of Petersburg, were married in St. Pauls church, Petersburg, at 4:30 p.m. Wednesday.

Mr. Mountjoy BAILEY, brother of the late Chapin BAILEY, died at his home in Prince William county last week, at the ripe old age of 96 years. For several years a resident of lower Loudoun.

Mrs. Mary WALLACE died at the residence of Richard ROOSE, in Town, last Friday night. Early in life she united with the M. E. Church, South and was a member through her life of nearly four score. Her funeral took place last Monday, Rev. W. G. EGGLESTON officiating. Interment took place in the cemetery at the M. E. Cemetery.

The death of Miss Sarah J. TAVENNER occurred at the residence of Mr. E. H. TAVENNER, in Town at 2 p.m. yesterday. Miss TAVENNER was born near Hamilton in 1814 and has resided in town through her entire life. She leaves two brothers. Her funeral will take place from Mr. TAVENNER's residence at 2 p.m. tomorrow. Interment in the M. E. Church cemetery, in town.

A licence for the marriage of Mr. Louis D. WINE to Elizabeth S. BUEHLER was issued in Washington on Tuesday. The bride comes from Gettysburg, Pa where was the home of Mr. WINE's first wife who died several years ago.

Mr. A. F. WELSH who went to Baltimore for medical treatment died there at the home of his brother. Rev. Mr. SHIPLEY preached a sermon after which his remains were conveyed to old South Fork for burial.

Mr. Wm. MONROE, an aged citizen of Bloomfield, died a few days since. He was the father of Mr. Madison MONROE, of Unison. He had been an invalid for a number of years.

Stephen PARKER, a very stout colored man, died very suddenly a few days since from an attack of colic.

Lovettsville: On Wednesday last Miss Rosa WENNER, of Taylortown, and Mr. Frank CARSON, of Goresville, were united in marriage at the M. E. Church, in this town, by Rev. M. E. McLINN.

Friday, 3 February 1893   Vol. XV, No. 41

Mr. Henry B. CLAGGETT, one of the oldest citizens of Alexandria, died at the residence of his daughter, Miss Bessie CLAGGETT, in Boston, Mass, recently from the effects of a stroke of paralysis received some days ago. He was more than eighty years of age.

Mr. Robert BENTLEY, a young man of lower Loudoun, died at the residence of his brother-in-law, Dr. B. F. NOLAND, at Farmwell, on Thursday last, in the 28th year of his age.

Cards are out for the marriage of Miss Christie ROGERS, daughter of Mr. A. H. ROGERS, of this country, to Mr. Robt. B. WILDMAN, of the firm of Wildman & Co., Leesburg which is to take place in that town the 8th inst.

Mrs. John GILL died at her residence near Taylor's Mill at 4 p.m. Wednesday. She leaves a husband and eight small children, one of whom is only six weeks old. Her funeral will take place from her late residence at 9 a.m. today. Interment in the M. E. Church cemetery in this town.

Capt. N. R. HEATON died of pneumonia, which occurred at his residence in Woodgrove, Wednesday evening. The deceased was a brother of the late Senator Henry HEATON. He was a prominent confederate soldier during the late war, and a member of the Democratic County committee.

Friday, 10 February 1893   Vol. XV, No. 42

Falls Church: Wm. H. ROBERSON, father of Wm. VEITCH, died at Providence Hospital, Monday night.

Mrs. Virginia HUTCHISON, wife of Robert P. HUTCHISON, formerly of this county, died at her home near Hickory Grove, on the 20th ult, in the 75th year of her age.

Maurice VANDEVANDER, a farmer of Fairfax was discovered in his barn on Monday night hanging by the neck half dead. He was resuscitated and yesterday sent to jail as a lunatic.

A shocking tragedy occurred at Paeonian Springs Wednesday morning. A negro woman, employed by T. D. MILTON, arose in the morning, leaving her child, an infant, asleep. When she returned some time after she was shocked to find that the child had smothered.

Friday, 17 February 1893   Vol. XV, No. 43

County Ct: Estates of Henry THURSTON, Godfrey SHELLHORN, Wm. THOMPSON and Jas. T. WRIGHT committed to sheriff. Wills of Mary J. WALLICE and Isaac VANDEVANTER admitted to probate. Mary J. TAYLOR qualified as Admr. of Thos. E. TAYLOR. J. W. GRUBB qualified as Admr. of Mr. GRUBB. A. W. PHILLIPS appointed committee of Rebecca J. WILLIAMS. Henry J. ST[E]VENS authorised to celebrate rites of matrimony. A. J. BRADFIELD qualified as Notary Public. Cornelius SHAWN qualified as Admr. of Landen D. ROBERTS. C. B. ADAMS qualified as Admr. of Caroline ADAMS.

The only child of Mr. Janney PURCELL of Round Hill died last Friday in the second year of its age.

Mr. Richard CLAGETT, of Gaithersburg, and Miss Leah PHILLIPS, of Leesburg, were married at the home of the groom, last week.

Mr. Samuel S. HOPKINS died Tuesday, at his residence. "White Hall," in Montgomery Co. Md. His death supposed to have been from heart disease.

Weddings are still the order of the day in Lovettsville. Thursday the 27th ult. Mr. Harry FRY and Miss Vida SMITH were made one, at the home of the bride's parents, Mr. and Mrs. John L. SMITH, near town, by Rev. M. E. McLINN. After the ceremony they started on a bridal tour of Johnstown, Pa, where Mr. FRY has been engaged in business for several years.

Herndon: Marriage of Miss Ella, daughter of Mr. Isaiah BREADY of this place to Mr. M. D. MOSS, of Roanoke, took place in the Congregational Church yesterday at 2 p.m. The ceremony was performed by Rev. Dr. MASON. They will make their home in Roanoke.

Fauquier: A little child of Mr. Arthur CAMPBELL, who lives near Little Georgetown, while playing about the room, in the absence of the grown people, caught on fire and was so badly burned that she died in a few hours.

Friday, 24 February 1893   Vol. XV, No. 44

Warner M. BROWN, son of Thomas and Elizabeth BROWN, died at the home of his parents in Hamilton, at 3:15 last Monday morning, in the 27th year of his age. About a year ago, while living in Nebraska was strickened with the Grip, from which he soon nearly recovered; but subsequent exposure in very severe weather, resulted in a relapse. The funeral took place at Friends meeting house, in Lincoln, Wednesday afternoon.

Friday, 3 March 1893   Vol. XV, No. 45

No marriages or death.

Friday, 10 March 1893   Vol. XV, No. 46

Deaths: Third month second, at her home, Lincoln, Va, Clarissa C. JANNEY, daughter of Eliza F. RAWSON and the late John JANNEY.

C. W. LITTLEJOHN, of Leesburg, died at 4:40 p.m. yesterday at Hagerstown, Md to which place he went about a week ago. His remains will be brought to Leesburg today.

Friday, 17 March 1893   Vol. XV, No. 47

Mr. Richard G. VICKERS, a brother of Mr. Julian VICKERS, is visiting his mother, Mrs. Sarah VICKERS, near Morrisonville. Mr. VICKERS has been residing for some years in Pittsburg.

Mr. Wm. DONALDSON and Miss Elnora LOWE were married at the home of the bride's parents in this town on Tuesday evening.

County Ct.: Wills of Norval SILCOTT, Jas. A. MAFFETT and Godfrey SHELHORN admitted to probate. L. T. NICHOLS qualified as Admr. of Isaac G. NICHOLS dec'd. C. W. S. TURNER qualified as Admr. of Alfred WELSH dec'd. C. W. S. TURNER, attorney, admitted to the bar. Adin C. WHITE qualified as Guardian of Julia WHITE. Geo. P. HUNTER qualified as Admr. of Mary STONE. Sheriff appointed Committee of Chas. H. LACEY. Wallace GEORGE qualified as Admr. of John GEORGE. Saml. P. MURRAY, colored, relieved from capitation tax. Sheriff appointed curator of estate of Mary HOUGH dec'd.

Friday, 24 March 1893   Vol. XV, No. 48

Mrs. Blanche MORGAN, nee GORMAN, who has been living somewhere in the West since leaving this vicinity, recently was bereft by death of her entire family – husband and three children.

Mr. Roger C. LUCKETT died at his residence in Baltimore on the 18th of this month. He was a brother of Samuel C. LUCKETT, who for many years was Secretary of the Loudoun Co Fire Insurance Co. and a brother of Josiah LUCKETT, of this town.

Friday, 31 March 1893   Vol. XV, No. 49

The town of Leesburg was shocked by the sudden death of Mrs. Lizzie A. WHITE, wife of Col. E. V. WHITE, which occurred at her home in Leesburg, last Thursday evening. Her remains were interred in Union Cemetery Sunday afternoon. Funeral services were conducted by Elder BADGER of the Baptist Church, of which the deceased was a devoted member.

Mrs. Martha CARR, relict of the late Joseph CARR, died at the residence of her son-in-law, Mr. Thos. G. ELGIN, near Leesburg, Tuesday morning.

Mrs. Pleasant WILLIAMS, widow of the late John WILLIAMS, died at her home near Luckets, Tuesday night, in about the 80th year of her age. Interment in Union Cemetery in Leesburg on Thursday. The same night, Mrs. HERNDON wife of Mr. Robt. HERNDON, died at the home of her father, Mr. John KIDWELL, near this town. Her remains were interred in Union Cemetery on Thursday.

Little Josie, the infant child of Ed. L. and Ruth H. BENNETT, died at the parents home near Clarks Gap, last Thursday evening aged 18 years.

Friday, 7 April 1893   Vol. XV, No. 50

Mahlon NICHOLS of Columbiana county, Ohio, died on March 29th, of pneumonia, in the 70th year of his age. He leaves a wife and seven children to mourn his loss. He was formerly a resident of this county.

Willie H., son of John GILL, died at the home of his father near Purcellville, Wednesday morning at 1:20 o'clock of typhoid pneumonia in the 18th year of his age. He was a member of the M. E. Church. His remains were laid to rest beside those of his mother, in Harmony cemetery, in this town yesterday.

Unexpected death of Chas. CARROLL, who died at his home in Baltimore Wednesday morning about 11 o'clock, a victim of consumption. Leaves a wife and a little daughter about 2 years old.

Anthony DIBRELL died at his home in Leesburg Monday afternoon about 5 o'clock, in the 53rd year of his age. Immediate cause of death was consumption. His remains were interred in the Union Cemetery, Leesburg. He was educated at Randolph Macon College. At the breaking out of the late war he was a clerk in a prominent business house in Richmond, he resigned and connected himself with the artillery of the confederate service and was a member of the Richmond Howitzers for four weary years. During the first year of the war he was stationed in Leesburg and after the close of the war married Agnes, daughter of the late Jas. H. CHAMBLIN of this town.

Mr. Jno. MIDDLETON, who died at his residence in this town, at 4 a.m. Thursday last. On the morning of the following day the deceased was buried in Sharon cemetery.

Friday, 14 April 1893   Vol. XV, No. 51

County Ct.: Wills of Sarah BIRDSALL, Mary TALLEY, Theomiah RHODES, N. R. HEATON and Anthony DIBRELL admitted to probate. Retail and barroom liquor licenses were granted to Survick & Whitmore, Clas. [Chas.?] R. LOWENBACH, Hickman & Bitzer, Shryock & Presgraves, Wm. H. BROOKS and Goodhart & Rollins. Ordinary licenses granted to A. D. WRIGHT and Nixon & Bro. J. B. McCABE qualified as Admr. of C. W. LITTLEJOHN. Wm. B. McCLELLAN, of Lincoln, qualified as Notary Public.

Friday, 21 April 1893   Vol. XV, No. 52

Mrs. William BEANS died near town last night. Funeral to take place at Harmony Church tomorrow; meet at house at 10 a.m.

Mr. Ed. NICHOLS left Leesburg on Monday for Libson [Lisbon?] Ohio, to attend the funeral of his brother, Judge W. A. NICHOLS.

The body of S. N. SIMPSON was interred in the Chapel burying ground, today. Mr. SIMPSON had been boarding with various families in the vicinity for a year. The first of January last, he was at Lost Corner, canvassing for a book, for which he was agent. About sundown of the 5th of January, he left the home of Randolph BARNHOUSE, intending to go to Mr. LOY's, which place he never reached. His sister living in Philadelphia was notified. Three months from his disappearance a man's body was found in the mouth of Seneca creek, a paper was discovered on his body, bearing the name of Noland SIMPSON, Lucketts, Va., also, bonds to the amount of $2,000.

Philomont, April 17: The death of J. I. BROWN at West End, Va. fills our hearts with sadness. Mrs. Mary ROBEY, mother of F. E. ROBY Esq. breathed her last on the 5th of April. She was in the 79th year of her age, and a consistent member of the Baptist Church. John F. NEWLON died very suddenly at this residence near Unison, Thursday the 13th of April. Mrs. BALL, the widow of the late Wm. BALL, died on the 14th inst., at the residence of her son-in-law Mr. Ashland LYNN.

Upperville: The wife of William ROBEY, after lingering for some time with disease, which baffled the skill of all the local physicians, died and was buried here on Thursday the 14th ult. William MOSS and Moses SCOTT, both octogenerians, the former living on his farm a mile distant, the latter in the village, are both active for men of their age.

Friday, 28 April 1893   Vol. XV, No. 52 [53]

Jackson M. MINOR farmer of this county died at his home near Taylortown, on Tuesday last, aged about 65 years.

The Telephone
Friday, 4 May 1894   Vol. XVII, No. 1

Bolington: Miss Ada LEMMEN has died after a lingering illness. Her remains were interred in the Rehobeth Cemetery, on Sunday 16th inst. Funeral services by Rev. M. E. McLINN. She was aged 13y 5m.

Circuit Ct.: C. C. WENNER qualified as Admr. of Sarah A. WENNER. Will of M. B. HUTCHISON admitted to probate, G. C. HUTCHISON and Chas. L. HUTCHISON, executors. Geo. T. SCHOOLEY and Chas. W. SCHOOLEY gave separate bonds as Executors of Thos. A. SCHOOLEY. John W. GARRETT qualified as Admr. of John F. NEWLON.

Mr. J. Robert BLACKMORE, of Fauquier county, died recently, aged seventy-five years, after an illness of a few hours. Mr. BLACKMORE was the youngest surviving member of his family, leaving a brother and two sisters, whose ages aggregate some 246 years. He had one brother killed by the Seminole Indians in the Florida war. He was a member of Turner ASHBY's old company during the war.

Thomas MURTAUGH, who was struck on the head at the Mahoneyville distillery, near Alexandria, by a falling plank on Thursday the 15th inst., died from the effects of his injuries Friday. He was a resident of West End, Fairfax county.

Mr. Josiah RINKER, an aged and respectable citizen, who resided near Gainsboro, Frederick county, died Tuesday. He was kicked by a horse Monday evening while entering his barn. He leaves a widow and three children.

E. B. GOLD, a student at the University of Virginia died Tuesday after an illness of several weeks. The remains will be taken to Berryville for interment.

[ISSUES MISSING]

Friday, 4 May 1894   Vol. XVII, No. 1

Circuit Ct.: Mrs. L. Jane OSBURN qualified as Executrix of Harrison OSBURN deceased. Mary E. MINOR qualified as guardian for Nellie W. MINOR. Estate of John HERNDON committed to Sheriff.

A very pretty wedding took place at St. Paul's Episcopal Church at 11 o'clock Wednesday morning when Miss Bertha EVERHART, adopted daughter of Mr. and Mrs. W. N. EVERHART was united in marriage to Mr. Arthur B. BURROWS of Washington City. Promptly at the appointed hour the wedding march played by Miss Carrie TAVENNER announced the arrival of the bridal company. Mr. Edgar MYERS of Hughesville and Miss Rose EVERHART, of Washington, best man and the bride's maid entered followed by the bride and groom. At the chancel rail they were met by Rev. R. R. S. HOUGH, who performed the ceremony of the M. E. Church South. They will locate in Washington, where Mr. BURROWS is engaged in business.

Mr. Daniel GREGG is the happy sire of three children – the youngest, a girl, will be one week old tonight.

Mrs. Jane JANNEY, wife of Dr. Nathan JANNEY deceased, died at the home of her brother, Rodney PURCELL, Sunday morning at 11 o'clock. She leaves two other brothers, Heaton PURCELL, near Round Hill, and Wm. PURCELL, of Baltimore. The funeral took place Tuesday morning at 10 o'clock. Relatives, including Wm. PURCELL and wife, of Baltimore. Interred in Friend's burying ground, at Lincoln.

Mrs. Gertrude TAYLOR, widow of the late Maj. Wm. TAYLOR, of Berryville, died in Richmond Tuesday morning of paralysis.

Friday, 11 May 1894   Vol. XVII, No. 2

Died at his home near Lovettsville, after a lingering illness, Monday night, John L. SMITH, aged about 55 years.

Friday, 18 May 1894   Vol. XVII, No. 3

Miss Jane EVANS died last Monday morning, at the home of her sister-in-law, Mrs. Louisa EVANS, in Hamilton, aged 76 years. Her funeral took place at Arnold Grove, Tuesday, Rev. C. T. HERNDON officiating.

Andrew ALDRIDGE, a brother of Mr. John ALDRIDGE of this county, died at "Caledonia," his country home near Charlestown, W. Va., on Wednesday morning May 9th. He had been in ill health for some time, but his death was unexpected.

A lovely wedding took place at 12 o'clock last Tuesday, in the Presbyterian Church, at Purcellville, when Mr. W. P. LOVE and Miss Laura HIRST were united by the bonds of wedlock, according to the impressive ceremony of the M. E. Church South, Dr. R. R. S. HOUGH. Rev. WILSON of the Presbyterian Church was also present.

County Ct.: Will of Nathan ROBERTS dec'd proved and Levin OGDEN and Saml. H. LORD, Executors. Nancy WYNKOOP qualified as Admx. of A. J. WYNKOOP dec'd. Robt. DODD qualified as guardian of Jno. G. DODD. Ida V. DODD qualified as guardian for Ruth V. DODD &c. Jno. G. UTTERBACH as guardian for W. H. DODD. S. C. CHANCELLOR qualified as Admr. of Margt. E. CHANCELLOR dec'd. S. C. CHANCELLOR qualified as Admr. of Lorman CHANCELLOR dec'd.

Mr. Charles Carroll MARTIN, of Washington city, died at his home in that city after a protracted illness, on Wednesday night, May 9th 1894. His funeral took place on Saturday last, interment at Rock Creek Cemetery. Mr. MARTIN married a Miss JOHNSON, of Leesburg, sister of Mr. S. J. JOHNSON, who with three children survives him.

Friday, 25 May 1894   Vol. XVII, No. 4

Thirty two years ago, at the old stone meeting house in Waterford, was celebrated the wedding of Franklin M. STEER and Mary F. DUTTON, and to commemorate friends assembled at "Sunnyside" Tuesday evening for a surprise.

Friday, 1 June 1894   Vol. XVII, No. 5

Dr. and Mrs. C. S. CARTER have issued cards for the marriage of their daughter Anne Page to Dr. W. J. S. STEWART, of Philadelphia. The ceremony is to take place 12 o'clock Tuesday, June 12th in St. James Church in this town.

Mrs. H. DIVINE, widow of the late Major Jas. F. DIVINE, of this town, died last Thursday evening, May 24th 1894, at the residence of her daughter, Mrs. Virginia Wise TREW, in Washington, in about the 80th year of her age. Most of her life was spent in her native Leesburg. She leaves a four daughters, Mrs. FURGUSON, Mrs. SHAW, and Mrs. TREW, of Washington, and Mrs. J. W. CONNOR, of this town. Her remains were brought here Saturday, and with services by Rev. J. W. GRUBB in the M. E. Church South in the afternoon, her remains were laid to rest in Union Cemetery.

Rose, the youngest child of Mr. J. Frank PEUGH, formerly of our town but now residing at Little Rock Ar., died on the 21st ult. aged 1y 2m.

Bolington: C. E. WOLFORD, who has been attending the U. S. Grant Theological University, of Chatanooga Tenn., graduated there a few days ago and has since married a lady graduate of the same school and will locate in Aniston, Ala. where he has been given a charge by the Alabama Conference.

The Orthodox church, at Silcott Springs, was the scene of a pretty wedding Wednesday, at 2 o'clock, when Mr. Frank HIBBS and Miss Edith SHOEMAKER were united in wedlock by Rev. C. T. HERNDON, of Hamilton. The ushers were Messrs. Henry PIGGOTT, of Silcotts Spring, and Humphrey HIBBS, of Leesburg. The waiters were Mr. James M. WHITE, of Purcellville and Miss Fannie BROWN, of New York; Mr. Walter OTLEY and Miss Minnie L. WOTRING, of Winchester; Mr. West HIBBS and Miss Mary HATCHER, of Purcellville; Mrs. Geo. SHOEMAKER, of Hamilton and Miss Kate HIBBS.

Friday, 8 June 1894   Vol. XVII, No. 6

Mrs. Ann MOORE, whose serious illness at the home of her daughter, Mrs. Albert GORE, in our town was mentioned last week, lingered until 9:30 Saturday evening, a life of nearly four score years. She came from her home near Wheatland, Wednesday, when apparently in good health, but took ill. The deceased was the widow of the late Geo. L. MOORE, and mother of Saml. L. and Dr. MOORE. She also leaves several daughters, two or more of whom have remained at home and ministered to her wants in her sickness. The funeral conducted by Rev. C. T. HERNDON, of the Baptist Church after which the body was interred by the side of her husband at the Catoctin burying ground.

Friday, 15 June 1894   Vol. XVII, No. 7

The coroner's jury in the case of Vernon Adam SHRY, who was shot and killed by Chas. E. HENLY, as reported last week, rendered a verdict of justifiable homicide.

County Ct.: Estate of John R. McNEALY dec'd committed to Sheriff. Wills of Brisco C. PANGLE, John L. SMITH and Ann E. HOUGH, admitted to probate. Chas. C. PANGLE qualified as Executor of Brisco C. PANGLE dec'd. Mary E. SMITH qualified as Executor of Jno. L. SMITH dec'd. Robt. R. WALKER and D. H. VANDEVANTER qualified as Executors of Ann E. HOUGH dec'd.

Miss Ann Page CARTER, daughter of Dr. C. Shirley CARTER, was married to Dr. J. W. S. STEWART, in St. James Episcopal Church, at Leesburg, last Tuesday. The bridesmaids were Misses Elizabeth BAKER of Washington, Sarah SHERRARD of Philadelphia, Henrietta TELGHMAN, of Baltimore, Evelyn BUCKNER of Baltimore and Sophie BROGDEN and May CHICHESTER of Loudoun. Mr. Murray STEWART, of Wilmington, brother of the groom was best man and the ushers were: Messrs. John P. ELTON of New York, S. D. FURGUSON of Washington, John GREGG of Harrisonburg, Va, T. F. MASON, G. M. CHICHESTER and C. Shirley CARTER Jr., a brother of the bride, of Loudoun. The ceremony was performed by the Rev. Berryman GREEN.

Mr. Nathan LODGE of this vicinity died suddenly at his home near our town last Saturday morning. While sitting in a chair he was attached by heart disease and died very suddenly. He resided through a long life of nearly 76 years in this vicinity. He leaves a fine farm and other property. His remains were Interred at Ebenezer burying ground on Tuesday, Rev. I. B. LAKE conducted the services.

Dr. L. A. BROWN, of this town, received a telegram Tuesday afternoon announcing the death of his father, J. R. BROWN of Washington city, on Tuesday morning after a somewhat protracted illness.

Wm. H. GRAY, son of the late Robert W. GRAY, of this town, died in Staunton last Thursday night. His remains were brought to Leesburg on Saturday and his funeral took place from the residence of his sister, Mrs. H. W. CLAGETT.

Friday, 22 June 1894   Vol. XVII, No. 8

Union: Thomas, infant son of Henry SAFFLE, died last week and was interred at Ebenezer, Rev. W. D. KEEN officiating.

Mr. John N. MINNIX, a native of Loudoun County, died at his home in Prince George Co., Md last Saturday.

Friday, 23 [29] June 1894   Vol. XVII, No. 9

A marriage license was issued in Washington to T. D. SHELTON, of Leesburg, and Lizzie BLACKNELL, of Jeffersonton, last Monday.

Mr. Stephen WILSON, of Round Hill, died at his home in that town about noon on Tuesday, and his remains were interred in Harmony burying ground, in Hamilton, yesterday.

Herndon, June 28th – Mr. Jno. OVERALL's son, Willie, aged 11 years, who died of diptheria, in Washington, Saturday morning last, was buried here Sunday afternoon.

William Giddings, infant son of Rev. Carter PAGE, who died at the home of his parents Brandy Station, Va. on Sunday last was buried in Union Cemetery, in this town on Tuesday.

As we go to press, Wednesday afternoon St. James' church is being readied for a wedding, which takes place at 8 o'clock Wednesday night. The contracting parties are Miss Netta Lee RUST, daughter of the late Col. A. T. M. RUST, of this county, and Mr. Wm. M. COULLING, of Richmond.

Friday, 6 July 1894   Vol. XVII, No. 01 [10]

Mrs. Emeline AYRES, widow of the late Thos. W. AYRES, died at the residence of Mr. Elijah RITICOR near Aldie, on Sunday morning last in about the 72^d year of her age. Her remains were interred in Union Cemetery this town, on Monday.

A colored man named Jos. BALDWIN was drowned while crossing the river at White's Ferry on Thursday afternoon last. BALDWIN was driving a horse belonging to a son of the late Judge W. A. STEWART, of Baltimore, from that city of the Plains, Va. He was a house servant of Mrs. STEWART's. Remains were buried near Martinsburg. On Friday evening, the remains were disinterred and taken to Baltimore.

Lucy ROBINSON, daughter of Esquire and Lucy ROBINSON, departed this life, June 28th in the 22nd year of her age.

Friday, 13 July 1894   Vol. XVII, No. 11

The *Alexandria Gazette* of last Friday said: Mrs. James M. BENTON, daughter of the late John D. HARRISON, of this city, died at Unison, Loudoun county, yesterday.

Mr. John B. GOOCH died at the home of his brother-in-law, Mr. TAYLOR, near Leesburg, last Monday, after an illness of about a month of typhoid fever, aged 23 years. His remains were interred at Leesburg on Tuesday.

County Ct.: Samuel W. HOUGH qualified as Admr. of Wm. M. HOUGH dec'd. Americus J. SAUNDER qualified as Admr. of Jno. STREAM dec'd. Russell PRICE qualified as guardian of Ruth and Ella PRICE. Will of Nathan LODGE dec'd admitted to probate. Volney OSBURN

qualified as Executor of Nathan LODGE dec'd. Sarah E. BROWN qualified as Admr. of Chas. MORTON dec'd.
Ridley PARKER (colored) was found dead in her bed Sunday morning.
United in marriage – contracting parties were the Rev. Chas. WOLFORD, of Bolington and Miss Julia McCALEB, of Morristown, Tenn. The marriage was at the home of the bride, Tuesday evening, May 22n, 1894. Bro. WOLFORD is pastor of St. Paul's M. E. Church, of Anniston, Ala., and is a member of the Alabama Conference.

Friday, 20 July 1894   Vol. XVII, No. 12

J. H. BRAMWELL, a large land owner in West Virginia, died recently in France. The town of Bramwell was named after him.
The wife of Mr. M. W. BURR, farmer of Jefferson county, W. Va, was found dead in bed Thursday morning.
Alexandria Gazette of last Saturday: Miss Susan CARTER died at the home of her brother-in-law, Mr. J. J. COCKERELL, near Manassas, on Tuesday. On Thursday her remains were taken to Middleburg, her former home, for interment.
Letter from Warrenton: Miss Mollie MIDDLETON, daughter of Mrs. S. C. MIDDLETON was married at high noon on the 12th to Mr. T. H. LAMBDON of the firm of Lambdon & Middleton, Washington D.C.
Mrs. Julia HAMMERLY was yesterday granted a divorce in Washington from her husband, J. A. HAMMERLY, on the ground of desertion. They were married in this city in 1867 and have five children. Mr. HAMMERLY is a residence of this city. *Alex. Gazette.*
Mrs. J. M. BENTON whose death has been announced. Rev. G. T. TYLER officiated at her funeral, assisted by Rev. W. B. KEENE. Her remains were taken to Middleburg Cemetery.
Died: Mrs. Susan C. JOHNSON, widow of the late Amos W. JOHNSON, died at her home near Lenah, Va. on June 19th, 1894, aged 73y 2m 10d. She leaves 1 son, 2 daughters and six grandchildren.
Died: Leesburg, on July 15th, at 11 o'clock p.m., Mary Agnes, only child of E. A. and Rose E. JOHNSTON, aged 10m 23d.

Friday, 27 July 1894   Vol. XVII, No. 13

Neersville: Miss Sarah RINEY, an elderly lady died yesterday morning, at the residence of H. COPELAND at Mechanicsville. Interment at Rehoboth today.
Clinton Harper, infant son of Geo. C. and Lillian H. HOUGH, aged 9m 12d, died at the home of its parents in Washington, last Tuesday. Its remains were brought to Leesburg and buried in the Union Cemetery on Thursday.
Mrs. Elizabeth M. BOUCHET, of Baltimore, died yesterday morning at Tilghman's Island, Md. of consumption. She was the widow of the

late J. M. BOUCHET. Born in 1744 [1844] in Loudoun County, her
parents being Marrow and Elizabeth BROWNE. *Alex. Gazette* 21st.
Death of Wilmer NICHOLS, son of Eli NICHOLS, near Philomont, from
typhoid fever. On Tuesday about noon his body was laid to rest in
Friends burying ground, at Lincoln.
Died: At Falls Church, Va, July 19th, Lewis Eli, infant son of Merton E.
and Carrie B. CHURCH. Aged 5m 7d.

Friday, 3 August 1894   Vol. XVII, No. 14

A marriage license was issued in Washington last Thursday, to Mr. B. F.
HOLLY, of Washington, and Miss Annie B. FERGUSON, of Round
Hill.
Hannah WILLIAMS, wife of James WILLIAMS, died Friday morning and
on Sunday afternoon her body was laid by the side of one of her
little children, in Friends burying ground at Waterford. She leaves
three little ones, the youngest only about two weeks old.
On Sunday, Mrs. Hannah CRAVEN, wife of Mr. Guilford CRAVEN, who
had been in poor health for some time, departed this life, at her
home near Lincoln. Interred at Short Hill burying ground on
Tuesday. She was a daughter of the late Timothy TAYLOR.
Mrs. Sarah E. LEWIS, wife of Samuel LEWIS of our town, died after a
brief illness last Saturday evening. Her funeral, on Tuesday, was the
first one to be conducted in the new Harmony Church, conducted by
Dr. HOUGH. She leaves several children, all grown or nearly so
except two. She was 50 years old. The aged mother of the
deceased attended the funeral.
Philomont: Mr. Eli NICHOLS and wife have sympathies on the loss of
their son, Wilmer.
Died: Morrell BEENS, son of A. H. and Monisa BEANS, died July 28th
1894 age 9m 6d.

Friday, 10 August 1894   Vol. XVII, No. 15

The funeral of John NICHOLS who was killed at the Bush Meeting
grounds, will take place tomorrow Saturday. Meet at the house at 10
a.m. and at Friends meeting house, at Lincoln, at 12 m.
At the great Bush Meeting at Purcellville last night, John NICHOLS, son
of Phineas J. NICHOLS, was instantly killed. Miss Mollie DUNBAR,
daughter of Mr. Harvey DUNBAR, near Upperville, perhaps fatally
injured. Lester SCHOOLEY, son of C. W. SCHOOLEY, recently of
North Fork, still alive but dangerously injured. Meeting grounds
seemed to be the center of a tornado.

Friday, 17 August 1894   Vol. XVII, No. 16

Bolington, Aug. 15, we chronical the death of Mr. Wm. MAIN, of
Knoxville, Md, who departed this life on Sunday 12th inst. Her

remains were laid to rest on Tuesday, the 14th. The deceased was a sister of Mrs. T. D. KALB.

On Monday of this week, Thomas CULLEN, near here, committed suicide by taking a dose of arsenic, of which he died on Monday night. His funeral will take place today.

Mr. Isaac HAWES, formerly of this county, died in Washington last week. His remains were brought to Loudoun on Friday and interred at Waterford.

Miss Ellen THOMAS, daughter of the late James THOMAS died at the home of her brother, Mr. Armstead THOMAS, near Leesburg, last Friday night. Member of the Presbyterian Church. Interred in Union Cemetery, on Sunday, Rev. Mr. WILSON of Waterford officiating.

Mrs. Nettie OFFETT, daughter of the late Dr. Chas. G. EDWARDS, of Waterford, in this county, and widow of the late Nichols OFFUTT, of Rockville, Md, died at the late home of Mrs. Ann S. WOOD dec'd in this town, on Wednesday morning Aug. 15, 1894. She was a member of the Presbyterian church. Her remains will be taken to Rockville today (Thursday) for interment.

Court: Wills of Jane A. EVANS, Henry M. HARDY and Ann S. WOOD admitted to probate. Presley C. EVANS qualified as Exor. of Jane A. EVANS dec'd. Chas. P. JANNEY qualified as Exor. of H. M. HARDY dec'd. Mary C. HELM qualified as guardian of Lizzie C. and Thomas M. HELM.

Died: Geo. R. ELGIN, husband of Sarah E. ELGIN, at his residence, 1012 7th St. NE, Washington DC, Aug. 10th. Interment in Leesburg.

Died: Mrs. Alcinda J. LOVE, died at her home near Hillsboro, Sunday Aug. 5, 1894, aged 56y 11m 27d. She connected herself with the M. E. Church about 10 years ago.

Friday, 24 August 1894   Vol. XVII, No. 17

A marriage license was issued in Washington on Monday to James F. PERKINS, of that city, and Mollie Orra BAUCKMAN, of Leesburg.

Friday, 31 August 1894   Vol. XVII, No. 18

Mrs. Dr. TURNER, only daughter of Townsend OSBURN, died at her home in Snickersville, Tuesday. Her remains were laid at rest in Ebenezer Cemetery yesterday. She leaves two children.

Death of Mrs. Sophia E. SHROFF, wife of P. E. SHROFF, occurred at the residence of her father, Mr. Jno. NORRIS, in this town, on Tuesday afternoon about 5 o'clock after a protracted and painful illness.

Married: Aug. 22, by Rev. J. T. BARBER, Wm. Clinton HERN, of Leesburg, to Ida LEONARD, of the same place.

Died: Fannie ADAMS, at the residence of her father, Mr. James ADAMS, at Mountain Gap, August 12th, in the 29th year of her age.

Died: Bessie L. DAYMUDE, of typhoid fever, at her home near Aldie, in the 16th year of her age.

Died: Elizabeth B. WORKS, at Sterling, Loudoun co., Aug. 18th, in the 89th year of her age.

[From Pennville (Ind.) *Gazette*] Joel BIRDSALL was born in Montgomery county, Md, on the 17th of the 11th month 1827; died at Balbec, Jay county, Ind., at the home of his daughter, Carrie V. SUTTON, 8th month, 6th, 1894, aged 66y 8m 10d. He was the son of John and Mary BIRDSALL, who moved with their family to Virginia in 1829. He was married to Jane C. BROWN, of Zanesfield, Logan county, Ohio, 3rd month, 7th 1855, and to them were born three children, Alvin J., who died at the age of two years and is buried in the Friends burying ground at Zanesfield; Carrie V., now the wife of James M. SUTTON; and Anna A., who died in 1881 at the age of 19 years. He survived his wife a years. [seven years] ... His funeral took place fro the Friends meeting house 8th month 8th, at 3 o'clock p.m. and laid to rest in the Friend's burying ground.

Harpers Ferry Sentinel of last week: Capt. John W. DOLL, the mayor of this place was taken sick last week with blood poisoning. On Sunday the end came about midnight. A number of years ago he was a popular conductor on the B. & O., afterwards he became the proprietor of the Hotel Conner. He was about 46 years of age.

Friday, 7 September 1894   Vol. XVII, No. 19

Philomont: Mr. Gilmore FURR of Bloomfield, Va was laid to rest a few days since. He lived to advance age. He was a member of Ebenezer Baptist church, Dr. I. B. LAKE his pastor preached his funeral.

Friday, 14 September 1894   Vol. XVII, No. 20

Among the marriage licenses issued in Washington Tuesday, was one to S. H. PEARSON and Mattie V. SILCOTT, both of Loudoun.

Charles E. BUCKNER and Miss Marie, daughter of Mr. William H. ROBINSON, were married by Rev. G. T. TYLER at the home of the bride's father near Paris, Wednesday morning, 5th instant.

County Ct.: Wills of Wm. G. FURR and Parmelia Ann PHILLIPS, admitted to probate. A. B. CHAMBLIN qualified as Exor. of Wm. G. FURR dec'd. B. F. PHILLIPS qualified as Admr. of Parmelia Ann PHILLIPS dec'd. Jno. W. GARRETT qualified as Admr. of Jno. CORNELL dec'd. Samuel JENKINS Jr. qualified as Admr. of Samuel JENKINS dec'd. Jos. A. DILLON qualified as Admr. of Ridley JOHNSON dec'd. Jos. S. HOUSE qualified as Admr. of Geo. F. COOPER dec'd. Estate of Mary E. HAMMERLY dec'd committed to Sheriff.

Wm. MEAD, son of the late Jos. MEAD, of this county, and a brother of Mrs. N. HEAD, died at his home in Bedford Co., Va, on Saturday, Sept. 1st, 1894. Mr. MEAD was in the 59th year of his age.

[*Berwick (Pa) Independent*] Wedding performed in Jane St. Methodist Church of New York was that in which Rev. Albert H. SMITH of the Berwick Baptist Church and Miss Minnie Adele CHAMBERLAIN, concert soloist of that city were made one. ...
Mrs. Jane POWELL, widow of the late Walter POWELL and mother of Mr. J. H. POWELL, died at her home at Fairfax C. H., on Sunday last, after a short illness of paralysis, aged 74 years. Mrs. POWELL was a Miss ROBERDEAU.

Friday, 21 September 1894   Vol. XVII, No. 21

A pretty home wedding took place yesterday (Wednesday) afternoon at the residence of Mr. and Mrs. J. D. SAUNDERS about 1 miles west of Leesburg, their daughter Lillie to Mr. Edward HULLER, of this town, by Rev. J. W. GRUBB, of the M. E. Church, South. Mr. Harry NORRIS and Mr. Ed. LAYCOCK were the only attendants. They will make their home in this town, where Mr. HULLER is manager for Mr. C. R. LOWENBACH.
Married: At Faith Chapel, Loudoun Co., by Rev. E. L. WILSON, Harvey A. TRITTAPOE and Miss Hatty E. UMBAUGH, Sept. 12th, all of Loudoun.

Friday, 28 September 1894   Vol. XVII, No. 22

Judge Thomas SMITH, of New Mexico, a son of the late ex-Gov. William SMITH, and Miss Lizzie GAINES, are to be married at Warrenton next month.
Marriage licenses were issued in Washington to Alder S. COOK and Carrie V. GORDING, both of Loudoun county; Silas E. ANDERSON and Pearl E. LOMAX, both of Fairfax County.
Charles PAXSON, son of Saml. PAXSON, died at Falls Church, last Monday morning, after a short illness of brain fever. The remains of the deceased were interred at Leesburg on Tuesday.
Maryland: The weddings of Frederick REYNOLDS of Washington and Miss Jessie Brooke STABLER of Sharon and Thomas Janney BROWN of Washington to Miss Elsie PALMER of Meadowbrooke will both occur in October.

Friday, 5 October 1894   Vol. XVII, No. 23

Cards are out for the marriage of Thomas Janney BROWN to Miss Elsie PALMER, daughter of Mr. and Mrs. Edward L. PALMER, of Baltimore, which is to take place in First Independent Christ Church, in that city on the 16th inst. at 6 p.m.
Mrs. HARDING, the mother of Mr. H. C. HARDING, of Farmwell, died last Friday and her remains were interred in Union Cemetery on Sunday.
Joshua GORE, son of Solomon and Rachel GORE, died at Hillsboro, Ohio, Friday September 14th, in the 89th year of his age.

Mrs. M. S. BISPHAM died on Sunday at her home in Fauquier County, near Remington.
The marriage of Miss Garnet PENDLETON, of Fauquier,, and Mr. Wm. WIRT, of Westmoreland county, took place in the Episcopal Church at Warrenton today.
Married: By the Rev. Geo. L. BITZER, September 26th, 1894 at the Manse, Leesburg, Mr. Edgar E. RUSK and Miss Mary E. VANSICKLER.
Married: On September 25, 1894, in Cumberland City, Md, by Rev. S. SHANNON, Pastor of Kingsley M. E. Church, Walter L. FURR, of Leesburg, and Lidie BIXLER, of Pittsburg, Pa.
Died: At his home in Snickersville, on September 14, 1894, Capt. Ashford WEADON, in the 82nd year of his age.

Friday, 12 October 1894   Vol. XVII, No. 24

A dispatch from Clarke county to the Richmond Dispatch, of the 6th inst. says that the friends of Miss Lee GIBSON, niece of Mr. H. C. GIBSON, of Loudoun, were surprised to hear of her marriage on Wednesday, 3d inst., in Washington, to Mr. B. T. MORTON, also of Clarke county. They will locate in Texas.
Mr. Richard A. VIRTS, formerly of Loudoun, died at his home in Brunswick, Md, in Thursday of last week, from an overdose of morphine taken to allay the pain caused by being bitten by a spider. Mr. VIRTS was about 28 years of age and leaves a wife and one child. His remains were buried at Rehoboth church.
Mrs. Susan WIGHTMAN, wife of Mr. A. J. WIGH[T]MAN, died at the residence of her son-in-law, Mr. John W. PUMPHEY, near Rockville on Oct. 1st, 1894, aged 55y 6m, after a long illness. The remains were taken to Loudoun County for burial.
Mrs. Amanda KELLY died at the home of her daughter, Mrs. Adelaide WALLACE, in this town, last Thursday night in the 76th year of her age. Her remains were interred in Union Cemetery Saturday afternoon, Rev. J. W. GRUBB, officiating.
County Ct.: Will of Octavia WYNKOOP dec'd admitted to probate. W. A. JOHNSON qualified as Admr. of W. W. JOHNSON dec'd. F. G. WELSH qualified as Admr. of Howard WELSH dec'd. Estates of Laura HARMON, John HAMMERLY and George NEWLON committed to Sheriff.
Miss Cora C. WRIGHT died early Monday morning at the residence of her mother, in Richmond of typhoid fever, making the third death in the family and house within a week from the same disease and the fourth within a few months.
Mr. W. S. EMBREY an aged citizen of Stafford died Tuesday morning at his home in that County, about 80 years old.

Friday, 19 October 1894   Vol. XVII, No. 25

Last Wednesday evening a dwelling house, the old home place of Messrs. Ras. and Jack MILBURN, on the mountain east of town was destroyed by fire and with it was burned a little colored girl, aged about four year, a child of Herbert COLE.

County Ct.: E. W. BIRKBY qualified as Admr. of John J. RATHIE dec'd.

Married: On the 3d of Oct. 1894, by the Rev. G. POPKINS, Miss Lula O. SLOPER to Mr. W. W. WILSON, all of Loudoun.

Died: At her home near Adamsville, Muskingum county, Ohio, October 2nd, Mrs. Hannah James COCHRAN, in her 75th year. A native of Loudoun county, and a sister of Messrs. Mason and Craven JAMES.

Friday, 26 October 1894   Vol. XVII, No. 26

Mr. H. Garland SKINKER of Middleburg and Miss Anna Lee RUCKER were married last week at the home of the bride's father, Mr. W. A. RUCKER, near Delaplane. Rev. Dr. I. B. LAKE performed the ceremony.

Married on Tuesday Oct. 11, at the Reformed parsonage, Frederick, Md, James Janney ORRISON and Clara Janette STOUTSBARGER, both of Loudoun County. The Rev. Dr. D. R. ESCHBACH officiated.

Friday, 2 November 1894   Vol. XVII, No. 27

Mr. Steve REED died at his home near Snickersville one day last week.

Mr. James HANVEY died of consumption at his home in Waterford last Friday evening about 4 o'clock.

Mr. Jacob HUMMEL died at his home in Bloomfield, Loudoun County, last week in about the 70th year of his age.

Mrs. ___ VANDEVANTER, widow of the late Gabriel VANDEVANTER, died at the home of her son, Mr. T. H. VANDEVANTER, near Waterford, Wednesday evening, aged 81 years. Her remains will be interred at Leesburg today at 12 o'clock.

The Washington News announced the death Wednesday morning of Mrs. Emma GOODRICH, wife of Mr. Earl S. GOODRICH, who spent several summers at the home of T. BROWN near Lincoln. The remains will be taken to Minneapolis, Minn, their former home, for interment.

Wilmer HAMPTON, of Round Hill, and Miss Belle HERRON, of this city were quietly married at the parsonage of Calvary Church by the Rev. Dr. GREEN on October 23.

Mr. Amos B. SLAYMAKER Sr. died at his home in Alexandria City, Tuesday afternoon, at an advanced age. The death resulted from blood poison. He was a former resident of this town where he at one time was engaged in business with Geo. W. JANNEY.

Tacy M. JEWETT, wife of Joseph H. JEWETT died at "Ingledew" their home in Lincoln, on last Sabbath morning, the 28th, in the 75th year of her age. Her funeral took place from the Friends Meeting House on third day, 30th, at 1 p.m.

Mrs. CULLEN, widow of the late Thomas CULLEN dec'd. sold her personal effects on Wednesday of last week and has gone to Baltimore to reside with her daughter.

Friday, 9 November 1894   Vol. XVII, No. 28

Marriage licenses were issued in Washington, Wednesday, to the following Loudouners: William SIMMS and Ida CRAVEN, Ethan R. McDONALD and Annie F. HAWES.

Mrs. Margaret EASTER, the well known author and poetess, died in Richmond on the 29th ult. Mrs. EASTER was a daughter of the late Danl. EASTER, who was born and reared in Loudoun county.

Rev. Dr. Saml. RODGERS, minister of the M. E. Church South, died at his residence in Baltimore last Thursday in the 70th year of his age. He was once pastor of the Leesburg Methodist Church.

Thursday morning last, in the presence of the members of the families of the contracting parties, Mr. Adin LAYCOCK, of the firm of Wildman & Co. and Miss Carrie McCABE, were united in marriage at the home of the bride's mother, Mrs. Amanda McCABE in this town. Rev. I. W. CANTER of Washington, assisted by Rev. J. W. GRUBB, performed the ceremony.

Philomont, Nov. 6 – Today at high noon at the village church the marriage of Miss Flora, daughter of Maj. Jno. CHAMBLIN to Mr. Wm. CHAMBLIN, a popular merchant of Bloomfield. Rev. Mr. TYLER officiating.

Mr. Silas KIDWELL died of consumption at his home near Fairfax Station on Saturday. He was about 45 years old.

Mr. Walters THOMPSON of Fairfax county, died at his home near Hunter's Mill on the 19th ultimo of paralysis. He was about 69 years old.

In Fauquier county, Wednesday, while Mrs. Wm. HART was riding from her home near Waterloo to a neighbor's, she was killed by a falling tree.

Friday, 16 November 1894   Vol. XVII, No. 29

Mr. Joel CRAVEN, of Washington city, a brother of Guilford CRAVEN, of Loudoun, is afflicted with a carbuncle on the back of his neck, which has developed what is believed to be a fatal case of blood poisoning.

R. H. HOSKINSON has a bran[d] new baby at his house – a boy.

Ditto T. L. RIDGFWAY – another boy.

County Ct.: Wills of Mary A. M. CURRELL and Mrs. Jane Cecelia VANDEVANTER admitted to probate. W. N. TIFFANY and Chas. B. MATHEWS qualified as Exors. of Mary A. M. CURRELL dec'd. T. H. and D. H. VANDEVANTER qualified as Exors. of Mrs. Cecelia

VANDEVANTER dec'd. Naturalization papers issued to Jno. D. LAMOTHE, a native of the Isle of Man, England. and he authorized to celebrate the rites of matrimony under the laws of this state.

Died: On the 12th inst. at the home of her daughter near Lovettsville, Sarah Ann SCHOOLEY, wife of the late Jonas P. SCHOOLEY, in the 86th year of his [her] age. Her remains were interred in the Lutheran Cemetery with the services of the Episcopal Church.

Died: On Saturday Oct. 13th, 1894, at his residence at George's Mill, William H. WRIGHT, in the 52 year of his age.

Married: On Wednesday, Nov. 7, 1894, by the Rev. Pascal HARROWER at the Church of the Ascension, West Brighton, Staten Island, Frances H. DeLANCEY to Archibald B. CASTLE, both of Leesburg.

Married: On the 29th of Oct., near Waterford, Miss Mollie JACOBS to Mr. Thomas GHEEN, by the Rev. G. W. POPKINS, all of Loudoun.

Married: On the 7th of Nov. 1894, Miss Sarah E. MADDOX to Mr. Philip A. HOWSER, by the Rev. G. W. POPKINS, all of Loudoun.

Col. John A. McCAULL, of opera fame died suddenly last Sunday at the home of his sister in Greensborough, N.C. Col. McCAULL was a brother of Capt. P. H. McCAULL, republican candidate in this district.

Friday, 23 November 1894   Vol. XVII, No. 30

Mrs. E. E. CHILDS died at her home in Harpers Ferry last Saturday.

Miss FOWLER, of 1338 Thirteenth St. has issued invitations for the marriage reception of her sister, Carrie Edith, and Mr. Lloyd SLACK, of Leesburg, on Wednesday evening, Nov. 21st, from 8 to 10 o'clock. The ceremony will be witnessed only by the immediate relatives.

Mr. Zenis MILBURN died last Sunday night, at his home about two miles south of Leesburg, aged 73 years. He died from the effects of cancer on his right breast. Upon the breaking out of the late war, Mr. M. joined Company A 8th Va Regiment, and was severely wounded at the battle of Ball's Bluff. He was a member of the M. E. Church South. He leaves a widow. On Tuesday his remains were interred beside those of his ancestors in the Grove Church burying ground, Rev. Dr. HOUGH officiating.

Neersville: Surprise birthday party for Mr. John GRUBB last Wednesday, for his 79th birthday.

Dr. John William SMITH, of Baltimore, formerly of Loudoun county, was married last Friday evening to Miss Annetta SCHOTT, at the First Methodist church of that city, performed by Rev. Dr. T. P. FROST. Father Mr. Simon P. SCHOTT gave her away. Miss Mamie C. SCHOTT, sister of the bride was maide of honor. They will live at 712 North Eutaw street on their return.

Married: Nov. 6th at Leesburg by Rev. J. T. BARBER, Mr. Lewis E. SHUGARS to Miss Annie V. ATHEY.

Married: On Nov. 14th at Anson M. E. Church, South, by Rev. C. B. SUTTON, Miss Minnie M. DAVIS and Mr. Milton E. THOMAS, all of Fairfax County.

Friday, 30 November 1894   Vol. XVII, No. 31

[*Zanesville Ohio Courier*, Nov. 21 – set free by his master he made a bold effort to carry away his slave wife] N. T. GANT – In 1822, on the 10th of May, he first saw the light of day on a plantation at Leesburg, Va. As he reached manhood the fine lineaments of his face, remarkable intelligence and close resemblance to caucasion features indicated white blood. It was not until Mr. GANT had been freed from slavery that his mother told him the truth. Identity of his father – Rev. Stephen J. RUSSELL, one of the greatest Methodist divines of the day and who at Baltimore during the war, made a memorable address. After Mr. GANT became rich his mother urged him to take the name of RUSSELL, but he refused. It was in 1844, that John NIXON, a rich slave owner of Leesburg, died leaving a will by the terms of which his slaves were freed and given sufficient money to transport them to a free state. N. T. GANT was among them. He married a beautiful young mulatto, the property of Miss C. A., but better known as "Miss Jane" RUSSELL, a spinster of old southern customs. When freed, the southern law prevented him from remaining near his wife. An agreement was entered that six weeks at 9 o'clock from the parting day, they should meet in an old stable on the Russell plantation. He came to Ohio, but returned in six weeks. They planned an escape, which included a counterfeit certificate of freedom for his wife. They left for Washington DC to stop with a support of the underground railroad, but when they arrived they found the supporter had been arrested. They confronted officers and the wife's papers would thought to be forged and both were thrown in jail. Miss RUSSELL arrived to take back her property and secured extradition papers to bring GANT to Virginia to make an example of him. Quaker Thomas NICHOLS gave Nelson money in jail and hired John JANNEY to take his case. The Quakers furnished $975 for Gant to purchase his wife. They returned to Zanesville and years later had a large amount of real estate and was worth $150,000 to $200,000. His son, N. T. GANT Jr. is a graduate of Oberlin college. The subject of this sketch is over 6' tall, 200 lbs. and uses very good English. [very long article]

Mrs. RUSE, an aged lady of Lovettsville, died last Sunday night, at the residence of her son, Joseph RUSE, aged 93 years. Interment at the Union cemetery, on Tuesday.

Mrs. Hannah NICHOLS, relict of the late Samuel NICHOLS, died at her home near Silcott Springs, on Tuesday, 20th inst., in her 79th year.

Mr. Milton W. CARPENTER and Miss Kate ANDERSON were married at Ebenezer Church, Wednesday evening, Rev. I. B. LAKE officiating.

Last Saturday evening, as two sons of Mr. Joseph LACY, who live near Bloomfield, were driving from home to the village their horse ran away throwing them out of the buggy. The older one, aged about 12 years died the next morning. The other lad, about 11 years old, was not seriously hurt. The funeral of the lad that was killed took place on Wednesday. Interment at Ebenezer.

Col. "Lige" WHITE married in Pennsylvania on Wednesday evening to Miss Margaret BAYNE.

Mr. Samuel H. PRICE, grandfather of Mr. Floyd PRICE, of this town, died recently at his house at Alma, Page county, Va, in the 82nd year of his age.

Died: Miss Mary Elizabeth MINOR, near Taylortown, Nov. 18th 1894, in the 62d year of her age.

Died: Mrs. Hannah JENKINS, daughter of the late Joseph L. WORTHINGTON, and widow of the late Norval JENKINS, at her home near Hillsboro, on Monday morning, Nov. 19th, at 4 o'clock, in the 47th year of her age.

Miss Hattie TODD, formerly of Manasses died at the home of her brother in New Jersey recently.

Mrs. Jane DULANY, living near Thoroughfare, died on Sunday morning, November 18, after a short illness from typhoid fever.

Friday, 7 December 1894   Vol. XVII, No. 32

Mr. W. S. KAHLE, formerly a resident of our town, died at his home in Middletown, Md, on the 23rd ult. in the 62nd year of his age. Mr. C. V. ANDERS, his nephew, of Hamilton, accompanied by his mother, attended the funeral, and remained in Maryland several days.

Marriage licenses were issued in Washington yesterday to Jacob B. CARSON and Nannie J. FILLER and William ROBINSON and Annie COOK all of Loudoun county, the latter couple from Round Hill.

Mrs. Elizabeth GRIMES, wife of Geo. W. GRIMES, died at her husband's residence in this town, about 2 o'clock last Thursday morning, Nov. 29th 1894, in the 38th year of her age. She had been in bad health for the past four or five years. Her funeral took place last Sunday afternoon from the Baptist church, Rev. J. T. BARBER, officiating. Interment was in Union Cemetery.

Marriage license was issued in Washington on Monday to Charles MERCHANT and Mamie BERRY, of Loudoun county.

Mr. John Q. JANNEY, aged 95 years, son of the late Amos and Mary Ann JANNEY, of Loudoun county, died in Baltimore last Friday.

Marriage license was issued in Washington last week to Geo. W. MILLS and Rosa V. WILLIAMS, of Loudoun Co.

Friday, 14 December 1894   Vol. XVII, No. 33

A report received yesterday that a young man named LICKY, living at what is known as Licky's Mill, was found dead in a field Wednesday morning. He left home in the evening and it is supposed death was cause by exposure to the cold rainstorm that prevailed throughout the night.

On Wednesday Mr. Will WELSH and Miss Nellie PAXSON were united in marriage, by Elder J. N. BADGER, at the home of the bride's father, Mr. S. B. PAXSON, near Hughesville.

Died: Aaron BEANS at his home in Cardington, Ohio, aged 70y 10m and _d. The deceased had been for fifty years or more, a resident of Waterford. In August 1881 he moved to New Straitsville, Perry Co., O., where he spent about 8 years of his life.

At high noon yesterday (Wednesday), Mr. Edward H. TRUNDLE, of Washington and Miss Mattie C. ELGIN, daughter of Mr. Thos. G. ELGIN, of this county, were united in marriage, at Sycolin M. E. Church, Rev. Dr. N. HEAD officiating. Miss Mamie ELGIN, sister of bride, was maid of honor and Mr. H. H. TRUNDLE, brother of the groom, was best man, and Messrs John SHUMATE and Howard ELGIN acted as ushers. They will make their home in Washington, where the groom is engaged in business.

A pretty wedding took place at the residence of Mr. and Mrs. J. V. QUICK, near Farmwell, Dec. 5, the contracting parties being their daughter, Sallie E. and Mr. R. L. ASKINS, of Washington. The bride was attired in dove-colored silk, trimmed with duchess lace, which was worn by her mother at her marriage 25 years ago. She carried a bouquet of Marchal Neil roses tied with white ribbon. The bridesmade, Miss A. RUPPERT, of Washington, carried LaFrance roses. The best man was W. V. QUICK, brother of the bride. They will make their home in Washington.

Friday, 21 December 1894   Vol. XVII, No. 34

North Fork: Cora, the infant daughter of C. W. SCHOOLEY, died very suddenly last Friday morning. Her remains were buried in Lake View Cemetery, at Hamilton, on Sunday.

North Fork: Leven POWELL, quite an aged man, who has been living with Mr. W. L. POWELL, for several years, was buried at "Llangollen" near Upperville, Saturday last.

The late Margaret E. MITCHELL's will, recorded in Washington recently, bequeaths to a widower, R. Fairfax MITCHEL, all the estate, which includes a house and lot at Round Hill.

Mr. Israel MYERS and Miss Helen JONES of our town Wednesday afternoon walked up to the Parsonage and had Dr. HOUGH unite them in matrimony, then strolled on to Mr. MYERS' dwelling in the west end of town.

The nuptial ceremony of Mr. Harry PEARCE and Miss Mary H. GORE was celebrated in Raymore, Missouri, at 12 M. Tuesday last, October 30th. The bride is a daughter of the late Amos GORE, of McArthur Township. They will be at home, No. 211 N-Detroit Street.

Died: Little Cora Mildred, infant daughter of C. W. and Emma SCHOOLEY, died at the home of her parents, at North Fork, aged 1y 22d.

Married: On the 28th of Nov. 1894, by Rev. J. W. GRUBB, Mr. Joseph E. MOFFETT and Florence A. MYERS, all of Loudoun.

Married: At Waterford, Dec. 19th, by Rev. E. L. WILSON, John W. VIRTS and Miss Emily J. CORBIN, all of Loudoun County.

Married: At noon on Wednesday, Dec. 19th, Mr. J. F. BRAWNER, of Aldie, and Miss S. Edmonia EDWARDS, at the bride's home in Leesburg. Rev. A. L. EDWARDS, uncle of the bride, performed the ceremony, assisted by Rev. Nelson HEAD, D.D.

Friday, 4 January 1895   Vol. XVII, No. 35

A telegram received by his mother, at Waterford, on Christmas day, announced the sudden death of Dr. PHILLIPS, at his home in Stockton, California. He leave a wife, but no children.

Sam RUSTIN, an aged negro preacher, died on day last week, at his home in Broad Run district.

Mr. Philip SOUDER died at his home very unexpectedly on Christmas day. He was about seventy-five years old.

William MYERS, son of Thos. MYERS, of Hughesville, died last Saturday morning, aged 28 years, and on Sunday afternoon his remains were interred in Lake View Cemetery, in Hamilton. Leaves a wife (daughter of R. W. THOMAS, of our town) and 2 little children.

Wedding of Mr. Edgar H. HIRST, of Purcellville, and Miss Daisy D. BROWN, of Ohio, at the home of her uncle, Mr. J. W. GARRETT, near Philomont, Thursday Dec. 20th 1894, at 9 a.m. Messrs. Will WHITE and Howard NICHOLS were the ushers. Elder Jos. N. BADGER of Aldie tied the nuptial knot. The bride was attired in a lovely travelling suit of dark blue.

Married: On December 18th, '94, by Rev. E. H. SWEM, R. Berry SWEET, of Washington, to Miss Ida V. ATTWELL, of Leesburg.

Died: At his home in Stockton, Cal., on the morning of 12 mo. 25th 1894, Dr. Thomas PHILLIP, in the 46th year of his age.

Philip SOUDER died very suddenly at his home in Lovettsville, on Christmas day. Heart failure was the cause. His remains were interred in the Union Cemetery, on the 27th inst.

Bolington: The infant son of R. H. HOSKINSON died last Sunday at 1 o'clock, aged 2 months. Interment at Hamilton yesterday.

Bolington: Miss Nannie VIRTS, of this vicinity, and Mr. Will. WILEY of Hillsboro, were united in holy wedlock, in Brunswick, on Thursday of last week.

Friday, 11 January 1895   Vol. XVII, No. 36

Died at her old home, Sunny Side, near Hillsboro, on the evening of January 3rd, 1895, Mary J. HOUSE, widow of the late E. C. H. HOUSE and daughter of Eli PIERPOINT, deceased. Born March 20th, 1826, in the vicinity in which she lived and died. A member of the Society of Friends from childhood.

Born to Mr. and Mrs. C. V. ANDERS, a son.

Mr. Austin ALLEN, formerly of our town, was married last Tuesday in Baltimore, to a Maryland lady whose name we have not learned.

Mrs. Julia BELL, wife of Mr. Albert BELL, died at her home, near Sterling Wednesday morning, aged 38 years. Her remains were interred at Arnold Grove, near Hillsboro, yesterday.

We learn of the death of John ALDRIDGE, which took place at his home, near Mt. Gilead, Wednesday night, about 9 o'clock, caused by congestion of the lungs. He was a member of the Baptist Church.

Wallace W. McDONOUGH, a stone-mason and brick-layer, died at his home in Leesburg last Friday morning, in his 47th year. He had been in failing health for the past year or two, a portion of the time confined to his bed. A widow and three children survive him.

The death of Caleb RUSSELL Jr. occurred in Chicago on the last day (Monday) of the old year. He had been afflicted with some bowel trouble which was aggravated by a cold contracted by exposure while acting as auctioneer at a public sale. The body was taken to his home in Iowa and laid to rest in the graveyard of Prairie Grove Meeting of Friends of which he was a member. His father, Caleb RUSSELL Sr. lived at what was then known as Purcell's Factory and there the son grew up to early manhood, when the father took his family and removed to Iowa, and the son remained. His wife, daughter of the late John FENTON and niece of Enoch FENTON of our county, was also from Loudoun, she with two daughters and two sons survive.

Died: On Friday morning, Jan. 4th, Welby Euglan, aged 4m 16d, only son of Laura and Albert E. GRAY.

Herndon: Mrs. Joseph M. RIDEOUT, on New Years morning, presented her husband with a fine boy. Miss Etta, the youngest daughter of Mr. Isaiah BREADY, died on the 23 ult. She had been sick nearly a year. Miss Edith an older sister, was also unwell but improving.

Obituary: George W. TAVENNER was born January 30, 1815, in Loudoun County. He was married in 1839 to Miss Juliet GALLOWAY, of Washington DC. They were blessed with thirteen children of whom eleven – 6 daughters and 5 sons, are living. Mr. TAVENNER came to this county in early 1841 and was a well known citizen in Vienna, until he removed to Laganda, about 15 years since. He was a butcher by trade. Some 19 years ago he lost his wife by death, and on October 23d, 1882, he was married to Miss

Cora RUSE of Hamilton, VA, who survives him. Eight weeks ago he stepped on a rusty nail, from which blood poisoning resulted and he died Nov. 30, 1894, aged 79y 10m. Mr. TAVENNER's funeral was held at the Lagonda U. B. Church, on Sunday morning. The remains were interred at Vienna. *Lagonda Ohio Paper.*

Peter COOPER and Miss Clara CASE were quietly married at the M. E. Parsonage, at Hillsboro, last Monday, Rev. J. P. FELTER officiating.

Mr. WILEY and Miss VIRTS married in Brunswick, last weeks report was incorrect. They were marred at the Lutheran Church, Rev. McLINN officiating.

In memoriam: On Dec. 12, 1894, at the residence of Samuel WRIGHT, Mrs. Emeline ARNOLD in the 77 years of her age. The last 11 years she could neither walk or stand upon her feet. She has gone to join the husband who preceded ?? years ago (at the age of 33 years) and five children, leaving but one daughter the wife of S. J. WRIGHT. She is buried in the Lutheran Cemetery on Thursday the 13th, just one week from her birthday when she would have been 7? years of age. [crease in paper]

Married: At Mt. Hope Baptist Church, Dec. 26th, 1894, Miss Emma V. LANHAM to Mr. Clinton I. COSTELLO, by the Rev. G. W. POPKINS, all of Loudoun.

Married: At the bride's residence on Christmas day, by the Rev. Geo. L. BITZER, John T. MORAN to Miss Minnie [? creased] E. CROSIN.

Married: Dec. 27, at the home of Mrs. EMMEUR, Washington DC, by Rev. J. MUIR, of the E street Baptist Church, Mr. Eugene BROWN, of North Fork, Va, and Miss Hattie COOK, of Warrenton.

Friday, 18 January 1895   Vol. XVII, No. 37

A marriage license was issued in Washington on Tuesday to Frederick C. G. PRATT, of London, England and Maggie R. ASHBY, of Loudoun county.

Miss Mary WARNER died at her home In Hamilton, Tuesday morning, and on Wednesday her body was laid to rest in the burying ground of the Methodist church, which she was a member. She was about 32 years of age.

In Ct.: Wills of Wm. H. WRIGHT, Craven JAMES, V. C. SAUNDERS, Wm. OSBURN and Samuel RUSTIN (col.) were admitted to probate. Laura G. WRIGHT qualified as Executrix of Wm. H. WRIGHT dec'd. T. B. JAMES and W. M. JAMES qualified as Executors of Craven JAMES dec'd. Henry SAUNDERS and Wm. H. SAUNDERS qualified as Executors of V. C. SAUNDERS dec'd. Jesse MOTEN qualified as Executor of Samuel RUSTIN dec'd. Jos. C. SOUDER qualified as Admr. of Geo. P. SOUDER dec'd. Court appointed H. H. RUSSELL Sheriff Admr. of Jonathan KEEN dec'd. Jos. M. DAVIS qualified as guardian of Mary G. and Annie E. BODMER.

Hon. C. E. NICHOL, who succeeds Judge KEITH in the 11th Judicial District, will hold court in Loudoun commencing the 21st inst. Judge NIC[H]OL was born in Brentsville, Prince William Co. on Feb. 22, 1854.

Married: On the 9th of January 1895, at her father's residence, near Oatlands, Miss Cassandra A. NIXON to Mr. Virgil C. SILMON, by the Rev. G. W. POPKINS, all of Loudoun.

Died: Near Purcellville, Jan. 7th 1895, Troy, youngest son of W. H. and Mary L. HUNT, aged 18m 4d.

Friday, 25 January 1895   Vol. XVII, No. 38

Dennis FENTON, of Clarke County, who was a contractor on the Gunpowder Water Works, Baltimore, died last week.

Co Ct.: Wills of Phoebe YOUNG and Elizabeth J. WHITE admitted to probate. Charles P. JANNEY qualified as Exor. of Elizabeth J. WHITE dec'd.

John Armstead CARTER died at his home near Unison last Saturday, aged 87 years. Mr. CARTER was well known in this county, which for some time he represented in the state Legislature. He was a member of the M. E. Church South.

Samuel CROCKETT died at his home, near our town, last Monday evening. He was about 95 years old. His body was taken to Baltimore on Wednesday and interred by the side of his wife who preceded him about 20 years. The deceased came to this country from Ireland when a young man and located in the vicinity of Baltimore where he engaged in contract work on public improvements. He subsequently located in Virginia, securing a contract on the proposed Loudoun & Hampshire railroad between Hamilton and Lincoln and located his family near the latter village. During the war he was loyal to the Union. He leaves seven children – 3 sons and 4 daughters.

We announce the death of S. Townsend TAYLOR, at his home, in Purcellville, about 11 a.m., Wednesday. He was taken sick on Sunday with pleurisy, but the immediate cause of death was through to be heart disease. His funeral will take place today, Friday at 1 p.m. He was a member of the Society of Friends, in the 50th year of his age.

Mountsville, Jan. 22, '95: We announce the death of John L. TRENARY, of Middleburg.

Fred ROBINSON, a retired hotel keeper of Point of Rocks, died very suddenly while sitting in a chair on Saturday last. He leaves a wife, but no children.

Died: In Greeley, Co., Tuesday morning, Dec. 18th 1894 of typhoid fever and brain disease, William Butler HOLLAND, aged 5y 6m, son of Mrs. Sallie B. and late John R. HOLLAND.

Married: Jan. 19th '95, in St. James P. E. Church, New York City, by the Rev. Frank H. NELSON, Mr. Robert Chas. EICHBURG, of Alexandria, Va, to Miss Rosina Mason HEFLIN, of Leesburg.

Wanted: Information no matter how incomplete, tending to prove that the ancestors of some of the present BROWNs or their kinsmen, of Loudoun not only came from Bucks Co., Pa, but were there [they] related to Jacob BROWN, the Quaker Soldier. Address: W. B. CARR, Hamilton, Va. 12-21-4t

Friday, 1 February 1895   Vol. XVII, No. 39

Mr. John JONES, who lived near New Baltimore, died on Thursday last. A native of Philadelphia and came to Fauquier about 15 years ago.

Henry WIDENOR, aged 60 years, a former resident of this county [Fauquier] and who had recently made his home in Taylor County, Ia., died Jan. 11th.

Court of Appeals: Mrs. Annie, lately divorced from her husband, Mason THROCKMORTON, brought suit against him and certain of his creditors holding deeds of trust on his land. Bill was dismissed.

Friday, 8 February 1895   Vol. XVII, No. 40

Miss Inez WHITE, daughter of Col. E. V. WHITE will be married to Mr. John D. GOLD, of North Carolina, at her father's residence in town, on Wednesday, Feb. 13th.

Died: Thomas EVANS, at his home, near Unison, Jan. 12th 1895. He leaves a wife, daughter and several brothers to mourn his death.

Died: David YOUNG, at his home near Bloomfield, Jan. 15th. He was a very old man.

Died: Miss Dorcas COOKSEY, at her home near Leesburg, Jan. 22, 1895, in about the 22nd year of her age. Her remains were laid to rest Jan. 27th in Leesburg Cemetery. She leaves a mother and several brothers and sisters.

Julia BELL, wife of A. B. BELL, died at her home, Smith's Switch, Jan. 9th, 1894, in her 38th year. She leaves a husband and several children. Her remains were laid to rest in Arnold Grove Cemetery.

Died at his home in Hillsboro, on Feb. 1st, 1885, Thomas CAMP, in the 64th year of his age. Mr. CAMP was the son of Isaac CAMP, of this county. He was born on a farm belonging to his father near Hillsboro. In early life he married Mary Jane GRUBB, a daughter of Joseph GRUBB, and a sister of Rev. James GRUBB, of Leesburg. By her he leaves three children.

Mr. Thomas E. CAMP, of Hillsboro, died there yesterday (Friday) morning of heart trouble. He was about 60 years old.

Cards are out for the marriage of Miss Carrie Bryant TAVENNER, of our town, daughter of Mr. E. H. TAVENNER, to Mr. Harry BECKER, of Washington city, which will take place at St. Paul's P. E. Church, Hamilton, next Tuesday at 12 o'clock.

Mr. G. D. HULFISH died at his home, at Silcott Springs Wednesday morning. For some time he was under treatment at Johns Hopkins Hospital.

William BROWN, son of the late Rev. Saml. BROWN, died at the home of his mother, at Farmwell, last Sunday, and on Tuesday his body was interred in the burying ground of the M. E. Church South, in Hamilton. The immediate cause of his death was Bright's disease.

Death of Miss Mollie CRIM, who departed this life at the residence of her brother Joseph CRIM, at Wheatland, last Saturday night, at 10 o'clock. She had been complaining for several days with brain fever. She leaves a father, mother, brothers and sisters. She was a member of the M. E. Church, at Rehoboth. The funeral services were conducted by her pastor, Rev. J. P. FELTNER.

Friday, 15 February 1895   Vol. XVII, No. 41

The social event of our town was the marriage of Miss Carrie Bryant TAVENNER, daughter of Mr. E. H. TAVENNER, to Mr. Harry BECKER, of Washington, which took place at the Episcopal Church, at noon last Monday. The bride was given away by her father and the ceremony of the Episcopal church was performed by Rev. LaMOTHE. Miss Maria TAVENNER, of Washington, was the bridesmaid and Mr. Leon DuFORTHE, of Baltimore was best man; and Messrs. Cloyd TAVENNER, of Washington and Edgar WILEY, of Hamilton, were ushers. The bride was becomingly attired in a travelling dress of French Phosphorous cloth.

At half past eleven yesterday (Wednesday) Feb. 13th 1895, a wedding took place at the residence of Col. E. V. WHITE in this town, the contracting parties being his daughter, Miss Inez, and Mr. Jno. D. GOLD, of Wilson, N. C. Elder E. V. WHITE, father of the bride was the officiating minister. Miss Mamie LEE, of Suffolk, Va was maid of honor, and Mr. Jos. M. GOLD, of Washington, brother of the groom, was best man. Messrs. Otis WILLIAMS, Eugene GIDDINGS, Ashton CLAPHAM and John H. NELSON, who acted as ushers. Mr. and Mrs. GOLD will make their home at Wilson, N. C. where the groom is engaged in the publication of *Zion's Landmark*, a paper of the Baptist denomination. The bride is the eldest daughter of Col. WHITE.

Joseph P. GRUBB died at his home near Hillsboro, on Saturday last, in the 87th year of his age. His wife died in 1889. They had five sons and three daughters, of whom the eldest son, Capt. Richard B. GRUBB was killed in the late war; and Samuel W. GRUBB has since died in Texas. Another son is the Rev. James W. GRUBB, the esteemed pastor of the M. E. Church, South, at Leesburg.

The burial was Sunday afternoon, of Mrs. CURRY, widow of the late John R. CURRY, of this town. The funeral took place from the

Presbyterian Church, where services were conducted by Rev. Geo. L. BITZER. The corpse was taken to Union Cemetery.

The wedding of Miss Adrienne Grey VIOLLAND and Mr. Byron J. KENYON took place Wednesday at the residence of the bride's parents, Maj. and Mrs. Eng L. VIOLLAND at Vienna Va.

Mrs. Frederick TERRETT died of apoplexy at her residence, near Fairfax Courthouse, Sunday morning, aged 70 years. Mrs. TERRETT was formerly a Miss STUART, of King George county.

Friday, 22 February 1895   Vol. XVII, No. 42

Rebecca BIRDSALL, widow of the late Benjamin BIRDSALL, was buried at Lincoln Tuesday afternoon. She was one of the oldest residents of the community. She leaves two daughters and two sons. She was a devoted member of the Society of Friends.

Mr. Chas. HOLLAND and Miss Mable JACKSON, both of this town, were married at the Presbyterian Manse on Tuesday evening last, Rev. G. L. BITZER officiating.

Marriage license was issued in Washington last week to Jas. MOORE, of Aldie, in this county, and Jennie BARRON, of Fauquier Co.

On Sunday, the 3rd of Feb. Rev. J. W. GRUBB buried his sister's husband, Mr. Thomas E. CAMP. On Saturday, Feb. 8th his father, Jos. P. GRUBB, died and the same day, the residence of Mr. GRUBB's mother-in-law, Mrs. NEALE, in Queen Anne county, Md, was totally destroyed by fire. Due to the impassable condition of the roads, Mr. G.'s father, who died on the 8th, could not be buried until Saturday last, the 16th.

William LAMBERT died on the 18th inst. at his home near Point of Rocks, Md, after several months illness. His granddaughter, Minnie, is lying dangerously ill, of brain fever.

A telegram was received on Tuesday, announcing the death of Mr. Mayo JANNEY of pneumonia, at his home in Washington.

Died: Mrs. Catherine HIBBS departed this life on Feb. 9th, '95, at her home near Evergreen Mills, Va. She was the mother-in-law of Thos. A. CARTER, She leaves several children. She was 73 years of age.

Friday, 1 March 1895   Vol. XVII, No. 43

Died: H. Clay OTLEY, at his residence near Philomont, on the 20th of Feb. 1895, in the 51st year of his age.

The remains of G. D. HULFISH who died at Silcott Springs on the 6th of Feb. on account of the severe storm was temporarily interred at his home, were finally laid to rest in Sharon Cemetery, Middleburg, on the 25th of Feb. He was in his 49th year. He leaves a wife and three children. He was a member of the Baptist Church for 27 years.

On Friday last, while Mr. BETTIS who lives on the farm of Mr. Wm. FLETCHER, near this place, was engaged in doing some work with his back to his daughter, she caught fire by a spark from a stove,

while asleep, for she was almost in a blaze when her father saw her and she was so badly burned that she died in a short while.
Philomont: Mr. H. Clay OTLEY died suddenly a few days since. He was thought to be improving, but was suddenly taken worse and died. His remains were buried at Lincoln on the 22d.

Friday, 8 March 1895   Vol. XVII, No. 44

Miss Ollie HALEY, a young lady of the Lincoln neighborhood is hopeless blind. At the time of the transit of Mercury last Autumn, she viewed that interesting spectacle through a piece of smoked glass, and when she awoke next morning she could not see. One of her eyes was removed in hope of saving the other but without avail and the other eye may have to be removed.

28th of Jan. 1895 was the occasion of the fiftieth anniversary of the marriage of Mr. Greenbery J. R. HOUSE, of Frederick Co., Md (brother of the late Eli C. H. HOUSE, of Loudoun) and Miss Mary M. GROVE, also of Frederick Co., Md. In 1845 they were united by Rev. A. P. FREEZE. Mr. M. J. GROVE, brother of the bride, read a poem. Mr. HOUSE is a retired farmer. His children are: Grove R., Franklin G. (County Commissioner of F___ Co.), Charles J., George C., Mrs. W. S. KEAFAUVER and Mrs. T. A. WILLARD. Mr. HOUSE was married at the age of 19 and his partner was in her 16th year. She was a daughter of the late Major G. W. GROVE, of Broad Run. The anniversary was celebrated on the same farm where the marriage took place 50 years ago. Their children all live within two miles of the farm.

Friday, 15 March 1895   Vol. XVII, No. 45

Mr. Romulous FERGUSON, father of Mr. George FERGUSON of this town, was paralyzed in his left side last Friday morning at his home near Aldie.

Lincoln: Mr. W. A. STROUD died Sunday morning near this place, after a brief illness.

Messrs. E. C. and C. R. SINE went to High View, W. Va. last week to attend the marriage of their brother, A. T. SINE of Springfield, Ohio to Miss Lillian B. KELSAN, of W. Va.

Co. Ct.: Wills of Samuel CROCKETT dec'd, Nancy DUNCAN dec'd, Jno. HIXSON dec'd, Catharine A. HIBBS dec'd, Sarah E. BENJAMIN dec'd, Mary C. HAYNES and Washington HAINES were admitted to probate. N. J. PURCELL, V. V. PURCELL and Logan OSBURN qualified as Exors. of Wm. OSBURN dec'd. Martha S. CROCKETT qualified as Executrix of Samuel CROCKETT dec'd. Geo. P. HUNTER qualified as Exor. of Nancy DUNCAN. K. B. COLE qualified as Executor of John HIXON. F. A. CARTER qualified as Exor. of Catharine A. HIBBS. C. C. GAVER qualified as Admr. of Sarah E. BENJAMIN. A. J. BRADFIELD qualified as Exor. of

The Telephone
Friday, 22 March 1895   Vol. XVII, No. 46

Washington HAINES. R. C. CRAVEN qualified as Admr. of Hannah CRAVEN. A. P. ALDRIDGE qualified as Admr. of John ALDRIDGE. Thos. E. LITTLE qualified as Admr. of Richard H. JONES. Estate of Stephen H. WILSON committed to Sheriff. Julia D. LITTLEJOHN qualified as Guardian of Forrest C. LITTLEJOHN, Paul V. LITTLEJOHN and Horace C. LITTLEJOHN. Jos. M. DAVIS qualified as guardian of Robt. R., Richard E. and Chas. C. SINCLAIR. Samuel J. BEATTY qualified as committee for Samuel SWANK. C. B. NORRIS qualified as guardian of Richard DAY. Jos. W. PAYNE qualified as Admr. of Lavinia FRAZIER.

Friday, 22 March 1895   Vol. XVII, No. 46

Married: On March 13, 1895, at the residence of the bride, Lenah, Va, by Rev. C. B. SUTTON, assisted by Rev. G. W. POPKINS, John H. BURTON, of Albemarle Co., Va and Miss Lottie R. SMITH, of Loudoun Co.

Mr. Henry C. LINDSEY, formerly of this county was run over and killed in the W. and O. railroad yard, at Alexandria, last Tuesday. Mr. LINDSEY was a native of Loudoun, 28 years of age and leaves a wife and three children. He was burned our a few weeks ago by the fire on North Patrick street.

Mrs. Eliza M. GIDDINGS, wife of Col. Wm. GIDDINGS, died at her home near Taylortown, last Sunday. She was about 70 years of age.

Mr. Presley EVANS died at the home of his niece, Miss Annie EVANS, in Hamilton last Sunday afternoon, aged nearly 80 years. He formerly resided in the Hillsborough neighborhood, but for some years he lived in Texas, where he was engaged in merchandising. His funeral took place on Tuesday at Arnold Grove near his old home.

Mrs. Jonah TAVENNER, who had been in ill health for a number of years, breathed her last on March 8th. She leaves a husband, two sons and a daughter.

Rehoboth Sunday School drafted a resolution of respect on the death of Mollie A. CRIM, who died February 2d, '95.

Mrs. Elizabeth ORRISON, widow of the late Arthur ORRISON dec'd, died after a lingering illness on Monday night last. Her remains will be laid to rest today, by the side of her husband, in Union Cemetery, near Lovettsville.

Death of Capt. James W. GRUBB, at Harpers Ferry, W. Va., March 7th. Capt. GRUBB belonged to the large family of that name in Loudoun. He was born about 1835, and was therefore about 60 years old. His boyhood was spent on a farm in Loudoun. He chose civil engineering as a profession and was engaged in that calling in 1861. He belonged to the 65th Va. militia, commanded by Col. Wm. GIDDINGS. When that regiment was called into the confederate service Grubb declined to follow and went to Maryland and enlisted in defense of the Stars and Stripes. He joined Co. A (Capt. VERNON) of Coles Md. Cav. After the Gettysburg campaign, July 1863, he obtained permission to recruit Co. C, for the Loudoun Rangers, and opened recruiting offices at Frederick Md. Upon the death of Capt. ANDERSON, in Nov. '63, Co's B and C were consolidated and Capt. GRUBB was elected Capt. On retiring of Capt. MEANS, in April 1864, Capt. GRUBB was the ranking officer, but waived his right to Capt. KEYES, Co. A. When the latter resigned on account of wounds, Capt. GRUBB commanded the battalion to the close of the war. After the war he settled in Bolivar and resumed his former profession as a surveyor. He was a republican in politics. In early life he married a Miss NEAR, who with three children survives him.

Mr. Robert Gray CAMPBELL, brother of Mr. Edgar LITTLETON, died in Louisville, Ky, on the 19th inst. of consumption, aged 49 years.

A marriage license was issued in Washington last week to T. Clayton ORRISON and Katie R. HILLERY, both of Lovettsville.

In the office of the Clerk of the County Court of Loudoun on Wednesday morning – the marriage of Chas. W. HILL, of Alleghany Co. Pa. and Miss Sarah E. CHAMBLIN, daughter of the late Ellzey CHAMBLIN, of Loudoun, Rev. Dr. HEAD performing the ceremony.

Friday, 29 March 1895   Vol. XVII, No. 47

Mr. Chas. MERCHANT, of Mt. Gilead, died Sunday morning, of old age, in his 97th year. Buried in North Fork burying ground Monday.

Charles MERCHANT, died at his home near Hughesville last Friday, in the 95th year of his age.

Wm. E. McPHERSON, a farmer residing about four miles east of Leesburg, died at his home last Sunday night, in the 68th year of his age. He was the father of James E. McPHERSON of this town.

On Thursday, March 7th, 1895, a wedding took place at the residence of Mr. P. MOSSBURG, of Maryland, the contracting parties being his daughter, Miss Josephene, and Mr. John C. HARVEY, of Virginia. Rev. DULANY and Mr. SMITH officiated. The bride was attired in a cream colored dress, trimmed in silk and satten, with gloves to match. The groom wore a full suit of black cloth.

Died: At the home of his grandfather, W. W. DIVINE, in Leesburg, at 3 o'clock a.m., on Friday, March 22d, 1865, of spasmodic croup, Joseph L., eldest child of Charles R. and Rata NORRIS, aged 3y 6m.

Friday, 5 April 1895   Vol. XVII, No. 48

Mrs. P. S. GOUCHNAUER died at her home in Upperville Tuesday.

Mr. R. O. HARRIS, died at his home in Purcellville, on the 1st inst. of consumption. He had been a sufferer for years. His remains were laid to rest in Short Hill burying ground on Wednesday.

Last Tuesday morning, without a word of warning, Mrs. Mary Ellen PUSEY died at her home near Hamilton. She arose in usual health that morning, about 10 o'clock her brother Hugh R. HOLMES noticed that her step was not steady and she could speak only a guttural sound. At 4:30 p.m. she died. On 24th of next September she would have been 71 years old. In 1867 she married the late Joshua PUSEY and lived at "Glenellen," near Waterford. She held his children in regard. The funeral took place Thursday morning, interment in the burying ground at Lincoln of the Society of Friends of which she was a member.

Friday, 12 April 1895 Vol. XVII, No. 49

April Ct.: Wills of Elizabeth JANNEY, Louisa BURGESS and Wm. A. STROUD admitted to probate. Phineas JANNEY, Samuel M. JANNEY Jr. qualified as Exors. of Elizabeth JANNEY dec'd. Estate of John R. McNEALA dec'd committed to Sheriff. Mary E. STEVENS qualified as Admx. of Louisa VINCEL dec'd. Jas. W. FURGUSON qualified as Admr. of Romulus FURGUSON dec'd. H. H. RUSSELL, Sheriff, appointed curator of the estate of Lavinia M. DODD dec'd.

Passed from life temporal to life eternal, April 2d, 1895, Mrs. Mary E. PUSEY, aged 70 years. ...

North Fork, April 11th – Mr. Wm. WEADON died Friday night. He was buried at the North Fork burying grounds, on Sunday last. He was 84 years old.

Suicide on Wednesday last, Mrs. DUNN, widow of the late Jno. DUNN, hung herself with a rope fastened to the rafters of the house, by getting on a chair and jumping off. Mrs. DUNN was about 65 years old and had been married twice, both husbands being dead. Her son, aged about 30 years (only survivor of her family) with whom she has been living was carrying in wood at the time of the sad event, thus being in the house at intervals. She had been in poor health. She was a member of the Catholic church, by which she was buried at Middleburg on Saturday.

Mr. Absolam RILEY died at his home near Harpers Ferry, on Saturday morning April 6th, of cancer. He had been a sufferer for years. His remains were buried at Ebenezer church, Sunday afternoon last. Age about 72 years.

Friday, 19 April 1895 Vol. XVII, No. 50

In memory of Francis B., son of James and Frances A. HENDERSON, of Lincoln, Va, departed this life in Beseon?, Mass., Nov. 9th 1894.

Alexander MURRAY, who lived on a farm near Goose Creek, went to Leesburg on Sunday and attended church, after which he went to the home of Mrs. DAVIS to dinner, While quietly sitting in a chair, the fatal numbness of paralysis effected his left side and extended to the right and on the following day he died.

Prof. Lawrence RUST, eldest son of the late Col. A. T. M. RUST, of this county, died at his home, near Gambier, Ohio, on Monday last. He had been in bad health for several years and his death was not unexpected.

Mr. C. B. RIPPON, one of the engineers of the Round Hill Milling Co., died at his home in Round Hill, on Monday of last week, of typhoid fever. He was about 40 years old and unmarried.

Swan BLACKMORE died at his home in Delaplane, Fauquier county from injuries received by a fall on the ice.

The funeral of the late Hambleton SHEPPERD took place in Warrenton Saturday.

Mr. John WOODYARD died at the home of Wm. CRAIG, near Bristow, Prince William county, Saturday. His death was due to injuries received a week previous, from being thrown into a barbed wire fence.

Friday, 26 April 1895 Vol. XVII, No. 52

Mr. Andrew CRIDLER, of this county, died at his home in Aldie, one day last week, at an advanced age. His remains were brought to Leesburg and interred in Union Cemetery on Thursday.

Lt. Harry HATCHER, of Col. MOSBY's command, died at his home in Fauquier county, last Tuesday.

Mr. Hermon HOGE, son of Mrs. Solomon HOGE, was married Tuesday, in Chicago, to Miss Emma WELLS, of Kenwood. They came to Morris last evening and went out to his home in the country. – *Morris (Ill.) Herald*, 2d inst.

Mr. Alexander N. BRECKENRIDGE died at his home in Washington city last Sunday. Mr. BRECKINRIDGE was a Lt. in Staunton Artillery C.S.A. He married a Miss WRIGHT (sister of Mrs. Francis CARTER) and lived with her on a farm near Middleburg until a few years ago when they removed to Washington, where he had secured a position in government employ.

[*Morris (Ill.) Herald*, Apr. 2] At 7:20 o'clock Tuesday morning the spirit of Townsend GORE took its eternal flight. He was over 75 years old when he dropped dead. He was born in Loudoun county, Aug. 4, 1819. It is not known at what exact date he moved to Ohio, but he was married to Ann Amanda HOGE, of Fauquier County in the late '40's. In the year 1865 they moved to Saratoga township, Grundy county, Ill., and they have resided in the same home in the same place that the aged husband and father died in this morning. He leaves a wife and eight children: William, of this city, Florence, Clinton, of Cripple Creek, Colo., Ida, Arthur, Clara, Herbert and Stanley. All except Clinton and William reside in Saratoga.

Married at Hillsboro April 16th by Rev. W. H. SAUNDERS, Mr. Wm. CREAMER, of Mechanicsville, to Miss Susie DERRY, of Neersville.

Miss Belle GRUBB, who has been afflicted for many years, departed this life today. A daughter of Mr. John GRUBB, of Neersville.

Mrs. Bud BAKER died last Sunday morning, after a lingering illness of several months.

Mr. Elijah CREAL, near Welbourne, who has been sick for some time, passed quietly away last Monday (15th inst.) evening. He leaves a wife, grown son and daughter. Just after the war he moved onto one of Thos. GLASCOCK's farms, where he remained until his death.

Friday, 3 May 1895   Vol. XVIII, No. 1

Mrs. FERGUSON, wife of Rev. S. G. FERGUSON, of the M. E. Church, South, died at Fredericksburg Thursday morning at her home after a short illness of pneumonia, aged about 45 years. She leaves a husband and seven children. The remains were taken to Charlestown, W. Va. for interment.

Miss Nancy STEWART, 81 years old, died near Meetz Station, Fauquier county, on Thursday morning.

Wm. A. WHITE, who would have been 80 years old on the 7th ultimo, died on Thursday in Warrenton.

Mrs. Sophia I. BOTTS, widow of the late Wm. BOTTS, sister of Col. John FAIRFAX and Aunt of state Senator Henry FAIRFAX, died at her home, Stafford county, a few days ago in her 73rd year.

Mr. W. W. WHITING, whose death in Alexandria, was announced last Sunday, was born in this county, but most of his life was spent elsewhere. In early days he worked on the "National Intelligencer," in Washington, and subsequently he conducted papers in Manassas, Fairfax C. H., and Alexandria.

Circuit Ct.: Jesse MOTEN qualified as guardian for Chas. Henry JACKSON. Estate of Catherine FELLOWS committed to Sheriff. Dr. Wm. B. LINDSEY qualified as guardian for Mary E. V. LINDSEY, Edna M. LINDSEY and Jesse Lee LINDSEY. Estates of Susan B. SMITH and Mary R. BELLESON deceased committed to Sheriff.

Friday, 10 May 1895   Vol. XVIII, No. 2

Rev. B. P. DULIN, Baptist minister, died at his home near Greenwich, Prince William, last week, aged 82 years. He went to bed seeming well and the next morning was found dead.

Mrs. GIBSON, mother of Col. Catlett GIBSON, died at her home in Culpeper, last Tuesday, aged 98 years.

Bolington, May 9 – Mr. David SLENTZ was stricken with appoplexy last Monday night and died Tuesday and his remains were interred at Lovettsville today. Mr. S. was probably 60 years of age.

Bolington – Mr. J. W. WENNER died on Wednesday night of last week, and his remains were interred at the Union Cemetery, Lovettsville, on Friday. He was also about 60 years of age.

Mrs. Lottie G. THOMAS, wife of Joseph B. Thomas, died at her home, near Snickersville, Wednesday evening, and her remains will be interred at Friend's burying ground, at Lincoln, at about 11 a.m. today.

Mrs. Virginia E. WARNER, wife of Mr. Geo. WARNER, died at her home near our town, last Friday evening, at 4 p.m., after a protracted illness, in the 58th year of her age. She was a member of Harmony M. E. Church South, where on Sunday her funeral took place.

Aldie was shocked by the sudden death last Friday of Capt. J. R. HUTCHINSON, a merchant of that place. he was attending to his usual duties in his store at the time. The interment took place at Middleburg, on Sunday. Mrs. HUTCHINSON is left alone to mourn.

The death of Mr. Wm. H. CASSADAY, who formerly resided on the farm near Waterford, is announced in the "Providence Independent," of Collegeville, Pa, on the 2d inst. He died at the family home – Ingleside – near Trappe, Friday morning, aged 84 years. Five children survive: Josephene C. GROSS, wife of Chas. H. GROSS, Esq., of Philadelphia; William H., Dr. C. E., E. R. and Irving C. CASSADY. Funeral service was held at the late residence of the deceased Monday evening at 7:30, conducted by Rev. Dr. FRY. The remains will be interred at Leesburg. Mr. CASSADAY came from Virginia in 1873 and engaged in farming the place where he died.

Married: On the 29th of April at Sterling, by Rev. A. WELLER, Mr. John M. GUNNELL, son of Orlando GUNNELL, Esq., and Miss Florence WALKER, all of Fairfax.

Died: Near Deepwater, Mo. April 16, 1895, Albert WRIGHT. The deceased was born near North Fork, June 1, 1809, and at the time of his death was 85y 10m 16d.

Died: At "Ingleside," Montgomery county, Pa, on the 26th of April 1865, William H. CASSADAY, formerly of Loudoun County, in the 84th year of his age.

Friday, 17 May 1895   Vol. XVIII, No. 3

Mrs. Sophia L. DELANY, wife of Michael DELANY, and who resided in Leesburg for some years, died at the residence of her son-in-law, Maj. B. L. WOODSON, in Kansas City, on Saturday last, in the 73rd year of her age.

Co. Ct.: Wills of Jno. R. HUTCHISON dec'd, Mary E. PUSEY dec'd, Robert Carter HARRISON dec'd, Catharine P. COCHRAN dec'd, Samuel T. TAYLOR dec'd, Elizabeth ORRISON dec'd and J. W. WENNER dec'd were admitted to probate. Laura B. HUTCHINSON qualified as Executrix of John HUTCHISON. Hugh R. HOLMES and Wm. PIGGOTT qualified as executors of Mary E. PUSEY. Elizabeth R. HARRISON qualified as Admx. w.w.a. of Robert C. HARRIS. Dr. J. Henry COCHRAN qualified as Exor. of Mrs. Catharine P. COCHRAN. Geo. T. WRIGHT qualified as Admr. of Charlotte

WRIGHT. Stirling MURRAY qualified as Admr. of Alexander MURRAY. T. S. ORRISON qualified as Admr. w.w.a. of Elizabeth ORRISON. J. T. McGAVACK appointed Guardian of Edward M. DUNBAR. H. H. RUSSELL, sheriff, appointed curator of the estate of John WATERS dec'd.

Warrenton, May 9 – H. C. YATES, postmaster here, died yesterday after a protracted illness. Deceased was a merchant here since 1865, was mayor, and for a number of years a member of the board of aldermen. He was chairman of the democratic county convention at the time of his appointment as postmaster. He was a prominent Mason. He leaves a widow and six children.

Friday, 24 May 1895   Vol. XVIII, No. 4

Mrs. Martha VANDEVANDER, widow of the late Isaac VANDEVANDER, died at her home near Leesburg last Sunday morning. She had been an invalid for several years.

Married, on Wednesday, 15th at the residence of the bride's parents, in St. Elmo, Alexandria county, Va. Mr. Thomas M. BOWIE and Miss Livie J. HAWS, daughter of W. A. and Mary J. HAWS, formerly of this county. The marriage ceremony was performed by Rev. J. H. BUTTLER, of Alexandria. Mr. and Mrs. BOWIE will at once settle in Alexandria.

Mrs. Effie L. BIRDSALL, whose maiden name was MANSFIELD, was divorced yesterday (Tuesday) by Justice COX from Dr. Charles W. BIRDSALL, of 1249 31st St, Georgetown, for desertion, dating from June 16, 1892. They were married May 27, 1887, at the First Baptist Church in Alexandria, and Mrs. BIRDSALL brought her suit for divorce Jan. 12 last. She claimed he urged her to go to Elmira, N.Y. in 1892, and that she has been obliged to depend upon friends and relatives for support since that time.

Neersville: At the residence of the bride's parents, on Wednesday, May 15th, Mr. Jos. H. DERRY was married to Miss Orra, only daughter of Mr. and Mrs. Richard MARSHALL.

Neersville: Cards are out of the marriage of Mr. Clinton HARDING and Miss Carrie, only daughter of Mr. and Mrs. N. B. RILEY on Thursday May 23rd.

Mrs. Clarissa SMITH, widow of the late Middleton SMITH, died at her home in this town last Saturday night at the advanced age of more than four score years.

The Indian Bureau, in Washington, has been informed of the death of Major W. L. POWELL, Indian Agent in Washington State. Major POWELL was a son of the late Col. H. B. POWELL, of Loudoun, and a brother-in-law of Hon. J. Randolph TUCKER.

Friday, 30 May 1895   Vol. XVIII, No. 5

J. T. LOVETT, a former resident of Loudoun county, died recently in Ohio. Mr. LOVETT was known by his neighbors as a very peculiar man, but they had no idea that he was a miser until after his death, when gold and paper money amounting to over $5,000 was found hidden in an old trunk in his house. *Charles Town Free Press.*

Last Saturday afternoon, while a force of hands in the employ of Mr. B. T. NOLAND were raising a barn at Mr. Edgar McCRAY's two miles east of our town, one of the timbers fell and struck a young man named Woodward DORRELL, son of Mr. Jas. A. DORRELL, of Round Hill, killing him almost instantly. On Sunday evening the body was laid in its final resting place in Hamilton Cemetery. He was about 20 years of age. A sister of this young man was so greatly distressed that she has been very ill.

Friday, 7 June 1895   Vol. XVIII, No. 6

Mr. James WIRGMAN, son-in-law of the late Solomon RUSE, died at his home in Romney, W. Va. last week, aged 91 years.

Mr. Washington SILCOTT, formerly of our town (father of J. Ed. SILCOTT) died at his home in Page Co., on 27th ult, aged 78 years.

Mr. R. J. N. REID and Miss Lucy MYERS were married, in Washington, last Tuesday, by Rev. R. R. S. HOUGH. They returned to Hamilton the same day.

Mr. Fenton VANDEVANDER, born and raised in Loudoun, died at his home in Springfield, Illinois, on the 4th of May, in his 83rd year. He was a cousin of Mr. Washington VANDEVANTER of this county.

Mr. James D. COPELAND, a former resident of Loudoun and a brother of Thomas F. COPELAND, who resided in Bethlehem, Connecticut, and who spent winter before last with his sister, Mrs. Z. T. WILEY, near Leesburg, died at his home in Connecticut on Tuesday last week, May 21st 1895.

Mr. John M. ATHEY, a former citizen of Leesburg, and a member of Loudoun Guard, Co. C. 17th Va Regiment, died at his home in Georgetown, on Thursday last, in the 77th year of his age. He was a member of the M. E. Church for many years. He had been a member of Loudoun Lodge, No. 26, Independent order of Odd Fellows, Leesburg, 40 years.

Samuel SWANK was picked up at his home near Lovettsville, on Saturday, about 3 o'clock, dead. It is supposed he suffered a sunstroke. He was 70 or 80 years old. His remains were buried in Union Cemetery on Sunday.

The infant son of Robert KELLEY was buried at Rehoboth on Wednesday of last week.

Married Wednesday: Mr. Rodney PURCELL and Miss Susan HATCHER of Purcellville. Mr. Maurice STRAUD and Ethel

SIMPSON. Mr. H. B. SIMPSON and Miss Ida F. MONROE, at the home of the bride, in Philomont.

Rev. Armstead FURR, a respected colored man, was buried today (Tuesday) at Willisville. He was paralyzed and only lived a few days after the stroke.

A telegram received in Leesburg on Wednesday, from San Antonio, Texas, announces the death of Charles E. CALDWELL, son of the late S. B. T. CALDWELL of this county, and a brother of Mrs. Ella C. MATTHEWS, of Leesburg. He was in the 59th year of his age and had been in declining health. After four years in the Confederate army, he left Loudoun at the close of the war in 1865, and has ever since resided in Texas.

Miss Mamie PRIEST, eldest daughter of Mr. John H. PRIEST, of Middleburg. died at her home last Thursday afternoon after a brief but severe illness, in the 20th year of her age.

Friday, 14 June 1895   Vol. XVIII, No. 7

Our town was startled yesterday morning by the report that Joseph LOW was found dead at his home, the old toll house at the east end of town. His little daughter Grace, probably twelve years of age, who had been living with him, came home in the evening and found the doors locked. By finding a window unfastened she found her father lying upon the bed dead. His funeral will take place at the Methodist Church, of which he was a member, just across the street from his house, today, at 2 o'clock.

A marriage licence was issued in Washington last Monday to Saml. QUEEN, of Leesburg, and Martha Ann WHEELER.

Miss Laura PIERCE (sister of Mr. Carroll PIERCE, one of the school teachers of Loudoun) was married at her home, near Rectortown, on the 11th inst., to Mr. Arthur A. RAWLINGS.

Miss Annie Lloyd MOORE, of Berryville, and Mr. William S. MOTT, of Glouchester county, were married in Grace Episcopal Church, Berryville, on Thursday.

At the home of Danial SHAFER and wife, at Clarks Gap, a wedding last Wednesday, when their daughter Mary united to N. Clifford NICHOLS, of the Leesburg bar. At 11:30 the ceremony of the Society of Friends. The bride was very becomingly attired in a white silk dress, with a beautiful bouquet of white roses. The waiters were: Howard NICHOLS and Mary HOGE, Joseph ROGERS and Emma NICHOLS (sister of the groom): Henry HOGE and Thamsin NICHOLS. On their trip north and west they will stop in the former home of the groom, in Belmont Co., Ohio. On their return they will make their home with the parents of the bride – an only child.

Co. Ct: Jos. H. JENKINS qualified as Admr. of Hannah JENKINS dec'd. Jno. W. GARRETT appointed guardian of Geo. E., Clarence and Elizabeth JORDON. Will of Mary E. WARNER admitted to probate.

Friday, 21 June 1895   Vol. XVIII, No. 8

J. W. DISHMAN qualified as Admr. of M. E. NOLLNER dec'd. Mary CONKLIN qualified as Admx. of Jos. R. CONKLIN dec'd. W. C. HEFLIN qualified as Guardian of Nora and J. and Bettie DODD. Estates of Catharine DUNN and Mary V. HOUSEHOLDER committed to sheriff. Will of A. N. BRECKENRIDGE admitted to probate. Bettie C. BRECKENRIDGE qualified as testimentary guardian of her children. Wills of Geo. W. BRYANT and Martha D. VANDEVANTER admitted to probate. Henry W. CREEL qualified as Admr. of Elijah G. CREEL.

De. Alman ROBEY, a flagman on the Washington Southern branch of the Pa. RR was killed about 3 o'clock Friday at Negys, Va, after a train stuck his heat by a platform. He was 24 years of age and resided at Herndon, Va. He was buried in Herndon.

About noon last Saturday while some workmen were engaged taking an old-fashioned heavy wooden pump out of the well, in the kitchen, at the home of the late Isaac NICHOLS, at Lincoln, Burr HAMILTON who lived at the place and was assisting with the work was struck on the head by the heavy pump stock and died at 8 o'clock next morning. His funeral took place at 2 p.m. on Tuesday, at Friends meeting house, he being a member. He leaves a wife.

Mr. Lewis Arthur TAYLOR, of Albemarle county, and Miss Sue E. STEPHENS, formerly of Warrenton, were married at the bride's home in Washington, on the 6th inst.

Friday, 21 June 1895   Vol. XVIII, No. 8

Mrs. Annie JANNEY, wife of Mr. Asbury JANNEY, and daughter of the late Thos. J. NICHOLS, died at the Baltimore City Hospital, last Saturday night, in the 54th year of her age. Death was the result of cancer of the stomach. Her funeral took place at Lincoln, Wednesday, at 10 a.m., and interred in Friend's burying ground.

The marriage of Miss Ara FLEMMING and Mr. Phillip HUTCHISON, a young farmer of Fairfax, took place at the residence of the bride's parents, Mr. Jos. FLEMING's at Chantilly, on Wednesday last Rev. A. WELLER officiated. The bride was neatly attired in white cashmere trimmed with silk, lace and ribbon. Their home is near Willard.

Purcellville: Mr. Sam. LAK?AN's baby was very ill Monday. Later, Mr. LA?HAN's little child died Tuesday night, about 7 months old. [page is creased]

Friday, 28 June 1895   Vol. XVIII, No. 9

The funeral sermon of H. Clay OTLEY will be preached by Rev. C. T. HERNDON in the North Fork Baptist church on Sunday, June 30th at 11 a.m.

Friday, 5 July 1895   Vol. XVIII, No. 10

Mr. John B. LOCKHART, brother-in-law of Mrs. Jas. H. MUSE, of our town, died suddenly at his residence in Washington, last Sunday. Funeral 4 p.m. Thursday.
Cards are out for the marriage of [torn] Lena, only daughter of Mr. Jos. and Sarah FRY, to Mr. Royal Lewis BALCH, at the New Jerusalem church, Lovettsville, on the 10th inst. at 11 a.m. After the 24th int. they will be at home at 2120 South 9th St., Philadelphia.
On Wednesday of last week, Mr. John F. KIDWELL, young man living with his father, J. F. KIDWELL Sr., near Leesburg, was fatally injured and died in a few hours. He was riding and fell, the horse dragged him to the barn. He was unconscious until he died.

Friday, 12 July 1895   Vol. XVIII, No. 11

An original widows pension has been granted Julia A. JACKSON (mother), Mountsville.
Co. Ct.: Will of Ann E. JANNEY admitted to probate; Samuel E. MICHOLS [NICHOLS] and James W. NICHOLS, Exors. Francis M. TINSMAN Admr. of James E. SLACK. Estate of William JAMES committed to Sheriff. Samuel E. ROSE Admr. of Rose HUGHES. Sallie A. SILCOTT guardian for Zula B. and Ella M. SILCOTT.
Mrs. Mary A. BURKE died at an early hour last Sunday morning, July 7th, 1895, she sank to rest in the 87th year of her age, more than 60 of which had been spent in Leesburg. Her funeral took place Tuesday afternoon, from her late residence on King street, conducted by Rev. J. W. GRUBB. Interment in Union Cemetery.
Miss Lena J. FRY, daughter of Mr. Joseph H. FRY, of Lovettsville, and Mr. Royal L. BALCH, of Phil. were married by Lutheran ceremony on Wednesday last in New Jerusalem Church. Rev. M. E. McLYNN performing the rite. At twenty minutes past eleven the bridal party marched in. The ushers and bridesmaides: Messrs. Hammond GROSS, Dr. A. HOUSEHOLDER, Marshall BOTELER, and Crum MARSHALL; Misses Marion HICKMAN, of Baltimore, and Lethia BALCH, of Philadelphia, sister of the groom. Miss Ruth McLYNN organist. The bride and maids wore white silk and the groom looked right handsome in a broad cloth cut-away suit. They will make their home in Philadelphia.
Mechanicsville: Mr. and Mrs. Walter EVERHART have a bran[d] new boy.
Mrs. Betsy FISHER, a very old lady, relict of John FISHER, died near New Baltimore Monday.

Friday, 19 July 1895   Vol. XVIII, No. 12

George W. JOHNSON, formerly of Loudoun, died at his home in Fairfax county, on the 20th inst., in the 69th year of his age. He was the father-in-law of Mr. Joseph FRY of this town.

Mr. Wm. KAIN, of Harper's Ferry was married to Miss Emma M. STOUTSENBURGER, of Loudoun county, at the residence of Mr. Thomas BOERLY, on Tuesday of last week by Father KELLY.

Friday, 26 July 1895   Vol. XVIII, No. 13

Joseph TURNER, colored, formerly of this vicinity, died at Mt. Pleasant last Wednesday.

A black TRILBY from Loudoun county, whose other name was FITZHUGH, was married in Washington last Friday. Her father, an old Virginia darkey, who wore a linen duster and a high hat was indignant because the license clerk expressed doubt as to his daughter's first name being TRILBY. The father had never heard of Du MAURIER or his famous heroine, and insisted that his daughter's name was TRILBY and always had been. The bridegroom, was little, but his name was Henry REDMAN. He was in the uniform of the Lincoln Coronet Band, and the couple were married in the clerk's office by an ancient colored divine, also from old Virginia. Miss TRILBY was not in her bare feet. She wore shoes and stockings. This fact was revealed when she raised her white satin gown from the dusty floor and "stepped high" to the platform. She also wore white cotton gloves.

Mr. John MISKELL, farmer of this county, died at his home near Point of Rocks, Tuesday afternoon, in about the 46th year of his age. He had been in bad health for some time. His remains will be interred in Union Cemetery, this town, today Thursday.

Friday, 2 August 1895   Vol. XVIII, No. 14

Mr. W. W. HOUGH a native of Loudoun county, and owner of the farm now tenanted by Mr. John W. ORRISON, near our town, died at his home in Washington, Monday morning, aged about 79 years. His health had not been good for some time.

Friday, 9 August 1895   Vol. XVIII, No. 15

Mr. Charles WHITE died at his home near Woodburn, last Saturday evening and his remains were interred at Hamilton Cemetery, on Monday. He was 62 years of age.

Mrs. Frank RINKER died at her home, at Waterford, Tuesday morning. She had been in frail health for about a year. Her funeral, on Wednesday.

Mrs. ___ DOWELL, aged 95, died at her home in Hamilton last Friday morning. Her funeral took place at Short Hill Sunday morning, where services were conducted by Rev. I. B. LAKE.

Mrs. Mary Ann BUTTS, mother of Mr. Calvin BUTTS, formerly one of the employees of Taylor's Foundry, near Lincoln, this county, but now a resident of Alexandria, died in Erie, Pa., last Friday and her remains were brought to Alexandria for interment.

Friday, 16 August 1895   Vol. XVIII, No. 16

A little child of Mr. John WILLIAMS, of Clarks Gap, about a year old, was buried at Harmony burying ground on Wednesday.

Co. Ct.: Wills of Mrs. Mary A. BURKE and David McCULLUCK admitted to probate. Estates of Catharine KINDALL and Jos. A. EDWARDS committed to Sheriff. W. S. MISKELL qualified as Admr. of Jno. H. MISKELL dec'd. Rev. Curtis LAWS granted right to perform the rites of matrimony.

Friday, 23 August 1895   Vol. XVIII, No. 17

Died: On the 6th of Aug. 1895, Mrs. Alberta E. RINKER, wife of Franklin RINKER and daughter of William and Ann E. HICKMAN, died at her home in Waterford, Va. The deceased leaves a husband and son. Mrs. RINKER was 41y 9m 7d.

Mr. Samuel J. COOK, aged about 40 years was struck by lightning and instantly killed. He was standing in the door of the house occupied by his father-in-law, George SMALLWOOD, when the bolt struck the house. The man's clothing and shoes were torn in pieces. Mr. COOKE leaves a wife and several children.

Friday, 30 August 1895   Vol. XVIII, No. 18

Mrs. Mary HARMON was tried at Fairfax C. H. last week for killing her husband, John R. HARMON, and was acquitted. The offense occurred on the 2nd of June when her husband who had not been living with her for several months attempted to enter through a window.

Robert, the little boy of Mr. and Mrs. R. B. WILDMAN died (last Sunday, we believe) at the home of his uncle, Maj. Wm. H. ROGERS, near Dover, where he had been taken in hopes that a change would benefit his health.

Friday, 6 September 1895   Vol. XVIII, No. 19

William HARMAN, a former resident of this city, died in Washington on Friday. The deceased was a nephew of the late C. HARMON – Gazette.

James W. WILLIAMS (son of the late William WILLIAMS) died last Thursday at 3 p.m. Just four weeks before he was taken sick, while in Washington, and at once proceeded to the home of his sister, Mrs. Louis PIDGEON, in Clarke County. His body will be laid to rest tomorrow near the place where as a member of the Society of Friends, he had worshipped, and laid by the side of his wife who died a year ago. A boy of about five summers and a baby about a year old survive.

Died near here, quite suddenly, last Thursday evening, at Mr. John HUNTER's, Mr. John Washington EDWARDS. Buried at St. Paul's Lutheran church, Saturday morning, at 10 o'clock. The funeral sermon was preached by Rev. SAUNDERS, of Hillsboro.

Friday, 13 September 1895   Vol. XVIII, No. 20

At the home of the bride's parents, Mr. and Mrs. Luther STEWART (colored) a pretty wedding took place Sunday Sept. 1st at 3:30 p.m. The bride, Annie BLANCH, was attired in a white albatross dress and carried a bunch of white lillies. The groom William H. BROWN work a stylish black suit.

Harmony church was the scene of a pretty wedding Tuesday morning, the 10th inst. The contracting parties being Mr. Samuel NICHOLSON, of Washington, and Miss Elizabeth WARNER, of Hamilton. At 11 a.m. the bridal party entered to the wedding march rendered by Miss Marguerite NICHOLSON, of Washington. They were met at the altar by the Rev. R. R. S. HOUGH. The ushers were Messrs. Malcram SPARROUGH, Robt. NICHOLSON and J. CRAMER, of Washington and Mr. Frank SMITH, of Hamilton. La Petite bride was becomingly attired in a green traveling dress and carried a bouquet of brides roses.

Mrs. Patience PURSELL, wife of Mr. Jas. H. PURSELL, died at her home near Round Hill, on Thursday last, in about the 70th year of her age. She had been an invalid for some time. She was a sister of the late Logan and Wm. OSBURN, and the last surviving member of a family of fourteen children, four sons and ten daughter. Her remains were interred at Ketoctin Baptist Church, on Saturday.

Co. Ct.: J. Edward WALKER qualified as Admr. of James W. WILLIAMS dec'd. J. B. NIXON qualified as Admr. of Hannah NIXON dec'd.

Died: Hannah SCOTT, in Waterford, 9th mo. 11th '95, in the 74th year of her age. Her funeral took place from her house, yesterday (Thursday) at 10 a.m.

Friday, 20 September 1895   Vol. XVIII, No. 21

Mrs. Emma THATCHER, died at Manassas last Friday after a brief but painful illness.

Mr. William C. REAMER aged 76 years, died yesterday at the Howard House after an illness of one week. He was born at Sideling Hill, Fulton Co, Pa. where for many years he was proprietor of the Sideling House. He represented Fulton co. in the Pa. Legislature in 1856 and 1857 and in 1859 removed to Martinsburg, W Va where he kept the old B. & O. Hotel. When he retired he resided with his son James, in Leesburg, for a number of years. His remains were interred in Union Cemetery at Leesburg.

Friday, 27 September 1895   Vol. XVIII, No. 22

Mr. Richard COLEMAN, of Herndon, Fairfax Co., died at the residence of his niece, Mr. N. W. JANNEY, yesterday. The deceased was 69 years old.

The relict of the late Lewis HAWLING, of Loudoun county, died last Thursday, in Washington city, at an advanced age.

Mrs. Elizabeth C. FOSTER, mother of Mrs. Robt. S. VANDEVANTER, of this county, died at her home in Norfolk, Va, on Wednesday, Sept. 4th at an advanced age.

Samuel W. GRUBB, an aged citizen of Milltown, died Sunday evening last, after a lingering illness of that dread disease, consumption. He had been sick for many months. His remains were laid to rest in the Union Cemetery on Tuesday. Funeral services conducted by Revs. McLINN and ALLENDER, at the Lutheran Church.

Mr. ___ GARRETT, an aged citizen of Lovettsville, died on Friday of last week. Interment at the Union Cemetery on Sunday.

Friday, 4 October 1895   Vol. XVIII, No. 23

Mrs. Rosalie Lewis, wife of Mr. Frank N. TILFORD, of Washington, and eldest daughter of the late Col. H. L. Dangerfield and Carter Freeland LEWIS, died on Saturday at the residence of her mother, at Audley, Clarke county.

Mr. Geo. W. GIBSON, who formerly resided not far from Paxson's P. O. died on Sunday at his home in Upperville, Fauquier Co. Mr. GIBSON was about 60 years of age and had been in bad health for some years.

Mr. S. M. GRANGER, of Zanesville, and Messrs. Chas. FOLLETT and Jno. D. FOLLETT, of Cincinnatti, arrived in Leesburg Tuesday evening and are registered at the Inn. The latter gentleman is to marry Miss Ida, youngest daughter of the late Col. A. T. M. RUST, this (Thursday) evening. The wedding is to take place at "Rockland" the residence of the bride's mother, about four miles from Leesburg.

Letter from Mrs. Rachel MEANS, of Brookland, DC. about a statement in the last issue, she states that instead of being a brother of the late Samuel MEANS that was injured by a trolly car, it was a son of that brother, Lewis Edward MEANS. He was fatally injured and died Saturday night. His funeral took place on Tuesday. He left a wife and four children.

Last Monday night at the home of Miss Susan GREGG, near Purcellville was a party for her 88th birthday.

Mr. J. Cleveland COLEMAN died at his home near Sterling last Sunday in the 59th year of his age. He was a member of the Board of Supervisors from Broad Run District, a member of the Democratic County Committee and a member of the County Electoral Board.

Friday, 11 October 1895   Vol. XVIII, No. 24

The wife of George P. HUNTER of Hillsboro, died yesterday of heart disease.

Mr. Geo. W. GIBSON, an old citizen of this county, died in Upperville Sunday last.

An "at home" wedding occurred yesterday evening at 6:30, when Miss Ida, youngest daughter of the late Col. A. T. M. RUST, of Loudoun county, was married to Mr. J. D. FOLLETT, of Cincinnati. The ceremony took place at Rockland, the home of the bride's mother, about 4 miles north of Leesburg. Rev. Harry B. LEE, of Charlottesville, uncle of the bride, performed the ceremony, assisted by Rev. Berryman GREEN, of Leesburg.

The marriage of Miss Daisy ENGLISH and Edgar CRIM is announced to take place on Thursday of this week in Frederick, Md.

Mrs. George HUNTER died yesterday at her home near Morrisonville. Her remains will be interred at the Union Cemetery to morrow.

Walter J. HARRISON died at his home in Leesburg at 10:20 Sunday night, Oct. 6th, 1895, in the 51 year of his age. About two months ago Mr. HARRISON received a paralytic stroke. He was the eldest son of the late Henry T. HARRISON, of this town, and a grandson of the late Walter JONES, of Washington City. He was born 7 March 1845. The second year of the late war found him with his younger brother, Henry, a student at Va. Military Institute. Upon the death of his father, Mr. HARRISON succeeded him as President of the Loudoun National Bank. He was a member of St. James Episcopal Church and order of Knights of Pythias. He was twice married, his first wife being a sister of Capt. E. B. POWELL; his second wife was Miss BENEDICT, of this town, who with four small children survive. A son by his first marriage is now grown. The funeral took place from his late residence on Market Street, at 3 o'clock Wednesday afternoon, Rev. Berryman GREEN, officiating, assisted by Revs. J. W. GRUBB, Geo. L. BITZER and C. T. HERNDON. He was buried in Union Cemetery.

Friday, 18 October 1895   Vol. XVIII, No. 25

Judge J. H. GRAY, who owned the farm formerly tenanted by Mr. E. J. NORTHRUP, about two miles east of Leesburg, died suddenly last Monday, in the office of his son-in-law, Mr. L. L. JOHNSON, in Washington City. He was 80 years of age.

Visiting – Nathan NICHOLS and Sarah HOGE were both natives of Loudoun. After their marriage they located in Belmont Co., Ohio, where they have since resided, engaged in farming.

Rev. Dr. George W. CARTER a few months ago married a young lady of Lynchburg. The parents of the bride, who was about nineteen, opposed the match, and the couple went to Washington where the ceremony was performed. Dr. CARTER was a divorced man.

Mechanicsville: Mr. William BLAKER wears a broad smile – it's a girl.
Mr. Lewis WRIGHT died at his home near Taylortown, in this county, on Monday, the 30th September, in the 83th year of his age.
Mrs. Mary PEARSON, wife of Mr. Geo. W. PEARSON, of this county, died at the residence of Mr. M. F. BROWN, near Leesburg, last Tuesday, October 10th, in about the 47th year of her age. Her funeral took place on Saturday. Interment at Mt. Zion.
Mr. Geo. W. INZER, a former citizen of Leesburg, died at his home in Washington last Friday morning, in the 59th year of his age. His remains were brought here on Sunday, the funeral taking place from the M. E. Church, Rev. J. W. GRUBB officiating. interment in Union Cemetery.
Co. Ct.: Wills of John W. DAILEY, Lydia LOVE and Walter J. HARRISON were admitted to probate. Florence J. DAILEY qualified as Executrix of John W. DAILEY. Mrs. F. S. COLEMAN qualified as Admx. of J. C. COLEMAN. R. S. and R. G. BURKE qualified Exors. of Mary A. BURKE. Thos. W. BUCKLEY qualified as Admr. of Thos. R. O'MEARA. Robt. R. WALKER qualified as Admr. of Hannah SCOTT. Geo. W. VIRTS qualified as Admr. of Saml. N. GRUBB. Louisa S. BASIQUE qualified as Admr. of Lydia LOVE. Henry HARRISON qualified as Exor. of Walter J. HARRISON. Estate of Edward EVANS committed to the Sheriff. Joshua L. RITICOR appointed committed for Joseph RITICOR, and qualified as such.

Friday, 25 October 1895   Vol. XVIII, No. 26

Mrs. JENKINS, widow of the late Reuben JENKINS, died at her home near Round hill, on Tuesday morning Oct 22nd. Mrs. JENKINS had passed her four score years and for some time past had been in bad health. Her funeral took place on Wednesday. Interment at Salem burying ground.

Friday, 1 November 1895   Vol. XVIII, No. 27

Mrs. Mary E. BIRD, wife of Mr. Chas. D. BIRD, formerly of this town, died at her residence in Baltimore, on Monday last, in the 58th year of her age.
Mrs. Fannie LAFEVER, widow of the late Peter LAFEVER, died at her home near Farmwell on Wednesday last. Her remains were buried in Union Cemetery, this town, on Thursday.
Mr. George REAMER, an aged citizen of this county, living near Taylorstown, died very suddenly on Monday of last week. He was afflicted with heart trouble and this is thought to have caused his death.
Mr. John J. TILLETT, of Manassas, who was connected with the business office of the Washington Times, died at Charlottesville, last Thursday night, of typhoid fever, in the 23d year of his age. His remains were interred at Manassas on Saturday.

Bolington, Oct. 30 – Mrs. Clara ORRISON, wife of James ORRISON, died at the residence of her grandmother, Mrs. STOUTZENBERGER, after a short illness of one week of typhoid fever and heart failure. Her remains were interred at the Union Cemetery, on Monday.

Oscar HOUSHOLDER, a former resident of his vicinity, but late of Montgomery Co., Md, died at his late residence on Sunday. His remains were brought here on Tuesday and laid to rest in the Union Cemetery. At the same time and place the funeral of George HEFNER took place. He was a resident of the Tankerville neighborhood and had gone on a visit to his son in Maryland, where died and his remains were brought to his old home on the same train that brought the remains of Oscar HOUSHOLDER.

Mrs. Mary Ann CONARD died of typhoid fever here on Monday evening, the 14th inst. Her remains were buried at Salem on Wednesday the 16th, funeral services by Rev. SAUNDERS.

Miss Sarah G. DEAHL, daughter of Mr. and Mrs. Horace P. DEAHL, of Berryville, and Mr. William MACKAY, a young life insurance man of Baltimore, were married at Berryville on the 22d.

Warrenton: Mr. Lewis Armistead BROWN and Miss Bessie WOOD, sister of Mr. D. P. WOOD, of this place, will be married in the Baptist Church here November 7th.

Mr. Horace JOHNSON, a brother of the late Wm. JOHNSON, of Warrenton, died at his home near Remington Monday last. He was a member of Mosby's command during the war.

Captain Joshua ELLIS, died suddenly at his home in Fairfax county last Thursday, supposedly from heart disease.

Friday, 18 November 1895   Vol. XVIII, No. 28

The mother of the SHIPMAN Bro's of our town died in her home in Lovettsville, aged 75 years.

Mr. John PHILLIPS was found dead lying on the floor of his bedroom, at the home of Mr. Townsend BELT, near Leesburg, last Monday morning. About a month age he came from the home of his son in Washington or Baltimore to make his home at Mr. BELTS. Some years ago he owned and operated what is known as the Oxley mill property two miles east of Leesburg.

Henry JANNEY, father of Mrs. Henry H. SMITH, of the Purcellville neighborhood, died at his home in Baltimore last Tuesday, after an illness of many weeks. He was born in Fairfax county and received his education at the Benjamin Hallowell School, Alexandria, Va. He married Miss Hannah SCHOFIELD, daughter of Mr. Joseph SCHOFIELD, of Washington, DC and removed to Ohio, where he began the boot and shoe business. He was a whig. At the close of the war he retired and went to Harford county, Md, where he farmer until about 1875. He then came to Baltimore where he resided until his death. He was a member of the Society of Friends. A widow and seven children survive him. The children are: Mrs. Henry H. SMITH, Joseph J. JANNEY, of the firm of POPE and JANNEY, Miss M. Elizabeth JANNEY, Miss Hannah H. JANNEY, Mrs. William E. WALTON, William H. JANNEY and Dr. O. Edward JANNEY.

Mechanicsville: Married at the bride's residence near here on Wednesday evening, Oct. 30th by the Rev. SAUNDERS, Mr. John MILLER, of Round Hill, and Miss Jennie HESKETT.

Died: Tuesday, Oct. 15 at her residence in Loudoun Valley, Mrs. Mary A. CONARD, in her 68th year. Her remains were buried at the Salem church, the services conducted by Rev. W. H. SAUNDERS, she had converted some 50 years ago. She leaves a daughter and son-in-law with family at her place of residence.

Friday, 15 November 1895   Vol. XVIII, No. 29

Mr. Samuel ARNETT informs the TELEPHONE that the village known as the Pot House, in the southwestern part of the county received its name from a pottery that was established there 85 or 90 years ago, by his great-uncle, William ARNETT.

Miss Margaret BLAINE, daughter of Robert G. BLAINE and niece of the late Jas. G. BLAINE, was married to Dr. H. J. CROSSON, in Washington last Tuesday.

Co. Ct.: Wills of James CRAIG and Ida M. SHOWER admitted to probate. Jno. C. RUST qualified as Admr. of George BEAMER dec'd. Reuben JENKINS Jr. and Joseph JENKINS qualified as Exors. of Reuben JENKINS dec'd. Geo. W. SPILLER qualified as Admr. of Martha SPILLER dec'd. Geo. W. SPILLER qualified as guardian of Alex. SPILLER. Olivia C. J. STRIBLING qualified as Admx. of Oliver J. C. CHAMBLIN dec'd. Estates of William GRAHAM and John I. COLEMAN committed to Sheriff.

Married: At Aldie, on Thursday Nov. 7th 1895, by Rev. W. F. DUNNAWAY, Mr. J. Ed. DOUGLAS and Miss Mary C. SKINNER, all of Loudoun.

Died at Live Oak, Florida, Nov. 10th 1895, Charles H., son of the late Dr. R. Herbert and Lily Selden TATUM, and brother of Mrs. Lucien B. TATUM.

Died: At Arcola, at 5:20 p.m. Saturday, Nov. 9th, of typhoid fever, Fanny MANKIN, wife of Dennis McCarty RAMSEY.

Friday, 15 [22] November 1895   Vol. XVIII, No. 29 [30]

Miss Evelyn, daughter of Chas. B. ADAMS, was married at the home of the latter, at Aldie, last Thursday, to Mr. Chas. McPHERSON, of Prince George county, Md.

A wedding took place December 11th, when Miss Mary Beverly CHICHESTER, daughter of Capt. Authur CHICHESTER, of Loudoun, will be married to Mr. Wilcox JENKINS, son of Mr. Joseph

JENKINS, of Baltimore. The marriage will take place at Ivon, the CHICHESTER country home, near Leesburg, after which the bride and groom will live in Wilmington, N. C., where Mr. JENKINS has been located for the past few years.

A marriage license was issued last week in Washington, to Flavius H. LODGE and Ella M. CONNOR, both of Round Hill.

Mr. Benj. D. RATHIE died last Thursday, at the residence of Mr. W. F. FLING near the Big Spring, in the 46th year of his age. He had been in ill health a long time. Interred in Union Cemetery, this town, on Saturday afternoon last, Rev. J. W. GRUBB officiating.

Died: George H. BOLON, at his home in Culpeper County, Nov. 10th 1895. The deceased was formerly a resident of Loudoun County.

Friday, 29 November 1895   Vol. XVIII, No. 31

Dr. S. S. NEILL, of Berryville, died Saturday morning at the age of 71 years.

Miss Nannie C. MASSY, daughter of the late E. W. MASSEY, of White Post, Clarke County, died last week at Garfield Hospital, where she had been for treatment.

On Thursday morning of last week, while yet the old folks slumbered, Miss Daisy FADELEY slipped out of her parents home, near Waterford, and hied away to Maryland and matrimony. Frank R. NEEDHAM, of Washington, and Miss Daisy G. FADELEY, of Loudoun, were married at Towson, yesterday. He is a son of Mr. Charles W. NEEDHAM, lawyer, who lives at 1730 16th St, Washington, She is a daughter of Mr. Charles W. FADELY, of "Rosemont" near Leesburg. They are 21 and 18 years respectively. They were married by Rev. W. E. ROBERTSON, pastor of Calvary Baptist Church.

Married: On the 21st of Nov. 1895 near Daysville, by the Rev. G. W. POPKINS, Miss Annie B. HEFFNER to Mr. W. T. MATHERS, all of Loudoun.

Friday, 6 December 1895   Vol. XVIII, No. 32

A pretty wedding took place near Daysville, at the residence of the bride's uncle, on Wednesday, Nov. 20th at 6 o'clock. The contracting parties were Willie MATHERS and Annie B. HEFFNER. Ceremony was performed by Rev. G. W. POPKINS. The bride was dressed in cream cashmere, trimmed with laces and ribbons and wore a long veil, fastened with lillies of the valley and carried a large bouquet to match.

Fauquier: Mr. William DIGGS, who went to Colorado some years ago, died on the 21st.

Fauquier: Mrs. MOORE, who lived in Paris, died at her home Saturday evening, aged 99 years. She had been bed ridden and blind. Her

daughter, Miss Fannie MOORE, aged 75, died about two weeks ago.
Fauquier: Miss Lucy PUTNAM, who lived near Orlean, died on Monday, November 18, aged 98 years.
A fifteen year old girl named RILEY committed suicide by hanging herself from a tree near Paris, Fauquier, one day last week.

Friday, 13 December 1895   Vol. XVIII, No. 33

Lewis McKenzie DIVINE, of Alexandria, died in Leesburg, of typhoid fever last Sunday.
Rev. R. R. S. HOUGH and wife went to Baltimore, on Monday, to attend the funeral of a brother of the later, Rev. STEPHENSON, who while standing in his pulpit, fell and died in a few hours.
Co. Ct.: Estates of Julia A. CHAMBLIN dec'd and Mary HUTCHINSON dec'd committed to Sheriff. Will of Lydia C. COGLE admitted to probate. H. A. TRITAPOE Guardian of Wm. E. TRITAPOE, executed a new bond. Jas. M. and Margaret A. BENTON's estates committed to Sheriff.
Joseph HOLDER, who lived on or near the mountain, east of Waterford, on Wednesday morning shot both is step-daughter and himself, he dying but his step-daughter is still living that night.
Mrs. Sallie COOPER, relict of John COOPER, died at her residence, near Morrisonville, on Wednesday evening of last week. Her remains were interred in the Union Cemetery on Sunday. She was 93 years old and a member of the Lutheran Church for many years. She leaves four daughters and two sons.
The wife of James W. MARSHALL, of Washington, DC, late of Paris, Fauquier, died on the 1st inst.
Mr. P. H. DELAPLANE died at his home "Kinsley," Buckland, on Wednesday, the 27th ult.
Mrs. Robert BLACKMORE, of Delaplane, died on the 27th ult., at 9 p.m., of consumption, aged about sixty years.
Cards are out for the wedding of Mr. C. C. DELEPLANE, of Delaplane, and Miss Mary W. McDONALD, or Warm Springs, Bath county, on the 11th inst.
A home wedding took place at "Ivon" the country home of Capt. A. M. CHICHESTER, near Leesburg, on Wed. morning, Dec. 11th 1895, the contracting parties being Miss Mary Beverly CHICHESTER, daughter of Mr. and Mrs. A. M. CHICHESTER, of this county, and Mr. J. Wilcox JENKINS, of Baltimore. The ceremony was performed by Rev. C. DENNEN, of Wilmington, N. C. The attendants were Miss Mary Richard CHICHESTER, cousin of the bride and Fred. J. JENKINS, brother of the groom. They will proceed to Wilmington, N. C. their future home.
Mr. Jonah PEUGH and Miss Mattie CROCKETT were married at 3 p.m. yesterday in Washington city. Mr. PEUGH is located at Altoona, Pa.

Mrs. Jacquelin MARSHALL died at her home, at Markham, on Saturday.

R. B. PAYNE, a merchant at Markham, Fauquier, committed suicide last week by shooting himself with a pistol.

Mr. Robert MINOR, an aged citizen of Fairfax county, died last week from a fall while crossing a small stream.

Mr. E. L. FLIPPO and Miss Fannie WORTHAM, both of Roanoke, were married in Paris, Texas, a few days ago. Mr. FLIPPO is a son of Rev. O. F. FLIPPO.

Friday, 20 December 1895   Vol. XVIII, No. 34

A marriage license was issued in Washington last Thursday to Clarence E. SCHOOLEY and Lizzie TIFFANY, both of Loudoun.

The remains of Mr. Crosby WILSON, who died at his home at Wheatland, on Monday, were interred at Harmony Methodist Church, on Wednesday. Mr. W. formerly resided in our town.

Wednesday morning three young gentlemen entered the home of Mr. and Mrs. John EVERETT. About the same time Rev. J. W. GRUBB, of Leesburg, was seen in the same vicinity. In a little while Mr. Henry WATSON, of Aldie, accompanied by his bride, Eunice, daughter of Mr. and Mrs. EVERETT, emerged. Miss Eunice's older sister is the wife of the groom's father.

On the same day, at 6 p.m., Samuel LEWIS, of our town, was married to Miss Jennie FRITTS, at her home in the Neersville neighborhood and yesterday he brought her to his home in Hamilton.

Bolington, Dec. 18 – David AXLINE, an aged citizen of this vicinity passed away on Wednesday evening of last week. He was afflicted and for the last five years bedfast, caused by paralysis. He was a member of the Lutheran Church. His remains were borne to Union Cemetery on Friday, the funeral services conducted by Rev. M. E. McLINN. He leaves two sons. His age was 86 years.

Cards are out for the marriage of Mr. Samuel R. POTTS and Miss Nettie SPATES, of Hillsboro, daughter of Mr. Thomas SPATES.

Fauquier: Mr. Harley F. KIRKPATRICK and Miss Annie B. SUTHERD, daughter of Joseph and Mary SUTHARD, were married on Dec. 11th, at the residence of the bride by Rev. L. H. CRENSHAW.

Joseph HOLDER, lived with his wife and five children, the oldest Lula CREEL, about 13 years of age, and the daughter of HOLDER's wife by a former marriage. On Wednesday morning HOLDER engaged men to kill his hogs. Tuesday evening he drank freely. On Wednesday morning he shot Lula then shot himself. The child died 11 o'clock Thursday morning. Holder was buried on Friday and his innocent little victim on Saturday.

Friday, 27 December 1895　　Vol. XVIII, No. 35

Mr. Edgar MYERS was married last Tuesday to Miss McKIMM at her home in Washington. They are now visiting the home of his father, Thomas MYERS, at Hughesville.

Married by the Rev. SAUNDERS, of Hillsboro, at Mr. John COCKERELL's on Wednesday evening, Dec. 18th, Mr. Samuel LEWIS of Hamilton and Miss Jennie FRITTS, of this place.

Cards are out for the double marriage of Misses Mary Emma and Virgie KIDWELL, daughters of Mr. John E. KIDWELL, of this place, to Mr. Dase GRUBB, of Hillsboro, and Mr. ___ WOOD, of Ohio, on Thursday, Dec. 26.

Thomas B. CLENDENING whose illness was mentioned last week, was buried at Hillsboro, at the Arnold Grove Church, on Friday morning Dec. 20th. He left a widow, son and daughter.

Friday, 3 January 1896　　Vol. XVIII, No. 36

A marriage license was issued in Washington last Saturday to Maurice W. BEAVERS and Sarah A. MATHERS, of Leesburg.

The engagement of Miss Robbie HENDRICKS, of Leesburg to Mr. Frank RITTENHOUSE, of Washington, has been announced.

Marriage licenses were issued in Washington last week to Thomas W. WEAVER and Dollie A. FURR; and James W. DAY and Nellie WILLIAMS, all of Loudoun county.

Mr. C. Means VANDEVANTER, one of the several brothers of that name who are well known in Loudoun, died one day last week, at his home in Washington, where he has resided most of the time since the war, in the 79th year of his age. His remains were interred in Union Cemetery, at Leesburg last Monday.

Mr. and Mrs. Abijah JANNEY, of Michigan, arrived last Saturday at the home of Mr. and Mrs. Harman GREGG, his uncle and aunt, at Purcellville – the latter being his father's sister. Mr. JANNEY is a son of Albert and Lydia Ann JANNEY. The latter was a NICHOLS and was raised at the place where Nathan T. BROWN now resides. His mother removed to Iowa when he was a lad.

Wm. JOHNSON and Sam VENY of Gum Spring neighborhood had a drunken quarrel, VENY attacked Johnson with a knife while the latter used a pistol and killed VENY.

Married at the residence of the bride's parent's, Mr. and Mrs. T. A. HITE of Bettsville, Ohio, on Thursday Dec. 26, Mr. David H. POTTS, formerly of Loudoun, but now of Gibsonburg, Ohio, and Cora E. HITE.

Friday, 10 January 1896　　Vol. XVIII, No. 37

Mr. J. Newton SHEPHERD, formerly a resident of Clarke county, died suddenly, Monday, near Charlestown, W Va.

Mr. Charles TAVENNER was married to Miss ___ SIMPSON at her home in Laurel, Md, on Tuesday, and in the evening brought her to the home of his parents, near town.

The family of Miss Mabel STUART, of Harpers Ferry, W. Va who recently disappeared from Camden Station, Baltimore have heard from her. Her sister, Miss Julia STUART, who lives at Bolivar, about a mile from Harpers Ferry received a letter postmarked Glencover, Queens county, N. Y. She also has a brother Mr. George STUART.

Joseph NICHOLS who has been ailing about two months, died at the home of his daughter, Mrs. Virginia HUGHES, near Hughesville, yesterday 'forenoon. He was afflicted with gangrene in one of his feet. He was in the 87th year of his age. He was on the board of directors of Loudoun Mutual Fire Ins. Co. Member of the Society of Friends and had for years been an elder of Goose Creek Meeting. His funeral will take place tomorrow (Sat.) 11 a.m. at the meeting house in Lincoln.

Mr. Oscar BRADEN died at the home of his nephew, Walter BRADEN about three miles north of town, last Saturday morning, the result of heart trouble. On Monday his remains were interred by the graves of his kinsmen, at Catoctin Church, near his home, Rev. E. S. WILSON officiated. He was an elder of the Presbyterian church, President of the Mutual Fire Insurance Co. of Loudoun, and in the late war commanded Co. K of the 6th Va Cavalry, in the Confederate army. He was in the 77th year of his age.

Friday, 17 January 1896   Vol. XVIII, No. 38

Jan. Ct.: Wills of Edward CURTIS, Randolph BARNHOUSE, and Oscar S. BRADEN admitted to probate. Martha CURTIS qualified as Executrix of Edward CURTIS dec'd. Edgar McCRAY qualified as Exor. of Oscar S. BRADEN dec'd. Franklin M. MYERS qualified as Admr. of Frances A. MYERS dec'd. Nelson W. and Edgar J. BARNHOUSE qualified as Exors. of Randolph BARNHOUSE dec'd. Naturalization papers issued to Jno. H. SVEDBURG, a native of Vosa, Finland.

Mr. Philip EVERHART, an elderly man living in the Sycolin neighborhood, died last Friday and was buried in Union Cemetery, this town, on Sunday, Rev. G. L. BITZER officiating.

Mr. Richard E. LEWIS, son of Mr. Harrison LEWIS, died last Friday at his father's residence near Aldie, and was buried in the Middleburg cemetery on Sunday.

Mr. Chas. L. POWELL, one of Alexandria's oldest citizens, died at his home there on Thursday night, of pneumonia. The deceased was a son of Hon. Cuthbert POWELL, of Llangollea, Loudoun county, and was born in Alexandria in 1804. He removed to Loudoun county in 1812. Subsequently he removed to the West, but returned to

Alexandria after the war, where for a number of years he conducted a school for boys.

Died on Friday, Jan. 10th at Waterford, Gertrude, wife of Charles MORELAND. For many years a member of the Methodist Church.

Friday, 24 January 1896   Vol. XVIII, No. 39

Thos. L. BALL was found dead in bed at the home of his cousin, Saml. H. BALL, at Swart's Mill house. He was apparently as well as usual the day before. He was a son of the late Henry BALL, about 50 years old, and unmarried. His remains were interred in Union Cemetery in Leesburg, Friday last, Rev. E. S. HINKS, officiating.

Circuit Ct.: Jas. L. WILSON, a native of Yorkshire, England, declared his intention to become a citizen of the United States.

Miss Maggie McGRAW, of Harpers Ferry, daughter of James McGREW, deceased, died very suddenly, last Saturday evening, at her brother's home.

Mr. Oden WRIGHT died of consumption at the residence of his mother, Mrs. H. V. WRIGHT, in this town about noon on Tuesday.

Friday, 31 January 1896   Vol. XVIII, No. 41 [40]

Mr. Maurice COST, formerly proprietor of the Hamilton Marble Shop, died at Western Port, W. Va. on the 21st inst. and his remains were interred there on the 23d. Death was caused by a complication of diseases. He leaves a wife and one child.

Major Thos. R. FOSTER died last Wednesday night at his home at Marshall, aged 79 years, He was a successful farmer in Fauquier. Three daughters and two sons, Captains J. W. and J. H. FOSTER survive him. During the war he served in the quartermaster's department of the Confederate army.

Miss Julia Eleanor MENARD, daughter of Mrs. E. D. MENARD, of our neighborhood, was to have been married at 11 a.m. yesterday, in St. Bartholomew's Church, Baltimore, to Mr. Albert G. PALMER of that city.

Mrs. Mary C. HAINES, widow of the late Washington HAINES, died at her home near our town, at 11 a.m. Wednesday, aged nearly 77 years. Death was due to old age. her funeral will take place from the house at 10:30 a.m. tomorrow, Saturday. Interment at Lake View Cemetery. Her consort died one year ago last Friday.

Thomas E. FISHER of Leesburg and Miss Lisa B. MUNDAY, of Morrisonville, eloped from their homes this morning and came to Frederick on an early train and as the Clerk was about to sign the license a Western Union messenger boy appeared with a message from the man's father that the son was not of age. The young couple left on an afternoon train for Pa. where they said their plans would not be frustrated again.

A marriage license was issued from the Clerk's Office in this town, on Tuesday, to Mr. Wm. E. ELLMORE and Miss Geneva MITCHELL, daughter of Mr. Wm. MITCHELL, both of Loudoun.

Mr. and Mrs. B. F. LEITH have issued cards for the marriage of their daughter, M. Olivia, to Mr. Alfred P. MEGEATH, the ceremony to take place at the M. E. Church at Aldie at 12 o'clock Feb. 6th 1886 [96].

Mrs. John BELL died at the residence of her son, Mr. C. C. BELL, in Hillsboro at an early hour Tuesday morning in about the 80th year of her age. Interment at Arnold Grove.

Matilda MOTON, wife of Jessie MOTON died at her home in this town last Thursday after a protracted illness. Her funeral took place Saturday afternoon from the colored M. E. Church. Interment in the colored cemetery, Rev. ___ NORWOOD officiating.

Mr. Thomas J. BROWN of this vicinity [Bolington] died on Monday evening about three o'clock of Bright's disease. He leaves a wife and four children. He was a consistent member of the Lutheran Church.

Yesterday on the farm of Col. R. H. DULANEY, Mr. David CARTER lost his left hand in a machine. He was the son of Mr. Furlong CARTER, about 25 years old, and has a wife and one child.

Friday, 7 February 1896   Vol. XVIII, No. 42 [41]

Jonathan BOYD a respected colored man, met a violent death at his home, near Paeonian Springs last Saturday. He went into the woods and was crushed under a limb of a tree that he had felled. His funeral took place at Waterford on Monday.

Joel L. NIXON, father of the Nixon Brothers, of Leesburg, died in that town last Sunday the result of a carbuncle which appeared on his neck a few weeks ago and subsequently erysipelas in his face. He was in the 70th year of his age. Col. NIXON was born near Leesburg, in March 1818. He engaged in mercantile pursuits. He was a Justice of the Peace in the old days. He also held a commission as colonel of the 57th Va militia. He serviced as Deputy Sheriff and retired from that position some 5 or 6 years ago.

Mr. W. H. TRIPLETT died at his home at Orlean, Fauquier county, of pneumonia. He was 62 years of age.

On Wednesday evening of last week, Mrs. McDONOUGH, widow of the late W. W. McDONOUGH of this town, and Mr. Thos A. BAKER, overseer of the poor for Mercier district, were married at the bride's residence in this town, Rev. J. W. GRUBB, officiating. The groom gave his age as 77, while the bride is considerably younger.

Mrs. S. P. ALLENDER died at her home near Morrisonville, Wednesday evening. Her remains were interred in the Union Cemetery, Friday.

Gideon HOUSEHOLDER of Lovettsville, who has been an invalid for several years, died last Sunday evening. Interment today at the Union Cemetery.

Kellars, W. Va.: Mr. John HOUZER died last Saturday at his home at the Virginia Ore Bank. Scarlet fever, Mr. John MINN has lost a son, 9 years of age, and a daughter is sick.

Died: Jonathan BOYD, suddenly at his home at Paeonian Spring, on the 1st of Feb. 1896, aged 68y 1m 17d. He leaves a wife and eleven children.

Friday, 14 February 1896   Vol. XVIII, No. 43 [42]

News received at Lincoln a few days ago of the death of William WILSON oldest son of Folger WILSON, of Richmond Indiana.

Co. Ct.: Will of Mary E. HAINES admitted to probate. A. J. BRADFIELD qualified as Exor. of Mary E. HAINES. O. J. PIERPOINT qualified as Admr. of Jonathan BOYD dec'd. C. C. WENNER qualified as Admr. of Thomas J. BROWN dec'd. C. J. C. MAFFETT qualified as Admr. of M. E. McFARLAND dec'd. C. C. GAVER qualified as Guardian of Elwood HAMPTON, minor over 14 years of age.

Friday, 21 February 1896   Vol. XVIII, No. 44 [43]

The wife of Mr. C. W. HAMMERLY died at her home at Woodgrove last Friday.

A marriage license was issued in Washington last week to Anton MAYOR of Minnesota and Dora T. FILLINGANE, of Lovettsville.

Philomont, Feb. 17 – Our Deputy Sheriff, Mr. Eugene MONROE buried one of his children, a little girl two years old. Mrs. Alice BROWN was laid to rest in the Friend's burial ground, at Lincoln, yesterday. She leaves two sons and one daughter. Mr. Turner DILLON, of our village and Miss Lutie CASTLE, of Wythe Co. Va went to Washington and were married last week.

Died: At the residence of her father, James CLIPP, on the 13th of Feb. 1896, Maggie, eldest daughter, in the 18th year of her age.

Friday, 28 February 1896   Vol. XVIII, No. 45 [44]

N. Clifford NICHOLS was called home on Monday to attend the funeral, on Tuesday the 25th, of his brother, Hon. J. Wilber NICHOLS, who died Sunday after a short illness of pneumonia, at his home, in St. Clairsville, Ohio.

Bolington, Feb. 26 – The remains of Mrs. Elias COOPER who died on Monday of last week were interred in the Union Cemetery on Friday. Mrs. J. M. VICKERS died of pneumonia on Saturday the 22nd and her remains were interred in the Union Cemetery on Monday. The marriage of Miss Effie REED and Mr. ___ EVERHART is announced to take place today at the residence of the bride's father, J. R. REED.

Mrs. J. A. ANDERSON died last Thursday night at the residence of her husband, Mr. James A. ANDERSON in this town.

Mrs. Laudolia E. WALLACE, wife of Mr. Lawson K. WALLACE, died Friday at her residence in this town, of pneumonia, aged 27 years.
Fanny JACKSON, a worthy colored woman, who had been living with the family of Mr. T. H. VANDEVANTER for several years, accompanied them when they moved from near Waterford to this town in January, was found dead in bed last Saturday morning at the Rock Spring where Mr. VANDEVANTER resides.
Mr. Jerome DAWSON, son of Mr. Jas. M. DAWSON, of this town, died at his father's residence on Monday last, of consumption. He was 30 years of age. His remains were interred in Union Cemetery yesterday (Wednesday) elder E. V. WHITE officiating.
On Tuesday evening of last week, Mr. Wm. J. GIDDINGS, son of Mr. Glen GIDDINGS of this county, and for some years engaged in business in Washington and Miss Mary WATERS were married at Trinity Church, Tacoma Park, near Washington, Rev. Dr. WATERS, uncle of the bride officiating.
Mr. Frank DANIEL died at his home near Mountain Gap on Sunday morning last of pneumonia in the 62nd year of his age. At 8 o'clock Sunday morning he passed away.

Friday, 6 March 1896   Vol. XVIII, No. 46 [45]

Miss Susan NICHOLS, daughter of Saml. NICHOLS deceased and sister of Wm. NICHOLS, of Hamilton, was buried yesterday at Friends burying ground, in Lincoln. She died at the home of her sister, Mrs. PIGGOTT, at Vienna, Fairfax County.
Isaac PRICE, of this place, for 30 years a member of the United Brethren Church, died very suddenly during one of the revival meetings. He leave a wife and seven children. He was a Federal soldier during the late war. In the battle of Winchester of '61 he was struck by a shell and in consequence of which both arms were amputated.
Columbia Ohio State Journal: J. W. NICHOLS of Belmont County, Ohio [brother of N. Clifford NICHOLS of Loudoun] was born in Belmont county 37 years ago and was of Quaker parentage. He attended school about 15 years ago at Ohio State university.

Friday, 13 March 1896   Vol. XVIII, No. 47 [46]

Mr. Samuel SHOWERS, citizen of Berryville, died on Tuesday aged about 70 years.
Miss Lizzie BRADEN died at her home, the residence of her brother, Mr. Walter BRADEN, last Saturday evening, and her remains were interred at Catoctin Church on Monday. She was about 50 years of age. It began with an attack of grip which resulted in pneumonia.
Just a week after the death of Miss Susan NICHOLS, her sister Mrs. John PIGGOTT died at her home near Vienna and on Tuesday her body was brought back to its native county and buried at Lincoln.

She was a daughter of Saml. NICHOLS, who resided near Philomont, and prior to moving to Fairfax she with her husband lived near Unison. Pneumonia was the cause of the death of both sisters.
Co. Ct.: Wills of David AXLINE and Gideon HOUSEHOLDER admitted to probate. Jno. W. AXLINE qualified as executor of Gideon HOUSEHOLDER. Jno. H. NELSON qualifies as Admr. of Susan T. NICHOLS. Mrs. Rose ALDER qualified as guardian of Irwin ALDER. E. F. RAPHAEL qualified as guardian of Cabel Y. PEPTON [PEYTON]. Fenton M. LOVE Sr. resigned as committee for Geo. M. MORRIS.
Tobias WILLIAMS, an aged citizen of vicinity of Lovettsville, died on Wednesday of last week. His remains were interred at the Lutheran Church on Saturday.
Last Tuesday afternoon, Mr. Chas. W. WEADON and Miss Ann E. SCATTERDAY were united in marriage at their home on the Haines farm. The ceremony was performed by Rev. R. R. S. HOUGH.

Friday, 20 March 1896   Vol. XVIII, No. 48 [47]

Mr. Jas. A. FLING, of Farmwell and Miss Edith GREEN, of Rockville, Md., were married at the Metropolitan church in Washington last Monday evening.
Mrs. Annie RINKER, wife of Wm. RINKER Sr. died at her home in Waterford, last Saturday and her funeral took place on Monday.
Mr. Thomas SWANN, grandson of the late Gov. SWANN, died at the home of his mother, in Baltimore, last Monday, from an attack, we understand, of Bright's Disease. He was 32 years of age.
Died, at Harpers Ferry, on Friday last, Mrs. Bettie SMITH, wife of Mr. Samuel SMITH, formerly of this county and a daughter of the late Thomas HOUGH, also of this county.
Mr. Chas. GAVER and Miss Dean ARTHUR were united in the bonds of wedlock, by Rev. C. T. HERNDON at the Baptist Parsonage last Wednesday morning.
Mrs. Esther CARROLL, widow of the late James CARROLL, died at her home in Baltimore last Friday. She had been in failing health for about a year.

Friday, 27 March 1896   Vol. XVIII, No. 48

Mrs. Chas. REAMER died at her home near Dover, last Thursday and on Saturday her remains were buried at Middleburg.
Robert STABLER died at his home, near Sandy Spring, Md, last Thursday, and his funeral took place on Saturday. Member of the Society of Friends. His widow was a native of Loudoun.
William SILCOTT, resident of Lincoln neighborhood died at his home last Sabbath morning and on Tuesday his funeral took place from the meeting house of the Orthodox Friends. A few weeks ago he

had a fall from the steps of his house,, which caused the breaking of one of his ribs. He was in the 84th year of his age.

Mr. Albert GREGG and Miss Mary HATCHER were married at the home of the bride's mother, in Purcellville, at 11 a.m. Wednesday, by the Rev. C. T. HERNDON.

The engagement is announced of Miss Eugenia TENNANT, daughter of Mrs. David B. TENNANT, to Mr. Henry FAIRFAX of Loudoun county. Since the removal of the family from Petersburg to Richmond, ...

Mrs. Susan CAVANAGH, widow of the late Martin CAVANAGH, of this county, died at her residence in Washington on Monday night, aged 60 years. Her remains were brought to Leesburg on Wednesday and interred in Union Cemetery.

Mr. John T. LAWS of Aldie died at his home on Tuesday evening. Mr. LAWS had been in bad health for some time; his son Rev. Curtis Lee LAWS, of Baltimore, and other children, and wife, were with him at the sad hour.

Fauquier: Mr. B. F. SMITH died Thursday morning of pneumonia at his residence near Bethel Academy, aged about sixty years.

Friday, 3 April 1896   Vol. XVIII, No. 49

Mr. Joseph A. WILLIAMSON, brother-in-law of Mrs. Dr. McGILL, of Leesburg, died at his home in Frederick Md, last Saturday.

Miss Nora E. PURCELL, daughter of Mr. J. F. PURCELL, and Mr. C. S. THOMAS, of Frederick Co. Md, were married at the Leesburg Inn, by Rev. E. S. HINKS, at 2 p.m. last Thursday. The wedding was quietly conducted in consideration of the recent death of the groom's father.

Last Monday morning Wm. POWELL and his son Aquilla were fatally overcome by gas in the Leesburg lime kiln. The old many was somewhat over 60 years of age and the son twenty odd.

Waterford: James BOYD was buried Tuesday.

Mrs. Mary Ellen HELM, widow of the late Joseph HELM died last Tuesday, at the home of her son-in-law, Mr. L. M. SHUMATE, in the 85th year of her age. Her remains were interred in the Leesburg cemetery on Friday afternoon, Rev. Dr. HEAD officiating. He was a member of Harmony M. E. Church South.

Mr. Edward COMPHER, formerly of Loudoun county, died at his parent's home near Jefferson, Frederick county, Md., last week.

Mrs. TYLER, wife of Mr. Douglas TYLER, died Tuesday night at her home near the Trappe, of pneumonia. Her funeral will take place today (Thursday) at 1 o'clock from St. James church.

Died: Mahala LUCAS, died at the residence of her daughter, Amanda MASON, on March 10th 1896, in the 92 year of her age.

Friday, 10 April 1896   Vol. XVIII, No. 50

Mr. Ben LOWE and Miss Orra THOMPSON, were married one day last week, by Rev. C. T. HERNDON.

Mr. Robert KELLY drove over to Loudoun county on Monday and returned with Mrs. Emma RECTOR. They stopped at the residence of J. D. HOLMES of Boliver, where the Rev. Louis HENCK joined in wedlock two happy hearts. The groom had lived 76 years in single blessedness and the bride of 62 summers is now enjoying her third marriage. – *Harpers Ferry Sentinel.*

Daniel MONDAY, a native of Loudoun county, died at his home in Winfield, Henry Co., Iowa about two weeks ago. He was born and raised in the vicinity of Waterford, and he was there married to the niece of his employer, Wm. B. STEER. About 40 years ago, with others of this section emigrated to Iowa, where he located and spent the remainder of his long life of about 85 years.

Dr. H. B. TRIST, son of the late Nicholas P. TRIST and a brother of Mrs. John W. BURKE, died in Washington at half past two o'clock yesterday from pneumonia. He was in the 65th year. Before the war Dr. TRIST was a surgeon in the U. S. Navy and was stationed on the ship Vandalia. Previous to that time he was a civil engineer. During the war he was in the Confederate army. After the war he became a practicing physician in Washington and Baltimore. – *Alex. Gazette.*

Married: On Tuesday Mar. 24th, 1896, at the residence of the bride's mother, by Rev. MOSS, John Edwin CARRUTHERS, formerly of Loudoun county, to Miss Emma Louis CARTER, all of Cumberland county, Va.

Married on the 17th of October 1896, by Rev Joseph T. KELLEY, of the Fourth Presbyterian Church, Washington DC, Charles M. HELFENSTEIN, to Miss Nannie McGILL. *Fred. Citizen.*

Married: Miss Annie C. GREENLEASE, daughter of the late J. H. GREENLEASE, of Loudoun and Mr. B. ROBINSON of Scranton, Pa, were quietly married Wednesday, Mar. 25th at 5 o'clock p.m., Rev. Dr. KELLEY officiating. They will reside in Pa.

Friday, 17 April 1896   Vol. XVIII, No. 51

A marriage license was issued in Washington Tuesday, to Wm. B. MINOR and ???da B. SMITH, both of Loudoun county. [page torn]

April Ct.: Wills of David F. DANIEL and Thos. SWANN admitted to probate. Alonzo DANIEL qualified as Executor of David F. DANIEL. Estate of Jno. BARNHOUSE committed to Sheriff. Edgar McCRAY qualified as Admr. of Mary E. BRADEN dec'd. Estate of Samuel T. JACKSON committed to Sheriff.

A marriage license was issued last week at Fairfax C. H. to Mr. Amos S. JENKINS of Loudoun, and Miss Mary B. WYNKOOP of Fairfax county.

James F. CONNER, second son of James W. and Louisa A. CONNER, and grandson of the late Maj. James F. DIVINE, died at the residence of his parents in this town, on Thursday morning last, April 9th in the 27th year of his age, after a long illness.

On Thursday last a quiet wedding took place in the parlors of the Hotel Linden in this town. The contracting parties were Mr. W. H. DANIEL, and Miss Magnolia MADDOX, both of this county. Performed by Rev. J. W. GRUBB, of the Methodist Church South.

Mr. W. B. MINOR, a public school teacher of Loudoun was married to Miss Armanda B. SMITH, of New York, formerly of Hillsboro, April 7th at the residence of the bride's brother, in Washington DC.

Mrs. Fannie HIRST, wife of Smith HIRST, died at her home in Purcellville March 28th 1896 of Bright's disease. Funeral was Sunday afternoon, March 29th, services by Rev. C. BALL and Mr. A. HOSKINSON.

Friday, 24 April 1896   Vol. XVIII, No. 52

Miss Nancy LANG died at her residence near Short Hill church, on Friday last at the age of 91 years. Her remains were interred in the burying ground at the church on Sunday, Rev. I. B. LAKE, officiating.

On April 18th after a wearisome illness, Margaret MYERS late of Old Farmwell, aged 72 years. She leaves a husband, two sons, one daughter, eight grandchildren and three great grandchildren.

Died April 22 '96, Mr. Samuel LANG at his home near Hillsboro. He had been an invalid for some time.

Died: Mrs. Mary A. MEADE died at her residence in Leesburg on Thursday last in the 85th year of her age after a long illness.

Mary PIGGOTT died at her home near Lincoln April 18th 1896. She was in the 80th year of her age and had spent her long life on the farm where she died, the home of Samuel P. BROWN. She was a member of the Society of Friends and was laid to rest in their burial ground, at Lincoln on Monday last.

[MISSING ISSUES]

Friday, 11 September 1896   Vol. XIX, No. 20

Joseph JACKSON, one of the oldest men of Frederick county was buried last Tuesday at Hopewell burying grounds of the Society of Friends. He had been confined to his bed for many years.

On Wednesday, the death of a little child, Katie G., daughter of Jas. H. BERN, who lives near the railroad a short distance west of Farmwell. The small child was struck by a locomotive.

Jacob CARSON, an old farmer of Goresville, committed suicide on Wednesday night. He leaves a widow and seven children, five sons and two daughters, all grown. His funeral took place Friday.

Died: Guilford White CUEN, in Lincoln on Aug. 4th, aged 3m 19d, son of Gustavus M. and Ida M. CUEN, of Washington.

Died: On Friday, Sept. 4th, 1896, at 2 p.m. at the residence of his aunt, Mrs. F. A. WALKER, Washington DC, Norman L., youngest son of T. S. and E. M. WRIGHT, of Woodlawn, Fairfax Co. in his 25th years.

Mrs. Sarah EAMICH, mother of Mrs. Luther H. POTTERFIELD, which whom she resided. She has been failing in health for some time. She died on the 21st of August and her funeral services took place on Sunday in the Reformed Church, of which she was a member. Three children survive: Mrs. L. H. POTTERFIELD, of Lovettsville, and Mr. George EAMICH, of the same place and Mr. John EAMICH of Morrisonville. She also leaves 6 grand children and 3 great grandchildren.

INDEX

ABEL
  Lillian E., 90
  R. B., 90
ACHANER
  E. P., 96
ACHER
  David, 61
  Harry, 61
ADAMS
  C. B., 121
  Caroline, 121
  Chas. B., 168
  Chas. H., 20
  Daniel, 26
  Evelyn, 168
  Fannie, 132
  Hoover, 29
  Ida, 86
  J. H., 54
  James, 132
  Lucy, 54, 83
  Marietta, 102
  Sallie J., 55
  William H., 21
ADIE
  Jas. L., 89
  Jennie, 72
  Mary J., 89
AFFETT
  Edna, 66
AISQUITH
  Charles W., 92
ALDER
  Irwin, 178
  James, 30
  Jas., 58
  Marietta, 30
  Rose, 178
ALDRIDGE
  A. P., 150
  Andrew, 126
  John, 126, 143, 150

ALEXANDER
  Burr T., 17
  E. M., 20
  Jno. H., 10
  John H., 10, 24, 117
  Malvina G., 17
  Mary M., 17
ALLDER
  Lute, 77
  Nathan, 77
ALLEN
  Albina P., 104
  Austin, 143
  Geo. W., 104
  Helen, 109
  Henry, 38
  Nimrod S., 41
  Ruth F., 104
ALLENDER
  Ashby, 57
  S. P., 175
ALLISON
  Geo., 100
  George, 100
  Richard, 100
ALLNUTT
  Calhoun, 55
ALTMAN
  H. E., 15
AMBLER
  Vincent, 105
ANDERS
  C. V., 140, 143
ANDERSON
  ___, 22
  Capt., 151
  J. A., 176
  James A., 176
  Kate, 140
  Nimrod, 91, 92
  Orion, 22
  Silas E., 134
ANDREWS

  Paul A., 55
ANKERS
  Jno., 89
  Saml., 5
APPLE
  Eugenia, 97
  Thos., 9
ARCHER
  Ellen D., 10
ARNETT
  Chas. E., 116
  Rodney, 46
  Samuel, 63, 168
  William, 168
  Wm., 63
ARNOLD
  Almeta, 49
  Almeta M., 49
  Bettie A., 49
  Bettie M., 49
  E. Sheldon, 49
  Elmer E., 8
  Emeline, 144
ARTHUR
  Dean, 178
ARUNDELL
  Chas. A., 117
ASHBY
  Maggie R., 144
  Turner, 125
ASHLEY
  Ella, 69
  Wm., 69
ASKINS
  R. L., 141
ATHEY
  Annie V., 138
  John M., 157
ATKINSON
  Prof., 101
ATTWELL
  B. R., 61
  Ewell, 42
  Florence M., 42

INDEX

Ida V., 142
ATWELL
___, 18
C. E., 102
E. Chas., 98
Ewell, 98
AULT
John, 101
AUSTIN
David, 92
AVERILLE
Wm. B., 89
AXLINE
David, 171, 178
Ely, 78
Jno. W., 178
AYERS
Thos., 29
AYRE
Wm., 5
AYRES
Emeline, 129
Thos. W., 33, 129

BADGER
Jos. N., 142
BAER
Dolly G., 70
James G., 70
Rutherford B. H., 70
William, 70
BAILEY
Chapin, 119
Mamie, 12
Mountjoy, 119
BAILLIE
John J., 68
BAKER
Bud, 154
Chas., 27
Elizabeth, 128
Frank, 108
Geo. S., 109
George, 7
Harlan, 99
J. R., 44, 45, 51

Jack, 4
Jos. D., 41
Mollie, 27
T. C., 41
Thos. A., 175
BALCH
Lethia, 160
Royal L., 160
BALDWIN
Dr., 112
Jos., 129
Jos. A., 22
M. K., 39
Mary, 112
Ruth, 39
BALL
C. Matt, 36
Elizabeth, 116
G. W., 16
Henry, 174
Henry A., 116
Mary B., 16
Saml. H., 174
Thomas, 47
Thos. L., 174
Wm., 99, 124
BALLENGER
Clinton C., 3
Dorcas O., 3
Edgar, 3
Rosa P., 64
BALLOU
L. D., 36
BANKS
Samuel, 106
BARBER
Emma M., 116
J., 99
J. T., 116, 132
BARNETT
Mrs., 86
BARNHOUSE
Edgar J., 173
Jno., 180
Nelson W., 67, 173

Randolph, 124, 173
BARRETT
Sarah A., 90
BARRON
Jennie, 148
BARROWS
M. A., 90
BARTLETT
N. H., 8
Rebecca H. V., 8
BASIQUE
Louisa S., 166
BASSELL
Etta, 76
Henrietta B., 102
J. Y., 74
John Y., 102
BAST
W. F., 106
BATCHELOR
Dr., 101
BAUCKMAN
Mollie O., 132
BAYNE
Margaret, 140
BEACH
Andrew, 97
Barbara, 97
Hattie, 10
BEALES
J. E., 44, 81
Mort. J., 114
Mortimer, 44, 71
Rodney, 84
S. Ella, 44
BEALL
Annie L., 115
Thomas B., 84
BEAMER
George, 168
Nelson, 117
BEANS
A., 96
A. H., 131
Aaron, 48, 141
Alice, 49

The Telephone
INDEX

Amos, 49
Amy A., 46
Flora, 48
H. P., 82, 115
Joseph A., 49
Lutie, 35
M. Lacy, 82
Maggie, 96
Martha, 49
Monisa, 131
William, 118, 124
Wm. A., 26
BEARD
  Eliza R., 41
BEATTY
  Samuel J., 150
BEATY
  Lulu B., 2
BEAVERS
  Delilah, 31
  Delilah H., 34
  Maurice W., 172
  Morgan, 52
  Thos., 31
BECKER
  Harry, 146, 147
BECKWITH
  J. B., 66
BEENS
  Morrell, 131
BELL
  A. B., 146
  Albert, 143
  C. C., 175
  Jos. W., 62
  Julia, 143, 146
  Roberta B., 26
BELL
  John, 175
BELLESON
  Mary R., 154
BELT
  Townsend, 167
BENEDICT
  Henrietta, 45
  Maria W., 106
  Miss, 165

BENEDUM
  Sarah A., 34
BENJAMIN
  Sarah E., 149
BENNETT
  Ed. L., 123
  Fannie, 81
  Josie, 123
  Ruth H., 123
  Sidnor, 13, 55
  Sydnor, 13, 57
  Virginia, 13
  Wm., 81
BENTLEY
  E. B., 12
  Mary A., 12
  Richard T., 21
  Robert, 120
BENTLY
  Annie, 29
  R. M., 29
BENTON
  J. M., 130
  James M., 129
  Jas. M., 170
  Margaret A., 170
  Nancy T., 50
BERKLEY
  Edmund, 71
BERN
  Jas. H., 181
  Katie G., 181
BERRY
  Amanda C., 10
  Mamie, 140
BEST
  Albert, 40
  Amanda T., 41
  Anna H., 89
  Bula, 89
  Edgar, 89
  Edward, 89
  Jno. Wm., 86
  John Wm., 84
  Parmelia A., 106
BETTIS
  Mr., 148

BEUCHLER
  Belle, 63
  J. R., 63
BIRCH
  Lee, 92
BIRD
  Chas. D., 166
  Mary E., 166
BIRDSALL
  Alvin J., 133
  Ann, 104
  Anna A., 133
  Benjamin, 148
  Carrie V., 133
  Charles W., 156
  David, 28
  Effie L., 156
  Elizabeth M., 11
  James M., 133
  Joel, 133
  John, 133
  Mary, 133
  Rebecca, 11, 148
  Sarah, 124
BIRKBY
  E. W., 136
  Edgar W., 12
  Susan, 97
  Thomas, 97
BISER
  W. G., 2
BISPHAM
  M. S., 135
BITZER
  Joseph R., 85
BIXLER
  Lidie, 135
BLACKFORD
  Thos. E., 73
BLACKMORE
  J. Robert, 125
  Robert, 170
  Swan, 153
BLACKNELL
  Lizzie, 129
BLACKWELL
  Leroy, 100

The Telephone
INDEX

BLAINE
  Jas. G., 168
  Margaret, 168
  Robert G., 168
BLAIR
  David, 3, 20
  J. E., 12
BLAKER
  William, 166
BLANCH
  Annie, 163
BLANCHARD
  H. C., 90
  H. W., 90
  Martha S., 90
  Ozias, 56, 90
BLANKENBAKER
  ____, 101
BLINCO
  James, 39
BLINCOE
  Chas W., 110
  John, 20
BLONHAM
  William, 118
BODMER
  Annie E., 144
  Jacob, 2
  Mary G., 144
BOERLY
  Thomas, 161
BOGER
  Ella, 78
  Ella V., 79
  Luther B., 2
BOLON
  George H., 169
BOLYN
  Somerfield, 31
  Summerfield, 39
  T. M., 39
  Tolliver, 31
BOND
  Alice W., 10
  Asa M., 10
  Beverley J., 77
  Carrie, 25

  Edward, 19
  John, 90
  Rev., 77
  Sarah, 19
  T. H., 25
BOOTH
  Charles, 34
BORDEN
  Daniel, 2
BOTELER
  Alexander R., 57
  Helen, 57
  Marshall, 160
BOTTS
  Sophia I., 154
  Wm., 154
BOUCHET
  Elizabeth M., 130
  J. M., 131
BOWIE
  Thomas M., 156
BOYD
  Daniel, 5
  J. Wm., 108
  James, 179
  Jonathan, 175, 176
BRABHAM
  Blanch, 98
BRADEN
  Lizzie, 177
  Mary E., 180
  Oscar, 173
  Oscar S., 173
  Walter, 173, 177
BRADFIELD
  A. J., 2, 50, 121, 149, 176
  Ivan C., 2
BRADLEY
  Julia, 78
BRADY
  A. P., 100
  Thos. C., 56
BRAMHALL
  Bettie, 22
BRAMWELL

  J. H., 130
BRANDON
  Betsy, 68
  Sallie, 112
BRAWNER
  J. F., 142
BREADY
  Edith, 143
  Ella, 121
  Etta, 143
  Isaiah, 121, 143
BRECKENRIDGE
  A. N., 159
  Alexander N., 153
  Bettie C., 159
  David A., 23
BRENT
  Robert, 80
BRINTON
  J. R., 14
BRISCO
  Francis, 12
BROAD
  Millard T., 112
BROGDEN
  Sophie, 128
BROOKS
  Ada, 24
  Philip W., 24
  Thomas, 103
  Wm. H., 93, 124
BROSIUS
  E. H., 113
  Lillie C., 113
  Samuel H., 111
BROWN
  A. P., 42
  Alice, 176
  B. F., 13, 14
  Bertie, 57
  Charles, 19
  Chas. J., 18
  Chas. L., 6
  D. H., 104
  Daisy D., 142
  David, 45, 110
  David H., 96

The Telephone
INDEX

Elizabeth, 122
Eugene, 144
Fannie, 127
Florence G., 38
Frances O., 28
G. W., 117
Hattie, 105
Isaac, 52
J. I., 124
J. R., 128
J. W., 28
Jacob, 146
Jane C., 133
Jas. E., 116
Jennie, 108
Jesse H., 45
Joshua P., 1
L. A., 15, 128
Lewis A., 167
Lizzie T., 41
M. F., 166
Martha J., 32, 70, 118, 119
Mary, 18
Mary L., 6
Mollie M., 21
Morris L., 15
Nathan T., 61, 70, 172
Rebecca, 96
Richard, 69
Rose, 20
Ruthie, 96
Sallie, 95
Saml., 40, 147
Samuel, 52
Samuel N., 101
Samuel P., 69, 181
Sarah E., 130
Sharon, 134
Susan P., 32
T., 57, 136
Thomas, 122
Thomas J., 32, 134, 175, 176
Thos., 17
Warner M., 57, 122
William, 147
William H., 32, 70, 118, 119, 163
Wm., 69
Wm. H., 1
BROWNE
 Elizabeth, 131
 Florence E., 27
 Marrow, 131
BROYDRICK
 T. J., 104
BRUIN
 Linnie, 91
BRYANT
 Edward, 97
 Geo. W., 159
BUCHANAN
 Martin N., 91
BUCKLEY
 Thos. W., 166
BUCKNER
 Charles E., 133
 Evelyn, 128
BUDD
 Isaac D., 9
BUEHLER
 Elizabeth S., 120
BUFFINGTON
 Armstead, 65
BURCH
 Edgar F., 19
 Mary, 19
BURDETTE
 C. C., 27
BURGESS
 Louisa, 152
BURKE
 John W., 180
 Mary A., 160, 162, 166
 R. G., 166
 R. S., 166
BURR
 M. W., 130
BURROWS
 Arthur B., 125
BURTON
 John H., 150
BUTLER
 David, 107
 Wm., 57
BUTTER
 ___, 13
BUTTS
 Calvin, 161
 Mary A., 161
 Mary J., 31
 Oliver G., 31
 Wm., 41
CALDWELL
 Charles E., 158
 S. B. T., 158
CALHOUN
 T. C., 101
CALLOW
 A. H., 108
 Albert H., 110
CAMP
 Isaac, 146
 Mary, 5
 Thomas, 146
 Thomas E., 146, 148
CAMPBELL
 Arthur, 121
 Robert G., 151
 S. A., 14
CARIE
 Annie E., 50
 James, 50
CARLIN
 W. H., 8
CARLISLE
 David, 52
 Joseph A., 27
 Julia, 48
 Mary A., 52
 Miss, 64
CARPENTER
 Josiah, 75

Milton W., 140
CARR
  David, 44, 75
  Hannah, 75
  John C., 38
  Joseph, 123
  Martha, 123
  Mary E., 44
  W. B., 146
CARROLL
  Chas., 123
  Esther, 178
  James, 104, 178
CARRUTHERS
  Joel, 100
  John E., 180
CARSON
  Frank, 120
  Jacob, 79, 181
  Jacob B., 140
  Roberta, 79
CARTER
  Ann P., 128
  Anne, 58
  Anne P., 127
  Armstead, 11
  B. G., 110
  C. S., 127
  C. Shirley, 128
  Cassandra, 70
  David, 175
  Elijah, 115
  Elizabeth O., 117
  Emma L., 180
  F. A., 149
  Francis, 153
  Francis M., 42
  Frank, 98
  Furlong, 175
  Geo. W., 11
  George W., 165
  Jno., 116
  Lillian, 111
  M. Elizabeth, 42
  Maria E., 116
  Oswell, 48
  R. J., 111
  Robt. S., 69
  Shirley, 74
  Susan, 130
  T. H., 106, 109, 110, 111, 114
  Thos. A., 148
  Wm. B., 1
  Wm. M., 70
CARTER
  John A., 145
CASE
  Anna A., 22
  Annie A., 21, 30
  Clara, 144
  Geo. W., 44
  Mabel, 44
  Mary F., 30
  Rosa B., 44
  W. W., 30
CASSADAY
  William H., 155
  Wm. H., 155
CASSADY
  C. E., 155
  E. R., 155
  Irving C., 155
  Josephene C., 155
  William H., 155
CASTLE
  Archibald B., 138
  Lutie, 176
CASTLE & MULLEN, 106, 117
CASTLEMAN
  M. M., 55
  Mrs., 42
CAVANAGH
  Martin, 179
  Susan, 179
CHAFFE
  Charles, 20
CHAMBERLAIN
  Dr., 117
  Minnie A., 134
  Mrs., 117
CHAMBERLIN
  ___, 61
CHAMBERS
  E. H., 28
CHAMBLIN
  A. B., 2, 133
  A. G., 2
  Agnes, 123
  Albert K., 52
  Clara, 2
  Ellzey, 47, 99, 151
  Eveline B., 2
  Flora, 137
  H., 110
  J. L., 114
  J. Lee, 113, 117
  Jas. H., 123
  Jessie, 52
  Jno., 137
  John, 3, 47
  John M., 117
  Julia, 114
  Julia A., 170
  L. L., 39
  Laura, 23
  Lee, 111
  Miss, 81
  Oliver J. C., 168
  Orland, 52
  R. C. L., 114
  Rosa, 23
  Sarah E., 151
  W. W., 98, 113
  Walter, 23
  Wm., 137
CHAMP
  Catharine, 31
  Catherine, 31
  Joseph, 29
  Joseph L., 31
  Kitty, 29
  Luke, 80
CHANCELLOR
  ___, 35
  Lorman, 126
  Margt. E., 126

S. C., 126
CHANDLEE
  Albert, 12
  Mahlon, 30
CHAPEN
  Charles, 47
CHAPIN
  Minnie, 47
CHEW
  Harry M., 87
CHICHESTER
  A. M., 170
  Authur, 168
  G. M., 128
  Mary B., 168, 170
  Mary R., 170
  May, 128
CHILDS
  E. E., 138
CHINN
  Charles, 63
  Chloe, 35
  Emory V., 8
  F. W., 36
  Francis, 63, 87
  Jno. L., 36
  John, 14
  John L., 35
  Kenny C., 25
  W. R., 11
CHURCH
  Carrie B., 131
  Chas. D., 67
  Julia, 67
  Lewis E., 131
  M. E., 16
  Merton E., 131
  Methel, 67
CLAGETT
  ___, 2
  H. O., 108
  H. W., 128
  Jennie, 110
  Richard, 121
CLAGGETT
  Bessie, 120
  H. O., 110

Henry B., 120
CLAPHAM
  Ashton, 147
  Elizabeth, 76
  J. H., 76
CLARK
  Kate, 23
  Mary E., 23
CLARKE
  Mary, 21
CLENDENING
  Thomas B., 172
CLENDENNING
  William, 13
  Wm. T., 28
CLEVELAND
  Andrew W., 59
CLINE
  Alfred, 79
  Alfred T., 96
  Bertha L., 47
  C. A., 69
  Chas. A., 47
  Corrie V., 96
  Fannie B., 96
  Gracie L., 96
  Mabel R., 96
  Mary, 79
  Mary A., 90
  W. B., 69
  William, 14
  Wm., 79
CLIPP
  James, 176
  Maggie, 176
CLOWE
  Hannah V., 27, 28
  William, 34, 43
  Wm. H., 45
COATS
  Calvin, 33
  Colvin, 36
  John, 74, 83
COCHRAN
  Catharine P., 155
  Hannah J., 136
  J. Henry, 155

COCKERELL
  J. J., 130
  John, 172
COCKERILL
  Baily, 20
COCKERILLE
  Sallie L., 105
  Sanford, 39
COCKEY
  Thos. B., 114
COCKEY
  Thos. B., 111
COCKRILL
  Mark, 12
COCKRILLE
  Nancy, 3
COE
  Frank, 91
  Hester, 91
  Robt., 117
  Samuel E., 107
COFFMAN
  Charles M., 53
COGLE
  Lydia C., 170
COLE
  F. M., 17
  Herbert, 136
  Jennie, 24
  K. B., 149
  Kendric B., 24
  Laura L., 108
  Mary E., 24
COLEMAN
  F. S., 166
  J. C., 67, 166
  J. Cleveland, 164
  John I., 168
  Richard, 164
COMPHER
  Edward, 179
  Elizabeth, 28
  Florian, 58
  John, 41, 73, 117
  Joseph, 74
  Luckett, 35
  Lucy, 2, 41

Lulu, 3
Millie, 117
Mollie, 73
CONARD
　Abner M., 50
　Arthur, 50
　Belle, 50
　Ebenezer J., 9
　Jno. W., 48
　Mary A., 167, 168
　Mary E., 48
　Steven, 60
CONKLIN
　Jos. R., 159
　Mary, 159
CONNER
　James F., 181
　James W., 181
　Lizzie, 101
　Louisa A., 181
　Sallie, 53
CONNOR
　Ella M., 169
　J. W., 127
　Jesse A., 101
　Laura V., 101
　Sevella Lee, 101
　Wm. E., 101
COOK
　Alder S., 134
　Annie, 140
　Hattie, 144
　Samuel J., 162
COOKSEY
　Bertie L., 53
　Catharine, 2
　Dorcas, 146
　Sallie, 3
COOPER
　____, 78
　Adam, 43, 83
　Edgar, 25
　Elias, 176
　Geo., 18
　Geo. F., 133
　George, 17, 115
　H. Clay, 5

J. W., 116
John, 17, 170
John W., 25
Lydia C., 2
M. Ella, 27
Mary E., 99
Peter, 144
Sallie, 170
Sarah A., 25
Tilghman, 6
Wm. F., 46
COPELAND
　H., 130
　James D., 157
　Jas. D., 15
　Lindsay, 87
　Lindsey, 84
　Linsay, 4
　Mary C., 57
　Thomas F., 157
CORBIN
　Emily J., 142
　James N., 58
　Jane, 40
　Silas, 35
CORDELL
　Jos. W., 31
CORNELL
　Jno., 133
　Leah, 79
CORNWELL
　Thomas F., 8
COS
　M., 7
COSBERRY
　Peter, 8
COST
　Carrie O., 55
　Maurice, 174
　Thomas J., 87
COSTELLO
　Clinton I., 144
　James, 60
　Robert, 105
　Robt., 106
　Walter L., 106
COULBOURN

Stephen D., 10
COULLING
　Wm. M., 129
COURTNEY
　____, 101
COX
　Justice, 156
CRAIG
　J. Asa, 65
　J. F., 65
　James, 168
　Phila, 23
　Wm., 153
CRAMER
　J., 163
CRAVEN
　Guilford, 131, 137
　Hannah, 131, 150
　Ida, 137
　Joel, 137
　Lillie B., 2
　R. C., 150
　Ross, 32, 52
　Sarah, 117
　William, 18
　William H., 19
CREAL
　Elijah, 154
CREAMER
　Wm., 153
CREEL
　Elijah G., 159
　Henry W., 159
　Lula, 171
CRICKTON
　Maud D., 48
CRIDLER
　Andrew, 153
　John, 34
CRIM
　Edgar, 165
　Joseph, 50, 147
　Lou, 116
　Lula, 117
　Mollie, 147
　Mollie A., 150
　P., 116

The Telephone
INDEX

Peter, 117
CRITTENDEN
 Henry T., 102
CROCKETT
 Martha S., 149
 Mattie, 170
 Samuel, 145, 149
CROMER
 Thos. K., 71
CROSEN
 Lizzie, 78
 Margaret, 105
CROSIN
 Minnie E., 144
CROSS
 Annie, 97
 Annie V., 19
 Benj., 85
 Ella, 104
 Jas. R., 104
 Katie C., 19
 William, 19
CROSSON
 H. J., 168
CROUNSE
 Amos, 51
CROZEN
 Maud, 85
CRUMBAKER
 C. Virginia, 19
CRUSEN
 John R., 28
CRUZEN
 Ann, 28
 Wm., 28
CUEN
 Guilford W., 182
 Gustavus M., 182
 Ida M., 182
CULAN
 Larry T., 48
CULLEN
 Jessie, 20
 N. J., 20
 Thomas, 132, 137
CUMMINS
 Levi, 22

CURRELL
 Mary A. M., 137
CURRY
 Ada, 37
 Herbert, 42
 John R., 147
 Mrs., 147
CURTIS
 Edward, 173
 Martha, 173

DABNEY
 Mary A., 12
 Richard H., 12
DADE
 Mattie, 85
DAFFER
 John, 81
 Mrs., 81
DAILEY
 Florence J., 166
 John W., 166
DAILY
 Maggie V., 1
DANA
 Mary S., 36
DANIEL
 Alonzo, 180
 David F., 180
 Elizabeth J., 4, 9
 Frank, 177
 J. H., 4
 W. H., 181
DARR
 Geo. W., 17
DAVIS
 A. H., 39
 Albert, 105
 Benj., 119
 Bessie L., 99
 C. G., 41
 Edwin, 15
 Ella, 41
 Ernest E., 72
 George W., 119
 H. M., 51
 J. M., 99

Jno., 119
 John H., 7
 John M., 99
 John W., 68
 Jos. M., 144, 150
 Mary, 41
 Milton B., 67
 Minnie M., 139
 Mrs., 152
 Oliver R., 45
 R. L., 28
 R. T., 96
 Richard T., 95
 Robert L., 15
 Rodney, 65
 Susan C., 55
 W. H., 70
 W. S., 70
DAWSON
 Jas. M., 177
 Jerome, 177
DAY
 James W., 172
 Richard, 150
 Washington, 73
DAYMUDE
 BessieL., 133
 John L., 78
DEAHL
 Horace P., 167
 Sarah G., 167
DEAN
 Chas. W., 109
 Reuben, 86
DEAR
 Sarah A., 90
DEBUTTS
 Bessie, 118
 Rebecca, 117
DELANCEY
 Frances H., 138
DELANEY
 L. A., 107
DELANY
 Michael, 155
 Sophia L., 155
DELAPLANE

192   *The Telephone*
INDEX

P. H., 170
DELEPLANE
  C. C., 170
DEMONET
  J. A., 99
DENHAM
  Caroline, 32
  Charlotte E., 32
  L. H., 32
DENNIS
  John W., 30
DENNISON
  R. L., 76
  R. Lee, 76
DEREAMER
  ___, 1
DERRY
  John P., 9
  Jos. H., 156
  Joseph P., 50
  Susie, 153
  Virginia, 50
  William, 9
  Willie A., 9
DETEWILER
  Edw., 47
DETWILER
  D. L., 89
DIBRELL
  Agnes, 123
  Anthony, 123, 124
DICE
  J. C., 92
DICKY
  Thomas W., 72
DIGGS
  William, 169
DILLON
  ___, 96
  J. A., 96
  J. W., 96
  Jos. A., 96, 133
  Turner, 176
DINSMORE
  Alonzo, 53
  Annie B., 53

Johnnie, 53
DISHMAN
  C. E., 86
  Charles E., 93
  Chas. E., 93
  Eddie E., 93
  J. W., 159
  Mary V., 93
  Rosa B., 93
DIVINE
  Ann, 38
  Arthur F., 70
  C. F., 38
  Cresford, 97
  Emily, 46
  H., 127
  James F., 77, 181
  Jas. F., 26, 94, 127
  Jessie, 70
  Joseph T., 19
  Lewis M., 170
  Rata, 52
  Sarah, 19
  W. W., 52, 151
  Winona S., 19
  Wm. W., 77
DIXON
  Albert, 71
  Mrs., 87
DODD
  Bettie, 159
  Ida V., 126
  J., 159
  Jno. G., 126
  Lavinia M., 152
  Lillie, 15
  Mary E., 117
  Nora, 159
  Robt., 126
  Ruth V., 126
  W. H., 126
  Wm., 31
  William, 33
DOLL
  John W., 133
DONALDSON

Elliot S., 37
  Margaret E., 57
  Robt. B., 57
  Wm., 122
DONOHOE
  Delia, 29
  Delila, 103
  John C., 29
  Robert L., 26
  Robt. L., 110
DOOLEY
  Harry G., 53
DORRELL
  Jas. A., 157
  Woodward, 157
DORRITEE
  Jas. H., 10
DORSEY
  Portia R., 48
DOTY
  Elmer, 3
DOUGLAS
  J. Ed., 168
DOUGLASS
  Archibald N., 109
  Catherine, 69
  Chas., 109
  Wm., 69
DOWELL
  Mrs., 161
DOWNING
  A. J., 75
DOWNS
  Annie E., 36
  Mason, 85
  Stephen, 36
DRAKE
  Dr., 12
  F. T., 70
DUFORTHE
  Leon, 147
DUGGER
  A. F., 73
DULANEY
  E. B., 103
  H. G., 40
  R. H., 175

The Telephone INDEX

DULANY
  Anne, 58
  H. Grafton, 51
  Hal G., 49
  Jane, 140
  R. H., 1
DULIN
  Alfred, 13, 14
  B. P., 154
  George C., 13
  Margaret, 13, 14
DUNBAR
  Edward M., 76, 110, 156
  Harvey, 131
  Herod H., 71
  Mattie F., 53
  Mollie, 131
DUNCAN
  Edward A., 10
  Nancy, 149
DUNN
  Catharine, 159
  Jno., 152
  John, 84, 86
DUTTON
  Emma, 20
  Emma S., 21
  John B., 20, 21, 87
  Mary F., 127
DUVAL
  Nellie, 1
DYE
  Joseph, 82

EACHES
  Jos. G., 36
  Thomas, 95
EAMICH
  Ada, 116
  Ada B., 117
  Frederick, 48
  George, 182
  John, 182
  John W., 116
  Sarah, 182

EASTER
  Danl., 137
  Margaret, 137
EASTERDAY
  Marvin P., 29
  Mary E., 29
  Wm. D., 29
EASTWOOD
  Mamie E., 7
EATON
  David, 33
EDWARDS
  Chas. G., 132
  Edmonia, 142
  Howard B., 56
  John G., 29
  John W., 163
  Jos. A., 162
  Lottie, 27
  Nettie, 132
  R. H., 67, 98
  S. R., 56
  Thos. W., 57, 58
EGGLESTON
  Evolyn, 82
  Georgie, 60
EICHBURG
  Robert C., 146
EISENBURG
  Prof., 64, 66
ELGIN
  Armistead M., 79
  Benj., 43
  Chas., 79
  Florence, 26
  Francis, 26
  Geo. R., 132
  Howard, 141
  I., 26
  Jas. W., 68
  Mamie, 141
  Marla L., 108
  Mary J., 26, 33, 68
  Mattie C., 141
  Maud L., 108
  Nannie T., 43

Nora E., 108
Sarah E., 132
Thos. G., 26, 123, 141
Willie L., 28
ELLIOT
  Jessie, 33
ELLIOTT
  Annie, 20
  Eli, 7
ELLIS
  Joshua, 167
ELLMORE
  Harvey, 47
  Wm. E., 175
ELLZEY
  William, 35
ELTON
  John P., 128
EMBREY
  Edward, 98
  W. S., 135
EMMEUR
  Mrs., 144
ENGLISH
  Catherine A., 52
  Charles A., 52
  Chas. A., 106, 119
  Daisy, 165
  John A., 106
ESKRIDGE
  Addie, 97
  John W., 8
ETCHER
  Chas., 109
  Chas. E., 109
  James, 109, 110
EVANS
  Annie, 150
  Edward, 166
  Jane, 126
  Jane A., 132
  Jno. P., 75
  Louisa, 126
  Presley, 150
  Presley C., 132

193

Thomas, 146
William H., 97, 98
EVERETT
  Eunice, 171
  John, 171
EVERHART
  Bertha, 125
  Christian, 64
  Eppie, 27
  Jno. B., 53
  Mr., 176
  Owen, 53
  Philip, 173
  Rose, 125
  W. N., 125
  Wallace G., 27
  Walter, 160
EWER
  May, 48

FADELEY
  Daisy G., 169
  E. B., 68
  G. B., 98
FADELY
  Charles W., 169
  Orra M., 14, 23
FAIRFAX
  F. W., 57
  Henry, 154, 179
  John, 57, 154
FAUNTLEROY
  Charles M., 20
  Frances, 20
  J. T., 104
  Lavinia, 104
FAWLEY
  Elizabeth, 10
  Jeremiah, 10
FEASTER
  George W., 70
FELLOWS
  Catherine, 154
FENTON
  Dennis, 145
  Enoch, 143
  John, 143

FERGUSON
  Annie B., 131
  George, 149
  Jno. H., 18
  Mary E., 88
  Mrs., 154
  Romulous, 149
  S. G., 154
  William, 94
  Wm., 55
FILLER
  Ella, 65
  Harry C., 27
  Nannie J., 140
  William B., 12
  William H., 11
FILLINGANE
  Dora T., 176
FISHER
  Betsy, 160
  Isaiah, 91
  John, 160
  Thomas E., 174
FITZHUGH
  ___, 161
  Blanche, 107
  Matilda, 106
FLEMING
  Jos., 159
FLEMMING
  Ara, 159
FLETCHER
  Fannie, 47
  Isaac, 33
  Joshua, 102
  Lula, 102
  Martha, 47
  Mary, 33
  Patterson, 84
  Wm., 148
  Wm. H., 47
FLING
  Alice, 94
  Geo. W., 31, 99
  Jas. A., 178
  Nora, 96
  Rebecca, 96

W. F., 169
FLIPPO
  E. L., 171
  O. F., 171
FOLLEN
  Rebecca, 57
FOLLETT
  Chas., 164
  J. D., 165
  Jno. D., 164
FOLLIN
  Theodore M., 53
FOOTE
  Mrs., 92
  Rev. Dr., 92
FORD
  Antonia, 110
FORREST
  Margaret E., 110
FORSYTH
  Wm. H., 68
FOSTER
  Columbia B., 76
  Elizabeth C., 164
  General, 95
  J. H., 174
  J. W., 43, 89, 102, 174
  James E., 89
  James R., 106
  Margaret, 106
  Mary E., 43, 89
  T. R., 102
  Thos. R., 174
FOWLE
  Geo. A., 94
  George A., 95
FOWLER
  Carrie E., 138
FOX
  B. L., 110
  Charles, 95
  Manly, 95
  Sylvester, 79
FRAME
  Charles, 98
  Chas. A., 55, 117

The Telephone
INDEX

Sue, 98
FRANCIS
  A. B., 85
  Willard, 85
FRANKLIN
  Ida E., 53
  T. W., 60
FRASIER
  Henry, 15
  Lizzie, 15
  Richard C., 15
FRAZIER
  Lavinia, 150
FRED
  Burr P., 100
  Frank L., 49
  T. Walker, 49
FREEZE
  A. P., 149
FRENCH
  J., 67
FREY
  Clara, 35
  T. Arthur, 86
FRITTS
  F. H., 41
  Jennie, 171, 172
  Mary B., 41
  Mrs., 47
  Polly, 85
FRY
  Annie S., 25
  Bertie, 114
  Bertie J., 112
  Charles, 112
  Claretta M., 35
  E. Frank, 116
  Ella E., 116
  Harry, 121
  Isaac, 34, 35
  John, 77
  John T., 25
  Jos., 160
  Joseph, 160
  Joseph H., 160
  Josephus, 25
  Josephus M., 26

  Lena, 160
  Lena J., 160
  Linnie, 77
  Malinda E., 25
  Margaret, 48
  Mary E., 87
  Minnie, 117
  Nannie D., 116
  Nettie, 77
  Peter A., 26
  Rebecca, 35
  Samuel H., 35
  Sarah, 160
  Wm. B., 25
FULENGANE
  Edward, 114
FULTON
  Margaret, 6
FUR
  Elzy, 67
  Fanny, 67
FURGUSON
  Jas. W., 152
  Mrs., 127
  Romulus, 152
  S. D., 128
FURR
  Armstead, 158
  Dallas, 87
  Dollie A., 172
  Frank N., 30, 31
  Gilmore, 133
  Henry, 12, 13
  J. P., 109
  Jno. W., 39
  Mrs., 82
  Walter L., 135
  Wm. G., 133
FUTZ
  Frank L., 71

GAINES
  Alice, 1
  Bertha M., 36
  George W., 1
  Lizzie, 134
GAINS

  David, 15
  Lucy L., 15
  Precilla C., 15
  Thomas A., 15
GALLEHER
  W. C., 108, 109
GALLOWAY
  Juliet, 143
  Wm. B., 91
GANT
  N. T., 139
GARDNER
  Chas., 28
  Mary E., 85
GARRET
  W., 46
GARRETT
  ___, 164
  Annie L., 10
  Ed. E., 107
  J. W., 142
  Jane H., 73
  Jno. W., 133, 158
  John W., 125
  W. E., 16
  Wm., 68
  Wm. E., 27, 28
  Wm. M., 33
GARRETT
  Mabel, 1
  Sadie, 1
  Wm. M., 1
GATES
  Charles J., 37
  Ida, 42
GAVER
  C. C., 31, 58, 87,
    92, 98, 110,
    149, 176
  Chas., 178
  Francis A., 73
  T. F., 4
GAYNOR
  Ann E., 45
GEORGE
  A. C., 93
  John, 122

The Telephone INDEX

Samuel W., 18
Sarah, 92
Wallace, 87, 122
GHEEN
  Thomas, 138
GIBSON
  Ada W., 26
  Annie, 9, 52
  Catlett, 154
  Douglas, 26
  G. B., 14
  Geo. W., 164, 165
  H. C., 135
  J. D., 50
  John, 9
  John N., 14
  Jos. A., 14
  Lee, 135
  Mrs., 154
  Owen, 52
  R. Emma, 6
  S. M., 6
  W. G., 15
GIDDINGS
  Chas. G., 48
  Eliza M., 150
  Ellen R., 42
  Eugene, 147
  Flossie, 113
  Glen, 177
  Nannie B., 9
  Wm., 9, 42, 150
  Wm. J., 177
GILL
  John, 120, 123
  Willie H., 123
GIST
  Elizabeth G., 89
  Henry C., 89
GLASCOCK
  Alfred, 14, 23
  Hattie B., 14
  May, 23
  Thos., 154
GOCHNAUER
  Jos., 46

GOCHNAUR
  W. L., 18
GOCHNAURER
  Preston, 52
GODFREY
  Wm., 33
GOLD
  E. B., 125
  Jno. D., 147
  John D., 146
  Jos. M., 147
GOLDEN
  Margaret G., 112
GOOCH
  John B., 129
GOODHART
  Andrew L., 54
  Chas., 53
  Chas. W., 54
  Luther, 53
  Goodhart & Rollins, 124
  Goodheart & Rollins, 93
GOODRICH
  Earl S., 136
  Emma, 136
GORDING
  Carrie V., 134
GORDON
  Henry, 40
GORE
  Albert, 50, 59, 127
  Amos, 142
  Arthur, 153
  Clara, 153
  Clinton, 153
  Florence, 153
  Henry, 59
  Herbert, 153
  Ida, 153
  Joshua, 134
  Mary H., 142
  Nannie, 50
  Rachel, 134
  Solomon, 134

  Stanley, 153
  Thomas H., 18
  Townsend, 153
  William, 153
GORMAN
  Blanche, 122
  Robert, 58
  Virginia E., 58
GOSSLING
  Letitia A., 25
GOTT
  Nora J., 38
GOUCH
  W. J., 78
GOUCHNAUER
  P. S., 151
  Sallie M., 18
GOUGH
  Julia, 40
GOULDING
  S., 48
GOVER
  E. M., 113
GRAF
  Frank G., 104
GRAHAM
  Robert, 102
  William, 168
GRANGER
  S. M., 164
GRAY
  Albert, 21
  Albert E., 143
  Arthur P., 31
  J. H., 165
  Jerome B., 40
  Jno., 21
  John, 74, 76
  Laura, 143
  Robert W., 128
  Welby E., 143
  Wm. H., 31, 128
GRAYSON
  David L., 23
GREBB
  Elizabeth, 32
GREEN

Annie E., 116
Edith, 178
Fannie B., 34
Fielding C., 116
Mary, 64
Sophia, 116
GREENLEASE
Annie C., 180
J. H., 180
GREGG
Albert, 179
D. S., 21
Dan, 88
Daniel, 126
H. W., 4
Harman, 172
John, 128
Laura R., 21
Roy R., 21
Susan, 164
GRIFFIN
George, 12
GRIFFITH
Gertie, 17
GRIGSBY
A. S., 113
C. M., 113
GRIMES
Elizabeth, 140
Geo. W., 140
Mattie, 56
GROSS
Chas. H., 155
Hammond, 160
Josephene C., 155
GROVE
G. W., 149
M. J., 149
Mary M., 149
GRUBB
Belle, 154
Benj., 17
Benjamin, 83
Betsey, 118
Clara B., 17
Dase, 172

J. W., 121, 127, 148
James, 6, 146
James W., 147, 150
Jane, 146
Jas., 6
John, 90, 138, 154
Jos. P., 148
Joseph, 146
Joseph P., 147
L. M., 17
Maggie V., 17
Margaret A., 83
R. W., 25
Richard B., 147
Robert, 59
Saml. N., 166
Samuel W., 147, 164
GUILLATT
Eleanor, 58
GULICK
George W., 27
John F., 70
GULLATT
Eleanor, 54
GUNNELL
John M., 155
Orlando, 155
GWARTHMEY
R., 49
GWATHMEY
Emma, 49
GYDER
Rachel, 27

HACKETT
Wm. T., 25
HACKLEY
Martha, 36
Wm. H., 36
HADDAY
___, 40
HAIGHT
Stephen S., 72

HAINES
Abraham, 7
Addison, 76
George W., 64
Harriet, 7
Manly, 37
Margaret A., 64
Mary A., 86
Mary C., 174
Mary E., 176
Sarah L., 7
Washington, 149, 150, 174
HAINS
H. F., 107
HALEY
Ollie, 149
HALL
James M., 119
John W., 59
R. C., 118
Robert C., 117
HALLOWELL
Benjamin, 117
HAM
Fannie, 86
HAMILTON
Burr, 159
Tom, 18
HAMMERLY
C. W., 176
J. A., 130
John, 135
John W., 105
Julia, 130
Mary E., 133
HAMPTON
Elwood, 176
Fenton, 80, 90
George, 61
J. N., 51
James, 106
Jno. A., 90
John, 37
John A., 106
Monena N., 51
Wade, 37

Wilmer, 23, 136
HANVEY
  James, 136
HARDESTY
  Ella J., 22
HARDING
  Albert, 8
  C. W., 94
  Clinton, 156
  Geneva, 82
  H. C., 134
HARDY
  H. M., 132
  Hanson, 78
  Henry M., 132
HARMAN
  William, 162
HARMON
  Allan C., 85
  C., 162
  John R., 162
  Laura, 135
  Mary, 162
HARPER
  Frank, 101
  J. W., 42
  Lillie, 101
  Lillie C., 100
  Nancy, 118
HARRIS
  James, 34
  R. O., 151
  Richard R., 27
  Robert C., 155
HARRISON
  Amos, 117
  Carrie, 47
  E. B., 97, 113
  Elizabeth R., 155
  Elsie C., 96, 97
  Henry, 62, 166
  Henry T., 165
  John D., 129
  Lalla, 98
  President, 3
  Robert C., 155
  Sadie, 97

Sarah, 59
Shep., 47
Walter J., 165, 166
HART
  Wm., 137
HARVEY
  John C., 151
HASLAM
  Emmie, 86
HATCHER
  Harry, 153
  Jonah, 4
  Joshua P., 72
  Mary, 48, 72, 127, 179
  Susan, 157
HATHAWAY
  James H., 100
HAVENER
  B. T., 13
HAVENNER
  Bessie L., 93
  Harmon, 91
  Jerre, 42
  L. Harmon, 92
  R. Virginia, 13
  Rachel, 36
  Thos. A., 73
  Vera M., 93
  Walter C., 93
HAWES
  Annie F., 137
  Isaac, 132
HAWKINS
  Phoebe A., 117
HAWLEY
  Ed., 43
HAWLING
  C. F., 21
  Chas. T., 78
  Lewis, 78, 164
  Wm., 78
HAWS
  Jennie, 80
  John, 80
  Livie J., 156

Mary J., 156
Samuel, 27
HAXALL
  Philip, 92
HAY
  Ann, 102
  Fenelon D., 25
  Geo., 102
HAYNE
  George, 3
HAYNES
  A. M., 8
  Mary C., 149
HEAD
  B. F., 56
  Benj. F., 90
  Clarence, 6
  Columbus, 91
  Eley, 56
  Emily J., 91, 96
  Geo. R., 56
  N., 133
  Nelson, 56
  Wm., 42, 90
HEATON
  Eppa H., 85
  Henry, 41, 120
  Jas., 41
  Louisa M., 41
  N. R., 41, 120, 124
  Senator, 40, 103
HEDGES
  C. S., 92
HEFFNER
  Annie B., 169
  Chas. W., 36
HEFLIN
  ____, 82
  Lee R., 74
  Rosina M., 146
  W. C., 159
  Wm. C., 117
HEFNER
  George, 167
HELFENSTEIN
  Charles M., 180

The Telephone INDEX 199

HELM
  Jos., 45
  Joseph, 44, 179
  Lizzie C., 132
  Mary C., 132
  Mary E., 179
  Mr., 24
  Thomas M., 132
HEMPSTONE
  W. D., 96
  W. Dade, 97
HENDERSON
  F. M., 3
  Frances A., 152
  Francis B., 152
  James, 152
HENDRICKS
  Robbie, 172
HENLY
  Chas. E., 128
HENSON
  Phebe C., 59
HERN
  Wm. C., 132
HERNDON
  Chas. T., 55
  John, 125
  John G., 76
  Louisa, 27
  Louisa H. L., 28
  Maggie, 76
  Robt., 123
  Travis, 27
HERNE
  John, 51
HERRON
  Belle, 136
HESKETT
  Jennie, 168
HESS
  C. B., 20
HIBBS
  Catharine A., 149
  Catherine, 148
  Frank, 84, 127
  Humphrey, 127
  Joseph, 10

Kate, 127
Mary, 10
West, 127
Wm., 10
HICKMAN
  Alberta, 162
  Ann E., 162
  John, 85
  Marion, 160
  William, 162
  Hickman & Bitzer, 93, 124
HICKS
  S. D., 3
HIGDON
  Charles, 3
HIGGINS
  Dennie, 10, 11
  Dennis, 88
  Harriet, 40
  Harriet E., 38
HILL
  B. Smith, 103
  Chas. W., 151
  D. W., 45
  James W., 92
  Joseph, 107
  Laura V., 71
  Rose, 107
HILLEARY
  Fannie, 67
  Harry L., 113
HILLERY
  Katie R., 151
HINDMAN
  S., 49
HIRST
  Annie A., 30
  E. H., 21, 22
  Edgar, 29
  Edgar H., 30, 142
  Fannie, 181
  Laura, 126
  Mamie, 46
  Mamie L., 47
  Mary F., 47

Smith, 46, 47, 181
Walter H., 82
HITE
  Cora E., 172
  T. A., 172
HIXON
  John, 149
  John W., 82
  Katie, 24
  Permelia, 82
HIXSON
  Jno., 149
HODGSON
  Cornelius, 76
  S. L., 76
HOEBER
  Arthur, 22
HOFFMAN
  Wm., 87
HOGAN
  Jas. W., 68
  Nicholas, 68
  Patrick, 65, 67
HOGE
  Amanda, 153
  Eli J., 32, 36
  Freddie, 5
  Geo. D., 34
  Grace, 52
  Henry, 158
  Hermon, 153
  Jesse, 52
  John H., 64
  Mary, 158
  Mary A., 30
  Mary E., 32
  Sarah, 165
  Solomon, 99, 153
  Thos., 30
  Thos. H., 30
HOGELAND
  Jane F., 5
  John J., 5
HOLDER
  Joseph, 170, 171
HOLLADAY

Annie E., 59
HOLLAND
  Chas., 148
  John R., 145
  Sallie B., 145
  William B., 145
HOLLINGSWORTH
  C. L., 25, 63
  Chas. L., 31
  Henry D., 25
HOLLY
  B. F., 131
HOLMES
  Elisha, 99
  Esther J., 99, 101
  Geo. W., 99
  H. R., 99
  Hester, 99
  Hugh R., 152, 155
  J. D., 180
  Jesse, 15
  Jessie, 99
  Kersey, 15
  Mary E., 152
  Samuel C., 28
  William, 28
HOLT
  Joseph, 37
HOLTSCLAW
  Emma, 16
  Gracie L., 16
  Luther J., 16
HOLTZCLAW
  Ashby, 105
  Martha, 94
  Susan, 94
HOOE
  Jas. R., 106
HOPKINS
  Samuel S., 121
HORSEMAN
  G. H., 20
  S. E., 14
HOSKINSON
  Clinton, 15
  Lennie E., 15
  R. H., 137, 142
  Virginia, 15
HOUGH
  Ann E., 128
  Bernard, 117
  Carrie, 16, 37
  Clinton H., 130
  Geo. C., 100, 130
  George, 116
  George C., 101
  H. A., 116
  Hannah, 118
  Ida A., 51
  J. T., 101
  Jennie, 71
  John, 71
  L. E., 37
  L. F., 50
  L. W. S., 45, 84
  L.N., 44
  Lillian H., 130
  Mary, 122
  Mollie, 84
  Mollie S., 86
  R. R. S., 170
  Robt. W., 51
  Rose, 82
  Samuel, 114
  Samuel W., 129
  Thomas, 178
  Virginia L., 19
  W. W., 161
  Wm. H., 88, 92
  Wm. M., 129
  Wm. N., 69
HOUSE
  Charles J., 149
  E. C. H., 112, 143
  Eli C. H., 149
  Franklin G., 149
  George C., 149
  Greenbery J. R., 149
  Grove R., 149
  Jos. S., 133
  Mary H., 112
  Mary J., 112, 143
HOUSEHOLDER
  A., 160
  A. Eugene, 27
  Dan P., 85
  Gideon, 175, 178
  Mary V., 159
HOUSHOLDER
  Oscar, 167
HOUZER
  John, 176
HOWARD
  Claton, 102
  George L., 90
HOWELL
  Flavius J., 32
  Jos., 85
  Joseph, 6
  Joseph W., 61
HOWSER
  Philip, 40
  Philip A., 138
HUGHES
  Amos, 31
  Elias, 46, 48
  John H., 11
  Rose, 160
  Virginia, 173
HULFISH
  Edwin, 91
  G. D., 147
  G. H., 148
  Garrett, 91
HULLER
  Edward, 134
HUMMEL
  Jacob, 136
HUMMER
  A. P., 27
  G. W. F., 61
HUMPHREY
  Thos. L., 30
HUNT
  Angie, 89
  Anzey, 86
  Anzie, 76
  J. T., 118
  Mary L., 145

The Telephone
INDEX

Troy, 145
W. H., 145
Wm. T., 2, 4
HUNTER
  Etta M., 107
  G. P., 54
  Geo. P., 122, 149
  George, 165
  George P., 165
  Jennie, 11, 12
  John, 3, 163
  R. J., 13
  W. H., 35
  William A., 35
HUNTON
  Lady, 49
HURST
  Benjamin, 62
HUTCHINS
  Stilson, 41
HUTCHINSON
  J. R., 155
  Laura B., 155
  Mary, 170
  Thos., 89
HUTCHISON
  Bettie, 16
  Beverly, 16
  Chas. L., 125
  Fannie, 83
  G. C., 125
  Henry B., 32, 36
  Jno. R., 155
  John, 155
  Julia, 93
  L. E., 15, 16, 116
  Llewellyn, 93
  Ludwell, 16
  M. B., 125
  Mary, 16
  Orion, 16
  Philip, 159
  Robert P., 121
  Sandford, 83
  Virginia, 121
  Wilmer, 10
HYNSON
  Anna N., 30
  Benjamin T., 30

INZER
  Geo. W., 166

JACKSON
  Chas. H., 154
  Fanny, 177
  Isaac, 17
  J. Fenton, 4
  Joseph, 181
  Julia, 62
  Julia A., 160
  Mable, 148
  Margaret A., 90
  Obadiah, 94
  Samuel T., 180
  Thos., 116
  Virginia, 61
JACOBS
  Annie, 23
  David E., 13
  Halie M., 68
  L. T., 23
  Leven T., 43
  Louise, 43
  Mollie, 138
  Rinard, 10
JAMES
  Alberta, 14
  Charles, 113
  Craven, 136, 144
  Delia P., 111, 113
  F. Leola, 73
  Floyd C., 72
  Frederick, 107
  Imogene, 2
  Jeanette, 113
  John E., 14
  Lillie, 107
  Mahlon, 45
  Mason, 60, 136
  Nellie, 14
  Rachel A., 87, 90
  Robt. M., 72
  T. B., 144
  T. Benton, 107
  W. M., 144
  Will, 31
  William, 2, 160
JANNEY
  Abijah, 172
  Albert, 172
  Amos, 140
  Ann E., 160
  Annie, 159
  Annie M., 58
  Aquila, 9
  Asa M., 66
  Asbury, 159
  Bessie, 64
  Charles P., 145
  Chas. P., 132
  Clarissa C., 122
  Cossie, 16
  Edgar, 9
  Eliza, 25
  Elizabeth, 107, 152, 168
  Ella, 16
  Ethel H., 55
  Geo., 22
  Geo. W., 136
  Hannah H., 168
  Henry, 16, 167
  Henry T., 41
  Jane, 126
  John, 10, 18, 122, 139
  John Q., 140
  Joseph, 58, 64
  Joseph J., 168
  Lydia, 66
  Lydia A., 172
  Mary Ann, 140
  Mayo, 148
  Millard, 5
  N. W., 164
  Nathan, 126
  O. Edward, 168
  P., 64
  Phineas, 64, 152
  R. W., 22, 23

Rodney, 18
Samuel M., 107, 152
Thamsin, 53
Thos., 55
William H., 168
JENIFER
　Henry E., 26
JENKIN
　___, 71
JENKINS
　Amos S., 180
　Charles, 27
　Ella A., 27
　Emma, 30
　Fred. J., 170
　Hannah, 140, 158
　Herbert L., 109
　J. Clay, 30
　J. Wilcox, 170
　Jos. H., 158
　Joseph, 168, 169
　Mary E., 29
　Nellie, 109
　Norval, 140
　Reuben, 33, 166, 168
　Rosa M., 30
　Samuel, 133
　Samuel M., 1
　Wilcox, 168
　Wm. G., 63, 82
JEWETT
　Jos. H., 4
　Joseph H., 136
　Tacy M., 136
JOHNS
　Mary, 4
JOHNSON
　Alpheus, 106
　Amos W., 130
　Charles, 53
　Edward A., 108
　Ella G., 20
　Emma, 77
　F. C. D., 5
　Frank, 48

George W., 160
Horace, 167
J. W., 7
Jane, 72
Kirke, 2
L. L., 165
M. Katie, 5
Miranda, 68
Miss, 126
Ridley, 133
S. J., 108, 126
Susan C., 130
W. A., 135
W. W., 135
Wm., 167, 172
Wm. H., 5
JOHNSTON
　C. W., 77
　E. A., 130
　Joseph E., 119
　M. E., 5
　Mary A., 130
　Myrtle, 86
　Rose E., 130
JONES
　Ann, 92
　Burr, 17
　Helen, 141
　J. A., 59
　J. C., 26
　James W., 74
　Jane, 17
　Jas. W., 59
　John, 146
　Lewen T., 25
　Lewin T., 22
　Lydia V., 73
　Paul, 119
　Richard H., 150
　W. R., 25
　Walter, 165
JORDAN
　E. C., 37
　E. Clarence, 37
　George, 5
　John L., 18
JORDON

Clarence, 158
Elizabeth, 158
Geo. E., 158
KAHLE
　W. S., 140
KAIN
　Wm., 161
KALB
　___, 60
　John, 77
　T. D., 132
KARNER
　Clara, 10
KATOR
　___, 18
KEAFAUVER
　W. S., 149
KEELER
　W. R., 108
KEELING
　Rosa B., 41
KEEN
　___, 55
　C. F., 78
　Charles, 78
　D., 16
　Hazel, 23
　J. J., 78
　J. W., 11
　John, 11
　Jonathan, 34, 144
　Lizzie, 78
KEITH
　Judge, 5, 145
KELLER
　Emily S., 71
KELLEY
　Robert, 157
KELLY
　Amanda, 135
　G. Frank, 18
　Robert, 180
KELSAN
　Lillian B., 149
KENLY
　Anna M., 30

The Telephone
INDEX

Edward, 30
Maria, 30
KENT
  N. H., 11
  Wm., 13
KENYON
  Byron J., 148
KEPHART
  Oscar M., 26, 27
KERCHEVAL
  Susan R., 52
KERN
  Mary M., 36
  Olivia, 8
KEYES
  Capt., 151
KIDWELL
  ___, 32
  Ann, 12
  J. F., 160
  John, 123
  John E., 172
  John F., 12, 160
  Mary E., 172
  Mary F., 8
  Silas, 137
  Thomas, 17
  Virgie, 172
KILGOUR
  James M., 9
  Robert, 9
KINCHELO
  James, 9
KINDALL
  Catharine, 162
KINES
  ___, 82
  Annie, 74, 107
  Gilbert, 74
  J. W., 74
  Lizzie, 74
KINGSLEY
  H. M., 72
  S. H., 72
KIRKPATRICK
  Harley F., 171
KITCHEN

Charles, 67
Thomas I., 64
KITIS
  R. H., 12
KOLB
  Wm., 21
KOZER
  Wilmer, 64
KRIIG
  Frederick V., 59
KUHLMAN
  Medora, 74

LA?HAN
  Sam., 159
LACEY
  Chas. H., 122
LACY
  Annie, 35
  B. F., 35
  Hattie, 110
  Joseph, 110, 140
  Mary, 110
  Mildred, 110
  P., 110
LAFEVER
  Fannie, 166
  Peter, 166
LAK?AN
  Sam, 159
LAKE
  John L., 110
  Thos. W., 91
  Walter S., 91
LAMBDON
  T. H., 130
Lambdon &
  Middleton, 130
LAMBERT
  Francis, 70, 93
  William, 148
LAMOTHE
  Jno. D., 138
LANDSTREET
  John, 75
LANG
  Nancy, 181

Samuel, 181
LANHAM
  Emma V., 144
  Minor, 56, 57
  Sarah C., 57
LANSFORD
  B., 79
LARNER
  C., 108
  W. H., 108
LATHAM
  Thos., 54
LAWS
  Curtis, 162
  Curtis L., 179
  John T., 179
LAWSON
  Chas. T., 53
  John, 90
LAY
  Craven, 53
LAYCOCK
  Adin, 137
  Ed., 134
  Florence R., 99
  Florrie, 49
  G. W., 48
  Geo., 20
  J. Wm., 99
  James H., 26
  Jos., 70
  Joseph, 69
  Mattie E., 26, 27
LEAVITT
  Benjamin, 86
  Luella, 86
Leavitt & Oglevee
  Co, 111
LEE
  Cassius F., 42
  Charles, 39
  David J., 83, 86
  Eleanor H., 62
  Evelyn, 103
  Evelyn B., 21
  Fannie, 42
  Geo., 63

The Telephone
INDEX

George, 94
Harry B., 165
Mamie, 147
Matthew P., 83
Mittie E., 92
Robert E., 71, 119
W. H. F., 71
William H. F., 71
LEFEVRE
  Henry, 100
LEITH
  B. F., 61, 175
  Lawrence, 61
  M. Olivia, 175
  May, 22
LEMMEN
  Ada, 125
LEMON
  Charles, 33
  Maggie, 33
LENNOX
  Hellen, 55
LEONARD
  Ida, 132
LESLIE
  Ida M., 51
LEWIS
  Ann S., 68
  Carter F., 164
  H. L. Dangerfield, 164
  Harrison, 173
  Hattie, 68
  Mary, 32
  Richard E., 173
  Rosalie, 164
  Samuel, 131, 171, 172
  Sarah E., 131
LICKEY
  Edgar, 40
  John W., 106
LICKY
  ___, 141
LIGGETT
  Catharine, 102

LIGHTFOOT
  Nannie C., 119
LINDSAY
  Effie, 3
LINDSEY
  Edna M., 154
  Effie E., 108
  Henry C., 150
  Jesse L., 154
  Mary E. V., 154
  Wm. B., 154
LIPPINCOTT
  Anna S., 30
  Ezra, 30
LIPSCOMB
  Judge, 82
LITTLE
  R. H., 86
  Robt. H., 83
  T. E., 86
LITTLE
  Thos. E., 150
LITTLEJOHN
  C. W., 28, 73, 122, 124
  Forrest C., 150
  Horace C., 150
  Julia D., 150
  Paul V., 150
LITTLETON
  Edgar, 151
LOCK
  Julia, 97
LOCKHART
  John B., 160
LODGE
  Flavius H., 169
  Joe, 23
  Joe L., 23
  Jos. A., 41, 70
  Laban, 73
  Mary, 89
  Nathan, 89, 92, 128, 129, 130
LOMAX
  Pearl E., 134
LONG

I. T., 113, 115
LONGCAR
  J. W., 52
LONGERBEAM
  Chas. E., 28
LORD
  Saml. H., 126
LOTT
  Mary E., 15
  Parkenson L., 15
LOVE
  Ada, 81
  Alcinda J., 132
  Curtis C., 58
  Dora, 81
  Edgar C., 58
  Eli, 38
  Eli A., 45, 46
  Fenton M., 178
  Fred S., 58
  Gertie, 89
  J. F., 81
  J. W., 112
  John, 45
  Lydia, 166
  Robt. R., 46, 58
  Rufus T., 58
  S. A. R., 58
  Saml. H., 4
  Samuel, 38
  Samuel H., 46
  Thos. E., 58
  W. P., 126
LOVELESS
  Martha, 73
  Walter, 80
LOVETT
  J. T., 157
LOW
  Grace, 158
  Joseph, 158
LOWE
  Ben, 180
  Elnora, 122
  Francis T., 12
LOWENBACH
  C. R., 93, 134

INDEX

Chas. R., 124
LOY
  Mr., 124
LUCAS
  Amanda, 179
  Henrietta, 72
  Luca, 64
  Mahala, 179
LUCIUS
  Chas. A. P., 58
  Hunter W., 53
  Kate, 76
LUCK
  W. J., 43
LUCKETT
  Josiah, 122
  L. Henry, 71
  Ludwell, 71
  Mary, 24
  Mary B., 43
  Mollie, 34
  Roger C., 122
  Samuel C., 34, 117, 122
  Wm. C., 24
  Wm. E., 31
  Wm. H., 43
LUNSFORD
  C. F., 29
  Jennie, 27
LUNT
  J. D., 75
LUPTON
  J. W., 57, 58
LYNCH
  Ella, 119
  Jennie, 98
LYNN
  Ashland, 124
  Clay, 94
  Jennie, 94
  Mrs., 80
  Wm., 80
  Wm. F., 101
LYON
  Geo. C., 39
  Mary E., 39

MACKAY
  William, 167
MACON
  Lee, 80
MADDOX
  Magnolia, 181
  Sarah E., 138
MAFFETT
  C. J. C., 2, 62, 176
  Henry, 8, 9
  Jas. A., 122
  Martha, 62
  Mollie, 11
  Norah, 89
  Wm., 62
MAIN
  Wm., 131
  Wm. Z., 60
MANKIN
  Fanny, 168
  G. T., 98
MANLEY
  John, 76
  Thos., 32
MANLY
  Susan, 61
  Thos., 68
MANN
  John, 60
  Katie, 39
  L. A., 60
  Mary, 39
  Samuel, 39
MANNING
  Jacob H., 59
  Katie, 81
MANSFIELD
  Effie L., 156
MARCUS
  M. T., 81
MARKS
  Thomas P., 27
MARLOW
  Dr., 32
  Fanny, 98

Geo., 117
Richard, 94
MARSHALL
  Crum, 160
  Jacquelin, 171
  James W., 170
  Orra, 156
  Richard, 156
  Wm., 109
MARTIN
  Charles C., 126
  Hattie, 15
  J. W., 74
  Sophia, 109, 112
MASON
  Amanda, 179
  Clara, 43
  Dr., 43
  J. F., 6
  John T., 64
  Julius, 14
  Maria, 14
  T. F., 128
  Temple, 64
  Thomas F., 98
  Wm. T., 79
  Wm. T. T., 79
MASSEY
  E. W., 169
MASSY
  Nannie C., 169
MATHERS
  Sarah A., 172
  W. T., 169
  Willie, 169
MATHEWS
  Chas. B., 137
MATTHEW
  Ella, 100
  Jessie, 100
  Lula H., 100
  Rodney, 85
  S. T., 112
  Wm., 100
MATTHEWS
  Ella C., 158
MAYOR

Anton, 176
MAYPOLE
  Mr., 64
McAFEE
  J. M., 105
McARTER
  Ann, 19
  Samuel, 19
  Thomas, 19
McCABE
  Amanda, 137
  Carrie, 137
  Charles P., 11
  J. B., 11, 124
  John, 11
McCALEB
  Julia, 130
McCARTY
  ___, 92
  M. M., 114
  Stephen W., 96
  W. M., 114
McCAULL
  John A., 138
  P. H., 138
McCLELLAN
  Wm. B., 124
McCLELLAND
  Sarah, 47
  William, 47
McCRAY
  Edgar, 23, 157, 173, 180
  Elizabeth, 31
  Wm., 31
McCREARY
  Robert, 8
McCULLUCK
  David, 162
McDANIEL
  James, 90, 114
  Ollie A., 117
  Rosanna, 90
  William, 78
McDERMOTT
  Owen G., 93
McDONALD

  Ethan R., 137
  Mary W., 170
McDONOUGH
  Jas., 73
  W. W., 175
  Wallace W., 143
McELROY
  Ellen J., 114
  Wm., 114
McFARLAND
  B. A., 84
  Julia, 73, 74, 85
  M. E., 176
  W. A., 52, 118
McGAVACK
  J. T., 156
  L. M., 5, 76, 110
McGILL
  Mrs. Dr., 179
  Nannie, 180
McGRAW
  Maggie, 174
McGREW
  James, 174
McGUIRE
  J. M. G., 42
  John, 42
McHENRY
  George, 89
McINTOSH
  J. L., 84
  Jas. L., 87
McKERNAN
  John, 66
McKIMM
  Miss, 172
McKIMMEY
  John, 36
McKINNEY
  Anna, 13
  Annie B., 14
  J. W., 13, 71
  Luther, 19
McLINN
  M. E., 85
McLOUGHLIN
  Alice, 58

  Catherine, 58
  Mary, 58
  Patrick, 58
  Thos., 58
McLYNN
  Ruth, 160
McMAHON
  Minnie V., 111
McNEALA
  John R., 152
McNEALEA
  John R., 94, 95
McNEALLEY
  John T., 111
McNEALY
  John R., 128
McPHERSON
  Chas., 168
  Frank T., 108
  James E., 151
  Wm. E., 151
McVEIGH
  Frank, 105
  James H., 66
  Mary E., 55, 56
  Townsend J., 2
  Wm. N., 16, 66
MEAD
  Jos., 133
  Wm., 133
MEADE
  Mary A., 181
MEANS
  Alice, 6
  Capt., 151
  Ellen, 25
  Lewis E., 164
  Rachel, 164
  Saml., 60
  Samuel, 25, 164
MEGEATH
  Alfred P., 175
MENARD
  E. D., 174
  Julia E., 174
  Mrs., 104
MERCHANT

The Telephone
INDEX

Charles, 140, 151
MERCIER
C. C., 75, 116
Chas., 115
Kage, 116
Wm. F., 75
MERKELL
Virginia H., 41
METZGER
Maria H., 50
W. A., 50
MEYERS
Mary, 11
MICHAEL
Florence J., 32
MIDDLETON
Jno., 123
Mollie, 130
S. C., 130
MILBURN
E., 80
Florence, 80
Jack, 136
Ras., 136
S. C., 70
Zenis, 138
MILHOLIN
Albert, 14
MILHOLLEN
Dixie, 75
E. A., 58, 76
Lelia, 70
MILLARD
___, 33
MILLER
J. A. M., 22
J. H., 103
J. M., 60
John, 168
Margaret J., 72
Rebecca, 50
Wm., 50
MILLS
Geo. W., 140
Harry, 102
John C., 36
Virginia, 29

Wm., 102
MILTON
Ann C., 88
John, 88
Mrs., 40
T. D., 88, 121
MINISTERS
ALLENDER, ___,
164
APPELL, A. G.,
51
ARMSTRONG, J.
E., 3
BADGER, ___,
33, 63, 123
BADGER, J. N.,
63, 141
BAILLIE, J. J., 78
BAILY, E. B., 81
BALL, B. F., 112,
118
BALL, C., 181
BALL, S. A., 1, 12
BALL, Saml., 57
BARBER, J., 99
BARBER, J. T.,
138, 140
BARR, David, 95
BEALES, C. F.,
13
BEALL, O. C., 1
BENTLEY, ___,
25
BITZER, ___, 99
BITZER, G. L.,
148, 173
BITZER, Geo. L.,
100, 135, 144,
148, 165
BOND, B. W., 23,
29, 37, 40, 42,
43, 47, 53, 55,
78
BOSMAN, ___,
107
BRANCH, H., 22

BRANCH, Henry,
16
BRIDGES, J. R.,
3, 12
BROWN, C. M., 3
BUSH, ___, 68
BUTLER, J. G.,
113
BUTTLER, J. H.,
156
CAMPBELL, J.
P., 23
CANTER, I. W.,
137
COE, ___, 10
COLE, W. C. P.,
20
CRENSHAW, L.
H., 171
CROMER, T. K.,
113
DAME, Nelson P.,
37
DAVENPORT, W.
G., 19
DAVIS, ___, 6,
19, 36
DAVIS, D., 77
DAVIS, Dr., 78
DAVIS, R. T., 4,
42, 66
DEIHL, ___, 17
DENNEN, C., 170
DICE, ___, 52
DICE, J. C., 26,
30
DINWIDDIE, ___,
49
DINWIDDIE, J.
C., 26, 37, 44,
53, 58, 68
DUDLEY, Thos.
U., 69
DULANEY, ___,
27
DULANEY, J. H.,
86, 112

The Telephone
INDEX

DULANY, ___, 65, 151
DULANY, J. H., 107
DUNNAWAY, W. F., 168
EDWARDS, A. L., 142
EGGLESTON, ___, 16
EGGLESTON, W. C., 84
EGGLESTON, W. G., 10, 29, 44, 48, 57, 62, 64, 65, 69, 70, 72, 73, 74, 79, 80, 81, 83, 99, 105, 111, 116, 118, 119
ESCHBACH, D. R., 136
EVANS, W. T., 8
FELTER, J. P., 144
FELTNER, J. P., 147
FRANCIS, A. B., 115
FROST, T. P., 138
FRY, ___, 155
FURR, Armstead, 62
GAINES, W. H., 56
GAINS, W. H., 8
GILL, A. J., 107
GREEN, ___, 20, 136
GREEN, Berryman, 128, 165
GREEN, S. H., 41
GRIFFITH, C. C., 112
GRIFFITH, Chas. G., 113
GRIGGS, Walter P., 97
GRUBB, J. W., 134, 135, 137, 142, 160, 165, 166, 169, 171, 175, 181
HADDAWAY, S. W., 28, 37
HALPENNY, ___, 117
HALPENNY, J., 116
HAMMOND, W. G., 42
HARROWER, Pascal, 138
HEAD, ___, 26, 27, 44, 61, 62, 151, 179
HEAD, N., 24, 29, 141
HEAD, Nelson, 21, 28, 42, 67, 90, 142
HEDRICK, D. C., 3, 27, 29, 31
HENCK, Louis, 180
HERNDON, ___, 87
HERNDON, C. T., 10, 15, 23, 25, 26, 31, 32, 50, 78, 98, 117, 126, 127, 128, 159, 165, 178, 179, 180
HERNDON, Chas., 35, 76
HERNDON, Chas. T., 109
HINGER, ___, 85
HINKS, E. S., 174, 179
HOPKINS, A. C., 27
HOSKINSON, A., 181
HOUGH, ___, 138, 141
HOUGH, Dr., 131
HOUGH, R. R. S., 125, 126, 157, 163, 178
HOWISON, ___, 107
I. B., 133
INGLE, Osbourne, 97
JACOBS, C. D., 86
KEEBLE, ___, 85
KEEBLE, J. W., 106, 110
KEEN, W. D., 128
KEENE, W. B., 130
KELLEY, ___, 180
KELLEY, Joseph T., 180
KELLY, ___, 161
LAKE, I. B., 23, 41, 52, 107, 128, 136, 140, 161, 181
LaMOTHE, ___, 147
LEAKIN, George A., 12
LEE, Harry B., 165
MASON, ___, 121
MASON, ___, 98
McLIN, E., 51

McLINN, ___, 90, 144, 164
McLINN, M. E., 51, 62, 64, 66, 77, 89, 109, 117, 120, 121, 125, 171
McLYNN, M. E., 160
MEADE, ___, 35
MILLER, P. H., 1, 3
MILLER, P. N., 8
MOFFETT, ___, 69
MOORE, J. H., 1
MOSS, ___, 180
MUIR, J., 144
NEEL, A. A. P., 29
NELSON, Frank H., 146
NICHOLL, W. D., 49
NORWOOD, ___, 175
NOURSE, Robert, 98
OWINGS, J. T., 38
PAGE, Carter, 42, 108
POPKINS, G., 136
POPKINS, G. W., 8, 16, 20, 27, 28, 62, 85, 138, 144, 145, 150, 169
POPKINS, Geo. W., 89, 112
POPKINS, George W., 111
PRICE, J. A., 101
READ, Miles S., 53
REED, Zack, 54

REID, Zack, 76
REILEY, A. R., 25
RINKER, H. St. J., 27, 34
RINKER, S. J., 1
RINKER, St. J., 25, 48
RINKER, St. John, 46
ROBERTSON, W. E., 169
RODGERS, Saml., 137
ROGERS, Samuel, 77
SAUNDERS, ___, 47, 163, 167, 168, 172
SAUNDERS, W. H., 153, 168
SCHINDLER, ___, 1, 8, 12, 19, 25, 34, 35
SCHINDLER, D., 3, 8, 11
SCHINDLER, Daniel, 26
SCOTT, ___, 71
SCOTT, R. A., 87
SCOTT, R. N., 116
SHANNON, S., 135
SHIPLEY, ___, 120
SHIPLEY, Chas., 110
SLATER, ___, 67
SMITH, ___, 151
SMITH, G. C., 117
STEVENSON, Jas. M., 15
SUTTON, ___, 105
SUTTON, C. B., 139, 150

SUTTON, M., 80
SWEM, E. H., 142
THOMAS, W. D., 56
TURNBULL, L. B., 4
TUSTIN, ___, 4
TYLER, ___, 137
TYLER, G. T., 130, 133
VICKERS, C. D., 85
WATERS, ___, 177
WELLER, A., 155, 159
WHITE, E. V., 6, 76, 85, 88, 107, 177
WICKLINE, J. L., 50
WICKLINE, J. S., 12, 35, 37, 39, 43, 51, 53
WICKLINE, W. S., 49
WIGHTMAN, J. T., 42
WILSON, ___, 126, 132
WILSON, E. L., 134, 142
WILSON, E. S., 173
WILSON, J. H., 53
WOLFORD, Chas., 130
WOOLF, John, 28, 38, 40, 53
WOOLF, Wm. E., 22
WOTRING, F. R., 22
ZERGER, J. E., 32

The Telephone INDEX

MINN
John, 176
MINNIX
John N., 128
MINOR
Jackson M., 117, 124
Louisa F., 2
Mary A., 117
Mary E., 125, 140
Nellie W., 125
Robert, 171
Spencer, 5
W. B., 181
Wm. B., 180
MISKELL
Jno. H., 162
John, 161
John H., 33
Lillie M., 33
Una M., 33
W. S., 162
MITCHEL
Fairfax, 76
R. Fairfax, 141
MITCHELL
Geneva, 175
James, 34
John, 46
Margaret E., 141
R. Tasker, 70
Rodney, 43
Sallie, 68
Wm., 175
MITZLER
Sarah J., 69
MOBERLY
Maria, 7
MOBLEY
Ida, 90
MOCK
Mary, 87
Mary J., 74
MOFFET
John, 41
MOFFETT
E. J. C., 18

Joseph E., 142
MONDAY
Daniel, 180
MONROE
Eugene, 176
Ida F., 158
Madison, 120
Wm., 120
MOORE
A. B., 51
A. L., 41
Ann, 127
Annie L., 158
Fannie, 170
Frank, 107
Geo. L., 127
Jas., 148
Jennie F., 22
John C., 17
Lilly C., 115
Mrs., 169
Mortime, 79
Saml. L., 127
MORAN
Geo., 105
H. W., 112
Jas. T., 99
John, 112
John M., 82, 99
John T., 144
John W., 44
Joshua G., 2
R. Y., 11
W. H. W., 44, 49
MORDECAI
___, 92
MORELAND
Carrie, 2
Charles, 174
Gertrude, 174
MORGAN
Amelia, 30
Annie, 30
Benjamine, 92
Blanche, 122
Goodiet, 58
Wm., 20

Wm. C., 30
MORIARITY
Thomas, 26
MORIARTY
Chas. T., 23
Daniel, 10
MORRIS
Geo. M., 178
John B., 31
Robert, 79
Sallie C., 79
MORRISON
Archibald, 61
Edward, 117
Francis H. S., 47
George, 110
J. H., 47
Saml., 41
Samuel, 30
MORTON
B. T., 135
Chas., 130
MOSBY
Col., 3, 153
John S., 48
Lizzie, 48
MOSLEY
Amelia, 91
MOSS
M. D., 121
William, 124
MOSSBURG
Josephene, 151
P., 151
MOTEN
Jesse, 144, 154
MOTON
Jessie, 175
Matilda, 175
MOTT
William S., 158
MOUNT
Charles E., 33
MOXLEY
Benj. F., 5
Emly A., 5
Maude C. P., 12

The Telephone
INDEX

MULLEN
  Arthur, 24
  Samuel H., 16
MUNDAY
  Eva V., 20
  Lisa B., 174
MURRAY
  Alexander, 152, 156
  Charles, 63
  Saml. P., 122
  Samuel, 38
  Stirling, 156
MURREY
  George, 38
MURTAUGH
  Thomas, 125
MUSE
  Jas. H., 160
  Sallie A., 111
MYERS
  C. F., 82
  E. F., 44
  Edgar, 105, 125, 172
  F. M., 5
  Fannie, 111
  Fenton, 45
  Florence A., 142
  Frances A., 173
  Frank, 48, 105, 111
  Franklin M., 173
  George W., 1
  Ish, 31
  Israel, 141
  Jacob, 77
  Katie, 17
  Lucy, 82, 157
  Maggie L., 5
  Mamie, 82
  Margaret, 181
  Mary, 40
  Mary R., 5
  Olivia, 8
  Randolph F., 44
  Robt. L., 87

Susan, 45
Thomas, 172
Thos., 142
Thos. J., 8
Will, 29, 48
William, 77, 142
Wm., 40, 82

NASH
  Arthur, 67
  Philip, 67
NEAL
  Ella J., 27
NEALE
  Mrs., 148
NEAR
  Miss, 151
NEEDHAM
  Charles W., 169
  Frank R., 169
NEEDLES
  Lida, 63
NEER
  John W., 90
NEILL
  S. S., 169
NELSON
  Frank, 86
  Jno. H., 178
  John H., 70, 147
  Louisa A., 68
NEVILLE
  ___, 40
NEWLON
  A. C., 119
  Chas. A., 9
  George, 135
  John F., 124, 125
  Monia, 119
  W. R., 99
NEWTON
  C. A., 46
  Fanuyl, 46
  Richard T., 8
NICHOL
  C. E., 145
NICHOLS

Arthur, 23, 111
Benton, 46
Ed., 76, 124
Edward, 76
Eli, 131
Emma, 158
Fenton M., 106
Hannah, 139
Howard, 142, 158
Isaac, 46, 51, 159
Isaac G., 85, 122
J. W., 177
J. Wilber, 176
James W., 160
Jas., 41
Jno. T., 111
John, 131
Joseph, 101, 173
L. T., 122
Laura, 41
M. B., 70
Mahlon, 123
Mary Ann, 101
N. Clifford, 158, 176, 177
Nathan, 165
Olivia, 46
Olivia B., 46
Phineas J., 131
S. T., 51, 111
Saml., 177, 178
Samuel, 139
Samuel E., 160
Susan, 177, 178
Susan T., 178
T. W., 70
Thamsin, 32, 158
Thomas, 139
Thos. J., 159
W. A., 124
Wilmer, 131
Wm., 177
NICHOLSON
  Marguerite, 163
  Robt., 163
  Samuel, 163
NIXON

Asbury, 70
Cassandra A., 145
George, 43
Hannah, 70, 163
J. B., 163
Joel L., 65, 175
John, 139
Levi, 2
Lewis, 55
Mary A., 43
Mary J., 65
W. W., 82
Nixon & Bro., 124
NOLAND
  B. F., 120
  B. T., 157
  Bessie L., 69
  Burr P., 23, 69
  C. Powell, 23
  Geo. W., 42
  S. T., 42
  Susan C., 23
NOLLNER
  M. E., 159
NORRIS
  C. B., 150
  Charles R., 151
  Chas. R., 52
  H. DeB., 59
  Harry, 134
  Jno., 132
  Jos. L., 52, 114
  Joseph L., 151
  Rata, 151
NORTHMORE
  Will, 86
NORTHRUP
  E. J., 165
NOURSE
  Kathleen A., 98
  Robert, 98

ODELL
  Ruth E., 42
OFFETT
  Nettie, 132

OFFUTT
  N. D., 67
  Nichols, 132
  Robert W., 108
OGDEN
  Levin, 126
OLIVER
  Jerome, 95
  John F., 95, 114
  Mary D., 114
O'MEARA
  Thos. R., 166
ORME
  Margaret, 94
  Thomas, 94
ORRISON
  Arthur, 150
  Clara, 167
  Elizabeth, 150, 155, 156
  J. H., 29
  J. W., 45
  James, 167
  James J., 136
  Jane, 32
  Jane E., 34
  John W., 67, 161
  Jonah, 64
  Loretta, 29
  Nancy, 64, 67
  T. Clayton, 151
  T. S., 156
  Wm. P., 59
OSBORN
  Herbert, 30
  Jos., 22
  Logan, 61
  Wm., 61
OSBORNE
  Bushrod, 84
  Jos., 84
OSBOURN
  Herbert, 114
OSBURN
  Alice, 23
  Clara, 22, 23
  Harrison, 125

  Herbert, 31, 37
  J. C., 23
  Jessie, 23
  Joab, 37
  L. Jane, 125
  Logan, 149, 163
  Martha C., 89
  Mortimer, 30
  Robert, 71
  Robt., 18, 36
  Townsend, 132
  Volney, 23, 129
  Wm., 144, 149, 163
  Wm. S., 30
OTLEY
  Flavius C., 30
  H. Clay, 148, 149, 159
  Jas. J., 82
  Jno. J., 30
  Walter, 127
OVERALL
  Jno., 129
  Willie, 129
OVERHALL
  Fannie, 68
OWENS
  Henry, 59

PAGE
  Carter, 9, 129
  Eliza M. A., 21
  Evelyn, 21
  William G., 129
  Wm. B., 21
PALMER
  Albert G., 174
  C. W., 67
  Edward L., 134
  Elsie, 134
  Fannie, 11
  Katie, 10, 11
  L. Frank, 88
  Mary F., 90
  Philip, 88
  Prudence V., 88

PANCOAST
  Joshua, 119
  Sarah, 119
PANGLE
  Brisco C., 128
  Chas. C., 128
  Jefferson H., 62
  Milton, 18, 54, 83
  Robert N., 54
PARIS
  Louisa A., 59
PARKER
  Ada, 76
  Ridley, 130
  Stephen, 120
PAXSON
  ___, 4
  Charles, 72, 134
  Edgar H., 10
  Griffith, 44
  John, 7, 8
  Nellie, 141
  S. B., 141
  Saml., 134
  William E., 98
PAXTON
  Amanda, 90
  Charles R., 4, 5
  Chas. R., 5
PAYNE
  Daniel, 39
  Jos. W., 150
  R. B., 171
  Theodore, 119
  Wm., 119
PEACH
  Selden, 43
PEACOCK
  James, 87, 88
  N. B., 62
  Noble B., 44
PEARCE
  Harry, 142
PEARSON
  Geo. W., 166
  Mary, 166
  S. H., 133

PENDLETON
  Garnet, 135
PENN
  William, 107
PERKINS
  James F., 132
PERRY
  Chas. E., 117
  Maiza, 42
PETERKIN
  Rebecca, 68
PEUGH
  J. Frank, 127
  Jas. B., 47
  Jonah, 170
  Rose, 127
PEYTON
  Cabel Y., 178
PHILLIP
  Thomas, 142
PHILLIPS
  A. W., 121
  Arthur W., 25
  B. F., 133
  Cella E., 53
  Dr., 142
  John, 167
  Leah, 121
  Mary, 20
  Parmelia A., 133
PIDGEON
  Louis, 162
PIERCE
  Carroll, 158
  Laura, 158
PIERPOINT
  Eli, 143
  Ella, 57
  Mary J., 143
  O. J., 176
PIGGOTT
  Alberta J., 14
  Bushrod, 1, 2
  Henry, 127
  Jesse, 96
  John, 177
  Martha B., 87

  Mary, 181
  Mary A., 87
  Mary E., 14
  Mary J., 117
  Mrs., 177
  Sallie E., 87
  Thomas H., 70
  Thos. H., 87
  Thos. J., 87
  Wm., 2, 45, 155
PINKET
  Cloey, 54
  Lewis, 54
PLASTER
  D. H., 59
  Fannie, 72
  Fannie L., 80
  Fanny, 59
  Geo.E., 59
  Henry, 81
POLAND
  Alexander, 25
  Margaret A., 25
POLEN
  Lena, 118
POLLARD
  Annie, 23
  Henry, 86
POLLEN
  Sarah A., 62
POLLOCK
  A. D., 39
  Thomas, 39
PONTON
  James, 41
PORTER
  A. J., 12
  Ida, 12
  John F., 72
  R. F., 57
  Robert F., 72
  S. L., 106
POSTON
  Alice I., 62
POTTERFIELD
  Harry, 112, 114
  Jannie E. A., 3

L. H., 50, 71, 182
Luther H., 182
Thos. L., 112
POTTS
 Clinton, 41
 David H., 172
 E. F., 4
 Gennie D., 4
 Ida, 81
 J. O., 4, 86
 James W., 113
 Jane E., 2
 John T., 81
 Jonathan, 50
 Martha J., 91
 Nannie, 4
 Samuel R., 171
 Virginia, 50
 Wm. B., 2
POWELL
 Aquilla, 179
 Chas E., 76
 Chas., 100
 Chas. E., 76, 101
 Chas. L., 173
 Cuthbert, 173
 E. B., 165
 Fannie, 46
 G., 46
 H. B., 156
 J. H., 134
 Jane, 134
 Leven, 141
 Lizzie, 76
 Louis H., 6, 9
 Lucien, 13
 Maria, 56
 Maria L., 56, 65
 W. L., 141, 156
 Walter, 134
 Wm., 179
POWER
 Carry J., 93
 Charles, 93, 94
 Cora, 93
 James, 85
 Sallie, 93

PRATT
 Frederick C. G., 144
PRESGRAVE
 Celia, 80
 E. W., 80
 J. T., 35, 80
 Mollie, 75
 Sarah A. E., 35
PRESTON
 Albert T., 111
 Ed, 96
 G. F., 60
 Lucy, 44
 Lydia A., 96
 R. M., 54, 117
PRICE
 Ella, 129
 Emily J., 54
 Floyd, 140
 Isaac, 177
 Jno., 28, 36
 Russell, 129
 Ruth, 129
 Samuel H., 140
PRICHETT
 Al, 110
PRIEST
 John H., 158
 Mamie, 158
PRINCE
 Rosa, 108
PUMPHEY
 John W., 135
PUMPHREY
 Elizabeth, 33
 John, 53
PURCELL
 Harriet N., 103
 Heaton, 126
 J. F., 179
 J. H., 61
 Janney, 121
 Logan, 114
 N. J., 149
 Nora E., 179

Rodney, 103, 126, 157
 V. V., 149
 Wm., 126
PURSELL
 Jas. H., 163
 N. J., 71
 Patience, 163
 V. V., 18, 36
PUSEY
 Joshua, 114, 152
 Mary E., 152, 155
PUTNAM
 Lucy, 170
QUEEN
 Saml., 158
QUICK
 J. V., 141
 Sallie E., 141
 W. V., 141
QUIGLEY
 Mamie, 19
RADCLIFFE
 Ann M., 7
 Mrs., 72
RAMSEY
 Dennis M., 168
RAPHAEL
 E. F., 178
RATHIE
 Benj. D., 169
 John B., 108
 John J., 136
 Joseph B., 112
 Sallie, 108
 Wm. P., 108
RATRIE
 Florence, 93
RAWLINGS
 Arthur A., 158
RAWSON
 Edward B., 69
 Eliza F., 122
RAY
 Clara, 86

The Telephone INDEX

REAMER
  Chas., 178
  George, 166
  James, 163
  William C., 163
RECTOR
  Alice C., 40
  Edward L., 105
  Edward W., 114
  Emma, 180
  H. N., 43
  Samuel, 43
REDMAN
  George, 8
  Henry, 161
REED
  Effie, 176
  Grant, 117
  J. R., 176
  Joseph, 83
  Landon, 38
  Rebecca, 38
  Sallie, 58
  Sarah C., 28
  Scott, 66
  Smith, 2, 83
  Steve, 136
  T. E., 68
  Thomas, 38
  Wm., 68
REEDER
  Scott, 66
REES
  Annie J., 102
  Jonah L., 102
  Mary, 102
REID
  Alice, 57
  Frank, 32
  Joshua, 117
  Marmaduke, 57
  Norman, 99
  R. J. N., 157
RESIDENCES NAMES
  Belmont, 77
  Caledonia, 126
  Carlheim, 4
  Clover Hill, 16
  Exeter, 5
  Forest Mills, 53
  Fruitland, 57
  Glenellen, 152
  Grafton, 21
  Green Hill, 99
  Hedgewood, 7
  Ingledew, 136
  Ingleside, 155
  Ivon, 169, 170
  Kinsley, 170
  Llangollen, 141
  Meadow Brook, 69
  Morven, 74
  Newstard, 15
  Oak Hill, 29, 114
  Oakland Green, 32
  Pagebrook, 21
  Ravenswood, 13
  Ravensworth, 71
  Rockland, 164, 165
  Rosemont, 169
  Sunny Side, 2, 112, 143
  Sunnyside, 127
  Temple Hall, 116
  The Whitley, 110
  White Hall, 121
RESSER
  Maggie, 58
REYNOLDS
  Clara V., 69
  Frederick, 134
RHODES
  Mary R., 4
  Nannie, 4
  Randolph, 4
  Theomiah, 124
RICE
  Jno., 40
  John Wm., 69
  Lena, 66
  Thomas B., 37
RICHARDS
  Alcinda, 93
  Leven, 48
  S. L., 81
RICHARDSON
  Chas., 43
  John M., 13
RICHIE
  Katie, 114
RICKARD
  L. Kate, 7, 8
RIDEOUT
  Joseph M., 143
RIDGEWAY
  Samuel, 90
  T. L., 137
RILEY
  ___, 170
  Absolam, 152
  Absolem, 104
  Carrie, 156
  Jas. W., 9
  Louisa, 104
  Minnie B., 9
  N. B., 156
  Rosa B., 53
  W. B., 27
RINEY
  Sarah, 130
RINKER
  Alberta E., 162
  Annie, 178
  Frank, 161
  Franklin, 162
  John L., 48
  Josiah, 125
  Susan, 48
  Wm., 178
RIPPON
  C. B., 153
RITICOR
  C. F., 116
  Elijah, 129
  Joseph, 166
  Joshua L., 166
  Mary C., 33

Robt. A., 66
Zilpha, 63, 66
RITTENHOUSE
  Frank, 172
ROBERDEAU
  Jane, 134
ROBERSON
  Wm. H., 120
ROBERTS
  Landen D., 121
  Nathan, 126
ROBEY
  Alman, 159
  Mary, 124
  William, 124
ROBINSON
  B., 180
  Esquire, 129
  Fred, 145
  Lucy, 129
  Marie, 133
  Rosa, 86
  William, 140
  William H., 133
ROBY
  F. E., 124
RODEFFER
  Ada, 1, 2
  Ada V., 3
  Anna, 3
  Hugh, 2
  Mary, 64, 66
RODGERS
  Mollie T., 28
ROE
  Edward, 5
ROESER
  Carl, 1
ROGERS
  A. H., 120
  Christie, 120
  Henry J., 38
  James H., 51
  Joseph, 158
  M. M., 21
  Milton, 38
  S. E., 76

Samuel, 22
Thos., 22
Wm. H., 162
ROLES
  Mary C., 67
ROLLINS
  Carrie A., 26
  Ella, 62
  James A., 62
  Jas. E., 62
  Samuel M., 93
ROLPH
  Emma M., 112
ROOSE
  Richard, 119
ROSE
  Ann D., 58
  Samuel E., 160
ROSS
  J. H., 110
  Jno. T., 100
  O. A., 72
  Robert, 66
  Sallie, 100
  Turner J., 110
  W., 72
ROWZEE
  Morgan, 3
  Sommerville A., 3
ROY
  Maggie, 98
RUCKER
  Anna L., 136
  W. A., 136
RUNER
  Wm., 1
RUPPERT
  A., 141
RUSE
  Cora, 144
  Elizabeth, 24
  Emanuel, 71, 73
  Joseph, 139
  Mrs., 139
  Michael, 24
  Solomon, 24, 28, 157

RUSK
  Edgar E., 135
RUSSELL
  ___, 48
  Brewis, 71
  C. A., 139
  Caleb, 11, 34, 143
  Edward, 69
  Elizabeth M., 11
  George, 86
  H. H., 45, 73, 110, 117, 144, 152, 156
  Hattie E., 73
  J., 7
  Joseph, 86
  Joshua, 1
  Llewelyn, 34
  Robt. E., 71
  Stephen J., 139
  Theodore, 11
  William, 88
  Wm., 73
RUST
  A. T. M., 129, 153, 164, 165
  Ida, 164, 165
  Jno. C., 168
  Lawrence, 153
  Netta L., 129
RUSTIN
  Sam, 142
  Samuel, 144
RYAN
  Catharine, 19
  John D., 93
RYON
  John D., 106

SAFFEL
  Mary, 68
SAFFELL
  Annie, 93
SAFFER
  John W., 91
  Thornton, 91

SAFFLE
  Henry, 128
  Thomas, 128
SAGLE
  W. H., 27
SAMPSELL
  Nixon, 42
SANBOWER
  Duana, 71
  Simon, 51
  Thomas, 49
  Thos., 50
SANDERS
  Sarah A., 77
  Wilson C., 77
SANTENYERS
  Bettie, 15
  John B., 15
  Mary E., 15
SANTMYER
  Rosa R., 99
SAUNDER
  Americus J., 129
SAUNDERS
  Henry, 13, 114, 144
  J. D., 134
  John H., 104
  Lillie, 134
  R. Neville, 114
  V. C., 144
  Wm. H., 13, 59, 144
SCANDLAN
  Albert T., 23
SCANLAND
  A. T., 81
  Albert, 23
SCATTERDAY
  Ann E., 178
SCHAFF
  Ray, 2
SCHOFIELD
  Hannah, 167
  Joseph, 167
SCHOOLEY
  Aaron, 118

Alfred, 55
Betsey, 118
C. W., 131, 141, 142
Chas. E., 32
Chas. W., 125
Clarence E., 171
Cora, 141
Cora M., 142
Cornelius, 54
Emma, 55, 87, 142
Florence, 55
Geo., 20
Geo. T., 125
Geo. W., 37
George, 118
George T., 106
Grace, 55
Honora M., 32
Horace P., 98
J. E., 98
James T., 18
Jas. B., 2
Jonas P., 138
Jonathan H., 54
Joseph E., 97
Laura, 54
Lester, 131
Lula E., 97, 98
Milton, 3
Narcissa L., 67
Reuben, 68
Sarah Ann, 138
Sherman, 55
Susan, 54
Thomas, 54
Thomas A., 118
Thos., 24
Thos. A., 125
W., 92
W. T., 112
Walter, 55
William E., 103
Wm., 63
SCHOTT
  Annetta, 138

Mamie C., 138
Simon P., 138
SCHROGGINS
  Annie, 117
SCHULKE
  Henry G., 107
SCOTT
  Hannah, 163, 166
  Jacob, 20, 21, 48
  John, 92
  Manerva, 53
  Mary A., 110
  Moses, 124
  R. A., 110
SCRIBNER
  Howard, 29
SEATON
  Arthur, 80
  Cornelius C., 62
  Ella, 35
  G. Ludwell, 36
  Irene, 78
  Mary E., 80
  Townsend, 52
  Wm., 35, 57
SEIFFERT
  G. R., 101
SELBAUGH
  Rosa J., 3
SELLMAN
  Ida, 98
SETTLE
  Newton, 39
  Thos., 36
SHAFER
  Danial, 158
  E. C., 113
  Mary, 158
  Susan, 49
SHAFFER
  Daniel, 50
SHARPE
  W. R., 16
SHAW
  Homer, 78
  Mrs., 127
SHAWEN

INDEX

A. T., 10
Fannie, 111
SHAWN
  Cornelius, 121
SHEETZ
  Arthur, 98
SHELHORN
  Godfrey, 122
SHELLHORN
  Godfrey, 121
SHELLHORNE
  Godfrey, 11
SHELTON
  T. D., 129
SHEPHERD
  J. Newton, 172
SHEPPERD
  Hambleton, 153
SHERMAN
  John, 13
SHERRARD
  Jos. H., 1
  Sarah, 128
SHIFFER
  Daniel, 66
SHIPMAN
  ___, 167
SHOEMAKER
  Alice, 60
  Basil, 51
  Basil W., 51
  Edith, 127
  Edwin, 82
  Elwood, 107
  Geo., 60, 127
  Sarah, 107
SHORTS
  Henry, 56
  Lettie, 56
SHOWER
  George T., 51
  Ida M., 168
SHOWERS
  Samuel, 177
SHREVE
  B. A., 29
  Eugenia, 29

  Francis E., 117
  Sallie N., 29
SHRIOCK
  John, 37
SHRIVER
  Amelia, 98
  David, 98
  Susan, 90
SHROFF
  P. E., 132
  Sophia E., 132
SHRY
  Christian, 44
  Christina, 45
  John H., 45
  Vernon A., 128
SHRYOCK
  Ailsey E., 90
  Jno. F., 93
  Shryock &
    Presgraves, 96, 124
SHUEY
  Laura, 19
  Lola, 62
SHUGARS
  Addison, 63
  Lewis E., 138
SHUGERS
  Mollie, 116
SHUMAKER
  Ann, 47
  Elizabeth, 23
  Frank, 65
  Sallie, 53
SHUMAN
  Wm., 99
SHUMATE
  Chilton, 102
  John, 141
  L. M., 179
  Lewis, 44
SILCOTT
  Armstead, 36
  Chas., 50
  Elizabeth, 73
  Ella M., 160

  Frank, 98
  J. Ed., 157
  Mattie V., 133
  Mortimer, 73
  Norval, 122
  Sallie A., 160
  Washington, 157
  William, 178
  Zula B., 160
SILL
  Andrew C., 116
SILMAN
  Gertrude, 107
SILMON
  Virgil C., 145
SIMMS
  Lee, 86
  William, 137
SIMPSON
  Annie, 109
  Annis, 110
  Augustus, 67
  Burr, 64
  Emily, 71
  Ethel, 158
  Frank, 80
  H. B., 158
  Harrison M., 104
  Henson, 70, 110
  J. H., 99
  J. T., 58
  John, 71
  John F., 66
  Julia, 99
  Lillian, 70
  Lillian E., 70
  Louisa N., 92
  Martha, 66
  Miss, 173
  Noland, 124
  S. N., 124
  Samuel, 82
  Samuel S., 67
  T. B., 67
SIMS
  Estelle E., 23
SINCLAIR

Chas. C., 150
Elijah, 73
Elizabeth, 73
James, 73
Richard E., 150
Robt. R., 150
SINE
  A. T., 149
  C. R., 149
  E. C., 149
SINGLETON
  Edward, 23
SKILLMAN
  James, 23
  L. F., 101, 102
SKINKER
  H. Garland, 136
SKINNER
  Alice, 25
  J. T., 25
  James, 2
  Lucy, 2
  Mary C., 168
  Peter, 34
SLACK
  James E., 160
  Lloyd, 138
  Nimrod E., 22
SLATER
  Julia A., 26
  Samuel, 26
  William, 83
SLAYMAKER
  Amos B., 136
SLENTZ
  David, 154
  John, 116, 117
SLOPER
  Lula O., 136
  Rhoda, 65
SMALLWOOD
  Annie, 30
  F. M., 30
  George, 162
  William, 75
SMART
  Fayette, 70

Frank T., 70
SMITH
???da B., 180
Achsah W., 18
Albert H., 134
Anna T., 7
Annie, 20
Armanda B., 181
B. F., 179
Bettie, 178
Chas. H., 3
Clarissa, 156
Daisy, 103
Ed., 109
Edward, 112
Edward J., 69, 76
Elen H., 7
Elizabeth B., 76
F. H., 47
Frank, 109, 163
Geo. W., 48
Hattie, 105
Henry H., 167, 168
Henry S., 76
Inez, 109
Jacob, 74
Jas. M., 86
Jennie, 35, 74
Jno. L., 128
Job, 46, 48
John, 28, 84, 105
John F., 24
John L., 121, 126, 128
John W., 138
Kate L., 27
Laura, 7
Lelia B., 62
Lizzie, 91, 92, 109, 112
Lizzie B., 32
Lottie R., 150
M., 93
M. M., 25
Marianna, 69
Mary, 41

Mary E., 128
Matthew, 93
Middleton, 156
Peter, 80, 86
Ruth H., 28, 33, 105
Samuel, 178
Samuel J., 35
Sandy, 62, 103
Sarah Ellen, 86
Susan B., 154
T. Towson, 100
Thomas, 134
Thomas R., 7, 20, 102
Venna, 62
Vida, 121
Vines, 103
W. P., 6
William, 134
Wm., 31
Wm. H., 65, 112
Zachariah, 59
SNOOTS
  Dolly, 34
  Henry, 94
  Presley, 38
  Sallie, 38
SOLOMON
  N. M., 52
SOMERVILL
  Louisa W., 76
SOUDER
  A. J., 119
  Emma V., 25
  Geo. P., 25, 144
  Jane, 119
  Jos. C., 144
  Philip, 142
SOWERS
  Daniel H., 115
SPALDING
  Maud, 31
SPARROUGH
  Benjamin F., 53
  Malcram, 163
SPATES

Nettie, 171
Thomas, 171
SPILLER
  Alex, 168
  Geo. W., 168
  Martha, 168
SPINDLE
  Lorinda, 17
SPINKS
  Alfred J., 86
SPRIGG
  Ida T., 76
SPRING
  Alice L., 38
  Annie, 58
  Charles, 49
  David W., 38
  Ed, 3
  Jefferson, 58
  Mary W., 1
  Mr., 57
SPURGEON
  Emma S., 37
SQUIRES
  John, 37
STABLER
  Jessie B., 134
  Robert, 178
STANLEY
  J. S., 96
STANSBURY
  J. J., 7
  M. A., 7
  Margaret A., 11
STANTON
  Frederick P., 77
  Mrs., 77
STAUBS
  Aaron, 113
  Charles, 113
STEADMAN
  David, 8
  Elizabeth, 8
  Olivia, 8
STEER
  Emma, 98
  Franklin M., 127

Harriet, 50
James D., 102
Robt. M., 98
Samuel L., 50
W. E., 110
Wm. B., 180
STEPHENS
  J. J., 7
  Joseph, 7
  Sue E., 159
STEPHENSON
  ___, 170
  Wm. H., 14, 25
STEVENS
  Henry J., 121
  Mary E., 152
STEVENSON
  Wm., 6
STEWART
  J. W. S., 128
  John, 17
  John W., 18
  Luther, 163
  Murray, 128
  Nancy, 154
  W. A., 129
  W. J. S., 127
STOCKS
  Christina, 67
  Eli, 4
  John, 60
  Mahlon, 5
  Matilda, 5
STONE
  Annie E., 54
  Bush, 2
  Frank P., 115
  Mary, 122
  Newton, 1
  Newton M., 2, 3
  Wm. J., 39
STOUFFER
  B. F., 69
STOUT
  Amanda E., 31
  Jacob, 108
STOUTSBARGER

Clara J., 136
STOUTSENBURGER
  Emma M., 161
STOUTZENBERGER
  Mrs., 167
STRASBERGER
  John, 5
STRAUD
  Maurice, 157
STREAM
  Jno., 129
  Samuel, 114
STRIBLING
  Olivia C. J., 168
STROTHER
  Annie D., 116
  John, 55
  Julia, 57
STROUD
  W. A., 149
  Wm. A., 152
STUART
  George, 173
  Julia, 173
  Mabel, 173
  Miss, 148
STULL
  Charles W., 107
SUDDITH
  John, 100
SULLIVAN
  Wm., 87
SUMMERS
  John, 72
  W. S., 39
  Wm. S., 117
SURVICK
  Bessie E., 25
  Survick & Whitmore, 96, 124
SUTHARD
  Joseph, 171
  Mary, 171
SUTHERD
  Annie B., 171
SUTTLE

The Telephone INDEX

Nelson, 39
Thos., 39
SUTTON
 Anna, 30
 Carrie V., 133
 James M., 133
 Jas., 30
SVEDBURG
 Jno. H., 173
SWAN
 Carita, 6
 Gov., 74
SWANK
 Eva R., 39
 Jno. W., 39
 Samuel, 150, 157
 Sarah E., 39
SWANN
 Thomas, 98, 178
 Thos., 180
SWART
 A. L., 109
 Elizabeth T., 11
 Henry, 11
 Henry S., 47
 Martha E., 109
SWARTZ
 Armida, 70
SWEENEY
 Jane, 33
 John H., 33
SWEET
 R. Berry, 142
SWEETSER
 W. D., 56, 90
SWOPE
 Medora, 114

TALBOTT
 T. Melville, 98
TALIAFERRO
 James M., 118
 John W., 119
TALLEY
 Maggie, 33
 Mary, 124
TARLTON

George W., 68
TATE
 Elizabeth, 25
 Mary, 16, 25
TATUM
 Charles H., 168
 Lily S., 168
 Lucien B., 168
 R. Herbert, 168
TAVENNER
 Benjamin, 116
 Carrie, 125
 Carrie B., 146, 147
 Charles, 173
 Chas., 110
 Clarence, 83
 Cloyd, 147
 E. H., 119, 146, 147
 Edgar, 106, 108, 110
 Emily, 106
 Emma, 9
 George W., 143
 Hiram, 24
 Hiram N., 33, 36
 James, 119
 John, 57
 Jonah, 150
 Levi, 64
 Lot, 43, 96
 Lott, 45
 M. D., 62
 Mahlon, 47
 Maria, 147
 Marie S., 73
 Mary, 96, 116
 Mary E., 108, 110
 Nimrod, 35
 R. W., 109, 110
 Rebecca, 57
 Rose, 110
 Sarah J., 119
 Susan, 47, 51
 Wm., 24, 104
 Wm. L., 106

Wm. P., 7, 104
TAYLOR
 ___, 129
 A. M., 60
 Bailey, 23
 Balie, 22
 Blanch, 23
 Charles E., 16
 Dr., 40
 Edward, 107
 Ella F., 29
 Gertrude, 126
 H. H., 43
 Hannah, 131
 Harry, 23
 Henry, 117
 Isabelle, 96
 J. W., 107
 Jno., 58
 Lewis, 89
 Lewis A., 159
 Mary J., 121
 Mortimer, 96
 Oscar, 29
 S. Townsend, 145
 Samuel T., 155
 Thomas E., 117
 Thos. E., 121
 Timothy, 131
 Virginia, 94, 95
 W. H., 16
 Wm., 126
TEBBS
 Julia, 97
TELGHMAN
 Henrietta, 128
TENNANT
 David B., 179
 Eugenia, 179
TERRETT
 Frederick, 148
THATCHER
 Emma, 163
THAYER
 B., 20
THOMAS

Armstead, 49, 132
C. S., 179
Ellen, 132
Frank, 16
Harry, 2
Henry W., 42, 43
James, 132
Lottie G., 155
Milton E., 139
Mollie, 32
Nora, 29, 48
Owen L., 110
R. W., 48, 142
Rebecca M., 16
W. W., 42
Wade E., 110
Will, 48
THOMPSON
　Allison, 36, 42
　Benjamin, 107
　Blanche M., 59
　David T., 58
　Eli, 21, 74
　Eliza, 66, 70
　Ernest L., 59
　Etta, 96
　Fannie, 21
　Franklin A., 96
　Howard, 32
　J. E., 109
　J. W., 108
　Jas. E., 112
　Maggie E., 12
　Mary H., 58
　Orra, 180
　R. J. C., 26, 66
　Robt J. C., 70
　S. Virginia, 108
　Samuel, 53, 58
　Summerfield, 58
　Walters, 137
　William, 36
　Wm., 121
THRASHER
　Elizabeth H., 6
　Ella F., 29

Luther A., 29
THRIFT
　Annie M., 8
　L. Francis, 62
THROCKMORTON
　___, 5
　Annie, 146
　Mason, 89, 146
THURSTON
　Henry, 114, 121
TIFFANY
　Lizzie, 171
　W. N., 137
TILFORD
　Frank N., 164
　Rosalie L., 164
TILLETT
　Caroline, 84
　John J., 166
　S. R., 32, 64
TINSMAN
　Cleveland, 19
　Francis M., 160
　J. M., 19
　S. J., 19
TITUS
　D. H., 25
　Geo. W., 18
　Martha A., 15
　Samuel, 15
　T. S., 15
TODD
　Hattie, 140
TOWNSEND
　Annie M., 58
　Carrie, 47
　Geo., 47
　Samuel, 58
TRENARY
　John L., 145
　Robert E., 48
TREW
　Mrs., 127
　Virginia W., 127
TRIBBY
　J. T., 49
TRIBY

Samuel, 51
TRILBY
　___, 161
TRIPLETT
　Miss, 92
　W. H., 175
TRIST
　H. B., 180
　Nicholas P., 180
TRITAPOE
　H. A., 170
　Wm. E., 170
TRITTAPOE
　Harvey A., 134
TRUNDLE
　A. C., 82
　Edward H., 141
　H. H., 141
TRUSSELL
　Charles, 60, 93
　Chas., 61
　Mary E., 32
TUCKER
　H. Tudor, 50
　J. Randolph, 50, 156
TURNER
　Ann, 78, 95
　C. W. S., 122
　Chas. W. S., 42
　Edward C., 58
　Joseph, 161
　Littleton, 83
　Lucy R., 92
　Mrs. Dr., 132
　Richard, 78
　Robt., 58
TWINING
　Sallie, 17
TYLER
　Douglas, 179
　Mrs., 179
　Thomas B., 66

UMBAUGH
　Hatty E., 134
UTTERBACH

Jno. G., 126
UTTERBACK
Benj. D. Jr., 116
Jas., 38
Mary, 103
Mary G., 103
Nancy M., 59
W. N., 59

VANDEUSON
T. A., 98
VANDEVANDER
Fenton, 157
Isaac, 156
Martha, 156
Maurice, 121
VANDEVANTER
A. C., 89
Albert, 114
C. Means, 65, 172
Cecelia, 138
Cornelius, 92
D. H., 16, 37, 128, 137
Dr., 86
Gabriel, 136
Isaac, 118, 121
Jane C., 137
Martha D., 159
Robert S., 76
Robt. S., 164
S., 92
T. H., 136, 137, 177
Washington, 157
VANSICKLER
J. B., 52
Jas. C., 61
Lula, 52
Mahala, 60
Mehala, 61
Mary E., 135
VAUGHN
Oscar L., 99
VEALE
Albert, 117

Rebecca, 117
VEITCH
Wm., 120
VENABLE
A. P., 12
VENNA
Roy W., 74
VENY
Sam, 172
VERNON
Capt., 151
VERTS
Elton, 79
VICKERS
Fred, 86
J. M., 85, 176
Julian, 122
Mabel, 85
Richard G., 122
Sarah, 122
VILLARD
Lee, 103
VINCEL
Louisa, 152
W. D., 77
VIOLLAND
Adrienne G., 148
Eng L., 148
VIRTS
___, 144
Annie, 65
Betsy, 51
Chas., 57
Edgar, 57
Elizabeth, 51, 54
Ella, 78
G. W., 65
Geo. W., 166
Harriet A., 54
Isaac, 108
Israel, 52
John W., 142
Lewis J., 9
Minnie, 108
Minnie L., 109
Mollie, 65
Mortimer M., 54

Nannie, 142
Richard A., 135
Susan A., 21
W. H., 65

WADSWORTH
Bessie, 86
WALDREN
Mary J., 43
WALDRON
H. C., 91, 101
Hiram C., 43
Lizzie, 15
WALKER
Beau, 23
F. A., 182
Florence, 155
H. E., 84
J. Edward, 163
James M., 45
Jas. M., 45
Martha, 52
Mollie, 52
R. R., 48
Robert R., 63
Robt. R., 114, 128, 166
Sallie, 20
WALL
Andrew, 100
WALLACE
Adelaide, 135
James M., 19
Jas. M., 21
Laudolia E., 177
Lawson K., 177
Lew., 19
Mary, 119
WALLICE
Mary J., 121
WALTER
Charles G., 97
WALTERS
Mary, 31
Mary N., 32
WALTMAN
H. Kate, 71

The Telephone INDEX

Kate, 101, 110
Lelia, 99
M. V. B., 71
William G., 101
WALTON
  Apple F., 115
  William E., 168
WARFORD
  Abel, 21
WARNER
  Annie G., 72
  Chas. E., 72
  Cora, 105
  Elizabeth, 163
  Florence, 106
  Gabrael, 60
  Geo., 155
  I. P., 33
  Isaac, 105
  Mary, 144
  Mary E., 158
  Richard, 92
  Theodore, 105
  Thomas, 92
  Thomas J., 104
  Virginia, 155
  Wm., 74
WASHINGTON
  Geo., 73
  Robt. W., 73
WATERS
  ___, 177
  Dan'l., 115
  Esther, 119
  Geo. W., 7
  J. F., 91
  James, 115
  John, 156
  Joseph, 119
  Mary, 177
  Susan, 91
  Tobitha, 87
WATKINS
  Bessie, 98
WATSON
  Henry, 171
  M. A., 101

WEADON
  Ashford, 135
  C. W., 73
  Chas. W., 178
  Fannie A., 72
  Frank, 75
  Nancy, 17
  T. W., 73
  W. C., 84, 85
  Wm., 74, 152
WEAVER
  Thomas W., 172
WEBB
  Rebecca, 99
WEBSTER
  Ella, 23
  Isaac B., 73
WEEDEN
  James, 113
WEILER
  Ollie, 16
WELCH
  William, 83
WELLS
  Emma, 153
  Frank N., 73
  Libbie J., 30
WELSH
  A. F., 120
  Albina, 103
  Alfred, 122
  F. G., 135
  Fayette, 32
  Florence, 23, 32
  Florence M., 111
  Howard, 23, 103, 135
  John, 39
  Seldon, 39
  Will, 32, 141
WELTY
  ___, 17
  Birtha, 59
  Elias, 46
  F. H., 59
WENNER
  C. C., 125, 176

  J. W., 154, 155
  Jennie, 25
  Mary V., 26
  Rosa, 120
  Sarah A., 125
WEST
  James J., 3
WHALEY
  A. M., 61
  J. W., 34
WHALLEY
  Emma F., 79
WHARTON
  Lulu, 23
WHEELER
  Johnson, 57
  Martha A., 158
WHITACRE
  Thornton, 38, 39, 41
WHITE
  A. C., 106
  Ada, 113, 115
  Adin, 49
  Adin C., 122
  B. V., 113
  B. Viers, 111
  Charles, 161
  Cornelia, 23
  E. V., 11, 45, 96, 113, 115, 123, 146, 147
  Eliza J., 86
  Elizabeth J., 145
  Furr, 109, 110
  Geo. W., 68
  George, 65, 79
  Gussie O., 86
  Hannah, 79
  Hannah E., 106
  Hattie V., 25
  Inez, 146, 147
  James M., 127
  Joshua, 74
  Julia, 122
  Levi, 5
  Lige, 140

The Telephone INDEX

Lizzie A., 123
Lou., 5
Mary, 19, 23
Richard, 11
Richard T., 11
Robert J. T., 40
Will, 142
Wm. A., 154
WHITE
  A. C., 74
  White & Bro, 106
WHITELEY
  Arthur, 86
WHITING
  Lean, 40
  W. W., 154
WHITLAY
  Adolphus, 59
WHITLOCK
  Henry, 91
WHITMORE
  John H., 114
WIARD
  Michael, 28, 36, 39
  William, 78
WICKLINE
  J. S., 45
WIDENOR
  Henry, 146
WIGHTMAN
  A. J., 135
  Orra J., 53
  Sallie, 22
  Susan, 135
WILDMAN
  J. W., 22
  John, 17
  John W., 36
  Mary G., 22
  R. B., 162
  Robert, 162
  Robt. B., 120
  Wildman & Co., 137
WILEY
  Annie, 82
  Clarence, 61

Edgar, 48, 83, 147
Goldie R., 14
Mary V., 61
Mattie, 39
Mattie R., 14
Mr., 144
Thomas H., 61
Thos., 60
W. S., 14
Walter G., 24
Walter R., 39
Will, 142
Z. T., 157
WILKINS
  James H., 115
WILLARD
  Dan B., 77
  Ella, 62
  Jas., 62
  T. A., 149
WILLIAMS
  Charley, 15
  Chas. A., 1
  Chas. W., 66
  Fannie, 11
  Geo. W., 63
  Hannah, 131
  Henry S., 106
  Howard, 79
  J. E., 30
  James, 105, 131
  James W., 162, 163
  John, 123, 162
  Nellie, 172
  Otis, 98, 147
  Pleasant, 123
  Rebecca J., 121
  Rev. Dr., 101
  Robt., 31
  Rosa V., 140
  Tobias, 178
  William, 111, 112, 162
  Wm., 114
WILLIAMSON

Joseph A., 179
Thos., 41
WILLIS
  James, 82
  R., 82
WILMARTH
  ____, 99
  Marbel, 23
WILSON
  Antoni, 6
  Crosby, 171
  Emily, 25
  Folger, 176
  Harry, 25
  Isaac, 76
  Jas. L., 174
  Jno., 15
  Sarah, 119
  Stephen, 129
  Stephen H., 150
  Thomas M., 84
  W. W., 136
  Will, 23
  Will H., 32
  William, 176
  William H., 76
WINE
  Louis D., 8, 13, 120
WINSTON
  Jay, 7
WIRE
  Geo., 104
WIRGMAN
  James, 157
WIRT
  Wm., 135
WISE
  Ella, 102
  Margaret D., 102
  Wm. N., 102
WOLFORD
  C. E., 127
WOOD
  Ann S., 132
  Bessie, 167
  D. P., 167

Daniel T., 69
Ham., 21
Hamilton, 22
Josiah, 11
Laura, 69
Leslie, 37
Mary, 22
Mr., 172
Sally, 55
Thomas, 37
WOODARD
  George R., 1
WOODS
  Blanche, 20
WOODSON
  B. L., 155
WOODWARD
  Geo. F., 38
  Hallie O., 3
WOODYARD
  John, 153
WOOLF
  Jno., 61
  Wm. A., 61
WORKS
  Elizabeth B., 133
WORSLEY
  T. L., 107
WORTHAM
  Fannie, 171

WORTHINGTON
  Joseph L., 140
WORTMAN
  Temple, 96, 97
WOTRING
  Minnie L., 127
WRIGHT
  ___, 153
  A. D., 124
  Albert, 155
  Charlotte, 156
  Cora C., 135
  E. M., 182
  Geo. T., 155
  H. V., 174
  Jas. T., 121
  John, 29, 32
  Klein, 19
  Laura G., 144
  Lewis, 166
  Norman L., 182
  Oden, 174
  S. J., 144
  Saml., 4
  Samuel, 6, 144
  T. S., 182
  William H., 138
  Wm. H., 144
WYCKOFF
  Harriet, 78

  Nicholas, 78
WYER
  H. H., 56
WYNDHAM
  Annie C., 1
  T. O., 1
WYNKOOP
  A. J., 126
  Fannie, 56
  James, 56
  Martha J., 26
  Mary B., 180
  Nancy, 126
  Octavia, 135

YAKEY
  Eliza, 108
YATES
  H. C., 156
YOUNG
  Benjamin, 106
  David, 146
  Henson, 38
  Howard, 100
  Phoebe, 145

ZEREGA
  A. L. B., 1
  Augustus, 6

Other Heritage Books by Patricia B. Duncan:

1850 Fairfax County and Loudoun County, Virginia Slave Schedule

1850 Fauquier County, Virginia Slave Schedule

1860 Loudoun County, Virginia Slave Schedule

*Clarke County, Virginia Will Book Abstracts:
Books A-I (1836-1904) and 1A-3C (1841-1913)*

Fauquier County, Virginia, Birth Register, 1853-1880

Fauquier County, Virginia, Birth Register, 1881-1896

Fauquier County, Virginia, Marriage Register, 1854-1882

Fauquier County, Virginia, Marriage Register, 1883-1906

Fauquier County, Virginia Death Register, 1853-1896

Hunterdon County, New Jersey 1895 State Census, Part I: Alexandria-Junction

Hunterdon County, New Jersey 1895 State Census, Part II: Kingwood-West Amwell

Genealogical Abstracts from The Lambertville Press, *Lambertville, New Jersey:
4 November 1858 (Vol. 1, Number 1) to 30 October 1861 (Vol. 3, Number 155)*

Genealogical Abstracts from The Democratic Mirror *and*
The Mirror, *1857-1879, Loudoun County, Virginia*

Genealogical Abstracts from The Mirror, *1880-1890, Loudoun County, Virginia*

Genealogical Abstracts from The Mirror, *1891-1899, Loudoun County, Virginia*

Genealogical Abstracts from The Mirror, *1900-1919, Loudoun County, Virginia*

Genealogical Abstracts from The Telephone, *1881-1888, Loudoun County, Virginia*

Genealogical Abstracts from The Telephone, *1889-1896, Loudoun County, Virginia*

Jefferson County, Virginia/West Virginia Death Records, 1853-1880

Jefferson County, West Virginia Death Records, 1881-1903

Jefferson County, Virginia 1802-1813 Personal Property Tax Lists

Jefferson County, Virginia 1814-1824 Personal Property Tax Lists

Jefferson County, Virginia 1825-1841 Personal Property Tax Lists

1810-1840 Loudoun County, Virginia Federal Population Census Index

1860 Loudoun County, Virginia Federal Population Census Index

1870 Loudoun County, Virginia Federal Population Census Index

Abstracts from Loudoun County, Virginia Guardian Accounts: Books A-H, 1759-1904

Abstracts of Loudoun County, Virginia Register of Free Negroes, 1844-1861

Index to Loudoun County, Virginia Land Deed Books A-Z, 1757-1800

Index to Loudoun County, Virginia Land Deed Books 2A-2M, 1800-1810

Index to Loudoun County, Virginia Land Deed Books 2N-2U, 1811-1817

Index to Loudoun County, Virginia Land Deed Books 2V-3D, 1817-1822

Index to Loudoun County, Virginia Land Deed Books 3E-3M, 1822-1826

Index to Loudoun County, Virginia Land Deed Books 3N-3V, 1826-1831

Index to Loudoun County, Virginia Land Deed Books 3W-4D, 1831-1835

Index to Loudoun County, Virginia Land Deed Books 4E-4N, 1835-1840

Index to Loudoun County, Virginia Land Deed Books 4O-4V, 1840-1846

Loudoun County, Virginia Birth Register, 1853-1879

Loudoun County, Virginia Birth Register, 1880-1896

Loudoun County, Virginia Clerks Probate Records Book 1 (1904-1921) and Book 2 (1922-1938)

(With Elizabeth R. Frain) *Loudoun County, Virginia Marriages after 1850, Volume 1, 1851-1880*

Loudoun County, Virginia 1800-1810 Personal Property Taxes

Loudoun County, Virginia 1826-1834 Personal Property Taxes

Loudoun County, Virginia Will Book Abstracts, Books A-Z, Dec. 1757-Jun. 1841

Loudoun County, Virginia Will Book Abstracts, Books 2A-3C, Jun. 1841-Dec. 1879 and Superior Court Books A and B, 1810-1888

Loudoun County, Virginia Will Book Index, 1757-1946

Genealogical Abstracts from The Brunswick Herald, *Brunswick, Maryland: Mar. 6 1891-Dec. 28 1894*

Genealogical Abstracts from The Brunswick Herald, *Brunswick, Maryland: Jan. 4 1895-Dec. 30 1898*

Genealogical Abstracts from The Brunswick Herald, *Brunswick, Maryland: Jan. 6 1899-Dec. 26 1902*

Genealogical Abstracts from The Brunswick Herald, *Brunswick, Maryland: Jan. 2 1903-June 29 1906*

Genealogical Abstracts from The Brunswick Herald, *Brunswick, Maryland: July 6 1906-Feb. 25 1910*

CD: *Loudoun County, Virginia Personal Property Tax List, 1782-1850*

www.ingramcontent.com/pod-product-compliance
Lightning Source LLC
Chambersburg PA
CBHW071228170426
43191CB00032B/1129